RETHINKING
THE
HENRICIAN ERA

RETHINKING THE HENRICIAN ERA

ESSAYS ON EARLY TUDOR TEXTS AND CONTEXTS

Edited by
PETER C. HERMAN

For Mummy, Christmas, 1996,

from Emily

UNIVERSITY OF ILLINOIS PRESS
Urbana and Chicago

© 1994 by the Board of Trustees of the University of Illinois
Manufactured in the United States of America
1   2   3   4   5   C   P   5   4   3   2   1

This book is printed on acid-free paper.

Library of Congress Cataloging-in-Publication Data

Rethinking the Henrician era : essays on early Tudor texts and
    contexts / edited by Peter C. Herman.
        p.   cm.
    Includes index.
    ISBN 0-252-02034-0 (alk. paper). — ISBN 0-252-06340-6 (pbk. :
alk. paper)
        1. English literature—Early modern, 1500–1700—History and
criticism. 2. Henry VIII, King of England, 1491–1547, in fiction,
drama, poetry, etc. 3. Great Britain—History—Henry VIII,
1509–1547—Historiography. 4. Politics and literature—Great
Britain—History—16th century. 5. Literature and society—
England—History—16th century. 6. Tudor, House of, in literature.
7. Kings and rulers in literature. I. Herman, Peter C., 1958–   .
PR413.R45   1994
820.9'002—dc20   93-12712
                                                            CIP

CONTENTS

ACKNOWLEDGMENTS

Several of the papers in the collection were first presented at a special session at the 1990 convention of the Modern Language Association of America in Chicago entitled "Rethinking the Henrician Era," and I thank the MLA for allowing us this forum.

I remain deeply grateful to all the contributors for signing on to a project with an uncertain future, sticking with it during its period of gestation, and giving me the benefit of their advice and encouragement. However, I must single out Paul G. Remley for his invaluable aid in preparing the manuscript in electronic form. Jean E. Howard and James V. Mirollo provided tactical advice at all the right moments. Ann Lowry, Arthur F. Kinney, Katharine E. Maus, and an anonymous reader for the University of Illinois Press rendered acute advice that significantly improved this volume. Pat Hollahan is, as one of the contributors put it, "a heck of an editor," and she saved me from many an embarrassing error. I am grateful to the University of Texas Press for granting permission to reprint Alexandra Halasz's "Wyatt's David." Penultimately, I want to thank as profusely as possible my wife, Meryl Maneker, for her unending patience and love. Truly, without her, this volume, and much else besides, would never have come to pass.

Finally, this book is dedicated to the memory of Florence Herman, who always supported me in every way. Without her, I would never have become a teacher.

Introduction:
Rethinking the Henrician Era

PETER C. HERMAN

I have chosen to call the period encompassing Henry VIII's reign (1509–47) "the Henrician era" rather than employing the more conventional term, "the early Tudor period," because the latter phrase encrypts a negative bias that this volume seeks to challenge. The "early" in "early Tudor" suggests immaturity, being interesting only as a precursor for later developments (e.g., the early Beethoven, the early Yeats), and the reception of this era's literature bears out this prejudice. Excepting Thomas More's *Utopia,* Henrician texts have not attracted much critical attention, and in no way does "benign" describe this neglect. In the first critical survey of pre-Elizabethan literature, John M. Berdan sets the tone by frankly admitting that the "earlier, cruder" writings of Henrician England gain merit only in the context of Elizabethan poetry: "The moment that such [inferior] work is placed in the scheme of things, that it is seen in relation to work admittedly superior, it gains a reflected interest. . . . The interest is not in the literature of the age so much as in the succeeding literature of the time of Elizabeth, which it conditioned."[1] In other words, Henrician literature is worth considering only insofar as it anticipates later developments. C. S. Lewis of course delivered the most damning comments in *English Literature in the Sixteenth Century* when he dismissed this period as "a drab age."[2] Nor did Henrician poetry much excite the New Critics, who, though less outspoken, ultimately were no more sympathetic to Thomas Wyatt and Henry Howard, earl of Surrey, let alone John Skelton, than were Berdan and Lewis. Thus, before the shift toward more theoretically and politically inclined analyses, the two dominant modes of criticism had very little positive to say about pre-Elizabethan literature.

The reasons for this marginalization are worth speculating on. Certainly, one explanation would be the different reputations enjoyed by the two monarchs. Elizabeth is and always has been immensely popular among literary critics and historians whereas Henry VIII, as an early editor of his writings puts it, reminds one more of Bluebeard than anyone else.[3] Charles Dickens called him a "disgrace to human nature, and a blot of blood and grease upon the history of England."[4] Jasper Ridley, Henry VIII's most recent biographer, reports that the catalogue of the British Library records only nineteen biographies of Henry in all languages. Mary, queen of Scots, on the other hand, rates seventy-nine, and Oliver Cromwell one hundred and two.[5] Given Henry's marital record and the distinguished list of those he condemned (John Fisher, Thomas More, Thomas Cromwell, and Henry Howard, earl of Surrey, among others), one can understand why critics might want to spend their scholarly lives in Elizabeth's more genial court. Also, pragmatically speaking, the later Renaissance affords many more opportunities for inquiry. From the 1580s onward, increasing numbers of poets, prose writers, and dramatists crowd the scene. Compared to the later sixteenth and seventeenth centuries, Henry's reign simply provides a much smaller vineyard, especially since it lacks an independent, commercial theater (although a popular, ideologically complex drama most certainly existed, as David Scott Kastan will demonstrate later in this volume). But these reasons, plausible in themselves if not terribly profound, still do not explain the paucity of interest in the Henrician era. After all, the Anglo-Saxon period could hardly be called inviting, and its surviving literature offers even fewer texts for analysis. Even so, Anglo-Saxon studies thrive. To more fully grasp the reasons underlying the Henrician era's unpopularity, we need to look at the role ideology played in the formation of the dominant view.

Immediately after Lewis condemns the pre-Elizabethans as belonging to the Drab Age, denouncing their poetry as "crude" and their prose as "clumsy, monotonous, [and] garrulous," he praises Elizabethan and seventeenth-century literature for "enrich[ing] the very meanings of the words *England* and *Aristocracy* [emphasis in the original]."[6] Now, some of Lewis's supporters have argued that he paid scant attention to temporal affairs because he believed that the universal truths of Christianity rendered the world's crises less than significant. As Lewis himself puts it in *The World's Last Night,* "nations, cultures, arts, civilizations, these are mortal, and their life is to ours [i.e., the Christian's], as the life of a gnat."[7] Consequently, the argument goes, Lewis could write "prolifically on eternal themes even as World War II raged about him."[8] However, as we now know, writing about "eternal themes" (such as the divine origin of the existing social order) usually covers a more temporal purpose.[9] Ideology, in its Althusserian sense, inheres as much in literary criticism as in literature, and Lewis's works provide no exception.

Lewis began writing *English Literature in the Sixteenth Century* during World War II, publishing it in 1953; and even though he never overtly refers to the bitter, depleted atmosphere of wartime and postwar England, Britain's economic and imperial decline clearly affect his judgments about the relative merits of Tudor/Stuart writing. Postwar Britain suffered from economic austerity and the double humiliation of ignominiously losing its empire and ceding international leadership to the United States, and (to oversimplify the case) Lewis reacted to this state of affairs by glorifying England's medieval and Renaissance past. In other words, Lewis's dismissal of pre-Elizabethan literature arises less from its alleged offenses against essentialized aesthetic standards and more from his nostalgia for the stable, ordered, and orthodox world of medieval Christianity, which of course Henry nearly destroyed through the break with Rome.[10] It was a world that (Lewis imagines) England dominated both culturally and politically, a world he associates with the reign of Elizabeth, not her father, because Henry introduced novelty into religion and chaos into the polity. A world, in sum, that deeply contrasts with England's debilitated condition during the time that Lewis produced *English Literature in the Sixteenth Century*. In this sense, Lewis's evaluations of Renaissance literature share the same conservative politics as those of his important contemporaries, J. R. R. Tolkien and E. M. W. Tillyard.[11]

The New Critical formalists of the 1950s and 1960s tended to push Wyatt and Surrey to the sidelines because they found their verse less amenable than Donne's or Marvell's to close reading. The New Critical practice of discussing "poems as poems," which entailed marginalizing the immediate social context, would not let them be particularly sympathetic to such texts as Wyatt's "My own John Poyntz," Surrey's politicized lyrics and translations, or Skelton's Wolsey satires. However, as Terry Eagleton points out, beneath the transcontinental New Critical worship of the verbal icon lies a nostalgia for a coherent, hierarchical, and aristocratic political order that bears considerable resemblance to Lewis's and Tillyard's politics.[12] The obvious differences between the two notwithstanding, both the New Critics and C. S. Lewis attempted to discover in literature an order they could not find in reality, and the reign of Henry VIII clearly embodied exactly the political instability they found so repugnant. Because of the anti-Henrician bias of these taste-makers, to this day Renaissance studies overwhelmingly favors the later Tudor/Stuart era.

The introduction, perhaps more accurately, the eruption, of theory into literary studies over the last decade or so has led to a massive over-haul of our previous notions of canon formation in general and the Renaissance in particular.[13] The political agenda informing Lewis's and Berdan's aesthetics as well as those underlying the New Criticism have been interrogated repeatedly and new political agendas have been set in their places. Renaissance texts have been subjected to any number of the newer critical approaches (e.g., neo-Marxism, the New Historicism, deconstruction, gay studies, and feminist studies, among others) that have displaced the New Criticism and the older historicism. Generally speaking, critics no longer search for objective meanings inhering in the text; instead they examine the various processes by which meanings are produced and legitimated; the interpretive community (fractious though it may be) is now as much a focus of attention as the ambiguous verbal icon. Furthermore, the older historicist paradigm of a pre-dominantly calm, static society whose literature reinforces authority has been replaced with a much more heterogeneous and transgressive cultural scene. This generation's Renaissance England privileges those voices that interrogate the hierarchical power structure set forth in such documents as "The Homily on Obedience" and "The Homily on Marriage." Having discerned that Renaissance texts are sites of conflict where authors, scribes, patrons, censors, publishers, and readers all have their part in determining meaning, theoretically inclined readers also recognize their own stake in the processes of literary or cultural criticism. In place of naively assuming the disinterestedness of one's own interpretations, these readers admit how their position as historical subjects necessarily conditions their reconstructions of the past. Rereading the past, in sum, constitutes an *intervention* rather than an objective reconstruction.[14]

And yet, despite all the transformations, interrogations, contestations, rewritings, rethinkings, re-presentations, and re-memberings of the Renaissance, one aspect of the Lewis-Tillyard picture retains wide acceptance: the assumption that the Elizabethan/Jacobean era takes precedence over the Henrician, that the term "Early Tudor Literature" really means "lesser Tudor literature." Even though practically all of the older constructions of the Renaissance have been challenged, Lewis's dismissal of pre-Elizabethan literature still holds, as does Berdan's view that it represents the inept first stirrings of what will later bloom into the glories of Elizabethan and Jacobean verse.

Most readers informed by recent critical developments have tacitly accepted the convention and so Henrician authors do not figure prominently, if they figure at all, in recent work. A quick glance over the indexes of such important general collections as *Literary Theory/Renais-*

sance Texts, Renaissance Historicism: Selections from "English Literary Renaissance," Representing the English Renaissance, The Historical Renaissance: New Essays on Tudor and Stuart Literature and Culture, Renaissance Rereadings: Intertext and Context, Rewriting the Renaissance, and *Contending Kingdoms: Historical, Psychological, and Feminist Approaches to the Literature of Sixteenth-Century England* palpably demonstrates how rarely critics address pre-Elizabethan texts.[15] The first three anthologies contain no such essays; the next three include one each; *Contending Kingdoms* has three. Although anthologies have been compiled on such diverse topics as reinterpreting Elizabethan or Jacobean literature, Shakespeare in the curriculum, non-Shakespearean drama, the politics of recent Shakespeare criticism, Tudor women and religious literature, Milton, and the canon set up by the New Critics, no anthology has yet been devoted exclusively to the literature of the Henrician era.[16]

This volume remedies this omission. The contributors show how the application of current theoretical approaches can enrich, complicate, and at times entirely revise our understanding of Henrician texts and contexts. The essays also intervene in ways other than simply arguing for better coverage of the Henrician era, although that remains a major aim of the volume. Several contributors contest the accepted canon of Renaissance literature either by showing that such previously slighted authors as John Bale and John Skelton are "better" than their current reputations allow or by recovering a lost poetic voice (e.g., Remley's treatment of Mary Shelton). In addition, these contributors challenge the older historicist practice of explicating a literary text by placing it in its putatively stable intellectual context by demonstrating how a shift in context radically alters the interpretation of a text (Greene and Herman), or by focusing exclusively on court culture (Howard) and cultural spectacle (Readings) rather than on poems and plays. Generally, these essays question the received notion of what constitutes an appropriate subject for literary analysis by crossing genre and discipline boundaries.[17] Finally, this volume attempts to shift the center of gravity of Renaissance studies away from the later Tudor/Stuart era and more toward the Henrician era.[18] No one denies that we should study Henrician literature because of its relationships to later literary production; however, the contributors also collectively assert that the era has its own integrity, its own issues, and its own problematics.

Although Berdan did not exactly err in asserting that Elizabethan writers relied upon their Henrician ancestors, his mistake (and Lewis's) lay in assuming that the Elizabethans refined the dross of the Henrician era. The relationship between the two ages is not alchemical but transformative, which accurately describes how many Elizabethans perceived the reign of Henry VIII. Because of their own complicated anti-Henrician agenda, Lewis and Berdan elide the fact that Elizabeth's reign began as a nostalgic return to the glories of the Henrician court. During her coronation procession, for example, someone called out, "Remember old King Henry VIII," and Elizabeth smiled approvingly.[19] Nor was this anonymous voice alone in viewing the new queen as Henry VIII redivivus. Sir Thomas Challoner, in the introduction to his epideictic poem on Henry which he presented to Elizabeth in 1560, called on the queen to emulate her illustrious father: "You, O Queen, can add to your own abundant fame the titles of your father Henry—no greater king ever ruled in our shores. O best one, how you are even better from the fame of your father. For a long while may years of praise proceed happily for you, and may they abound in new honors. Yet nothing will be more worthy than for you, descended from a noble lineage, to be like your noble father. So like him in appearance, lovely heroine, be like him in deed and duplicate his great works."[20] Elizabeth certainly did learn from Henry's example, especially his use of spectacle in reinforcing the myths surrounding the Tudor dynasty and his use of erotic discourse as a tool of policy.[21]

Somewhat ironically, the writers of the Elizabethan "Golden Age" considered the Henrician era as the standard by which they measured and legitimated themselves. For the Elizabethans, the Henrician era constituted their "Golden Age" of literature. In appropriating the figure of Colin Clout for his inaugural, if also anonymous, poem, Spenser seeks to domesticate Skelton's wild energies for his purposes even as he uses Skelton's satiric mantle to justify himself and his project. Similarly, Richard Tottel relied on "the honorable stile of the noble earle of Surrey, and the weightinesse of the depewitted sir Thomas Wyat" to prove that "our tong is able in that kynde to do as praiseworthely" as Latin, Greek, or Italian.[22] And when the fin de siècle atmosphere set in during the last decade of Elizabeth's reign, such popular writers as Thomas Deloney (*Jack of Newburry*) and Thomas Nashe (*The Unfortunate Traveller*) set their fictions in the "good old days" of Henry VIII, whom Nashe calls "the terror of the world and fever quartane of the French . . . the only true subject of chronicles."[23] The Henrician era, in sum, constitutes the ground upon which the Elizabethan era consciously and problematically depended.[24]

I have divided the essays in this collection into three overlapping groups. The first deals with more general themes and with Renaissance humanism; the second analyzes specific authors; and the third looks at the problematics of Shakespeare's representation of the Henrician era.

The first three essays explore how the Henrician court constituted a site for the production, dissemination, and contestation of ideology. Skiles Howard looks at the function of dancing during the early years of Henry VIII's reign. Dancing has conventionally been interpreted as an emblem of cosmic harmony (bodies moving in imitation of the heavenly spheres); Howard, however, through her analysis of Elyot's *The Boke named the Governour* and the reports of court entertainments in Hall's *Chronicles,* argues that dancing functioned as a means for expressing and reinforcing both the political and the sexual hierarchies of the Henrician court. For example, the pageant in which Anne Boleyn made her debut at court, known as the "assault on the *Chateau Vert,*" enacts the chivalric rescue of maidens from the Castle of Scorn, but "Scorn" in this context means female refusal of male advances and the forced "rescue" of the "damsels in distress" inscribes upon the bodies of the participants the roles of female submission and male domination. Dance, in other words, served as a vehicle for the transmission and legitimization of gender roles. Sir Thomas Elyot also makes this clear when, following his naturalization of the dance as an expression of divine harmony, he demonstrates how dancing enforces gender distinctions by formalizing the prescribed roles for males and females: men lead, women defer.

In "Mary Shelton and Her Tudor Literary Milieu," Paul Remley argues that the courtly love lyric and even medieval antifeminist verse were appropriated by women of the Tudor aristocracy as a means of challenging the inequities of Henry's reign. The inscription of poetry in a private manuscript established a site autonomous from the power of the state. Citing the striking parallels between the predominant themes of the poetry of the Devonshire manuscript and the lives of its many contributors, Remley shows how Shelton and collaborators carefully manipulated courtly tropes, creating an amateur verse as contestatory in its own way as anything produced by Wyatt and Surrey. Specifically, Remley seeks to recover two previously unrecognized female voices. The first is that of Mary Shelton, who, in her occasional verse and in her dual capacity as scribe and ad hoc editor, used the Devonshire volume as a vehicle to document the oppression of contemporaries by the court and to record her own personal disillusionment with some of the men of her day, particularly in their treatment of women. The second previously neglected voice is that of Margaret Douglas, an aristocrat in line to the throne who was jailed in the Tower along with her lover, Thomas Howard, as a result of their impolitic love affair and possible secret marriage. Shelton herself appears to have copied out the unique group of epistolary love poems exchanged by Douglas and Howard, which employs the conventions of courtly verse to comment obliquely upon the circumstances of their incarceration.

John N. King continues the examination of how the language of universals masks the inculcation of political values through his analysis of the reciprocities between religion and politics. Looking at the images of Henry in the illustrations for the title pages of the Coverdale Bible (1535) and the Great Bible (1539), as well as the Davidic images in the king's private psalter, King shows how Henry VIII's artists appropriated images and symbols previously identified with the papacy and transferred them to the king, who as an autonomous head of both church and state owed no allegiance to any foreign superior. In their concern to legitimate the Reformation by visually identifying Henry VIII with Moses, David, and the Evangelists, King suggests that these artists also call attention to the politicization of religion. This essay also intends to show that the deliberate construction of the monarch as a "cult" figure began not with Elizabeth, as many have assumed, but with her father.

Janel Mueller, in "'A Whole Island like a Single Family': Positioning Women in Utopian Patriarchy," argues that women occupy a highly ambivalent position within More's commonwealth. On the one hand, More's vocabulary suggests inclusiveness. The passages on Utopian moral philosophy and religion contain numerous uses of indefinite personal pronouns (e.g., *qui, quisque,* and *quisquam*) that suggest More's sexual egalitarianism. Similarly, Utopian manual labor practices do not differentiate between the sexes, although the Utopians do provide for biologically linked differences in physical strength. Even so, More's language gives way to gender-specific pronouns and privileges the male perspective at key moments, thereby underscoring that Utopian women never escape subordination to a male. For example, both men and women may view each other naked before marriage, but the text then elides the feminine perspective and only talks about the prospective husband. However, even though *Utopia* refigures women as subservient members of a patriarchy, More further complicates the position of women within *Utopia* by using them as models for Utopian ethics and spirituality.

W. Scott Blanchard and Peter C. Herman both examine what might be called the poetics of marginality in the works of John Skelton, a figure who is only beginning to be read with the same degree of attention accorded his more courtly (and more courteous) contemporaries.

Blanchard looks at the complicated matter of "territorialization" (i.e., the definition of various forms of boundaries, political and otherwise) in Skelton's political satires. Blanchard argues that even though Skelton vehemently protested Wolsey's blurring of the distinction between church and state, his strategies in the satires accomplish the same effect on the notions of authorship available to him. Just as Wolsey shuttled between the clergy and the laity, Skelton occupies the ambiguous middle ground separating modern notions of authorship and older traditions of religious dissent in which the author either is anonymous or takes on the identity of the community. Ironically, Skelton's authorial strategies enact precisely the dissolutions of discrete boundaries that the poems so vociferously denounce.

Next, Peter C. Herman offers a revisionary interpretation of Skelton's much maligned poem, *The Tunnynge of Elynour Rummynge*, in light of Bakhtin's theory of grotesque realism. Rather than finding this text expressive of Christian orthodoxy or cultural misogyny, Herman argues that *Elynour Rummyng* valorizes female autonomy and challenges the expectations of female subservience. After arguing that the "grotesque" and perpetually leaky bodies of Elynour and her customers contest patriarchal attempts at corporeal enclosure, Herman situates Elynour's business within the shift in ale-brewing from a trade dominated by women to a trade dominated by men. Just as their bodies contest the patriarchal construction of the "closed" female body, their economy (no men enter Elynour's alehouse) contests male economic rule.

With W. A. Sessions's contribution, the volume begins to focus on the poetry produced by the court of Henry VIII. The current concern with the intersections between politics and poetry, summed up in Puttenham's nice phrase "cunning princepleasers," has done much with later writers, such as Spenser, Sidney, and Marvell, but relatively little with Wyatt and almost nothing with the earl of Surrey. Sessions argues that by examining the later Tudor appropriations and reinterpretations of Wyatt and Surrey as well as the earl's own interpretations of Wyatt we can recover the process by which these two transform the medieval concept of the poet as a craftsman into the Renaissance notion of the poet as an orphic voice of communal honor and nobility. Obviously, courtiers and aristocrats wrote poetry well before Wyatt and Surrey, but these two together transformed what Castiglione might have called an ornament into a vocation essential for the well-being of the nation.

The next three essays deal with three aspects of Wyatt's poetry: the use of religious verse as a vehicle for expressing political concerns; the place of women with his version of Petrarchan discourse; and the complicated relationship between Petrarchism and the discussions of the New World.

Alexandra Halasz demonstrates the centrality of political and poetic concerns in Wyatt's paraphrases of the seven penitential psalms. In this sequence, Wyatt creates a perspective from which one may judge the values of a system in which Henry is the absolute monarch of both church and state. Wyatt inscribes not only a "privileged" perspective but its cost. As poet, Wyatt addresses Henry with a consciousness of loss. Like Nathan, he can call the king to account, but unlike David's prophet, he cannot do so from a position of innocence or spiritual purity.

Barbara Estrin looks at Wyatt's lyric poetry from a feminist-Lacanian perspective, exploring how Wyatt's "I," rather than the Lady, functions as the self-igniting inspiration that Marvell would later refine in "The Garden." Wyatt incorporates the woman, turning her physical body into his poetic body, thereby remaining in the safely semiotic realm challenged by the menacingly sexual woman of "They Flee from Me." In his Petrarchan imitations Wyatt responds to the woman whose sexual and verbal powers encroach upon ostensibly exclusive male domains (i.e., sexual aggressiveness and writing) by rendering her into the woman who means too little. To be slightly less than Petrarch in the translations renders the "she" slightly other than Laura and so to withhold laurelization.

Roland Greene, reminding us that Petrarchism is more thematically capacious than most critics allow, suggests how erotic discourse also served as a medium for the deliberation of issues pertaining to the New World. Greene shows that the extended time that Wyatt spent as an ambassador at the court of Charles V would have exposed him to the intense debates over the morality of the European presence in the New World. After offering a sketch of Wyatt's late diplomatic career and his place in the international group of European poets concerned with New World themes, Greene suggests how several of Wyatt's lyrics (including "They Flee from Me," "The Long Love," and "What Rage Is This?"), in addition to their erotic/political themes, also meditate upon the European experience in America.

David Scott Kastan turns to the "bilious" John Bale, in Thomas Fuller's notorious phrase, to demonstrate that the relations between dramatic representation and early modern politics, much studied in terms of Shakespeare's history plays and the Stuart masques, is no less revealing and complex in Henrician drama. Kastan sets Bale's *King Johan* in its relation to the government propaganda of the Cromwellian phase of the Reformation. While responding to the government's call for popular images of Catholic perfidy and English resistance, the play nonetheless reveals, in its very act of advancing the claims of the emerging Protestant nation, an unnerving instability in its own polemical assertions as well as in the imperial claims. Bale's play, like the nation it would help bring into being, appeals to historical and scriptural authorizations that neither history nor the Bible can actually provide.

Bill Readings brings the anthology to a close with a consideration of Shakespeare's representation of the Henrician court in *Henry VIII*. In so doing, he problematizes the current versions of when and how the Renaissance began. Readings also seeks to trouble the New Historicist versions of a politicized drama because Shakespeare's texts are concerned not so much with the politics of spectacle as with their condition as spectacle. We seem to be in a world almost identical to Guy Debord's society of spectacle and Baudrillard's simulacra, where everything exists as representation only of itself. Readings calls into question the New Historicist understanding of the politics of Renaissance theater by suggesting that Shakespeare's text and Henrician court politics per se are displaced toward the condition of spectacle in ways that render problematical a grasp of the past.

Although the contributors generally employ the same theoretical tools that have been used to alter our understanding of the later Renaissance, the essays themselves express a wide and contradictory variety of theoretical positions. *Rethinking the Henrician Era* comes at a time when one safely can assume that the polemical battles over the legitimacy and permanency of theoretical approaches are over and done with; consequently I perceive no need either to justify the new, more politically inflected forms of criticism or to privilege one school of literary interpretation over another. This does not mean that oppositional criticism has been neutralized through co-optation by the "establishment"; quite the opposite, for the theoreticians have won the field.[25] Not everyone practices the same form of literary or cultural criticism, and not everyone favors the newer modes of criticism, but theory has become an undeniable fact of life in the profession.[26] It is impossible to attain an advanced degree in literature without significant grounding in the various forms of literary theory, and one simply cannot publish on Shakespeare or Wyatt without taking into account Stephen Greenblatt's work on these authors as well as the various critiques of Greenblatt's work. The same goes for Stanley E. Fish on Milton, Annabel Patterson and Louis Montrose on the pastoral, Phyllis Rackin on Shakespeare's history plays, and Jonathan Goldberg on Spenser. Nor does it seem likely that we will ever return to the time when one could assume that meaning unproblematically inheres in the text itself or claim that

Shakespeare's plays explore the question "What is man?" without reflecting on whether "Man" includes slightly more than half of humanity too.[27]

Consequently, while the following essays explore a common theme—rethinking the Henrician era—I have tried to be as theoretically inclusive as possible. Thus, the essays range from John N. King's and William Sessions's more "traditional" scholarship to Bill Readings's postmodernism to Paul Remley's combination of gender-related readings and paleographical analysis. The contributors implicitly (and occasionally explicitly) disagree with each other, and the theses of some essays even might be considered incompatible. Through its multiplicity of approaches, interpretations, and assumptions, this anthology intends to intervene in the current debates over political correctness by providing a forum in which diverse critical approaches may coexist, challenging, accusing, and complementing each other. Pluralism, whether critical or political, may risk looking like fence-sitting; nonetheless, given the current emphasis in Renaissance studies (and in most of these essays) on contestation and resituating the marginal, to omit essays predicated upon a critical viewpoint that I or some of the contributors may not practice or like would constitute the imposition of precisely the coercive hegemony that these essays, and literary theory in general, do their best to challenge. In other words, those of us who espouse dialogism in our theory should not be monologic in our practice.

If this book sparks further debate about the Henrician era, if it nudges a reader into reexamining a text that he or she might have considered unworthy, or significant only as it presages later writers, then this volume will have succeeded—especially if that nudge ends up altering a syllabus or two.

Notes

1. John M. Berdan, *Early Tudor Poetry: 1485–1547* (New York: Macmillan, 1931), viii.

2. C. S. Lewis, *English Literature in the Sixteenth Century, Excluding Drama* (London: Oxford University Press, 1954), 1.

3. *Miscellaneous Writings of Henry the Eighth,* ed. Francis Macnamara (Waltham: Golden Cockerel Press, 1924), 7.

4. Quoted in Lacey Baldwin Smith, *Henry VIII: The Mask of Royalty* (London: Jonathan Cape, 1971), 15.

5. Jasper Ridley, *Henry VIII* (New York: Viking, 1985), 9.

6. Lewis, *English Literature in the Sixteenth Century,* 1.

7. Quoted in Michael Nelson, "C. S. Lewis and His Critics," *Virginia Quarterly Review* 64.1 (1988), 12.

8. Ibid., 12.

9. See, for example, Jonathan Dollimore, "Introduction: Shakespeare, Cultural Materialism, and the New Historicism," in *Political Shakespeare: New Essays in Cultural Materialism,* ed. Jonathan Dollimore and Alan Sinfield (Ithaca: Cornell University Press, 1985), 5.

10. Lewis's nostalgia also manifests itself in his dislike for the "liberal" Christianity of his day on account of its departures from what he construed as orthodox doctrine. See Nelson, "C. S. Lewis," 7–8.

11. Norman F. Cantor, *Inventing the Middle Ages* (New York: Morrow, 1991), 205–44. Cantor finds a similar dynamic at work in Lewis's other works, including the Narnia saga, and in Tolkien's *Lord of the Rings* trilogy.

12. Terry Eagleton, *Literary Theory: An Introduction* (Minneapolis: University of Minnesota Press, 1983), 46–47.

13. The books heralding the arrival of a new critical movement in Renaissance studies are (in chronological order) Stephen Orgel, *The Illusion of Power: Political Theater in the English Renaissance* (Berkeley and Los Angeles: University of California Press, 1975); Stephen J. Greenblatt, *Renaissance Self-Fashioning: From More to Shakespeare* (Chicago: University of Chicago Press, 1980) and his introduction to *The Forms of Power and the Power of Forms in the Renaissance* (*Genre* 15 [1982], 3–6); Jonathan Goldberg, *James I and the Politics of Literature: Jonson, Shakespeare, Donne, and Their Contemporaries* (Baltimore: Johns Hopkins University Press, 1983); and Dollimore and Sinfield, *Political Shakespeare.* Jean E. Howard has written what remains the best summary and critique of the New Historicism in all its various guises, "The New Historicism in Renaissance Studies," *English Literary Renaissance* 16 (1986), 13–43, reprinted in *Renaissance Historicism: Selections from "English Literary Renaissance,"* ed. Arthur F. Kinney and Dan S. Collins (Amherst: University of Massachusetts Press, 1987), 3–33. See also Alan Liu, "The Power of Formalism: The New Historicism," *ELH* 56 (1989), 721–71, and the essays collected in *The New Historicism,* ed. H. Aram Veeser (New York: Routledge, 1989), especially Stanley Fish, "Commentary: The Young and the Restless," 303–16.

14. Despite (or perhaps because of) the widespread acceptance of this critical sensibility in leading journals, university presses, and graduate schools, there is still considerable resistance, if not outright hostility, toward theoretically informed analyses. In Renaissance studies, Richard Levin has become something of an apostle for this group. See his "Feminist Thematics and Shakespearean Tragedy," *PMLA* 103 (1988), 125–38, and "The Poetics and Politics of Bardicide," *PMLA* 105 (1990), 491–504. See also the essays attacking Levin collected in *Shakespeare Left and Right,* ed. Ivo Kamps (New York: Routledge, 1991).

15. *Literary Theory/Renaissance Texts,* ed. Patricia Parker and David Quint (Baltimore: Johns Hopkins University Press, 1986); *Renaissance Historicism; Representing the English Renaissance,* ed. Stephen J. Greenblatt (Berkeley and Los Angeles: University of California Press, 1988); *The Historical Renaissance: New Essays on Tudor and Stuart Literature and Culture,* ed. Heather Dubrow

and Richard Strier (Chicago: University of Chicago Press, 1988); *Renaissance Rereadings: Intertext and Context,* ed. Maryanne Cline Horowitz, Anne J. Cruz, and Wendy A. Furman (Urbana: University of Illinois Press, 1988); *Rewriting the Renaissance: The Discourses of Sexual Difference in Early Modern Europe,* ed. Margaret W. Ferguson, Maureen Quilligan, and Nancy J. Vickers (Chicago: University of Chicago Press, 1986); and *Contending Kingdoms: Historical, Psychological, and Feminist Approaches to the Literature of Sixteenth-Century England,* ed. Marie-Rose Logan and Peter L. Rudnytsky (Detroit: Wayne State University Press, 1991).

16. In addition to the anthologies listed above, see *Shakespeare Reproduced: The Text in History and Ideology,* ed. Jean E. Howard and Marion O'Connor (New York: Methuen, 1987); *Shakespeare in the Changing Curriculum,* ed. Lesley Aers and Nigel Wheale (London: Routledge, 1991); *Staging the Renaissance: Reinterpretations of the Drama in Renaissance England,* ed. David S. Kastan and Peter Stallybrass (New York: Routledge, 1991); *Shakespeare Left and Right; Silent But for the Word: Tudor Women as Patrons, Translators, and Writers of Religious Works,* ed. Margaret P. Hannay (Kent, Ohio: Kent State University Press, 1985); *The Politics of Discourse,* ed. Kevin Sharpe and Steven Zwicker (Berkeley and Los Angeles: University of California Press, 1985); *Remembering Milton: Essays on the Texts and Traditions,* ed. Margaret Ferguson and Mary Nyquist (New York: Methuen, 1987); and *Soliciting Interpretation: Literary Theory and Seventeenth Century English Poetry,* ed. Elizabeth D. Harvey and Katharine E. Maus (Chicago: University of Chicago Press, 1990).

17. I am indebted to the anonymous reader for the Press for helping to clarify this paragraph.

18. I am not suggesting that the Henrician era has been completely ignored. Stephen Greenblatt, for example, has written brilliant essays on More, Tyndale, and Wyatt in *Renaissance Self-Fashioning,* the work most often cited (or accused) of constituting the originary moment of the New Historicism. But few critics other than Greenblatt have given this era their sustained attention; indeed, Greenblatt might be called the exception who proves the rule. However, during this anthology's gestation, there has been some movement toward according the Henrician era the same degree of attention given to later Renaissance literature. In particular, see Jonathan Crewe, *Trials of Authorship: Anterior Forms and Poetic Reconstruction from Wyatt to Shakespeare* (Berkeley and Los Angeles: University of California Press, 1990 [I have borrowed the gravitational metaphor from 12–13]); Alistair Fox, *Politics and Literature in the Reigns of Henry VII and Henry VIII* (London: Basil Blackwell, 1989); and Greg Walker's two books, *John Skelton and the Politics of the 1520s* (Cambridge: Cambridge University Press, 1988) and *Plays of Persuasion: Drama and Politics at the Court of Henry VIII* (Cambridge: Cambridge University Press, 1991).

19. Quoted in J. E. Neale, *Queen Elizabeth* (New York: Harcourt, Brace, 1934), 59.

20. Sir Thomas Challoner, *In laudem Henrici Octavi,* trans. and ed. John B. Gabel and Carl C. Schlam (Lawrence, Kans.: Coronado Press, 1979), 25.

Challoner apparently wrote his poem sometime between 1545 and 1546, but decided against presenting it to the aging, increasingly irascible king. It sat on his desk until Elizabeth ascended to the throne. Then he rewrote the beginning, added a new introduction, and presented his repackaged poem to the queen as a New Year's gift. On the poem's background, see Gabel and Schlam's introduction, 10–13.

21. See Sydney Anglo, *Spectacle, Pageantry, and Early Tudor Policy* (Oxford: Clarendon Press, 1969), and Peter C. Herman, "Henry VIII," *Dictionary of Literary Biography* (forthcoming).

22. Richard Tottel, "The Printer to the Reader," *Tottel's Miscellany,* ed. Hyder Edward Rollins, rev. ed. (Cambridge: Harvard University Press, 1966), vol. 1, 2.

23. Thomas Nashe, *The Unfortunate Traveller,* in *The Unfortunate Traveller and Other Works,* ed. J. B. Stearne (1971; reprint, Harmondsworth: Penguin, 1971), 254.

24. Crewe, *Trials of Authorship,* 48–49.

25. On the ambiguities of co-optation, see Gerald Graff's excellent essay, "Co-optation," in *New Historicism,* 168–81.

26. See n. 14, above.

27. For some marvelously crude examples of sexist Shakespeare criticism, see Richard Levin, "Reply to Bristol and Greene," in *Shakespeare Left and Right,* 58.

"Ascending the Riche Mount": Performing Hierarchy and Gender in the Henrician Masque

SKILES HOWARD

A recent biography of Anne Boleyn describes her debut at the English court in a Burgundian pageant, the "assault on the *Chateau Vert*." Cast as Perseverance, Anne was one of eight court ladies personifying the feminine virtues of Beauty, Constancy, and Bounty who were "protected from assault" by eight boy choristers of the royal chapel representing "the contrary feminine vices" of Disdain, Jealousy, and Scorn. Eight courtiers, including King Henry himself, played the masculine virtues of Nobleness, Attendance, and Loyalty.[1]

> The men entered, led by Ardent Desire dressed in burning crimson satin. . . . Desire begged the ladies to come down, but when Scorn and Disdain announced that they would resist, he called on the courtiers to take the ladies by force. To a peal of cannon, synchronized from outside, Henry led the attack, bombarding the castle and its garrison with dates [and] oranges, to which the "ladies" . . . replied with a barrage of sweetmeats and rose water until Lady Scorn and the rest of the boys retreated. . . . Female coldness having fled before masculine ardour, the warm and soft qualities were taken prisoner and brought out of the castle to dance.

Ives's description presents the entertainment as a benign, even trivial amusement: a chivalric rescue of feminine warmth and softness from a prison of Petrarchan scorn, heroically accomplished by male ardor discharged in delectable volleys of candied fruit, the triumphant liberation of "warm and soft" femininity celebrated in joyous dancing.

The pageant, though, had another side that Ives suppresses, and operated with more complexity than he acknowledges. Hall's description of the event, from which the biographer borrows, is more cryptic and less sentimental: after the successful assault on the castle, "the lords took the ladies of honor as prisoner by the handes, and brought them doune, and daunced together verie pleasauntly."[2] Since the courtly dancing to which the ladies were led "as prisoner by the handes" signified a "concord"[3] achieved by their pleasant submission to masculine dominance, the jolly rescue is really a mock rape, tolled in the synchronized peal of a cannon. The articulation of "masculine dominance" through a scenario of forcible abduction defines the practice of dancing, and the festivity of the Henrician era to which it was central,[4] as a privileged site for the production of hierarchy and gender difference.

That courtly dancing was a patriarchal practice might seem to be self-evident; however, it has not, as yet, been the subject of a feminist or historicist engagement,[5] an omission perhaps attributable to a lingering residue of critical logocentricism. The relative neglect of the Henrician masque, the spoken words of which, if any, were not recorded,[6] may be a result of the same tendency. In this essay, therefore, I seek to establish courtly dancing as an important bodily discipline that constructed hierarchy and gender difference, and, in the Henrician masque, was at the center of a constellation of nonverbal practices that consolidated political power in the sovereign by performing the work of social stratification.[7]

The Henrician masque emerged at the beginning of an absolutist trajectory that continued through the Stuart era,[8] and in fact performed some of the work for which the Jacobean masque has been credited. The connection of dancing and power in the Jacobean masque has long been established, with dancing recognized as a privileged instrument in the dissemination of imperial "harmony."[9] In the early modern era, the activities on the sublunary dancing place were dignified as a reflection of the motions of the heavenly bodies.[10] Accordingly, in the Jacobean masque, danced and spoken poetry confirmed the "cosmic harmony" centered in the king, and the revels between masquers and spectators extended this harmony outward and downward into the court, uniting performer and audience in a communion of aspiration, and transforming each in turn. Dancing, Ben Jonson observes, demonstrates the excellence of the dancer and elevates the spectator—"an exercise / not only shews the movers wit, / but maketh the beholder wise, / as he hath powre to rise to it."[11]

Similar transformations, however, are attributed to the practice of dancing during the Henrician era by Sir Thomas Elyot who, in *The Boke named the Governour* (1531), advocates the study of dancing as a moral exercise. For Elyot, dancing is a text written on the body that mnemonically preserves important discursive values within the dancer as subject, and transmits these by means of the dancer as object:[12] "Let all they that haue their courage stered towarde very honour or perfecte

nobilitie: let them . . . either them selves prepare them to daunce, or
. . . beholde with watching eien other that can daunce truely" (sig.
L3v). For Elyot as well as Jonson, dancing is more than an amorous
pastime or an invigorating sport; both praise it as exercise that imbues
in the dancer the aristocratic values of "wit," "honour," and "nobilitie,"
and through the dancer, ennobles the beholder "as he hath powre to
rise to it." It is important, in this connection, to note that dancing had
not only its defenders but its opponents: the appropriation of dancing
as an instrument of power and a code of power relations is attested to
by an opposition that was organized along religious lines, with Catholics and Puritans deploring the practice that courtly Protestants
praised.[13]

It was, in fact, during the Henrician era that courtly dancing in England evolved as a discursive practice instrumental in courtly self-fashioning.[14] Anticipating by centuries phenomenological theorists of the
constitution of social reality through language and gesture, Elyot, in his
apology for dancing, anatomizes the ways in which dancing is "performative," or, in Judith Butler's words, a "stylized repetition of acts . . .
which are internally discontinuous" and arbitrary, "renewed, revised,
and consolidated" over time to create the perception of a social identity.[15] Elyot's defense of dancing locates its salubrious effect in its rehearsal of social roles, defining the dancing couple as a model of aristocratic
gender relations,[16] recording a choreography of gender and rank, and
celebrating a pedagogy of dancing.

The courtly dancer, however, was more than a receptive cultural
vault; in the early modern era, dancing was no longer a spontaneous and
improvised response to sexual, seasonal, or religious mysteries, but was
actively rhetorical, "a forensic oration whose purpose was to persuade."[17] In his *Orchésographie* (1581), the French cleric Toinot Arbeau
explains that "dancing is a kind of mute rhetoric by which the orator,
without uttering a word, can make himself understood by his movements and persuade the spectators that he is gallant and worthy to be
acclaimed, admired, and loved."[18] Codified, instructed, and rehearsed,
courtly dancing, like oratory, explicitly sought to control response; like
the orator, the dancer could not only "make himself understood" by his
audience, he could make himself believed. Dancing therefore functioned not only to preserve and transmit beliefs but to change them,
both circulating social norms and negotiating new formations.

The courtly dancing Elyot defends is a fully framed political discourse, an elaborate system of interrelated ideas and terms—kinetic,
spatial, and visual—that organizes a way of conceptualizing the world
and the body, one that naturalizes itself, and excludes others.[19] The dis-

course of dancing visually articulates on and through the dancing body[20] the physical signs of hierarchy and gender difference, reflecting social pressures and managing social conflicts. Significantly, the word "discourse" etymologically derives from *discurrere,* moving "back and forth," or "running to and fro,"[21] suggesting both the protean nature of dancing as cultural artifact and the means by which it stimulated a social metamorphosis. Inherent in the meaning of "discourse" is the iconicity of transformation, and the paradoxical materiality and evanescence of dancing.

On the Continent, the circumstances and forms of social dancing began to change radically toward the end of the fourteenth century. In the Middle Ages, it is believed, dancing most often took place in the open air where it was freely accessible, and men and women of all conditions danced together in a round or a chain, singing their own accompaniment. When the elite moved indoors to dance, around the beginning of the fifteenth century, dancing began to take two discrete forms—"country" or popular dancing, still improvised outdoors in mixed groups, and "courtly" dancing, choreographed by a dancing master and performed indoors in heterosexual couples to the accompaniment of professional musicians.[22] Popular and courtly dancing embodied the fundamental social distinction between those who worked with their hands and those who did not: dances of the working people mimed their occupations,[23] but in courtly dancing, gesture was considered "a fault to be refined."[24] Throughout Europe, court festivity was informed by the same images and the same assumptions,[25] and certainly, in the case of dancing, the same practices; cultural trends that emerged in Italy in the fifteenth century manifested themselves in England in the sixteenth, as Henry VII returned from exile in France to introduce the customs and dances of the Burgundian court.[26]

The festive practices imported to England from the Continent adapted well to the needs and preoccupations of a governing class in the process of reforming. Social mobility increased during the reign of Henry VII as a new landed nobility sprang up from the gentry and merchants. The rapid population growth experienced at the beginning of the sixteenth century and the attendant fluctuations in prices affected different strata of society more or less, improving the fortunes of some, while those of others declined. The accelerated circulation within the social hierarchy of the early sixteenth century is witnessed by the rise of both Wolsey and Cromwell from humble origins to the heights of government. Country knights were imported to court as a power base, and ambitious younger sons moved in and out, fodder for a growing bureaucracy, as Henry VII sought to restore, and Henry VIII to consolidate, the power of the Crown in relation to the established magnates.[27] The newly or temporarily elevated had to be transformed rather quickly into disciplined and useful courtiers. The feudal warrior ethic, based on honor in battle, had been replaced by a hierarchal "network of patronage";[28] honor was no longer won by brave deeds but by adroit manners that promoted princely trust and social acclaim. In the absence of martial rigor, the importance of an aestheticized physical training— less overtly aggressive, but equally competitive—was emphasized.[29]

Courtly dancing, like civility, instructed the ambitious if unrefined courtier in a way to prepare and present his credentials by means of an "outward bodily propriety" that affirmed the power of those he sought to represent.[30] In a period of social transition, behavior became a new heraldry by which the courtier created his nobility and signaled his allegiance, for in the "upward training of the body," achieved by tedious and painful means, the principle of hierarchy was blazoned on the upright figure of the dancing courtier.[31] Furthermore, in a time of uncertainty, when fortunes were being made and lost, when heirs were failing or were produced in superfluity, dancing served a talismanic function, producing through a socially oriented physical training the illusion of social control: whatever his place in the hierarchy, the dancer might reassure himself that his exertions would improve his social position as certainly as his posture.

In *The Boke named the Governour,* Elyot elaborates an ideal of dancing practice at the center of which is the reassurance that "nobility," moral and social, is created in the actions of courtly dancing. Citing Greek pedagogy, which conveniently coincided with Tudor exigency, Elyot prescribes dancing as a means by which "children of gentill nature or disposition may be trayned into the way of vertue with a pleasant facilitie" (sig. L2v), noting that many "wise men and valiant capitaines [of antiquity] imbraced dauncinge for a soveraigne and profitable exercise" (sig. K6r). The "soveraigne" exercise of dancing, then, profitably reinscribes on those "men" with the nature or disposition for gentility the requisite characteristics. Elyot, however, is careful to veil the hegemonic function of dancing practice, which is naturalized as an imitation of "the wonderfull . . . order of the celestiall bodies . . . and their motions harmonicall" (sig. K5r), and sacramentalized as "matrimonie" (sig. L1v).

The "right courtier," Elyot explains, is constituted through his performance of the Measures, a kind of Platonic-way-through-the-Beautiful-to-the-Good[32] that structures the moral elevation of the dancer from the "firste morall vertue called prudence" (sig. L3r) to the quality of maturity (sig. L4v). In the Measures, a procession of couples inched forward in an elegant unison, executing five simple steps in different sequences, beginning and ending with an "honour" which enclosed varying combinations of "singles," "doubles," sideways "*branles*," and retreating "*reprises*."[33] Training the body to perform these steps, Elyot asserts, simultaneously trained the spirit.

The "singles"—a step forward, a pause, then another step—are, in Elyot's interpretation, "two unities separate in pacinge forwarde: by whom may be signified providence and industrie" (sig. L6r). The "brawle" (*branle*), "a meane between two extremities" (sig. L4v), sways from side to side; suspending forward motion, it inspires that "celeritie and slowness" which betoken an excellent virtue (sig. L4r). The "double," three slow steps and a pause, instructs in the three branches of prudence—election, experience, and modesty (sig. M2r). The "*reprise*," a step diagonally backward, teaches circumspection (sig. L7r). In practicing those movements, the dancer learns his social lessons. He learns to move in concert with others and to relinquish improvisation; to pace forward slowly, circumspectly, and deliberately, tracing and retracing his steps; to advance steadily while not straying from his designated place. Dancing the Measures assures the courtier of achieving nobility by the mastery of a formalized "mobility."

Clearly, Elyot recommends dancing not because it is "timeless" but because it is timely, a discipline to be undertaken "not only [for] pleasure, but also profite and commoditie" (sig. Lr).[34] The humanist appeal of "profit and pleasure" is widened, with the addition of "commoditie," to include the ambitious courtier. The movements of the dance are touted as both moral and tactical, for the Measures begins with the "honour" which signifies that "at the beginninge of all our actes, we should do due honour to god, which is the roote of prudence. . . . And that in the begynnynge of all thinges we should advisedly, with some tracte of tyme, beholde and forsee the success of our enterprise" (sig. L4r). The "honour" imbues the dancer with the spirit of reverence, the foundation of all moral virtues. Governing relations between superiors and inferiors, "honour" is, at the same time, the spine of hierarchy.[35]

A display of reverence is doubly prudent, for it not only pleases the superior, it affords the courtier the opportunity to pause, collect his thoughts, and concentrate on the "success" of his "enterprise." The moral ascent that commences with a gesture of reverence is coterminous with a kind of early modern career-building, so that he who performs the gesture can ultimately become both a "wise man" and a "valiant captaine," foregoing neither worldly nor otherworldly success. The performance of respect to those above and the extraction of deference from those below not only conferred advantage upon the courtier himself, his actions reinforced the hierarchical social order from which the notion of "honour" emerged.[36]

The hierarchy valorized by courtly dancing was, of course, patriarchal, with the interests of male supremacy served by gender constructions that inscribed feminine dependence to preserve the sanctity of family and inheritance.[37] Officially charged with political significance under the Tudors by the "diplomacy of marriage" employed by Henry VII,[38] the subject of marriage and its fruits was understandably a matter of concern for Henry VIII, since the Tudor claim to the throne was somewhat tenuous, and his contributions to the succession, less than decisive. The decline or extinction of a line was of general concern as well, for lesser families were in a similar, if less conspicuous, danger of dying out.[39] Strengthening the patriarchal family through a cultural privileging of marital relations also served to strengthen the power of the state by correspondingly weakening the feudal ties of extended kinship that challenged Henry's absolutist ambitions.[40]

Paired in heterosexual couples that visually articulated the preoccupation with patriarchal marriage, Elyot's dancers display an array of gendered virtues in support of the principle of male dominance: "A man in his naturall perfection is fierce, hardy, strong in opinion, covetous of glorie, desirous of knowledge. . . . The good nature of a woman is to be milde, timerouse, tractable, benigne, of sure remembrance, and shamfaced" (sig. L1v–L2r). Elyot establishes masculine preeminence by marshaling behind him all the characteristics of "naturall perfection" which his negative image, woman, lacks. These antinomous traits, Elyot suggests, are learned through, and expressed in, deportment. The man demonstrates in his "more vehement" movements "the courage and strength that oughte to be in a man," and his partner, in movements that are "more delicate and with lesse advancing of the body," shows the "pleasant sobernesse that should be in a woman" (sig. L2r).

In a dance, of course, movement is everything, and a metonym for the opposition as a whole. As the gentleman conventionally begins the dance,[41] he assumes the active role; the lady follows and completes him by supplying what he lacks. The "associatinge of man & woman in dauncing, they both observing one nombre and tyme in their meuvinges," which "signifie[s] matrimonie" (sig. L1v), articulates an ideal of a marital order "nat begonne withoute a speciall consideration." The gender construction of male dominance was always part of a larger plan, Elyot emphasizes, the result of a "conjunction" not fortuitous but "necessarye." Courtly dancing practice established, then reinforced, the socially stabilizing parameters of gender difference that Elyot naturalizes as divinely sanctioned, obscuring their human fabrication and utility.[42] Elyot's monolithic model of dancing practice does not acknowledge the resistances the practice actually generated, but the clarity of his assertions illuminates the workings of the practice in the tightly controlled form of the masque.[43]

The Henrician masque performed the work of social stratification in two important ways: first, through the formalization of structures of hierarchy and gender in dancing and gesture, as Elyot so carefully explained; and second, in the incorporation of the monarch as exemplum into the spectacle.[44] The function of dancing in the Henrician court masque may best be understood not only through the example of the "assault on the *Chateau Vert*" but in comparison with an earlier English disguising, the visit of the Commons of London to Richard II prior to his accession in 1377.

> [I]n ye night were 130 men disguizedly apareiled and well mounted on horseback . . . and their faces covered with vizards . . . when they were come before ye mansion they alighted on foot and entered into ye haule . . . shewing a pair of dice . . . which dice were subtilly made that when ye prince shold cast he shold winne. . . . And then ye prince caused to bringe ye wyne and they dronk with great joye   And ye prince and ye lordes dansed on ye one syde, and ye mummers on ye other a great while and then they drank and tooke their leaue and so departed.[45]

This is a vivid picture of the medieval mumming on a grand scale, but it leaves one important question unanswered. The Commons of London, "130 men disguizedly apareiled," confirm Fortune's favor with weighted dice; Richard entertains his welcome guests; and all dance, "ye prince and ye lordes . . . on ye one syde, and ye mummers on ye other." But with whom did princes, lords, and mummers dance? Were there women in the court that night? Did the mummers dance with them? This account has been cited as evidence of a "division" between masquers and spectators, one that was "healed" when the two groups began to commingle in the masques of Henry's reign.[46] However, it can also be offered as evidence of dancing between masquers and spectators, unless the "130 men disguizedly apareiled" danced by themselves.[47] What is important is that neither the presence nor the absence of women has been textualized, the woman simply absorbed into the "ungendered" masculine body.[48]

The Epiphany masque of 1512 early in Henry's reign traditionally marks the occasion upon which the ostensible division between masquer and spectator was repaired by the importation of the festive customs of the Italian *maschera*.

> On the daie of the Epiphanie at night, the king with . . . xi. other were disguised, after the maner of Italie, called a maske, a thyng not seen afore in Englande, they were appareled in garmentes long and brode, wrought all with gold, with visers and cappes of gold & after the banket doen, these Maskers came in, with six gentlemen disguised in silke, bearing staffe torches, and desired the ladies to daunce, some were content, and some that knewe the fashion of it refused, because it was not a thyng commonly seen. And after thei daunced and commoned together, as the fashion of the Maske is, thei took their leaue and departed, and so did the Quene, and all the ladies. (Hall 526)

This masque retained many features of earlier festivity, vizards, torches, surprises.[49] But whatever it was that was "not seen afore"—details of masking dress, the dance between masquers and spectators, or something else entirely[50]—while the dancing in 1512 may have "healed" one division, it created another in a newly formalized distinction between men and women.

Hall's description of the Epiphany masque furthermore juxtaposes the two salient and related characteristics of the Henrician masque: the staging of the monarch into the court spectacle and the formalization of gender distinction in dancing and gesture. Richard was a participant in the pageant in the sense that the cast of dice was a ritual confirmation of the prince's fortune. However, it was his visitors who were the performers, "covered with vizards" and supplying the "subtilly made" dice; he merely played himself—fortunate prince and gracious host. Henry, however, is imbedded within the spectacle.[51] He is one of twelve masquers, his preeminence disguised by the same "visers and cappes of gold" as worn by the others, and, "desir[ing] the ladies to daunce," he behaves in the same way. However, his true identity, though hidden, is not unknown; clearly, it was known to Hall. As the king, his behavior is exemplary: while seeming to be part of a community of masquers engaged in spontaneous revels, in fact, he leads them in a rehearsed performance of a new ritual which confirms his power much as the weighted dice confirmed Richard's good fortune.

This ritual involves and verifies a view of what it is to be a gentleman, with Henry as royal paradigm. Unlike the description of the earlier mumming, from which women were literally if not actually absent, this passage is remarkable for its emphasis on gender difference and in its elaboration of gender roles. In the mumming of 1377, the woman was, if present, an undifferentiated part of universal man; if absent, unremarked. However, in Henry's court, men and women are precisely distinguished, and the ritual of gaining feminine consent is central: the gentlemen masquers invite the ladies to dance; some ladies accept the invitation and some "that knewe the fashion of it refused."

Gender is the fundamental category here, separating masquers and ladies and regulating their interaction. Gender is defined by characteristic actions: gentlemen "desire" the ladies to dance, ladies do not "desire" the gentlemen. Although in theory ladies may accept or refuse a masquer's invitation, few apparently exercise the latter option, for most dance and common together, "as the fashion of the Maske is." Roles are consistent throughout: the ladies follow the gentlemen's lead from beginning to end, responding in the affirmative to the gentlemen's "desire" and departing after the gentlemen have finished. Far from hiding women amongst the brambles of universal man, or failing to note their absence, as did the chronicler of Richard's mumming, Hall cultivates men and women in separate rows, trimming them into monitory forms according to patterns implicitly inspired by the desires of the monarch.

One project of the Henrician masque, disguised as entertainment and perhaps entertaining in itself, was that of social segmentation, a kind of "division of the kingdom" into discrete units which, once established, were sanctioned to interact in a strictly regulated way. Both the Tudor disguising and the later masques shared a common structure: they began with the entrance, often in a pageant-wagon, of the disguisers, usually divided into two groups, of men and women. The disguisers danced alone and then together; descended into the hall to dance the dances they had rehearsed; and returned to the pageant-wagon which conveyed them out.[52] The proceedings were ordered and unambiguous, with roles clearly defined, groups of masquers segregated in space and time, and interactions between them carefully governed. The participants in courtly festivities were assigned to oppositional categories—those of "masquer" and "spectator," and "lord" and "lady." Boundaries were marked by habiliment, behavior, and locality: symmetrical numbers of masquers were dressed identically in conspicuous opulence; they enacted an emblematic relationship for an assortment of spectators; and they were restricted by the structure of the masque, and to a particular space within the hall. Once established, the integrity of these groups was rigorously maintained: persons did not move into or out of a group at their own discretion, and the time, place, and form of any interaction between them was conventionally predetermined.

A taxonomic preoccupation did not, of course, descend upon the court at the instant of Henry's coronation; the same tendencies were evident toward the end of the reign of Henry VII, at the marriage of Henry's older brother Prince Arthur to Katherine of Aragon, later Henry's first wife. The marriage was celebrated with an elaborate pageant in which eight disguised ladies were liberated from a castle by eight goodly knights who arrived by mountain-shaped pageant-car, and the sixteen, half in English dress and half in Spanish, danced together; after they had departed, "the duke of York and a few very distinguished members of the audience descended into the hall and danced basse dances."[53] During the festivities on another evening, twelve knights descended from an arbor and danced "many different dances," and were followed by twelve ladies who emerged from a giant lantern to "dance alone and then [couple] with the knights." In yet another pageant, after the lords had danced, the ladies descended and with them "daunced there a long season many and divers roundes and newe daunces." These pageants record the festive reproduction of hierarchical opposition: men and women, liberators and prisoners, masquers and very distinguished members of the audience, those in Spanish costume and those in English dress. The artificiality of these categories is aestheticized by the symmetry of the subdivisions: sixteen dancers in the castle masque are divided into four groups uniform in gender and nationality. Discrete groups are isolated in space and time: twelve lantern ladies dance alone and establish their difference before coupling with twelve knights from the arbor, and masquers and ladies likewise dance separately before they dance with the lords and ladies of the court.

The division of a commonwealth of revelers into symmetrical groups in distinctive dress seems an unremarkable and innocent form of amusement, and one not particularly saturated with social import; today it is a comfortingly familiar nineteenth-century operatic convention. However, the uniform dress of English masquers was apparently unique to sixteenth-century England, not a characteristic adopted from the fifteenth-century Burgundian court, since Hall remarks admiringly on the variety of French masquing dress on the Field of the Cloth of Gold.[54] The English emphasis on fixed and stable groups indicates a singular preoccupation with, and anxiety concerning, social fluidity, and an attempt to promote and achieve an enduring structure. The masquer and spectator, lord and lady, remained for the entirety of the entertainment in his or her predetermined role, acting only in concert, and in the manner prescribed in the conventional scenario. He or she neither wore inappropriate clothes or changed them, for the identical apparel of the masquers was an emblem of social cohesion, related to the sumptuary laws which increasingly striated the society.[55] Court celebrations, then, rehearsed many of the means by which the equilibrium of an unstable society might be restored: affiliation, glamorized by costly costumes, was promoted; unison movement and a suggestibility to direction were honored; and a tendency toward unsanctioned personal forays was eliminated.

If the structure of the pageant rehearsed social expectations, the dancing itself rehearsed intimate relations. The *basse* dances, "divers roundes and newe daunces," regulated interactions between men and women in the ways explained by Thomas Elyot. In the courtly round, lords and ladies paired in heterosexual couples reflected the amorous songs of the troubadours; later, the dancing couple of the *basse* dance and "newe daunces"—the "bargenettes, pauvions, turgions, and roundes" to which Elyot refers (sig. K7v)—"signified matrimonie" as they practiced gender difference. The dances within the masques, like the masques as a whole, served to regulate the opportunity and the terms of interaction between men and women: the gentleman was required to "desire" a lady to dance, and the lady, to respond correctly at the proper time, in harmony with her immediate community, and with the partner selected for her—she was not permitted to emerge at her pleasure from a giant lantern and couple posthaste with any knight or guest she fancied.

Early in the reign, an elaborate pageant served as a model for the articulation of the hierarchical opposition of "gentle and base" that structured relations both inside and outside the court.[56] At the celebration in 1511 of the queen's "churching" at Richmond, an "uprising" against the courtiers of the "Garden of Pleasure" followed the pageant and dancing (Hall 518–19). After supper, the lords and ladies retired to the richly hanged "white Hall" to view an interlude of the gentlemen of the chapel. When the entertainment was finished, "the mynstrels beganne to playe, and the lordes and ladies beganne to daunce." The king, meanwhile, departed unnoticed, and returned with the richly dressed disguising: "When the tyme was come, ye sayd pageant was brought forth into presence, & then descended a lord and lady by coples, & then the mynstrels, which were also disguised also daunced, and the lordes and ladies daunced, that it was a pleasure to beholde." As the lords and ladies prepared to retire, "rude people ranne to the pageant, and rent, tare, and spoiled the pageant." The king, "in token of liberality," had "appointed the ladies, gentlewomen, and the Ambassadors to take the [gold] letters of their garments." As they did so, "the common people perceiving ranne to the king, and stripped hym into his hosen and doublet, and his companions in likewise . . . wherefore the kings guard came suddenly and put the people back. . . . and all these hurts were turned to laughing and game" (519). This pageant opposes the "unlettered" masses—rude people who run, rend, tear, and spoil—with the lords and ladies who are orderly enough to descend by couples, civil enough to dance sufficiently well to be a "pleasure to beholde," liberal enough to give away their golden letters, powerful enough to withstand an uprising, and good-natured enough to laugh it away. The lords and ladies give a performance that naturalizes a system of dominance and aristocratic entitlement.

The hierarchical model of social relations circulated by the dancing and gesture of Henrician masque was reinforced by visual emblems of social ordering that replicated the structuring principle. The year after the masque of Epiphany, the disguisers of a pageant emerged from a "riche Mount . . . set full of riche flowers of silke." "On the top stode a goodly Bekon geuing light, round about the Bekon sat the king and five other . . . the Mount . . . came before the quene, and the king and his companie discended and daunced: then sodenly the Mount opened, and out came six ladies . . . and thei daunced alone. Then the lordes of the Mount took the ladies and daunced together: and the ladies re-entered and the Mount closed" (Hall 535). This pageant erects characteristic boundaries between the men "[o]n the top . . . round about the Bekon" and the ladies who emerge from the base, and imposes behavioral sanctions in the forms of precedence—the king and his "companie" descend and dance, then the mount opens, then out come the ladies.

Furthermore, the setting is itself an icon of social structure, with actual height denoting social elevation, the king and the other male masquers, already atop the "riche Mount" as it appears in the hall, naturalized as an eternal presence. That the monarch is the chief luminary is somewhat ponderously allegorized by the location of scenic illumination: in medieval pageants, the light originated outside the hierarchical peak, produced by common torchbearers who cast a circle of light around the masquers; here, however, the masquers, towering over the spectators, appear to be the very source of light. Masquing ladies, in contrast, are visibly subordinated, entrapped within a pyramidical mount that opens to liberate them only after the king and his company have descended and danced. That the ladies' dance follows that of the lords emphasizes their separate and secondary status, one further underlined when the lords of the mount take the ladies and dance together. Never on equal footing, the ladies are "conveighed out of the hall" in the lower portion of the firmly closed mount.

The visual trope of the "riche Mount," then, reinscribed a hierarchy that was specifically gendered. This mount of hierarchy was a familiar sight in Henrician masque, displaying the monarch and his courtiers upon a lofty promontory and disgorging ladies from its base. If the ladies were, on occasion, elevated above the men, as happened in the pageant of the *Chateau Vert*, they were also imprisoned and isolated, helpless in the "nether end" of a castle tower (Hall 631). When Lady Scorn and her company of choirboys, fighting from "under nether the basse fortresse of the castle," are "driven out of the place and fled," then the ladies are "taken as prisoners by the handes, and brought . . . doune." In most pageants, though, the ladies are emplaced firmly beneath the lords throughout, as at the entertainment for the French ambassadors in 1527. Following a debate on the relative importance of riches and love, a mount appeared, covered with rich stones, roses, and pomegranates, and eight lords, who "descended from the mounte and toke ladeys and daunced divers daunces" (723). Eight other ladies then emerged from a cave to dance with the lords, but were suddenly interrupted when six lords with masks and long garments, masquers who were "not knowne," entered and "tooke Ladies and daunsed lustely about the place" (724).

Related to the images of "lusty" masculine dominance circulated in courtly dances and replicated in iconic settings, the form of the monarch's appearance in pageants and masques enforced the notion of male privilege. Typically, Henry, in the company of a number of other lords, disguised himself in spectacular apparel, surprised the spectators with an impromptu or staged intrusion into the hall, danced rehearsed dances with the ladies, and disvisored as dramatically as possible. In the Epiphany masque, Henry deftly inserts himself into the spectacle, his primacy concealed by the identical dress worn by the other knights. "[A]ppareled in garmentes long and brode, wrought all with gold," the masquers are clearly of the aristocracy, but social distinctions among them are effaced by their impenetrable costume and masks. Yet the preeminence of the king, though concealed, is not unknown, so that Henry enacts not a "spectacle of rule" but a spectacle of role, the paradigm of the new patriarch.[57]

"[A]fter the banket doen," Henry leads the masquers, sharply delineated by their dress and the light from the "staffe torches" that surrounds them, in a bold intrusion into the relatively passive company. "[F]ierce, hardy, strong in opinion, covetous of glorie, desirous of knowledge" expressed in commensurate "advancing of the body," the masquers desire the ladies to dance; some of the ladies, those "tractable [and] benigne" were content, but the "timerouse, of sure remembrance, and shamfaced" declined "because it was not a thyng commonly seen." After the masquers and ladies "daunced and commoned together . . . thei took their leaue and departed." Henry's was an example that the court had, perforce, to follow;[58] but concealing his identity, and therefore not acknowledging the court's obligation to imitate him, Henry rehearsed them in hierarchy and gender difference in a way that denied the hegemonic reality of his actions.

In one respect, though, Henry's performance was inimitable. Unlike the rest of the court, Henry frequently changed roles during the masque, and this source of dramatic excitement was an important emblem of his power. Often, he began the festivities as a spectator, but when the attention of the court was occupied with the performance, he surreptitiously "shifted himself" and returned as a masquer. After one Shrove supper, "began the daunsyng and every man toke muche hede to them that daunsed. The kyng percevyng that, withdrew hym selfe sodenly out of the place, with certayn other appoynted for that purpose [and returned with the lords in opulent masking dress] of blew Velvet and Crymosyne with long sleves, all cut and lyned with clothe of golde" (Hall 514). Unlike other courtly participants, the identity of the king is not fixed—he has the license to change his apparel as well as his estate during the masque.

On some occasions, the king abruptly withdraws when the attention of the court is occupied with the dancing, and returns visibly more impressive, adorned with the regulated perquisites of the aristocracy, in an emblem of the male performative. On others, as after the pageant of the "riche Mount," he sheds masquing dress to return in royal guise, the most impressive role of all: "Then the Kyng shifted himself and came to the Quene, and sat at the banqute which was very sumpteous" (Hall 535). Henry, then, is repeatedly seen to descend into the anonymity of masquing lords, to startle the spectators with an unexpected entrance, and—recalling Henry Richmond—to rise like a "riche Mount" above the other lords as he disvisors. Henry's assertion of the right to the ultimate mobility, that of remaking himself king, coincides with the strategic concentration of the court on his performance as a man, so that when Henry performed in a masque, dancing was an exercise that indeed showed the mover's power to rise, and enlightened the beholder to it, strengthening the hierarchy from the courtly base of commoning dancers to the top of the mount.

A century later in *Henry VIII*, Shakespeare conflates the pageant of the "assault on the *Chateau Vert*" with another chronicled banquet held at York Place,[59] dramatizing the "first dance" of Henry and Anne that culminated in the Reformation.[60] As a Lord flirts heatedly with

Anne, one of the Cardinal's guests, the banquet is interrupted by the entrance of

> A noble troupe of Strangers,
> For so they seeme; th'have left their Barge and landed,
> And hither make, as great Embassadors
> From forraigne princes.[61]

The intrusion, however, is not an embassy but a masque:

> Hoboyes. Enter King and others as Maskers, habited like Shepheards, usher'd by the Lord Chamberlain. They pass directly before the Cardinall, and gracefully salute him. (754–57)

"Out of the great respect they beare to beauty," the "shepherds" have left their flocks and "[c]rave leave to view these ladies, and entreat / An hour of Revels with 'em" (762 65). The Cardinal bids the masquers "take their pleasures" (769), the masquers choose ladies, and the King chooses Anne (770), to whom he extends the courtesy of a kiss. The Cardinal offers the now overheated King some "fresher ayre . . . [i]n the next Chamber," and the scene ends as king and company withdraw to continue the festivities:

> Lead in your Ladies ev'ry one: Sweet Partner,
> I must not yet forsake you: let's be merry,
> Good my Lord Cardinall; I have halfe a dozen healths
> To drink to these fair Ladies, and a measure
> To lead 'em once again; and then let's dreame
> Who's best in favour. Let the Musicke knock it.
> (812–17)

In this short scene, Shakespeare borrows the devices of the Henrician masque—the sudden intrusion of the masquers into the banquet, the disguised king, the commoning of masquer and spectator—to unravel the "apparatus of royal power" that Hall and Elyot so painstakingly constructed out of the same material. Shakespeare shows, in a sensual fantasy that owes much to the anti-dance writing of Catholic and Puritan critics, dances that are "merry," not "moral," characterized by consuming heat, not by stately restraint, an instrument of male appetite, not of masculine control. However, that Shakespeare dramatizes as a dance an event that was both conclusive and generative is a tacit acknowledgment that the dancing of the court masque was a practice that transformed English society and empowered the monarch, if perhaps not quite as Elyot had envisioned.

Through dancing and spectacle, the Henrician masque reproduced the concentration of authority at the patriarchal pinnacle, and circulated rituals of power that informed later ages and generated resistances at multiple sites. The Henrician masque is nowhere credited with the "perfection" of Jacobean masque that resides in the unity of the elements of decor, poetry, music, and dance. But, in effect, Henrician pageants and masques were equally unified, if not around a verbal text. Had the pageant and dancing by themselves proved inadequate, certainly a spoken text would have been required and preserved;[62] but in the Henrician era, the discursive function of the masque was sufficiently realized by the rehearsal in miniature of the principles of social ordering, and the terpsichorean elevation of the sovereign. If, in Jean Howard's words, ideology is "the obviousness of culture, what goes without saying, what is lived as true,"[63] then the ideology of dancing involved rendering natural, even enjoyable, a society stratified according to rank and gender under an absolutist ruler. In the Henrician masque, this enjoyment operated through the danced interludes and the participation of the sovereign. Practice makes a practice "perfect," and naturalizes it as well: how many, even today, fail to question whether it is "natural" for the gentleman the "desire" the lady to dance, rather than the reverse?

Notes

I would like to acknowledge the contributions of Jean E. Howard, David Scott Kastan, and Peter C. Herman to the preparation of this essay.

1. Eric W. Ives, *Anne Boleyn* (Oxford: Basil Blackwell, 1986), reconstructs the scene from the accounts of Hall and others (48–49).

2. Hall's *Chronicle*, 1548, 1550 (London, 1809; reprint, New York: AMS Press, 1965), 631.

3. Sir Thomas Elyot, *The Boke named the Governour* (London: Thomas Bertheleti, 1531; facsimile reprint, ed. R. C. Alston, Menston, Eng.: Scolar Press, 1970), sig. L1v.

4. Enid Welsford's observation, made in *The Court Masque* (New York: Russell and Russell, 1927), that dancing was "the *raison d'être* of the whole performance" (166), is often cited as a point of reference, as by Stephen Orgel in *The Jonsonian Masque* (New York: Columbia University Press, 1965), 5. In comparison with the attention recently lavished on Elizabethan and Jacobean festivity, the Henrician masque has received little critical scrutiny. An important exception is Gordon Kipling's *The Triumph of Honour: Burgundian Origins of the Elizabethan Renaissance* (The Hague: Leyden University Press, 1977). Earlier studies on the development and structure of the English masque include Paul Reyher, *Les Masques Anglais* (New York: Benjamin Blom, 1909); Welsford, *Court Masque;* E. K. Chambers, *The Elizabethan Stage*, vol. 1 (Oxford: Oxford University Press, 1928), and *The Mediaeval Stage*, vol. 1 (London: Oxford University Press, 1903); and Glynne Wickham, *Early English Stages,*

vol. 1 (London: Routledge and Kegan Paul, 1959), and *The Medieval Theatre* (Cambridge: Cambridge University Press, 1974). Two works on the seventeenth-century masque, Orgel's *Jonsonian Masque* and John C. Meagher's *Method and Meaning in Jonson's Masques* (Notre Dame: University of Notre Dame Press, 1966), contain valuable material on the Henrician masque.

5. The writing of dance historians on the Renaissance (though not on the modern and postmodern eras) is still largely informed by humanist tropes—see, for example, the recent article "Skill and Invention in the Renaissance Ballroom," by Anne Daye, in *Historical Dance* 2, no. 6 (1988–91), 12–15. Literary commentators, however, are beginning to acknowledge dancing as a social practice: Harry Berger, Jr., "'Against the Sink-a-Pace' Sexual and Family Politics in *Much Ado About Nothing*," in *Shakespeare Quarterly* 33 (1982), 302–13, and Harold Jenkins, "The Ball Scene in *Much Ado About Nothing*," in *Shakespeare: Text, Language, Criticism,* ed. Bernard Fabian and Kurt Tetzli von Rosador (Hildesheim: Olms, 1987); these, however, focus upon the dances as ancillary to the written texts, and do not examine either the technique or ideology of the practice in depth. Mark Franko's valuable work, *The Dancing Body in Renaissance Choreography* (Birmingham, Ala.: Summa, 1986), an important study of the semiotics of the "dancing body," does not include the paradigm of gender.

6. Wickham, *Early English Stages,* vol. 1, 221. It should be noted that the descriptions of the Henrician masque by Hall and others are very brief, which complicates analysis, and focus upon the opulence of the settings and masquing dress.

7. My analysis is informed by Michel Foucault's theories concerning the disciplining of the body in *Discipline and Punish: The Birth of the Prison,* trans. Alan Sheridan (New York: Vintage, 1979), and *Power/Knowledge,* ed. Colin Gordon (New York: Pantheon, 1972); and the work on civility of Norbert Elias, *The Civilizing Process* (New York: Pantheon, 1978), and Frank Whigham, *Ambition and Privilege: The Social Tropes of Elizabethan Courtesy Theory* (Berkeley and Los Angeles: University of California Press, 1984). Behind my reading of Elyot is Foucault's image of the "docile body" that is "manipulated, shaped, trained, which obeys, responds, becomes skilful and increases its forces . . . one which may be subjected, used, transformed, and improved" (*Discipline and Punish,* 135–55 [cited at 136]). While Foucault assumes that a body's docility is defined by parameters of class, and that the bodies of the lower classes are systematically transformed and used by institutions that serve to maintain the control of the upper classes, and although he discusses the "docile body" as an invention of the "classical age," the characteristics of, and operations upon, the body that Foucault identifies as manifestations of eighteenth-century institutional oppression of the underclass accurately describe those that the early modern courtier inflicted upon himself.

8. Perry Anderson, in *Lineages of the Absolutist State* (London: New Left Books, 1974), observes that Henry VIII was practically an absolutist monarch (122); his discussion of the Tudor era has influenced my readings of the masques, and my assertions.

9. Stephen Orgel has formulated the widely cited paradigm: "what the

spectator watched he ultimately became. The most common method of effecting this transformation was to have the production culminate, literally and dramatically, in the revels, the dance between the masquers and members of the audience" (*Jonsonian Masque*, 7).

10. The trope of the cosmic dance figures prominently both in Renaissance defenses of dancing and in later commentary; Meagher traces from antiquity the notion that the harmonies of music and the motions of dancing were replications of cosmic order (*Method and Meaning*, 58–61, 82–86). This trope was also a site of resistance: John Northbrooke is careful to begin his diatribe against dancing, in *A Treatise Against Dicing, Dancing, Vaine Playes and Interludes* (London, 1577; reprint, London: Shakespeare Society, 1843) with a refutation of the supposed cosmic origins of dancing (146).

11. Ben Jonson, *Pleasure Reconciled to Virtue*, in *Ben Jonson*, ed. C. H. Hereford, Percy Simpson, and Evelyn Simpson, 11 vols. (Oxford: Clarendon Press, 1925–63), vol. 7 (1941), 269–73.

12. Eric A. Havelock, in *Preface to Plato* (Cambridge, Mass.: Belknap Press, 1963), suggests that dancing served as a mnemonic device in the oral culture of Greece, with the sequence of physical motions required by the performance of a speech strengthened by the associated patterns of danced movement (151). Pierre Bourdieu, in *Outline of a Theory of Practice* (trans. Richard Nice [Cambridge: Cambridge University Press, 1977]), cited as epigraph to *Ambition and Privilege*, observes that movement functions as an abbreviated cultural reminder.

13. The morality of dancing was defended by courtly servants like Elyot and Sir John Davies in his poem "*Orchestra*"; and its immorality was reviled by Puritans like John Northbrooke and Catholics Erasmus and Vives. Juan Luis Vives denigrates dancing for both men, in *Linguae Latinae exercitatio* (1539), and women, in *De institutio foeminae christianae* (1523), translated by Richard Hyrde in 1540 as *The Instruction of a Christian Woman*. Here, Vives argues against dancing at great length, emphasizing its lasciviousness and the consequent danger it poses to women of a downward transformation—the cause, as he puts it, "that so many yonge women lye pockye, and scabbed, in spittals, and lazer houses, and go a begging," sig. D3r. As Constance Jordan points out in *Renaissance Feminism* (Ithaca: Cornell University Press, 1990), although Vives strongly voiced injunctions against a woman's rule, Mary ruled anyway, however briefly (118–20). According to Hall, she danced, too— emerging out of a "riche mount" and dancing with the masquers at the entertainment for the French ambassadors in 1527 (*Chronicle*, 723–24). Jordan goes on to assert, in the matter of woman's rule, that Elyot's *Defense of Good Women* (1540) "functions (whether intentionally or not) as a refutation of Vives' *Instruction*" (119); perhaps the defense of dancing in the *Governour* was written in response to Vives's sentiments. Elyot seems to have prevailed, for there is little evidence in Hall for "not dancing" in the Henrician court, among either men or women.

14. Stephen Greenblatt, in *Renaissance Self-Fashioning: From More to Shakespeare* (Chicago: University of Chicago Press, 1980), discusses "repetition

as self-fashioning," emphasizing the importance of the "repetition of the self-constitutive act" (201) such as Elyot theorizes were the movements of courtly dancing.

15. See Judith Butler, "Performative Acts and Gender Construction," in *Performing Feminisms,* ed. Sue-Ellen Case (Baltimore: The Johns Hopkins University Press, 1990), 271–78, and Susan R. Bordo, "The Body and the Reproduction of Femininity: A Feminist Appropriation of Foucault," in *Gender/Body/Knowledge: Feminist Reconstructions of Being and Knowing,* ed. Alison M. Jaggar and Susan R. Bordo (New Brunswick: Rutgers University Press, 1989). Butler writes that "the phenomenological theory of 'acts,' espoused by Edmund Husserl, Maurice Merleau-Ponty, and George Herbert Mead . . . seeks to explain the mundane way in which social agents *constitute* social reality through language, gesture, and all manner of symbolic social sign" (270).

16. See Judith Lynne Hanna, in *Dance, Sex, and Gender: Signs of Identity, Dominance, Defiance, and Desire* (Chicago: University of Chicago Press, 1988), on the dancing couple as a model of gender relations (12).

17. Peter Herman's description, private correspondence.

18. Toinot Arbeau, *Orchésographie* (Langres: Jehan de Preyz, 1588, 1589, and many reprints), trans. Julia Sutton (New York: Dover, 1967), 16.

19. Catherine Belsey's definition has influenced my formulation; in "Disrupting Sexual Difference: Meaning and Gender in the Comedies," in *Alternative Shakespeares,* ed. John Drakakis (London: Methuen, 1985), she describes "discourses (or knowledges)" as "a set of terms and relations between terms in which a specific understanding is inscribed" (166).

20. Franko suggests that a model of the "dancing body" may be assumed as is a model of civility—"a systematic and generalizable perspective on movement quality within choreographic descriptions" (*Dancing Body,* 4).

21. Hayden White, *Tropics of Discourse: Essays in Cultural Criticism* (Baltimore: The Johns Hopkins University Press, 1978), 3.

22. "It would not be seemly," Messer Federigo warns, "for a gentleman to honor a country festival with his presence where the spectators and the company are persons of low birth," in Baldesar Castiglione, *The Book of the Courtier,* trans. Charles S. Singleton (New York: Doubleday, 1959), 101. On elite withdrawal from popular culture, see Peter Burke, *Popular Culture in Early Modern Europe* (New York: Harper and Row, 1978), esp. 29 and 270; Walter Sorell's *Dance in Its Time* (New York: Doubleday, 1981), 3; and Carl Sachs, *World History of the Dance,* trans. Bessie Schonberg (New York: W. W. Norton, 1937), 300–301. The Italian dancing treatise that commemorates this withdrawal, Domenico da Piacenza's *De arte saltandi et choreas ducendi* (or *De la arte di ballare et danzare,* in Paris, Bibliothèque Nationale, fonds it. 972), is dated ca. 1425. The authoritative text on courtly dancing is, somewhat paradoxically, the *Orchésographie* of the middle-class French cleric Toinot Arbeau; the most complete English text, *The Maner of Dauncing of Base Daunces after the Use of Fraunce* . . . printed by Robert Copeland (1521; facsimile ed., Sussex: Pear Tree Press, 1937). For reconstructions of sixteenth-century dances,

see Ingrid Brainard, *The Art of Courtly Dancing in the Early Renaissance* (West Trenton, Mass.: I. G. Brainard, 1981), which has an excellent bibliography, and Mabel Dolmetsch, *Dances of England and France: 1450–1600* (1949; reprint, New York: Da Capo, 1976).

23. Burke, *Popular Culture*, 30.

24. Franko, *Dancing Body*, 46.

25. Roy Strong, *Art and Power* (1973; reprint, Woodbridge, Suffolk: Boydell Press, 1984), 31.

26. Whigham notes that dancing was an indispensable supplement to classical studies in the program of humanist education transmitted from Italy to England through Bruno and Alberti (*Ambition and Privilege*, 13). Kipling discusses the Burgundian influence on English dancing practice, and specifically the integration of dancing into the pageant setting (*Triumph of Honour*, 104–6).

27. John A. Guy, *Tudor England* (Oxford: Oxford University Press, 1988); G. R. Elton, *England under the Tudors*, 3d ed. (London: Routledge, 1955), and *Reform and Reformation: England, 1509–1558* (Cambridge: Harvard University Press, 1977); Conrad Russell, *The Crisis of Parliaments* (Oxford: Oxford University Press, 1971); Mervyn James, *Society, Politics and Culture in Early Modern England* (Cambridge: Cambridge University Press, 1986). Russell (5–13), Guy (31–37, 44, and 49) and Elton (*England*, 7–15) discuss social mobility; Elton (*England*, 43–46 and *Reform*, 27) and Guy (156 and 165) note the royal "courtship" of the country gentry; and James (307–20) and Elton (*Reform*, 25) discuss the transition from warrior to courtier society.

28. Elton, *Reform*, 25.

29. James discusses the transition from a feudal to a courtly concept of honor, stressing the competitive component of the latter (*Society, Politics and Culture*, 307–20, esp. 312–13).

30. Elias, *Civilizing Process*, 55, 79–80, and 100–102.

31. Georges Vigarello, "The Upward Training of the Body from the Age of Chivalry to Courtly Civility," in *Fragments for a History of the Human Body, Part Two*, ed. Michel Feher with Ramona Naddaff and Nadia Tazi (New York: Zone Press, 1989), esp. 152 and 154. Elias also notes the connection between personal and social structure (*Civilizing Process*, 201).

32. Vigarello emphasizes the Platonic resonances of posture ("Upward Training," 153).

33. The *basse* dance, "Queen of Measures," reigned on the Continent from the beginning of the fifteenth century to the middle of the sixteenth. There were differences between the Italian *bassadanza*, the Burgundian *basse* dance, and the English Measures, but "despite the differences in choreography from region to region, [the *basse* dance] is reducible to an identity which was exemplary for the Renaissance" (Franko, *Dancing Body*, 50). Dolmetsch identifies the Measures as "the transformed English *basse* dance of the Elizabethan period" (*Dances of England and France*, 49). Arbeau, in 1588, observes that the *basse* dance is long outdated, but describes it nevertheless (*Orchésographie*, 51–56).

34. Dedicated to King Henry, *The Governour* apparently pleased him well enough to secure the writer's appointment to the court of Charles V.

35. James, *Society, Politics and Culture*, 312–13.

36. Lawrence Stone, *The Family, Sex and Marriage in England, 1500–1800* (London: Weidenfeld and Nicolson, 1977), asserts that respectful gestures strengthened the hierarchy (177). Judith Lynne Hanna, in *To Dance Is Human: A Theory of Non-Verbal Communication* (Chicago: University of Chicago Press, 1979), notes that dancing "is part of those networks of social stratification that organize the interconnected activities of members of a society" (25).

37. See *Making a Difference*, ed. Gayle Greene and Coppélia Kahn (London: Methuen, 1985), 3–4.

38. Elton, *England*, 71.

39. Guy, *Tudor England*, 49.

40. See ibid., 81–83, on Henry's ambitions; and Stone on the strengthening of the patriarchal family (*Family, Sex and Marriage*, 133–38).

41. Arbeau, *Orchésographie*, 52.

42. An instance of what Whigham terms "the mystification of the contingent as absolute" (*Ambition and Privilege*, 67).

43. As Diane Macdonell observes in *Theories of Discourse: An Introduction* (Oxford: Basil Blackwell, 1986), "prevailing practices, by subordinating women, [can] promote a gendered resistance" (36). In fact, courtly dancing did promote a sort of resistance within the masque, as when the masquers "daunced lustely" with one another; but resistances were more fully articulated later on the popular stage.

44. In the analysis of the masques that follows, I will not deal with issues of occasion, nor will I focus on the diversity of dancing practice: since my project is the introduction into the critical mainstream of an operational and ideological model of dancing in the Henrician masque (comparable to Whigham's model of civility), I will, in the interests of clarity, resist the urge to note and to account for the points at which the model dissolves. This will be the subject of later studies—my own, and, I hope, those of others. It is evident, however, that Henry enjoyed dressing up like the popular hero Robin Hood (Hall, *Chronicle*, 513); and that the Henrician masque was notable for its incorporation of popular elements that, in Jacobean times, were rigidly segregated in the antimasque.

45. London, British Library, Harley 247, in J. Stow, *A Survey of London*, ed. C. L. Kingsford (Oxford: Clarendon Press, 1908); passage cited in Welsford, *Court Masque*, 3–39; Chambers, *Medieval Stage*, vol. 1, 394–95; Wickham, *Early English Stages*, vol. 1, 207; and Reyher, *Masques Anglais*, 3–4.

46. Wickham, *Early English Stages*, vol. 1, 208.

47. There were dances performed by men, such as the sword dances or the Morris, a popular dance also performed at court. Although best known as a sixteenth-century dance, there may have been a fourteenth-century equivalent; see Arbeau, *Orchésographie*, 177, and Welsford, *Court Masque*, 26–30 and 119–20.

48. Peter Stallybrass, "Patriarchal Territories: The Body Enclosed," in *Rewriting the Renaissance: The Discourses of Sexual Difference in Early Modern*

Europe, ed. Margaret W. Ferguson, Maureen Quilligan, and Nancy J. Vickers (Chicago: University of Chicago Press, 1986), notes the assumption of an "ungendered" male body by writers as diverse as Bakhtin and Elias, following the example of "early Elizabethan proclamations on apparel that legislate men's dress but are silent on women's" until 1574 (125). Franko, in his "working model for the relationship of the social dancer to his audience," makes the same assumption (*Dancing Body,* 3), as do other commentators on this passage, including Chambers, Reyher, Welsford, and Wickham. And so does Elyot, in promoting courtly dancing as the exercise of masculine "nobility."

49. Chambers, *Medieval Stage,* vol. 1, 151.

50. Welsford (*Court Masque,* 130–35) and Orgel (*Jonsonian Masque,* 27) speculate on what was "not seene afore." Although critics now agree that the dance of masquer and spectator was the thing "not afore seen," Hall sometimes characterizes details of dress that way, as in *Chronicle,* 719. Welsford suggests (137–40) that the "real novelty" was "the introduction of a new element of gallantry and intrigue," consistent with the introduction of gender roles. This is the one example of women's refusal to dance that I have found in Hall, which seems to indicate that Vives's influence in the matter of dancing was not decisive.

51. Not, as Stephen Orgel observes in *Illusion of Power: Political Theater in the English Renaissance* (Berkeley and Los Angeles: University of California Press, 1975), as James was, part of the spectacle as spectator (16).

52. Welsford, *Court Masque,* 122.

53. C. L. Kingsford, *Chronicles of London* (Oxford: Oxford University Press, 1905), 234, cited in Welsford, *Court Masque,* 120–21; Wickham, *Early English Stages,* vol. 1, 208–9.

54. Welsford asserts that the English uniformity of dress was singular, citing Hall (*Court Masque,* 143).

55. Wilfred Hooper, in "The Tudor Sumptuary Laws" (*English Historical Review* 30 [1915], 433–49), observes that Henry VIII's first parliament passed a "lengthy" sumptuary law in 1510 that continued earlier restrictions but imposed forfeiture of the offending apparel, outlined measures for its recovery, and gave the sovereign the right to make exemptions (433). Where certain women under the earlier acts were exempted, women were excluded in the 1510 law. See Stallybrass on the ungendered male body in sumptuary legislation, n. 48 above.

56. See Whigham's discussion, "The Tropes of Social Hierarchy," *Ambition and Privilege,* 63–88.

57. David Kastan, "Proud Majesty Made a Subject: Shakespeare and the Spectacle of Rule," in *Shakespeare Quarterly* 37 (1986), 458–75. Kastan rightly suggests that representations of proud kingship on the public stage may have "weakened the structure of authority" (461); however, within the Henrician court, the representation of an ideal of masculine "gentility" by the king served to enforce its authority.

58. As Stephen Orgel observes, "no one could refuse [to dance] for long, knowing that beneath the disguise danced the king," and no one could refuse

to emulate him, for "[w]hen the monarch has moved into the masque world, the court is obliged to follow" (*Jonsonian Masque,* 27).

59. Alan Brissenden, *Shakespeare and the Dance* (Atlantic Highlands, N.J.: Humanities Press, 1981), 103.

60. Wickham, *Medieval Theatre,* 165–66.

61. *The Famous History of the Life of King Henry the Eight,* in *The First Folio of Shakespeare,* Norton Facsimile, prepared by Charleton Hinman (New York: W. W. Norton, 1968), vol. 1, 2, 740–43.

62. Wickham suggests that the words spoken on these occasions were "superfluous" (*Early English Stages,* vol. 1, 221).

63. Jean E. Howard, "Scripts and/versus Playhouses: Ideological Production and the Renaissance Public Stage," *Renaissance Drama* 20 (1989), 31–49, esp. 37.

Mary Shelton and Her Tudor Literary Milieu

PAUL G. REMLEY

Recent humanistic scholarship has drawn attention to reforms promoting the education of women during the reign of Henry VIII. Nevertheless, while several studies have addressed the attainment of literacy by certain women of the Tudor aristocracy,[1] there has been surprisingly little discussion of the details of their efforts as prose-writers, poets, copyists, and collectors. Surviving specimens of their writing range from copywork, glosses, and marginalia to holographic letters, substantial devotional works, and original poems.[2] The present study offers the first thorough survey of contemporary evidence for the life and literary activities of Mary Shelton, prominent member of the Norfolk gentry and sometime attendant of Anne Boleyn. Shelton has been mentioned most often in connection with the private lives of prominent Tudor poets.[3] She is, in some accounts, the waspish inamorata who spurned the love of Thomas Wyatt and, in others, the confidante and reputed adulterer whose trysts with Henry Howard, earl of Surrey, are recorded among documents from the proceedings that led to the poet's execution. The names of Shelton and one of her sisters, Margaret, crop up repeatedly in rumor and innuendo issuing from periods when Henry was seeking a new concubine or spouse. The life-records of the Shelton sisters, however, have never been examined with regard to the contributions of women of the Henrician court to early Tudor literary culture or political developments of their time. The Shelton family moved in aristocratic circles that were affected directly by the upheavals of Henry's reign, maintaining a prominent presence at court during the years bridging the trial and execution of Anne Boleyn in 1536 and the appropriation of church property at the close of the 1530s. Although the political and financial fortunes of the Sheltons within the upper echelon of Norfolk society continued for decades, no single discussion has yet adduced more than a small fraction of the available evidence for their family history.[4] In particular, Mary Shelton's activities in the 1530s as a collector of poetry and composer of her own informal verse have never received much attention, presumably because the details are less sensational, if less speculative, than those of her tumultuous life. The present essay seeks to demonstrate that Shelton, long consigned to the shadows of Wyatt, Surrey, various other Howards, and members of the Douglas family, has her own special place in Tudor literary history. Her contributions to the so-called Devonshire manuscript (now London, British Library, Additional 17492; sigil *D* in most scholarly apparatus)[5]—a complex miscellany of courtly poetry, extracts from medieval texts, and literary arcana that dates from the 1530s—represent one of the earliest surviving written efforts by a woman living in Tudor England. While the limitations of Shelton's achievement, specifically the judgment that her original poetry is simply not very impressive, will always preclude her elevation to a canonical stature, the evidence set out below may at least justify a shift of position away from the margins and toward the center of the pages of the Devonshire manuscript, itself one of the fundamental documents for the establishment of the corpus of Tudor poetry. Finally, I hope to show that the literary endeavors of Shelton and her collaborators witness the use of a neglected poetic technique in which the deliberate rearrangement of individual phrases and entire stanzas drawn from the common stock of English—often Middle English—courtly poetry creates a novel effect that is, in its own way, as subversive as any achieved by Wyatt or Surrey in their translations and adaptations of works by continental poets.

Mary Shelton is the only copyist whose handwriting can at present be identified securely in the Devonshire manuscript, a document that to date has been exploited mainly in the service of the canon of Wyatt's poems. This statement and much of the discussion below are informed by a new study of the handwriting of Shelton and her collaborators that has involved extensive consultation of the Devonshire manuscript itself. The materials assembled here throw new light on a range of topics, most conspicuously the development of writing conventions in the early sixteenth century and the emergence of various types of amateur script deriving from the more formal secretary hands. Beyond these paleographical concerns, evidence preserved in the Devonshire manuscript attests to the emergence of secular literacy in the first half of the sixteenth century, the circulation of private literary manuscripts among the Tudor aristocracy, and the simultaneous (and rarely acknowledged) cultivation of Middle English and contemporary Tudor poetry that accelerated during the 1530s after the appearance of such medieval col-

lections as Thynne's 1532 edition of Chaucer. Previous treatments of
Shelton's handwriting have produced two cursory and largely incompatible assessments of her involvement in the production of the Devonshire manuscript. Raymond Southall viewed Shelton as the main archi-
tect of the volume and held her personally responsible for the copying
of items on dozens of leaves.[6] These include a remarkable exchange of
original poems by Margaret Douglas and Thomas Howard, composed
while the couple were held in confinement after the revelation that they
had undertaken a clandestine and impolitic betrothal, and a series of
extracts transcribed from a copy of Thynne's Chaucer. Richard Harrier
challenged much of Southall's analysis, regarding Shelton as only an
occasional borrower of the Devonshire manuscript whose contributions
are limited to entries scrawled on a few leaves.[7] Harrier's diminution of
Shelton's contribution to the manuscript continues to exert an influence on critical opinion. Shelton's "scrawl," for example, is characterized by S. P. Zitner, in a comment on the cultivation of letters by members of Surrey's circle, as an indictment of "the deforming limits of the
age: Mary Shelton writes a scrawl, but she transcribes Chaucer and
Hoccleve as well as Wyatt."[8] Shelton's entries in the volume, I hope to
show, should not be dismissed as mechanical exercises in transcription
punctuated by a few haphazard scrawls. Her method, however hastily
conceived, involves a deliberate attempt to recast poetry written by others as a new and proprietary sort of literary text. Under scrutiny, typical
entries reveal an attempt, in one instance, to document the sense of
outrage felt by her circle at the unjust imprisonment of two close ac-
quaintances (Margaret Douglas and Thomas Howard) and, in another,
to protest the mistreatment of women by self-serving lovers. The reliable identification of Shelton's handwriting and the establishment of
the facts of her life are thus of much more than antiquarian interest,
since it is only through the positioning of her written efforts within the
Devonshire manuscript that any argument may proceed regarding Shelton's use of the volume as a vehicle for representing her own personal
circumstances and those of her collaborators.

Mary Shelton's historical identity has been misconstrued frequently
by literary scholars. The single notice offered by Southall for Shelton's
life at court ("Anne [Boleyn] herself remarked that Weston, one of the
Councillors charged with having been her lover, was not hers but Mary
Shelton's") seems to perpetuate a tradition inspired by a mutilated and
notoriously unreliable letter from William Kingston to Thomas Cromwell, which perhaps contains a reference to Mary's sister Margaret Shelton, who, according to some accounts, served briefly as a concubine of
Henry VIII.[9] Harrier, in his remarks on Shelton, confuses the woman

in question with the daughter of her brother, the younger John Shelton, and his wife Margaret Shelton (née Morley).[10] The Mary Shelton who contributed to the Devonshire manuscript was in fact the daughter of Anne and John Shelton, eponymic citizens of the town of Shelton, Norfolk, whose family fortune had been established in the late fifteenth century by the knight Ralph Shelton.[11] The family residence, Shelton Hall, which now lies in ruins, was an imposing structure surrounded by a towered, twenty-five-foot wall and a wide moat; the Sheltons also provided their town with an elaborate English Gothic perpendicular church.[12] The family, however, seems to have spent most of the 1530s living in London and environs at various royal apartments. Mary Shelton's mother, Anne Shelton (née Anne [sometimes Amy] Boleyn), was an aunt of Queen Anne and the Sheltons were numbered among Boleyn's most loyal partisans. Anne Shelton was charged with the governance of Princess Mary in the mid-1530s, gaining a reputation as a harsh disciplinarian in courtly gossip, and her employment as royal tutor may illuminate both the fact of her daughter's literacy and the unique pedagogical background of the Devonshire manuscript.[13] Anne's husband, the elder John Shelton, was steward of the households of the princesses Mary and Elizabeth, personally commanding their domestic guard.[14] The extreme dates for the life of the Sheltons' daughter Mary extend from 1512 (the date of the marriage of Anne and John Shelton) to ca. 1560 (the date of her death, shortly after the beginning of her second marriage).[15] Mary Shelton may thus have reached her middle twenties in the 1530s, when she made the bulk of her entries in the Devonshire manuscript, but it is also possible that she was considerably younger. She would not marry Anthony Heveningham until the mid-1540s and gave birth to one son and three daughters after that date.[16] It is worth remembering that Shelton's contemporary Mary Fitzroy (née Howard), one of the two other women who can be securely linked to the Devonshire manuscript, was aged about fourteen or fifteen when she married Henry Fitzroy in 1534.[17] On the basis of the evidence set out so far, it may safely be concluded that Shelton was introduced to courtly circles by her parents, possibly at an early age, and that, given her mother's occupation and the family's standing generally, she had access to some of the best women's schooling of her day.

Despite the existence of records to indicate Mary Shelton's presence at court from 1534 onwards,[18] few of these documents offer any glimpse of her as an individual or corroborate the witness of her entries in the Devonshire manuscript. The most important of those that survive is an anecdote originating with William Latymer, the chaplain who purchased many religious books for Anne Boleyn, describing the severe

chastisement of Mary Shelton by the queen for the crime of having presumed to copy some irreligious poetry ("ydill poeses") in a book of
prayers.[19] Latymer's report demonstrates at a stroke the fact of Shelton's attendance on Boleyn and her early fondness for secular poems,
characterized in his account as "tryfels" and "wantone toyes." It also
suggests the dangerous and necessarily covert effort that the preservation of secular poetry, such as that contained in the Devonshire manuscript, would sometimes have required. There appears, moreover, to
have been a specifically literary subcurrent in the events preceding Boleyn's fall. The queen availed herself of an opportunity to bolster her
deteriorating authority by asserting forcefully the privileged status of
religious texts in the lay curriculum. Caution is necessary in considering all of these points, since Latymer's rhetorical prose is concerned
above all to depict Boleyn as a godly queen. Given the partisan affiliations of the anecdote's source, our faith in the historical reliability of the
reportage should perhaps be subordinated to the evidence it provides
for Shelton's literary milieu. As Latymer's chronicle has only recently
appeared in print and many other relevant documents remain inedited,
however, the proper interpretation of many of the strange resonances
of the scandal instigated by Mary Shelton's "wanton" verse must for
now remain speculative. While it is possible that Boleyn viewed *any*
cultivation of secular poetry among her attendants as constituting a significant problem of discipline, the crux of the offense attributed to Shelton may have been the entry of such verse in an instrument of devotion. One conclusion, however, is beyond dispute. Latymer states
outright that before Anne's action the enjoyment of popular verse by
the young women of her household had been commonplace. The new
poetry had clearly attracted a youthful audience and Shelton is implicated in its development.

The episode of the disrespected prayerbook has recently been connected with the badly documented tradition maintaining that one of
the Shelton sisters, perhaps Mary or her sister Margaret, served briefly
as Henry's concubine in a stratagem on the part of Boleyn's supporters
to distract the king's attention from his failing marriage.[20] In the event,
the execution of Boleyn (on May 19, 1536) does not appear to have
affected the standing of the Sheltons at court. Mary Shelton, moreover,
appears to have been a main figure in another intrigue, this one arising
after the death of Jane Seymour in 1537. In a letter dated January 3,
1538, John Husee, servant of Arthur Plantagenet Lisle, viscount and
royal deputy of Calais, submitted a report to his employer following a
visit to Henry's court on New Year's Day in which he wrote: "The election lieth betwixt Mistress Mary Shelton and Mistress Mary Skipwith. I
pray Jesu send such one as may be for his Highness' comfort and the

wealth of the realm. Herein I doubt not but your Lordship will keep silence till the matter be surelier known."[21] The precise nature of the "election" for which Mary Shelton was supposedly under consideration is hard to determine, but a recent, unabridged edition of the Lisle letters countenances the most natural interpretation: Shelton was one of several women who were regarded as candidates likely to be chosen to serve as the fourth wife of Henry VIII, if only in the mouths and ears of courtly rumormongers.[22] Whatever the circumstances surrounding the rumored "election," Mary Shelton next appears as a resident of St. Helen's, Bishopsgate, a socially prominent convent school.[23] Geoffrey Baskerville has remarked that St. Helen's seems to have "catered more for the *nouveaux riches,* the daughters of the merchant princes of London. It is obvious that these young women were not being educated for nothing."[24] Though the first impulse is to connect Shelton's sudden installation at St. Helen's with some undocumented debacle at court, possibly related in some way to Husee's dispatch, it should also be recalled that the period 1539–40 was the time of final suppression of the English religious houses and Shelton's family stood to profit from the apportionment of royally confiscated properties. Mary Shelton's younger sister, Gabrielle Shelton, had been a nun of Barking in residence at Carrow Priory near Norwich since at least 1536 and at the time of its suppression in 1538 the establishment was granted to her father, the elder John Shelton.[25] The Sheltons may have hoped to achieve a similar stroke in the final years of the dissolution with the cooperation of their daughter Mary. John Shelton, however, died on December 21, 1539, at the age of sixty-two and the family suffered a series of financial setbacks that continued at least into the early 1540s.[26] During this period, Mary Shelton's name seems to drop out of the historical record.

Whatever her circumstances in the years immediately following the death of her father, Mary Shelton seems to have maintained an association with Tudor literary circles at least until the mid-1540s. Surrey's eulogistic sonnet on the death of Thomas Clere, the poet's attendant and close friend, suggests that one of the Shelton sisters had been his lover until he died on April 14, 1545:

> Norfolk sprang thee, Lambeth holds thee dead,
>   Clere of the County of Cleremont though hight
> . . . Shelton for love, Surrey for Lord thou chase:
>   Aye me, while life did last that league was tender.[27]

Previously unnoticed confirmation that the Shelton sister mentioned in Clere's epitaph is in fact Mary is available in a land grant to her that was made in October 1546 under the terms of Clere's will.[28] After the death of Clere in 1545 Mary Shelton, as noted above, married Anthony Heveningham, a prominent figure among the Suffolk gentry.[29] There is no incontrovertible record of Shelton's participation in any literary undertaking after her marriage, but she continues to be linked with Surrey by contemporaries. The poet instructed his servant, Hugh Ellis, to deliver a letter (now lost) that he had written to Mary Heveningham (née Shelton) with the following note: "I pray delyver this letter w^t all spede to Mrs. Heuingham, whom yew shall fynde at heromes Cheltons [Jerome Shelton's] howse in London, or els will be ther wth in iij days."[30] As this letter was probably written in the summer of 1546, Mary Shelton apparently remained in contact with Surrey and perhaps his circle for at least twelve months after the death of Clere. Surrey's note to Ellis was brought forward as evidence at a December 1546 meeting of the Privy Council in its examination of the charges of treason that had been brought against him. A comment written on the back of the note in the course of the inquiry led by Richard Southwell shows that the standing of Heveningham (Shelton) as confidante of Surrey was viewed with extreme suspicion and suggests that she may have been interviewed at a later stage of the investigation about Surrey's affairs: "Y^r maye please your good Lordshippes to examyn Mes Henygham, late Marye Shelton, of theffect of th'earle of Surrey his lettre sent unto her; for y^t ys thowght that menye secretes hathe passed between them before her maryag and sethens."[31] The inquiry does not appear to have brought any further details of the friendship to light and, at this juncture, the record of the life of Mary Shelton (later Heveningham), apart from her several appearances in legal documents as a name on a page, comes to an end.

In the final tally, it remains difficult to form any distinct impression of Shelton's character on the basis of these few surviving historical notices.[32] Beyond her fondness for "ydill poeses," which she evidently retained at least from about 1535 until 1546, she seems, as S. P. Zitner has remarked, "to have been a woman of spirit."[33] Although this impression is borne out to some extent by Shelton's contributions to the Devonshire manuscript, it should be noted that received critical assessments of Shelton's temperament—occasioning elsewhere the adjectives "waspish" and "vitriolic"—sound unduly condescending. No one would characterize Wyatt or Surrey as "men of spirit" simply because of some controversial episodes in their public affairs or their use of poetry to promote unpopular views. (In turning below to the content of Shelton's own words, as preserved in the Devonshire manuscript, I have attempted to avoid unsubstantiable characterizations of Shelton's demeanor and to acknowledge possible multiple interpretations of her words when these seem reasonable.) Several tangible points, however, emerge from the preceding analysis. Regardless of the historicity of the specific incident in Latymer's account, the inappropriate cultivation of secular poetry by a young woman could be viewed in Shelton's time as a serious infraction. The rumored association of Shelton, a woman with a known interest in popular verse, with the poet Surrey after her marriage to Heveningham also was seen as a breach of propriety, though there is admittedly a suggestion here of something more than an exclusively literary exchange. Surviving records thus afford some basis for the belief that Shelton's poetic efforts were regarded with suspicion by certain contemporary authorities. The analysis of her entries in the Devonshire manuscript in the following discussion will provide specific evidence to indicate that some suspicion may have been justified. Shelton was capable of engaging the work of her contemporaries with a combative turn of mind and, on occasion, she used the Devonshire manuscript itself as a means to convey her disillusionment with some of the inequities of her day, particularly in relations between the sexes.

The Devonshire manuscript is a paper composition-book, bound in quarto, whose leather binding, embossed without the use of gold leaf in an ornamental "capstan" design, has been used to date its production between 1525 and 1559.[34] This small volume now contains 114 of its original leaves, with fragments of what may once have served as flyleaves mounted on endpapers added when the manuscript was acquired by the British Museum in the nineteenth century. At least a dozen and according to some estimates more than twenty contributors have added entries in a variety of hands ranging from fine examples of ornamental Tudor secretarial script to unpracticed scribbles. The manuscript preserves about 185 items of verse, but it is impossible to obtain an exact figure as many of these are fragments, medieval extracts, or the like, and others are divided up differently by various editors. Certain entries are not poems at all, but rather such ephemeral jottings as single names, ciphers, anagrams, pen-trials, and brief expressions of good will. Nearly half of the leaves have been left blank, a detail neglected in all accounts of the manuscript, and this has necessitated the use of a dual system of citation in the present study.[35] The leaves that contain writing were filled in a largely haphazard fashion. Writers seem to have added entries over the course of years, in some cases from early adolescence onwards, and the passage of time has affected the aspect of their scripts. There is no assurance that the contributions of a particular copyist will be grouped together in any one part of the book or that their relative position accords with the chronological sequence of their entry. The varying quality of writing instruments and ink, the presence or absence of ruling on particular leaves, and other factors also serve to differentiate individual entries. The Devonshire manuscript was almost certainly maintained as an informal volume but beyond this nothing is known for certain about its origins and use. It may have served an entire household as a sort of commonplace book that was shown to friends and visitors or it may have circulated quietly among a small circle of friends as a private collection. Traditional descriptions of the manuscript as a "courtly anthology," a "family album," and the like should be set aside until the origins of the book have received closer scholarly attention than they have in the past. Finally, despite ambitious attributions of handwriting by earlier scholars, the possibility is remote that an unsigned passage entered by Mary Shelton or any other occasional contributor may be identified exclusively on the evidence of script. No such ascription will be made in the present study without the support of additional evidence.

Mary Shelton's entries in the Devonshire manuscript may be divided, mainly for the sake of convenience, into two discrete categories: original contributions and copywork. The original entries include several instances of her signature, brief comments on individual items of courtly poetry, and three intriguing compositions in verse, which Shelton herself describes as "dogrel," whose obscure thematic content apparently refers to her own immediate circumstances. The identification of Shelton's copywork offers many problems because of the paleographical difficulties outlined above and because of the backlog of unsubstantiated critical pronouncements on the subject. In 1871, Edward A. Bond of the British Museum maintained without elaboration that the copy of Surrey's poem "O happy dames" on fols. 59r–v [55r–v] was made by Mary Shelton and this view has persisted.[36] In 1962, Raymond Southall attempted a complete reckoning of Shelton's contributions, citing entries on fully twenty-six leaves that he regarded as witnessing about twelve distinct stints by Shelton as copyist.[37] In 1975, Richard Harrier challenged much of this analysis, arguing that "Southall lumped a distinct hand, which does range throughout the volume, with that of Mary Shelton."[38] Harrier's conclusion that Shelton herself was incapable of producing more than an unpracticed "scrawl," as noted above, has sometimes been taken as an indication of her limited involvement in the production of the manuscript and even as an indictment of the failure of efforts to educate women in her time.

The following survey of Shelton's contributions to the Devonshire manuscript represents the result of an attempt, on the one hand, to reconsider previously proposed instances of her handwriting in the volume with as few preconceptions as possible, and, on the other, to look beyond the formal aspects of her scripts to the contents of the poetry they preserve. Two general principles have been borne in mind throughout this undertaking. First, the primary criterion for identification of an individual's handwriting in the Devonshire manuscript should be the formation of its letters rather than its general aspect.[39] If any entry is to be attributed to Shelton or anyone else, the paleographical element in the argumentation should proceed from the shapes of individual letters, the sequence of their strokes (or *ductus*), peculiarities of ligature, and so on. Second, no contribution should be attributed to Shelton or any other historical figure exclusively on the basis of handwriting analysis. Wherever possible, corroborating evidence should be brought forward to support any such identification, whether it inheres physically in the manuscript or resides in the content of the texts that have been copied out on its leaves.

Mary Shelton's single most prominent contribution to the Devonshire manuscript is a signature, "**mary shelton**," written in a notably idiosyncratic script and now preserved on the first of the fragmentary flyleaves (mounted on fol. 3r [1r]).[40] Shelton's signature is carefully written in a dark ink, as if to a ruled line, and differs from all other examples of her handwriting in that its strokes, notably the hooked minims of the *m* and *n*, are written one after the other, typically *sine pedibus*, with a deliberate lifting of the pen.[41] The signature contrasts with the other contents of the flyleaf, which include several peculiar jottings (two of which resemble chi-rho symbols), an apparent monogram ("R.N.") in a looped setting, and miscellaneous scribbles and fragments of words that have faded over time.[42] The signature also differs markedly from two other certain occurrences of the name "mary shelton" in the Devonshire manuscript, both of which tend toward a cursive appearance.[43] Shelton's letter-forms here are noticeably larger in size than those in her other signatures. Though it falls far short of professional scribal quality, the flyleaf signature remains Shelton's most deliberately calligraphic effort in the volume and it is difficult to avoid the suspicion it is meant to serve as a record of ownership or, in any event, as a forthright assertion by Shelton of her involvement in the production of the manuscript.[44] Even if Shelton's possession of the volume is regarded as temporary or intermittent, her contribution of two other signed passages to this collection of courtly poetry is striking, particularly in view of Latymer's anecdote about her chastisement by Boleyn over the copying of "ydill poeses" and the politically controversial nature of some of the entries discussed below. The most important point to be taken here, however, is that Shelton's signatures show incontrovertibly that her handwriting was not restricted to a "scrawl" and that, in fact, she was capable of practicing any one of several distinct scripts on different occasions.

Shelton's two signatures within the main body of the volume, those on fols. 10r [7r] and 25v [22v], stand below examples of her continuous handwriting. These original entries comprise, respectively, a direct and negative response by Shelton to the lyrical advances of a prospective courtly lover (fol. 10r [7r]) and an attempt at a rudimentary sort of verse composition (25v [22v]). The thematic content of the poem that incurs Shelton's response may be summarized as follows: The opening stanza finds the poet—Wyatt himself, according to several editors[45]—"suffrying in sorow" and "desyryng in fere," imploring his unnamed addressee to "ease me off my pain." He repeatedly declares his intention to persevere with the phrase ". . . to serve and suffer styll I [or he] must," which concludes each stanza. It is not made entirely clear that the object of the poet's despair is a woman until the lyric's penultimate line (34: "tyll she knowythe the cause . . ."), but there can be little doubt that the poem was written as an appeal for the love of Mary Shelton: the initial letters of the seven stanzas of the Devonshire text form the acrostic SHELTUN. Following a line that once contained an ascription of authorship (fol. 10r [7r]: "ffynys [. . .]"), where the letters of the poet's name or initials have now been obliterated, Shelton adds the following retort: "ondesyerd sarwes / reqwer no hyar / mary mary shelton."[46] Shelton's comment provides a remarkable example of an overtly critical rejoinder to a courtly lyric by a contemporary reader who is almost certainly the intended recipient of the verse. While this comment has been noted previously by several critics, it does not appear to have been acknowledged that the comment "fforget thys," written beside the first stanza of the same poem, provides strong evidence in support of Harrier's contention that Shelton herself was the active annotator whose marginalia at various points encourage some unknown user(s) to memorize or perform favorite entries; see, for example, the comment "lerne but to syng yt" on fol. 97r [81r] beside the Wyatt *dubium* "Now all of chaunge."[47] The comment "fforget thys" beside the SHELTUN acrostic is otherwise hard to explain, unless it is assumed that its stanzas were composed by an exceptionally notorious poet.

Although it has been suggested on the basis of Shelton's signed response to the unsuccessful suitor that she had a "waspish" demeanor, it seems equally probable that her words are meant ironically, offering a private recognition of the absurd spectacle of a man determined to get his way through protestations of extreme humility. On at least one occasion, moreover, Shelton offers a favorable response to an anonymous poet who regrets the absence of his lover in the five-stanza lyric "What nedythe lyff" on fols. 47v [43v]–48r [44r]. Shelton here appends the following four-line, slant-rhymed doggerel, one of three such wholly original (and seemingly improvised) compositions that she contributes to the Devonshire manuscript:

> And thys be thys ye may
> Asuer your selff off me,
> No thyng shall make me to deney
> That I haue promest the.[48]

Elsewhere, however, Shelton's *dogrel* clearly provides a vehicle for her anger or despair. After lamenting some unspecified bereavement or loss, one of her lines asserts "not as my nowen I do protest" (i.e., "I do not protest on my own [*or* for my own sake? *or* as does my beloved?]").[49] Although the literary merit, in a subjectively normative critical sense, of Shelton's original entries is minimal, it is a striking fact that three of them—the signed rejoinder, the comment "fforget thys," and the lines ending with the phrase "I do protest" in her signed *dogrel*, however inscrutable—embody an element of explicit dissent.[50] It will be argued below, moreover, that Shelton may be implicated in the preservation of a controversial exchange of epistolary verse by two prisoners of the court and that Shelton's semi-original Chaucerian entries in the final written leaves of the Devonshire manuscript sometimes reveal a force of presence that rivals her signed rejoinder in intensity.

It is possible that certain instances of Shelton's scribal work in the Devonshire manuscript, although these mainly reproduce the words of other poets, should be regarded as an early form of "protest literature" because of their thematic content. The first sequence of poems in the manuscript with no apparent connection with Wyatt or his circle occupies fols. 29r [26r]–32v [29v]. Eight items preserved on these leaves, including seven original poems and a pastiche of lines from Chaucer's *Troilus and Criseyde,* bear unique witness to an exchange of epistolary love-poetry by Margaret Douglas and Thomas Howard composed while the couple were incarcerated.[51] Douglas and Howard were arrested less than a month after the execution of Anne Boleyn, following the discovery that they had presumed to undertake a private betrothal.[52] Howard was imprisoned in the Tower of London and Douglas was initially held in the Tower and later enclosed at Sion Abbey on the Thames. The most commonly cited explanation for the harsh treatment of the couple involves Margaret's position as a potential successor to the throne, which meant that the royally uncountenanced association was a treasonable offence.[53] The Douglas-Howard poems provide a rare example of a literary exchange whose historical background is absolutely inseparable from the content of its texts. Evidence internal to this poetry shows that Howard (Anne Boleyn's uncle and half-uncle to the poet Surrey) viewed himself as having loved a woman above his station; he admits to Margaret that "ye desende from your degre" (7.19) while asserting his own "tytle wych is good and stronge, / That I am yowrs and yow ar myne" (4.11–12) and conveying his hope that one day "ower hartes shalbe off one estate" (1.8). Howard refers to the circumstance of their incarceration directly in his poetry ("Alas that euer pryson stronge / Sholde such too louers separate!" [1.5–6]) and in one capricious rhyme likens his captivity to that of a hawk in a *mew*, or moulting-cage:

> . . . And shortly to get hus owt off thys place:
> Then shall I be yn as good case
> As a hawke that gets owt off hys mue,
> And strayt doth seke hys trust so true.[54]
> (3.26–28)

Howard seems to have taken receipt of both letters and poems from Douglas, and he repeatedly cites the pen as the instrument that mediates their forcible separation (e.g., "To yowr gentyll letters an answere to resyte, / Both I and my penne there to wyll aply" [7.1–2]).[55] Douglas hoped too that she would one day be reunited with her lover. In one of her own compositions—also among the earliest surviving examples of original poetry by a Tudor woman and of much higher metrical quality than Shelton's doggerel—Margaret Douglas seems to invoke this theme in a way that recalls Howard's reflections on the disparity of their social standing: "Unto god dayly I make my prayer / To bryng vs shortly both in one lyne" [6.23–24]).[56] Pessimistic sentiments and explicit allusions to death, however, become more frequent as the sequence of poems progresses. The final lines of the last item, which recast an excerpt from the lament of Troilus on the impending departure of Criseyde, are meant to serve as Howard's epitaph:

> But whan ye comen by my sepulture
> Remembre that yowr felowe resteth there,
> For I louyd eke, thowgh I vnworthy were.[57]
> (8.28–30 [Troilus 4.327–9])

In the event, Thomas Howard died in the Tower of London on October 31, 1537, reportedly as the result of a bout of shivering fits.

The pastiche of lines from *Troilus and Criseyde*, presumably put together either by Howard or Douglas—or perhaps by Shelton[58]—exemplifies another exceptional feature of their poetical correspondence. Although the content of the verse refers directly to their immediate circumstances, its vocabulary is traditional and, in many cases, specifically medieval in origin. The striking simile of the moulting-cage, for example, is arguably Chaucerian in derivation (compare *Troilus* 3.1784: "As fressh as faukoun comen out of muwe"). In all of his poems Howard declares his love in terms drawn from the conventional vocabulary of courtly verse (e.g., "my hart ys plyte" [1.4], "suche faythful loue" [1.12], "my trust so trew" [3.7], and so on), and he plays off these phrases by employing a distinctive sort of theme-and-variations technique. With the phrases noted here, compare "my hart ys persed" (2.2), "my harte ys prest" (2.13), "trusty and trew" (3.21), "my hart ys set" (4.5), "my faythful and louyng make" (7.14), and so on. The diction of Margaret Douglas's surviving reply to Howard proves that she had in fact taken delivery of his verse-epistles, as she adapts entire lines of his poems to her own use, introducing her own echoic effects.[59] Where Howard had written, for example, "My loue truly shall not decay / For thretnyng nor for punysment" (3.15–16), Douglas responds poetically, "From me his loue wyll not decay" (6.8) and "Wyth thretnyng great he hath ben payd / Off payne and yke off punnysment" (6.9–10). The imitative style employed by Douglas and Howard deserves further study, particularly with reference to the composite Chaucerian texts discussed below and the traditional notion that Tudor poets regarded themselves first and foremost as literary "makers."

In view of the furor caused by the impolitic betrothal of Douglas and Howard, it is perhaps surprising that their personal exchange circulated at all in a contemporary document such as the Devonshire manuscript, particularly if received critical judgments are upheld that would characterize the volume as a publicly maintained "courtly anthology" or a frequently exhibited family guest book. It may thus be worth considering briefly how the Douglas-Howard exchange came to be preserved in the Devonshire manuscript. Southall declares without hesitation that the whole sequence of poems was copied into the manuscript by Mary Shelton, but fails to support his claim with any systematic analysis of script.[60] Southall's identification of Shelton's hand on these leaves is denied outright by Harrier: "The neat hand of ff. 26r–29v is not the scrawl of Mary Shelton."[61] Harrier, however, here draws an untenable connection between the aspect of a given hand in the Devonshire manuscript and the identity of the copyist who is supposed to have produced it. Shelton's signed entries, as shown above, prove that she was capable of practicing more than one type of script and at one point Harrier himself envisions her producing both "her scrawl" and "possibly what Mary Shelton would have produced had she tried to do a copyist's work" on a single leaf of the manuscript.[62]

Three observations may be offered in support of Southall's attribu-

tion of the handwriting in the copy of the Douglas-Howard exchange
to Mary Shelton. First, an analysis of script permits—but cannot be tak-
en to prove—such an attribution.[63] Second, the appearance of neatness
in this section of the manuscript may reflect the previously unrecorded
fact that the leaves containing the Douglas-Howard items are ruled (albeit somewhat haphazardly) in pencil and may thus be distinguished
from the preceding leaves, which lack ruling or any other sort of enhanced layout. Third, very strong evidence to indicate that Shelton was
in fact the copyist who preserved the Douglas-Howard exchange is
found in a hastily written sequence of characters that appear at the foot
of fol. 29v [26v], which, according to Harrier, "looks like a genuine
signature or name used in direct address."[64] Harrier transcribed this
inscription as *margrt* and saw in it a possible signature of Margaret
Douglas.[65] Under scrutiny, however, the characters reveal a sequence of
strokes and ligatures that bear close comparison with those seen in
Mary Shelton's three certain signatures (the reading "Mary Sh——lt—
—" is almost certain, in my view) in the Devonshire manuscript. It thus
appears that Southall's claims for fols. 29r [26r]–32v [29v] can be sub-
stantiated by reference to the signature first noted by Harrier.[66] It was
Shelton and not Margaret Douglas who left her hurried and perhaps
surreptitious mark at the foot of fol. 29v [26v], establishing her subjectivity in what may now be regarded as a genuine example of her copywork. Mary embraced the opportunity to preserve the controversial
Douglas-Howard exchange for posterity—or for some other purpose
which, at this distance, must remain unfathomable—and it appears that
she did so with sufficient enthusiasm that she chose to document this
activity with a hasty (or deliberately disguised) signature. Shelton certainly would have been in a good position to facilitate the secret correspondence of Margaret Douglas and Thomas Howard during their confinement. Her father, as noted above, was in command of one segment
of the palace guards and it has not been recorded previously that her
brother, Thomas Shelton, was groom porter of the Tower of London,
where Howard was held until his death.[67] The inclusion of the Douglas-
Howard exchange in the Devonshire manuscript is hardly surprising if
the volume is viewed as a private document in which some of Henry's
disillusioned subjects were able to give voice to their dissent. Shelton's
attempt to preserve and perhaps circulate the poems in question arguably constitutes as forthright an act of protest as Douglas and Howard
had committed in undertaking their clandestine exchange.[68]

Southall and Harrier are in agreement that the copyist who entered
the Douglas-Howard poems in the Devonshire manuscript also added
a long sequence of medieval extracts from Chaucer and other writers

which serves to conclude the whole written portion of the volume. Southall detected the hand of Shelton in both cases and the identification of Shelton as copyist of the medieval extracts has recently been reasserted by Zitner.[69] My own collation of letter-forms supports this rare instance of scholarly consensus on these texts, which would hold the same individual responsible for the entry of the Douglas-Howard poems and the Chauceriana. No formal demonstration of Shelton's involvement in the copying of the extracts will be offered here beyond the evidence set out above in connection with her identification as the copyist of the Douglas-Howard exchange, though the question, in my view, deserves further attention. More important for the appreciation of the element of protest in the literary endeavors of Shelton and her collaborators, I feel, is the clarification of the thematic content of the medieval extracts themselves. These excerpts from the work of Chaucer and other medieval poets have been viewed most often as the remnants of some kind of courtly game or amusement. John Stevens took them to indicate the performance at court of certain scenes from *Troilus and Criseyde*, perhaps in the presence of Henry himself, suggesting that "'[to] rede and here of Troilus' became an occupation of dalliance and a spur to 'luf-taking', a sentimental education."[70] My own reading of the Devonshire Chauceriana, however, suggests that the transcription of these medieval borrowings was undertaken in a less convivial spirit.

The group of Middle English extracts in question derives from Thynne's edition of Chaucer, first issued in 1532.[71] Despite the archaic origins of these passages, much of their value inheres in their witness to the immediate impact of printed texts on the reception of medieval poetry in the Tudor period. Three of the four legitimate Chaucerian borrowings are from *Troilus and Criseyde* and one is from *Anelida and Arcite*. It is worth noting that the non-Chaucerian extracts—these include stanzas in Middle English from Hoccleve's *Lepistre de Cupide*, the poem *La belle dame sans mercy* (usually ascribed to Richard Roos), and an anonymous antifeminist poem with the incipit "Loke wel aboute" (titled *Remedye of Love* in the version known to Shelton)—are printed by Thynne within the corpus of Chaucer's work.[72] Mary Shelton clearly thought that these poems were written by Chaucer, and all may be regarded in the context of the present discussion as Chauceriana.

Before attempting a "reading" of the final series of Chaucerian extracts in the Devonshire manuscript, I should acknowledge two circumstances that have placed limitations on the scope of the present inquiry. First, no discussion of the processes by which Chaucer's poetry came to be excerpted and recast as "new" composite verse by late medieval and early modern redactors would be complete without fuller consideration than can be offered here of the evidence of two related manuscripts. These are the nearly contemporary Welles manuscript (Oxford, Bodleian Library, Rawlinson C. 813 [ca. 1533/34 x 1538]), a recently edited Tudor courtly miscellany including "erotic dream visions that sound much like Wyatt; love epistles clearly written to be sent from a woman to a man"—and, not surprisingly, a pastiche of extracts from *Troilus and Criseyde*—and the earlier, late medieval Findern manuscript (Cambridge, University Library, Ff. 1. 6 [s. xv 1]), which also excerpts Chaucer.[73] Second, the course of the following analysis has been complicated, on the one hand, by a tradition of textual editing that has sought consistently to dissociate Tudor verse from its manuscript context, and, on the other, by a paucity of theoretical work on the phenomenon of the Tudor anthologies, including such collections as Arundel-Harrington, Blage, and Fayrfax, however deeply mined by canonists.

Rather than participating in some sort of courtly amusement, Shelton, I would argue, in the selections she makes from her copy of Thynne, finds a voice for her indignation at the treatment of women of her time by hypocritical lovers. To consider the extracts in the sequence in which they appear in the Devonshire manuscript, the first stanza from Hoccleve praises the good heart of a woman and lists its virtuous qualities (Thynne fol. 373r = Devonshire manuscript 113v [89v]); the next condemns the man who broadcasts his relations with a woman, specifically by boasting that "he her body hath don shame" and thereby bringing her a "sclaundrous name." The stanza suggests rather that the "sclawnder" is in fact his (371v = 113v [89v]). In her excerpt from "Loke wel aboute" (366v [end of second column] = 114r [90r]), Shelton alters the line "The *cursydnesse* yet and *disceyte* of women" to read "The *faythfulnes* yet and *prayse* of women," turning a stanza asserting the impossibility of conveying in writing all of the deceitful qualities of women wholly to their praise. The excerpts from *La belle dame sans mercy* condemn hardheartedness in a man and praise the faithfulness and "service" of a good man in love (290v [end of second column] and 290r = 114r [90r]). Shelton's third and final citation of Hoccleve employs the exemplum of Jason and Medea to illustrate the plight of the faithful woman betrayed by a deceitful man (373r = 116r [91r]). The first of the authentic Chaucerian borrowings, from *Anelida and Arcite*, again condemns the faithless man, here with the simile of a rotten mast in a tempest, and includes the line "Wher ys the truthe off man?" (293v = 116r [91r]). The extracts from *Troilus and Criseyde* continue the theme. In the first, Shelton alters the pronouns in Pandarus's conversation with Criseyde to turn the application of the lines to her own circumstances (178v [start of first column] = 116r–v [91r–v], following *Troilus* 2.337–51). She complains thereby that her lover would not care about "my" death (Chaucer: "his"), sees in him the character of a "mocker" (Chaucer: "iaper"), and doubts that he will "make amendes off so crewel a dede." In these stanzas and those that follow it becomes clear that Shelton has been victimized by scandal and, apparently, wronged by one man in particular. The first stanza of the next extract describes love as "the most stormy lyfe" and laments the powerlessness of women in the face of adversity. The second condemns the "wyckyd tonges" which "speake us harme" and suggests that as soon as men's physical desire has ceased so also ceases their love, referring in the final lines to the end of a romance (181r = 116v [91v], following *Troilus* 2.778–91). The final extract from Chaucer, which also constitutes the final item of the Devonshire manuscript, condemns those who would characterize love as a "vyce" or a form of servitude ("thralldom"). These people are envious, simpleminded, or incapable of loving because of their wickedness. The written portion of the Devonshire manuscript then concludes on a vaguely optimistic note, stating that such individuals have never known true love. The Chaucerian extracts as a group thus bear comparison with the Douglas-Howard exchange, which, despite the bitterness and pessimism of some of its lines, finally stands as a defense of its subjects' right to love at will.

Shelton's familiarity with the Chauceriana she borrowed from Thynne was sufficient to allow her to turn the application of entire passages to her own situation and, perhaps, to extend it ironically to other aspects of life among the Henrician aristocracy. Though the bitterness of Shelton's objections here should not be exaggerated, her words may embody a cynical recognition that a man, however uncivil in his treatment of women, frequently may keep his good name while the women are condemned. Perhaps the most important point to emerge from the discussion above is that what has previously been regarded by all critics as an instance of mechanical copywork on the order of a handwriting exercise in fact preserves a previously neglected and highly personalized composite text assembled and, in a sense, edited by a young woman of the Tudor aristocracy. Indeed, Shelton interacts with the medieval texts she copies in the Devonshire manuscript in a way that transcends the largely artificial distinction, maintained in the preceding discussion as a matter of convenience, between the production of new compositions ("original entries") and more conscientiously scribal reproduction of texts ("copywork").

Stevens's view of the Chauceriana as a prop for some sort of courtly amusement is particularly hard to reconcile with the thematic content of the verse itself, but the very fact that he was moved to propose what would otherwise seem to be an intuitively reasonable hypothesis may point the way toward an appreciation of the subtle force of these passages. The medieval extracts indeed appear at first glance to be trifles and may well have been regarded as such by some contemporary observers of Shelton's activities. On closer examination, however, they are revealed to be deeply implicated in their copyist's personal affairs. One might even risk adducing a parallel with the translations and imitations of Petrarch and other continental poets undertaken by Wyatt, Surrey, and their contemporaries, which typically involve the adaptation of traditional source material to reflect the poets' own circumstances. Shelton, to pursue the analogy, extends the parameters of creative *imitatio* by altering the diction of native English poetry and reenvisioning its context to depict her own situation. The resultant composite text, similar to some of Wyatt's later *terza rima* satires, wholly belongs neither to its source nor to its redactor but rather represents something of a literary amalgam. Even a cursory reading of Shelton's idiosyncratic pastiche suggests that the successful apprehension by modern critics of the postmedieval resonances of Middle English erotic and antifeminist poetry, particularly in the first half of the sixteenth century, may in the future demand consideration of significantly more complicated questions than have been raised in previous discussion.

Before closing, I will offer a summary appraisal of the evidence for Shelton's literary milieu. The following comments attempt to identify other individuals who may have collaborated with Shelton in the production of the Devonshire manuscript and poets whose work was privileged (insofar as it was collected) by members of her circle, some of whom may also have been contributors. For the first time, moreover, specific textual evidence will be set out to establish a reliable range of dates for Shelton's entries in the volume. Apart from Shelton, the only figures who can be connected confidently with the possession of the manuscript on the basis of internal evidence are two individuals who have been mentioned above: Margaret Douglas and Mary Fitzroy. On fol. 76r [68r] a French-speaking contributor has entered the following salutation: "Madame margeret / et madame de Richemont / Je vodroy bien quil fult."[74] Harrier correctly notes that the "margeret" in question may well be Margaret Douglas and that Mary Fitzroy, as wife (or widow) of Henry Fitzroy, duke of Richmond, would almost certainly have styled herself duchess "de Richemont." He also recognizes that the identification of specific contributions to the Devonshire manuscript by Douglas or Fitzroy "could safely be done only if one had at hand a holograph letter also signed by [one or the other] writer,"[75] but—presumably because of the historical obscurity of Shelton—Harrier follows earlier critics in developing an unsubstantiated narrative recounting the origins of the manuscript in which Douglas and Fitzroy emerge as main figures, Shelton's contributions are minimized, and the whole collection is characterized as a "Howard family album."[76] The present study has found no evidence to support this view.

One long-standing judgment regarding the volume that may surely stand, however, concerns the preeminent position of Wyatt among the circle that produced the Devonshire manuscript. The manuscript, perhaps to a greater extent than any other single contemporary document, has provided a steady source of Wyatt apocrypha, but the fact remains that even in the most restrictive summation of the canon to date, that of Richard Harrier, the manuscript offers fully seventy-three witnesses to Wyatt's poetry.[77] This number is greater by dozens than the total of what is in fact the next most common attribution of items in the volume—anonymous. Strictly in terms of number of contributions, the most popular named poet after Wyatt is the unfortunate Thomas Howard, with five or six certain compositions on fols. 29r [26r]–32v [29v] and proposed examples of his work found elsewhere in the collection (including two poems signed "T.H.").[78] Surrey is the only other poet represented whose critical fortunes have approached those of Wyatt, but only *one* of Surrey's poems has been identified in the manuscript. It is hard to reconcile this state of affairs with the supposed early ownership of the volume by Henry and Mary Fitzroy during Henry's close friendship with the young Surrey in the 1530s (the scenario envisioned by Southall and Harrier) or with Shelton's known association with Clere, and thus Surrey, in the 1540s. One simple solution to the problem, which will receive additional support below, would involve the dissociation of both Henry Fitzroy and Clere from the fortunes of the volume and the dating of its compilation to the mid to late 1530s. A few other, lesser-known members of Shelton's circle can be identified by name. One "E.K.," presumably Edmund Knyvet of Buckenham Castle, Norfolk, sergeant-porter of Henry VIII and sometime tennis rival of Mary's Shelton's lover Thomas Clere, contributes at least three poems.[79] Anthony Lee, usually identified as one of Thomas Wyatt's brothers-in-law, has one ascribed poem.[80] One peculiar poem on the virtues and vices of women, which may be read either as a celebration of women or as antifeminist poetry depending on the division of lines adopted by the reader, is ascribed to Richard Hattfeld, as yet unidentified.[81] The contributions of other individuals whose names and initials are preserved in the Devonshire manuscript appear to be entirely ephemeral.[82]

The political argument of the present essay—the project of Shelton and her collaborators is implicated in debacles such as the Douglas-Howard affair and may even have been viewed as potentially subversive by the authorities of the court—demands some literary-historical support for the traditional but heretofore unsubstantiated view that the writing of the relevant leaves of the manuscript was in fact contemporaneous with the events in question.[83] The only reliable dating criteria yet adduced have involved anterior termini. For example, the Douglas-Howard poetry on fols. 29r [26r]–32v [29v] must have been composed before October 31, 1537, the date of Howard's death—but may have been copied out at *any* time after that. Insufficient critical notice has been taken of the presence of other datable poems in the volume, mainly by Wyatt. Securely dated items include Wyatt's *terza rima* poems "My nowne John poyntz" and "My mothers maids" (on fols. 101v [85v]–103r [87r] and 103v [87v; lines 1–13]), whose use as models of Luigi Alamanni's Provençal satires, published in 1532–33, fixes a terminus post quem for their composition.[84] The Petrarchan rendering "So feble is the therd" (fols. 53r [49r]–54v [50v]) is datable by Wyatt's autographic caption in the Egerton manuscript ("In Spayne") to between June 1537 and June 1539.[85] At least eight passages in six different poems have been identified in which the manuscript preserves lines that agree with the unrevised versions of the texts in the Egerton manuscript, to which Wyatt added a series of autographic corrections between 1536 and 1542; the only datable Devonshire entry incorporating some (but not all) of the Egerton revisions is the cited poem written in Spain (1537–39).[86] Again, this sort of evidence can only be used to date the composition of texts preserved in the Devonshire manuscript, not the compilation of the volume itself, and, strictly speaking, can only provide earlier termini. In view of the collocation of dates in the mid to late 1530s, however, two suggestions may be offered here. First, such termini may appear more plausible as dating criteria when it is recognized that the Devonshire manuscript is the sort of collection in which batches of poems by Wyatt and others were entered as soon as they became available. Second, the assumption that the bulk of the entries were completed by circa 1537–42 (fixed by the dates of Wyatt's arrival in Spain and his death on October 11, 1542) and quite possibly at the earlier part of that period accords well with two otherwise irreconcilable facts: (1) the association of Mary Shelton with Thomas Clere (and thus with Surrey, whose sonnet proves the link) during the early 1540s and into the middle years of the decade; and (2) the vast discrepancy between the numbers of poems by Wyatt and Surrey in the collection.[87] A dating of the Devonshire manuscript to around 1534–39 seems most plausible and the volume may be viewed as a product of the period in which Wyatt's career as a poet was well under way and Surrey's was at an early stage. The contents of the Devonshire manuscript would thus provide contemporary witness to years bounded by the fall of Boleyn and the dissolution of the religious houses, which saw the occurrence of the upheavals that had the greatest immediate impact on Shelton and her family.

For a general impression of Shelton's literary circle, I have little to add to the succinct appraisal of S. P. Zitner: "a romantic but not mawkish circle of young aristocrats whose public and personal lives were intense and closely knit."[88] Particularly striking is the heterogeneity of the clique, which my colleague F. J. Levy characterizes as a "group of people, men and women together, good poets and not-so-good, working together at a literary enterprise," contrasting this with the later sixteenth-century notion of the literary Areopagus (usually taken to include Sidney, Spenser, Greville, and Dyer, among others), and suggesting that the range of collaborators witnessed by the Devonshire manuscript stands closer to that ideal. At one end of the spectrum, we have the contributions of an accomplished poet, Wyatt—though his poetry still would not appear in print for more than ten years—and at least one effort of a young Surrey; at the other end, there are numerous instances of verse preserving the sentiments of amateurs, previously neglected members of the manuscript culture that embraced the new poetry of the 1530s. In developing their poetic voices, these literati were prepared to look in the direction of native Middle English poetry as well as that of the better-known models from Italy and France. The traditional focus of critical work on the emergence of Tudor poetry has perhaps been too narrow. Indeed, the parameters of Henrician humanism may be more reliably established through the further examination of documents such as the Devonshire manuscript. Biographical research on the lives of marginal figures in the history of letters should not be dismissed as cheering for the underdog. Through such means we may obtain a more sound comprehension of poetic monuments produced in imperfectly known literary environments.

While it may seem facile to assert that the social milieu of a Tudor literary miscellany determined the nature of the texts which it preserves, in the present instance the evidence for the influence of daily events on the contents of a book would seem to be incontrovertible. Mary Shelton's spurning of an aspiring lover's poetic voice in a candid subscript, her manipulation of Chaucerian extracts to condemn hypocritical lovers, her recasting of antifeminist poetry to read in praise of women, and similar undertakings would seem to support the case prima facie. The

Douglas-Howard exchange is concerned exclusively with the immediate situation of its poets. The hierarchies of "estate" and "degre" acknowledged by Howard in his poems to Douglas had in fact incurred the forcible separation of the couple. It might even be argued that Mary Shelton and her companions, because of the times in which they lived, were subject to a peculiar blurring of the distinction between the traditional ideals of Chaucerian and Petrarchan love-poetry and the social and political exigencies of life at court. The most that can be said for certain is that there are striking parallels between the favored themes of the poetry of the Devonshire manuscript—the necessity of secrecy in love, the disastrous consequences of impolitic love affairs, and so on— and daily life at Henry's court and in his prisons.[89] Further comparisons might be drawn between the ostensible fictions of the Devonshire poems and the contents of documents brought forward as evidence in the legal proceedings that led to the execution of Boleyn and her alleged lovers. These often incorporate the exaggerated reports of courtiers who characterize their subjects as conversing in strings of literary clichés. By the time of Surrey's prosecution, jurists typically examined letters which, if not outright fabrications, strove for a literary sort of verisimilitude. Taken together, the available evidence suggests that the literary activities of Mary Shelton and the compilation of the Devonshire manuscript itself, in addition to witnessing the cultivation of contemporary poetry and a revived interest in Middle English, also embody a covert yet dissentient response to some of the incivilities of the Henrician court.

Notes

The staff of the Students' Room of the Department of Western Manuscripts at the British Library generously assisted in my consultation of the Devonshire manuscript. I would like to thank Éamonn Ó Carragáin and Neil Wright for discussing early drafts with me and Jonathan Goldberg for providing helpful references. I am most deeply grateful to Jane Stevenson, Peter Herman, F. J. Levy, Sharon L. Jansen, Fiona Robertson Remley and several readers for the press for submitting sets of written comments that substantially improved the final form of this essay.

1. See, e.g., Maria Dowling, "Women and the New Learning," in her *Humanism in the Age of Henry VIII* (London: Croom, 1986), 219–47, her "Anne Boleyn and Reform," *Journal of Ecclesiastical History* 35 (1984), 30–46, and her recent general survey, "A Woman's Place? Learning and the Wives of Henry VIII," *History Today* 41 (June 1991), 38–42, with additional references; Retha M. Warnicke, *The Rise and Fall of Anne Boleyn: Family Politics in the*

Court of Henry VIII (Cambridge: Cambridge University Press, 1989), esp. 131–62 and 246–51; Eric William Ives, *Anne Boleyn* (Oxford: Basil Blackwell, 1986); and Constance Jordan, "Feminism and the Humanists: The Case of Sir Thomas Elyot's *Defence of Good Women*," in *Rewriting the Renaissance: The Discourses of Sexual Difference in Early Modern Europe*, ed. Margaret W. Ferguson, Maureen Quilligan, and Nancy J. Vickers, Women in Culture and Society (Chicago: University of Chicago Press, 1986), 242–58.

2. For some ground-breaking work in this area, see especially Jonathan Goldberg, *Writing Matter: From the Hands of the Renaissance* (Stanford: Stanford University Press, 1990), 122–26 and 137 55. On Tudor women writers, see also essays collected in *Silent But for the Word: Tudor Women as Patrons, Translators, and Writers of Religious Works*, ed. Margaret P. Hannay (Kent, Ohio: Kent State University Press, 1985), esp. at 1–91; and *The Renaissance Englishwoman in Print: Counterbalancing the Canon*, ed. Anne M. Haselkorn and Betty S. Travitsky (Amherst: University of Massachusetts Press, 1990). These sources, however, do not mention the activities of Shelton and her sal laborators. Cf. also *Letters of Royal and Illustrious Ladies of Great Britain from the Commencement of the Twelfth Century to the Close of the Reign of Queen Mary*, ed. Mary Anne Everett Wood, 3 vols. (London: Colburn, 1846), and comments on Wood's sources in *The Lisle Letters*, ed. Muriel St. Clare Byrne, 6 vols. (Chicago: University of Chicago Press, 1981), vol. 3, 218–19. See also the generously documented if obsolescent survey by Dorothy Gardiner, *English Girlhood at School: A Study of Women's Education through Twelve Centuries* (London: Oxford University Press, 1929), 169–82.

3. There is no standard biography of Shelton and as far as I can ascertain no study has devoted more than a few sentences to her. The introductory comments in this and the next paragraph, all of which will be developed below, are based on brief and mainly unsubstantiable references to Shelton in the following studies: Edward A. Bond, "Wyatt's Poems," *Athenaeum* 2274 (May 27, 1871), 654–55; Raymond Southall, *The Courtly Maker: An Essay on the Poetry of Wyatt and His Contemporaries* (Oxford: Basil Blackwell, 1964), esp. 17–25 and 171–73, and "The Devonshire Manuscript Collection of Early Tudor Poetry, 1532–41," *Review of English Studies* n.s. 15 (1964), 142–50; and Richard C. Harrier, *The Canon of Sir Thomas Wyatt's Poetry* (Cambridge: Harvard University Press, 1975), esp. 23–29.

4. There is no record of the family, for example, in the *Dictionary of National Biography* (hereafter cited as *DNB* from *The Compact Edition of the Dictionary of National Biography*, ed. Leslie Stephen et al., 2 continuously paginated vols. [London: Oxford University Press, 1975]).

5. The manuscript has no known early connection with Devonshire and acquires its familiar name from its early modern provenance in libraries of the Cavendish family and successive dukes of Devonshire; see *Index of English Literary Manuscripts, Volume I: 1450–1625, Part 2 (Douglas-Wyatt)*, compiled by Peter Beal (London: Mansell, 1980), 589.

6. Southall, "Devonshire Manuscript," 146; cf. his *Courtly Maker*, 19.

7. Harrier, *Canon*, 27.

8. Sheldon P. Zitner, "Truth and Mourning in a Sonnet by Surrey," *ELH* 50 (1983), 509–29, at 513–14.

9. Ibid. Southall, however, seems here to have misinterpreted comments in the secondary source which he cites, i.e., Agnes Strickland, *Lives of the Queens of England from the Norman Conquest,* intro. John Foster Kirk, 16 vols. (Philadelphia: Barrie, 1902–3), vol. 3, 309, n. 2. Kingston's lacunose dispatch, the primary source for Boleyn's alleged remark, contains a gap where the name of Weston's alleged lover once appeared, and the phrase "Mistress Skelton" appears only as a conjectural restoration in the modern printed edition of the letter, in *Letters and Papers, Foreign and Domestic, of the Reign of Henry VIII Preserved in the Public Record Office, the British Museum, and Elsewhere in England,* arr. and cat. John Sherren Brewer, James Gairdner, and Robert Henry Brodie, rev. ed. Brodie, 21 vols. in 37 (1862–1910; reprint, London: HMSO, 1920 [hereafter cited as *LP*]), vol. 10 (1536), 334–35 (no. 793). See further Paul Friedmann, *Anne Boleyn: A Chapter of English History, 1527–1536,* 2 vols. (London: Macmillan, 1884), vol. 1, 249; *Lisle Letters,* vol. 3, 397, and below, n. 20.

10. Harrier, *Canon,* 26. This Mary Shelton married John Scudamore of Hertfordshire, not Anthony Heveningham, as Harrier claims, and has no connection with the Devonshire manuscript. See further Stanley Thomas Bindoff, *The House of Commons 1509–1558,* 3 vols., The History of Parliament (London: Secker, 1982), vol. 3, 312, and *The Visitacion of Norffolk,* ed. Walter Rye, Harleian Society Publications 32 (London: Harleian Society, 1891), at 247.

11. A genealogy of the Shelton family drawn up during the sixteenth-century Norfolk visitation is preserved in London, British Library, Harley 1552, ink fol. 112v, pencil fol. 106v, and is printed in *Visitacion.* Mary Shelton was one of eight children (five daughters and three sons) who were born before Anne Shelton came to court in the 1530s. For discussion of the Norfolk visitation and families such as the Sheltons who shared their patronymic with their local towns, see M. J. Sayer, "Norfolk Visitation Families: A Short Social Structure," *Norfolk Archaeology* 36 (1974–77), 176–82. The Shelton family arms appear in British Library, Sloane 1301, fol. 377v: see Edward J. L. Scott, *Index to the Sloane Manuscripts in the British Museum* (London: British Museum, 1904; reprint, Wolfboro, N.J.: Longwood, 1971), 492.

12. *Census 1971: England and Wales* (London: HMSO, 1977) sets the population of Shelton, Norfolk, at 244. A contemporary drawing of Shelton Hall is reproduced by David Yaxley, *Portrait of Norfolk* (London: Hale, 1977), 3d plate foll. 160, who discusses the Sheltons at 147–48. On the church, see A. Hassell Smith, *County and Court: Government and Politics in Norfolk, 1558–1603* (Oxford: Clarendon Press, 1974), 195–96. On the early prominence of the family, see R. Virgoe, "The Recovery of the Howards in East Anglia," in *Wealth and Power in Tudor England,* ed. E. W. Ives, R. J. Knecht, and J. J. Scarisbrick (London: Athlone Press, 1978), 1–20, at 10–11.

13. The primary sources for Anne Shelton's tenure at court may be summarized as follows: *LP,* vol. 9 (1535), 188, 198, 230, and 293–94 (nos. 566, 594, 681, 873); 10 (1536), 103 and 117–18 (nos. 282 and 307.2); 13 (1538),

pt. 2, 538 (no. 1280, sec. f.55); *Calendar of Letters, Despatches and State Papers Relating to the Negotiations between England and Spain, 1485–1558,* ed. G. A. Bergenroth et al., 13 vols. (London: Longman et al., 1862–1954), 5, pt. 2, 182 (no. 70) and 576 (note). See also discussion by Friedmann, *Anne Boleyn,* vol. 1, 267 and 272, and vol. 2, 123–24, 143, and 196–98.

14. For the elder John Shelton's stewardship and sphere of influence, see *LP,* vol. 11 (1536), 7 (no. 7), and discussion by Friedmann, *Anne Boleyn,* vol. 2, 62; Philip W. Sergeant, *The Life of Anne Boleyn,* 2d ed. (New York: Appleton, 1924), 206; and *Lisle Letters,* vol. 5, 11. John Shelton's name is cited frequently in connection with business transactions throughout the 1530s and the prosperity of his family continued to increase until his death in 1539. See below, n. 26.

15. For the date of the marriage, see Francis Blomefield, *An Essay towards a Topographical History of the County of Norfolk,* 2d ed., 11 vols. (London: Miller, 1805–10), vol. 5, 266–68, and for Shelton's second marriage and death, ibid., vol. 5, 93–94.

16. See below, n. 29.

17. *DNB,* 698, *s.n.* Fitzroy, Mary.

18. The first recorded royal gift in favor of Mary Shelton, previously unrecorded in this context, probably occurs in a document dated January 1, 1534, in a list of New Year's gifts given by the king, which includes a reference to a "Mistress Shelton"; see *LP,* vol. 7 (1534), 5 (no. 9).

19. Latymer writes: "[Anne Boleyn] gave streight commaundement that all tryfels and wanton poeses should be eschued upon her displeasure. After that there was a booke of prayers whiche belonged to one of her maydes of honour called Mrs [i.e., "Mistress"] Mary Shelton presented unto her highnes where in ware writton certeyne ydill poeses. . . . [A]t the lengthe the pensive gentilwoman (to whome the booke apperteyned) was discovered. Whereupon the quene her majestie, calling her before her presence, wonderfull rebuked her that wold permitte suche wantone toyes in her book of prayers"; Oxford, Bodleian Library, C Don 42, fol. 31r–v, cited from *William Latymer's Chronickille of Anne Bulleyne,* ed. Maria Dowling, Camden Fourth Series 39 = Camden Miscellany 30: 23–65 (London: Royal Historical Society, 1990), 62–63. Cf. also Dowling, *Humanism,* 233 and 245, n. 32, and Warnicke, *Rise and Fall of Anne Boleyn,* esp. 131–62, 246–51, and 287, n. 52.

20. Most early discussions of the episode identify Margaret Shelton as the concubine and stress the political ramifications of the consortium; see, e.g., Friedmann, *Anne Boleyn,* vol. 2, 56–57, including the French text of the letter translated in *LP,* vol. 8 (1535), 104 (no. 263). Henry's attention is said to have shifted to a new woman by September 1535; see Friedmann, ibid., 138. Margaret Shelton apparently disappears from the historical record after her marriage to Thomas Woodhouse of Kimberley; see *Visitacion,* 247 and 322. Her name does not appear in the will of Anne Shelton codified December 19, 1555; see Blomefield, *Essay,* vol. 5, 266–68, and *Index to Wills Proved in the Consistory Court of Norwich, II: 1550–1603,* compiled by Margaret A. Farrow, ed. Percy Millican, Index Library Series 73 (London: British Record Society, 1950),

150. Several recent discussions have conjecturally identified Mary Shelton as the concubine; see, e.g., Warnicke, *Rise and Fall of Anne Boleyn*, 183, and commentary in *William Latymer's Chronickille*, 63, citing the opinion of Helen Baron. The frequent confusion of Mary with Margaret (sometimes "Madge" or "Marg.") may reflect the similarity of *y* and open-looped *g* in Tudor secretary script; see, e.g., Anthony G. Petti, *English Literary Hands from Chaucer to Dryden* (Cambridge: Harvard University Press, 1977), 16. The fundamental issue that has yet to be addressed by modern scholarship, however, is whether *any* Shelton sister had such an association with Henry.

21. *LP,* vol. 13 (1538), 9 (no. 24).

22. *Lisle Letters* (vol. 5, 11) referring to "Mary Shelton, upon whom . . . it would appear from Husee's guarded and confidential reference, that the King had been casting an appraising and appreciative eye. His pious hope that the royal 'election' might be 'for his Highness' comfort and the wealth of the realm' suggests another wife rather than a mistress, but as it is an apparently unique piece of Court gossip one can only say that this comment and his caution both suggest there were some grounds for thinking it might be serious." Shelton might also have been considered to be a suitable candidate for a "royally sponsored marriage endowment" the king hoped to arrange (ibid., 13). In April 1538, for example, Henry countenanced the marriage of Skipwith and Lord Tailboys (*LP,* vol. 13 [1538], pt. 1, 296 [no. 795]). As the king had secured dynastic succession with the birth of Edward, Henry's advisors were too busy searching out political alliances that could be achieved through a marriage to a woman from one of the European nobilities (e.g., Christina of Denmark and, of course, the ultimately successful Anne of Cleves) to consider seriously a woman of the Norfolk gentry such as Shelton; Husee may well have been the recipient of a false lead.

23. A list of pensions and grants to religious communities dated January 29, 1539, preserved among the records of the Courts of Augmentations shows Shelton receiving a special royal stipend of £4; see *LP,* vol. 14 (1539), pt. 1, 600 (no. 1355).

24. Geoffrey Baskerville, *English Monks and the Suppression of the Monasteries* (London: Cape, 1937), 207. Shelton's name appears immediately below that of the prioress and above the names of fourteen nuns, none of whom is said to be in receipt of a stipend from the Crown. On St. Helen's, see also John Edmund Cox, *The Annals of St. Helen's, Bishopsgate, London* (London: Tinsley, 1876) and Gardiner, *English Girlhood*, 136, with references.

25. Geoffrey Baskerville, "Married Clergy and Pensioned Religious in Norwich Diocese, 1555" (*English Historical Review* 48 [1933], 43–64 and 199–228, at 219), who notes further that in 1536 a "nun of Barking, Gabrielle Shelton, was living in Carrow Priory near Norwichap. . . . She had a slightly larger pension than that enjoyed by Miss Paston [Margerie Paston, daughter of William Paston]." William Page, *The Victoria History of the County of Norfolk* (6 vols. [Westminster: Constable, 1901–6]), discusses the history of Carrow Priory, noting that "[t]he site and revenues were granted in 1538 to Sir John Shelton" (vol. 2, 351–54, citing *LP,* vol. 13 [1538], pt. 2, 407 [no. 967.28]). This would seem to correct the statement of Baskerville, ibid., that

John Shelton "had bought [Carrow Priory] from the Crown" by 1536; cf. also T. H. Swales, "The Redistribution of the Monastic Lands in Norfolk at the Dissolution," *Norfolk Archaeology* 34 (1966–69), 14–44.

26. See Blomefield, *Essay,* vol. 5, 266. A controversy surrounding the execution of Shelton's will was officially resolved when two lawyers who had advised Shelton before his death were imprisoned; see Bindoff, *House of Commons,* vol. 3, 312, Stanford E. Lehmberg, *The Reformation Parliament: 1529–1536* (Cambridge: Cambridge University Press, 1970), 86 and 154–55. The problems of the Shelton family continued at least until 1542, when the younger John Shelton was forbidden to leave London pending resolution of a complaint filed by a foreign merchant and an English brewer relating to his father's outstanding debts; see *Acts of the Privy Council of England,* ed. John Roche Dasent et al. (London: HMSO, 1890–), n.s. vol. 1 (1542–47), 14; cf. also Public Record Office, [*Publications*], List and Index Society, 160, 35 (Ref. C 78, roll 4/27 [=1–3 Edw. VI]), Sir William Turvile v. Sir John Sheldon alias Shelton: "Breach of ꞇꝋᴠꞙꞏꜱꜱᴛ ꝋᵲ ꜱꝋᴛᴛꝇꝋꝳꝋꜱᴛ ꝳꜱꝉꝇꝋ ꝃꝋᴛᴠꝋꝋꝋ ꝕꝉꜱꝋꜱꝉꝉꝉ ꝋꝳꝃ Ꝉꜱꝋꝇꝃꝋꝋ ꝋꝳꝃ ꝃꝋꝉ ꝋꝋꝉꝋꝋᵲ Ꝉꝋ volves lands or rents unspecified." The younger Shelton persevered and had a successful career in politics though the family's resources would not return to the level they reached in the 1530s in his lifetime; see Bindoff, *House of Commons,* vol. 3, 312. For the later sixteenth-century prominence of the Sheltons, see Hassell Smith, *County and Court,* 35, 195–96, and 354.

27. The text is cited from Henry Howard, Earl of Surrey, *Poems,* ed. Emrys Jones, Clarendon Medieval and Tudor Series (Oxford: Clarendon Press, 1964), 34; cf. notes on 129–30. For a thorough study of the sonnet, see Zitner, "Truth and Mourning"; cf. also commentary by William A. Sessions, *Henry Howard, Earl of Surrey,* English Authors 429 (Boston: Twayne, 1986), 124–27.

28. *LP,* vol. 21 (1546), pt. 2, 168 (no. 332): "lands in Hockham Magna, which Thomas Clere by his will bequeathed to the said Edward [Belingham] and Mary, by the name of Mary Shelton, one of the daughters of Sir John Shelton." It is still by no means clear that Clere was Mary Shelton's lover, as Harrier and others have suggested, when she made the bulk of her entries in the Devonshire manuscript.

29. The marriage is recorded by Blomefield, *Essay,* vol. 1, 175, and vol. 5, 93; cf. *Visitacion,*. This was Heveningham's second marriage; he died about twelve years later. For other notices of Heveningham, some of which mention Mary Shelton, see also *Calendar of the Patent Rolls Preserved in the Public Record Office: Edward VI (1547–53),* 6 vols. (London: HMSO, 1924–29 [hereafter cited as *CPREdwVI*]): (1 Edward VI), pt. 3 (1547–48), roll 801 for May 26, 1547, 89; *CPREdwVI* (2 Edward VI), pt. 3, roll 810 for May 11, 1548, 360; *CPREdwVI* (2 Edward VI), pt. 7 (1548–49), roll 814, m. 23, 117; *CPREdwVI* (4 Edward VI), fine roll of 1551, m. 13, 358; and *Calendar of the Patent Rolls Preserved in the Public Record Office: Philip and Mary (1553–8),* 4 vols. (London: HMSO, 1937–39), (1 Mary), pt. 1 (1553–54), no. 864 for February 18, 1554, m. 6d, 24. In view of her remarriage, it is not clear whether Mary Shelton was ever entombed with her first husband, Heveningham, according to the terms of his will.

30. For text and discussion, see Edwin Casady, *Henry Howard, Earl of Sur-*

rey, MLA Revolving Fund Series 7 (New York: Modern Language Association of America, 1938), 22–23 and 181–82; cf. *LP,* vol. 21 (1546), pt. 1, 715 (no. 1426).

31. Text cited from *LP,* vol. 21 (1546), pt. 1, 715 (no. 1426). Surrey was eventually convicted of treason on the basis of other testimony and executed on January 19, 1547.

32. For completeness, it may be noted that Shelton (Heveningham) has been identified as the subject of two works by Holbein, one a formal portrait and the other a drawing, but both attributions are controversial; see *Drawings of Henry Holbein in the Collection of His Majesty the King at Windsor Castle,* ed. Karl Theodore Parker, 2d ed. (Oxford: Phaidon, 1945), 43 (no. 26), and *Holbein: The Paintings of Hans Holbein the Younger,* ed. John Rowlands (Oxford: Phaidon, 1985), 142 (no. 55). Note also an apparent allusion to Shelton's striking appearance in a letter from John Hutton to Cromwell dated August 1, 1537: "The duchess of Milan [i.e., Christina of Denmark, widow of Francesco Sforza] . . . is 16 years old, very tall—taller than the Regent, of competent beauty, soft of speech, and gentle in countenance. She wears mourning after the manner of Italy. . . . She resembles one Mistress Shelton that used to wait on queen Anne"; printed *LP,* vol. 12 (1537), pt. 2, 419 (no. 1187). In addition to acquiring this apparent reputation for Criseyde-like couture, Shelton seems to have been known for her generosity in giving expensive gifts. An inventory of jewels from the first half of the sixteenth century records a ring "with a pointed diamond, which was sent to her [i.e., one 'Mistress Holland'] as a token from Mistress Mary Shelton, as she said"; text printed in *Works of Henry Howard and of Sir Thomas Wyatt the Elder,* ed. George F. Nott, 2 vols. (London: Longman, 1815–16), vol. 1, cxvii–ix.

33. Zitner, "Truth and Mourning," 513.

34. The cover measures 158 x 236, the inner pages 153 x 230. At present there exists no adequate codicological description of the volume. A regrettable amount of space in these notes is given over to refuting red herrings promulgated by the standard entry in *Catalogue of Additions to the Manuscripts in the British Museum in the Years 1848–1853,* comp. Edward A. Bond, 6 fascs. in 1 (London: British Museum, 1868), vol. 1, 23. For a more recent description, see *Index,* comp. Beal, 589. Comments here follow Southall, "Devonshire Manuscript," 142, reproduced in his *Courtly Maker,* 171, and followed in part by Harrier, *Canon,* 23. The dates given there in fact correspond almost exactly to the extreme limits that I establish above for Shelton's literary activities.

35. The modern foliation has been entered in pencil only on pages that contain text and thus offers no reliable representation of the physical state of the manuscript. In the present essay, the first part of the reference "fol. 98v [82v]," for example, indicates the true position of the leaf in the manuscript and the second refers to the inaccurate modern foliation cited in all previous treatments of the volume except for that in *Works,* ed. Nott.

36. See Bond, "Wyatt's Poems," 655, and subsequent comments by Agnes Kate Foxwell, *A Study of Sir Thomas Wyatt's Poems* (New York: Russell, 1911), 127; Kenneth Muir, "Unpublished Poems in the Devonshire MS.," *Proceed-*

ings of the Leeds Philosophical and Literary Society: Literary and Historical Section 6 (1944–45), 253–83, at 254; Southall, *Courtly Maker,* 173, and "Devonshire Manuscript," 144, and Harrier, *Canon,* 25, and Zitner, "Truth and Mourning," 513. Harrier in a subsequent notice seems to admit some doubt about Bond's assertion, remarking that "O happy dames" is "probably in Mary Shelton's hand" (*Canon,* 51).

37. Southall, *Courtly Maker,* 172–73, and "Devonshire Manuscript," 144–45. Southall detects Shelton's work on fols. 3r [1r] (the flyleaf signature), 6r [3r] (in the first group of entries in the manuscript), 25v [22v], 29r [26r]–32v [29v], 33r [30r], 44r [40r]–48r [44r], 59r–v [55r–v], 66r [58r]–68r [60r], 69v [61v]–70r [62r], 73r–v [65r–v], 75v [67v]–76v [68v], 104r [88r], 113v [89v]–114r [90r], and 116r [91r]–117r [92r] (the last group of medieval extracts in the manuscript). Southall claims that his account of the production of the manuscript "was arrived at simply by collating the disposition of the hands in the manuscript with the known histories of Mary Shelton ([Hand] A), Mary Fitzroy (B), and Margaret Douglas (C)" (*Courtly Maker,* 173), but he does not document his study by reference to so much as a single primary or secondary source or offer any impression of the features of Shelton's handwriting. Southall's assertions may strike some readers as fictive in the extreme, but it is worth recalling that one of Wyatt's more cautious editors, Joost Daalder, praised Southall for producing "the best complete transcripts of E [Egerton] and D [Devonshire] which I have seen" (*Sir Thomas Wyatt: Collected Poems,* ed. Daalder [London: Oxford University Press, 1975], vi) and my own collations of letter-forms have in the event borne out some of his impressions regarding Shelton's stints as copyist.

38. Harrier, *Canon,* 27.

39. Facsimiles and guides consulted in the preparation of the present paper include Lewis Foreman Day, *Penmanship of the XVI, XVII and XVIIIth Centuries* (London: Batsford, 1911); Charles Hilary Jenkinson, *The Later Court Hands in England from the Fifteenth to the Seventeenth Century,* 2 vols. (Cambridge: University Press, 1927; reprint, New York: Ungar, 1969); *Specimens of Sixteenth Century English Handwriting Taken from Contemporary Public and Private Records,* ed. C. B. Judge (Cambridge: Harvard University Press, 1935); H. C. Schulz, "The Teaching of Handwriting in Tudor and Stuart Times," *Huntington Library Quarterly* 5 (1943), 381–425; James Wardrop, *The Script of Humanism* (Oxford: Clarendon Press, 1963), and Petti, *English Literary Hands;* see also bibliography in Goldberg, *Writing Matter,* 329–42.

40. A photographic facsimile of the flyleaf fragments is printed in *The Poems of Sir Thomas Wiat,* ed. Agnes Kate Foxwell, 2 vols. (London: University of London, 1913), vol. 1, plate facing 251.

41. Exceptions are the *l,* to which a short horizontal stroke has been added at the line of writing, and the second, hooked minim of the final *n.* The signature also bears witness to a letter-form that may help to distinguish Shelton's handwriting elsewhere in the Devonshire manuscript, a peculiar form of *t* that resembles an incomplete *c* with a cross-bar.

42. One of the most frequently repeated theories of the origin of the vol-

ume—that it was originally presented as a wedding gift and that Margaret Douglas (styling herself "Howard") was its main owner—are based mainly on two of these faded inscriptions ("m[——]ayg[——]" and "marg[——] how[——]"), but these readings are doubtful and the fragmentary words in question appear to be scribbles or pen-trials; cf. Foxwell, *Study*, 125, and Harrier, *Canon*, 23, with references.

43. An imperfectly formed, smudged attempt at the same formal signature occurs on fol. 25v [22v]. A third instance of the name "mary shelton," moreover, which occurs on an earlier leaf (fol. 10r [7r]), is more current in aspect than either of the two attempts at a formal signature. The *m*, *a*, *n*, and a variant form of Shelton's *h* are all written without lifting the pen and the *ry* ligature is written very hastily. The signature, however, does maintain the distinct *l* and *t* of the flyleaf autograph. It also exemplifies Shelton's customary initial *s*, which is composed of a long vertical stroke with an oblique, hairline headstroke.

44. Kenneth Muir and Patricia Thomson, for example, state outright that the Devonshire manuscript "belonged to Mary Shelton who copied, and probably composed, some of the poems"; see *Collected Poems of Sir Thomas Wyatt*, ed. Muir and Thomson, Liverpool English Texts and Studies (Liverpool: Liverpool University Press, 1969), xiv.

45. The poem "Suffrying in sorow" is printed as Wyatt's in *Poems*, ed. Foxwell, vol. 1, 257–58; *Collected Poems*, ed. Muir and Thomson, 176–77 (no. 165), and *Sir Thomas Wyatt: The Complete Poems*, ed. Ronald A. Rebholz (London: Penguin, 1978), 268–69 (no. 210), among "Poems Attributed . . . after the Sixteenth Century." Harrier states that the song "must be excluded from the Wyatt canon" and "may be by Thomas Clere [Shelton's lover in the 1540s]" (*Canon*, 41 and 45); it is silently excluded from the Wyatt canon in *Wyatt: Collected Poems*, ed. Daalder.

46. For various transcriptions of Shelton's partly legible response, see *Poems*, ed. Foxwell, 1, 258 (note); Southall, *Courtly Maker*, 17; and Harrier, *Canon*, 23 (quoted here) and 38. The apparent meaning of the comment is "[You offer an] undesired service; [I] require no hire," though Zitner suggests an alternative reading, "undesired sorrows require no ear" ("Truth and Mourning," 509–29). The repetition of Shelton's first name has inspired the fairly elaborate explanation that some unidentified writer "later realized another Mary (Mary Fitzroy [née Howard, the poet Surrey's sister]) was also identified with the book" (Harrier, *Canon*, 23) and wished to avoid confusion by expanding the name. Examination of the manuscript, however, reveals that the commentator (almost certainly Shelton herself, given the evidence of handwriting and the acrostic preserved by the verses in question) first wrote her first name, then stopped because of pen-failure, canceled the name, and resumed by writing "mary shelton" in full.

47. Harrier, *Canon*, 27: "Another activity of Mary Shelton is evident. . . . After the bulk of the volume had been filled in, she went through it marking certain poems for copy, memorization, or musical performance." The entries in question include the marginalia on 97r [81r] ("lerne but to syng yt"), 7r [4r], 12v [9v], 15r [12r], 16v [13v], 17v [14v], 27r [24r], 86v [70v], 87v

[71v], 88v [72v], 89r [73r], 89v [73v], 94r [78r], and 96v [80v] (all of which contain the comment "and thys"), and 20r [17r] ("and thys chefly"). Southall does not essay any attribution of the marginalia. The attribution to Shelton finds support in certain combinations of characters (e.g., the sequence *thy* in fols. 7r [4r; marginalia], 29r [26r: Howard poems], and 73v [65v: four-line doggerel]). In all, the marginalia offer the following letters for comparison with Shelton's work: *a, b, c, d, e, g, h, l, n, o, r, s, t, u,* and *y*. There is also a striking agreement between the less acute form of *h*, terminating to the left below the line of writing, observed in the Douglas-Howard poems and in the marginalia; Shelton's autographic *th* extends the cross-bar of her characteristic *t* to begin the following *h*. The agreement in the forms of initial *ff*, certain forms of final *s*, and medial *y* is also striking. One possible objection to the proposed identification of hand might be based on dialectal or orthographic considerations: Shelton's signed doggerel of fol. 25v [22v] attests the spelling *bot* ("but"); the marginalia on 97r [81r] have *but*.

48. Text printed by Muir, "Unpublished Poems," 268 (no. 20); ascription to Shelton by Southall, *Courtly Maker*, 17.

49. Taken as a whole, this four-line doggerel by Shelton, which appears on fol. 25v [22v]), is extremely difficult to interpret. The whole entry, which apparently refers to Shelton's personal circumstances, has been transcribed by Harrier as follows: "awel I hawe at other lost / not as my nowen I do protest /bot wan I haue got that I hawe mest / I shal regoys among the rest / mary shelton" (*Canon*, 23). The sense apparently runs along the lines: "All I have another [person?] lost; I do not protest on my own [?]. But when I have got what I have missed [*or* most?], I shall rejoice among the rest." A third, almost completely illegible "ryme dogrel" by Shelton on fol. 73r [65r] has not been printed. The first line of the text (following transcription by Muir, "Unpublished Poems," 282) apparently reads, "how many myle to meghelmes," i.e., "How many miles [*or* meals?] until Michaelmas," which suggests that Shelton may have made some of these informal entries on festive occasions.

50. To sum up, Shelton's original entries in the Devonshire manuscript are here held to include the following: three certain signatures, the rebuff of the poet of "Suffrying in sorow" (indicated by her signature and the context of the acrostic), three slant-rhymed verse compositions (one indicated by her signature and the other two by prosodic form and script), and the marginalia guiding a user of the volume in the memorization of certain pieces (indicated by script and manuscript context). Taken together, the signed entries exemplify more than twenty different letters of Shelton's alphabet, several of which appear in variant forms, and these have proved useful in the analysis of possible instances of Shelton's copywork set out below. The signed entries offer examples of Shelton's *a, b, d* (two forms), *e, g, h, I* (pronoun), *l, m, n, o, p, q, r, s* (two forms: initial/medial and final), *t* (also in ligatures *st* and *th*), *w* (or *uu*, which often does duty for single *u* and *v*), and *y*. The letters *c, f,* and *i/j* (lowercase), *k, x,* and *z* do not occur in Shelton's signed entries.

51. The sequence of poetry is printed in full by Muir, "Unpublished Poems," 261–66, whose text is cited here. The numbers that have been assigned

to the poems here (1–8 inclusive followed by line number: "1.1," e.g., denotes the first line of the first poem) correspond to the following texts: (1) "Now may I morne," 261–62 (no. 7); (2) "Wyth sorowful syghes," 262 (no. 8); (3) "What thyng shold cawse me to be sad?" 262–63 (no. 9); (4) "Alas that men be so vngent," 263 (no. 10); (5) "Who hath more cawse," 264 (no. 11); (6) "I may well say," 264 (no. 12); (7) "To yowr gentyll letters," 265 (no. 13); (8) "And now my pen, alas" [=Chaucer, *Troilus and Criseyde*, 4.prol.13–14, 4.288–308, and 4.323–9], 265–66 (no. 14).

52. See *DNB*, 563, *s.n.* Douglas, Margaret. The date of the incarceration of Douglas and Howard, June 8, 1536, provides the first secure terminus post quem for any of the entries in the Devonshire manuscript. On the basis of some of Howard's phrases, e.g., "my none swete wyfe" (4.21 and 7.23) and "yowr louyng husband" (7.18), it has been suggested that the couple had begun to live conjugally as well. Caution is required on this point since Douglas and Howard address each other elsewhere with less formal epithets, e.g., "louer swete" (1.20), "faythfull louers" (2.8), "faythfullyst louer" (6.4); Howard at one point suggests that the couple were merely "yntent / Yn gods laws for to be bownd" (2.11–12). Note also Douglas's entreaty in a letter to Cromwell, "And I beseech you not to think that any fancy doth remain in me touching him . . . being a maid as I am" (*Letters*, ed. Wood, vol. 2, 292–93).

53. Harrier remarks that, "As a niece of the king, Lady Margaret was for a time close to succession to the throne, since both Elizabeth and Mary had been declared illegitimate. . . . This act [of betrothal] was treasonable, since it involved a successor to the throne" (*Canon*, 24). One may suspect that the king's personal disapproval may also have played a part, since the diplomat Castillo reports in 1534 that "Henry has a niece whom he keeps with the queen, his wife, and treats like a queen's daughter, and that if any proposition were made to her he would make her dowry worth that of his daughter Mary"; see *DNB*, 563, *s.n.* Douglas, Margaret.

54. In another peculiar sequence of lines, Howard imagines that the couple's oppressors should be bound in their love-tokens and run aground on Goodwin Sands, dangerous shoals off the coast of Kent: "And they that wold other bate or stryfe / To be tyed wythyn ower louyng bandys, / I wold they were on Goodwyn Sandys" (7.26–28).

55. Compare also "To wryte off them" (2.8); "Yff I shuld wryte . . . / Wyth penne yn letters" (3.8–11); "As tonge or penne can yt repet" (5.16); "And now my pen, alas, wyth wyche I wryte, / Quaketh for drede of that I muste endyte" (8.1–2 [=*Troilus* 4.prol.13–14]).

56. For Howard's hope of release, compare "shortly togyther that we may goo" (2.20); "Desyryng god . . . / . . . to get hus owt off thys place" (3.23–25); "god . . . / Wyll send us ryght where we haue wrong" (4.18–19).

57. The thirty-line centonization of Chaucer comprises *Troilus* 4.prol.13–14, 4.288–308, and 4.323–29; Criseyde's name has been omitted to leave space for Margaret's, which seems to have been entered and then expunged.

58. Given Shelton's fondness for the reorganization of extracts of medieval verse—later in the volume she reworks many lines from *Troilus and Criseyde*

(see below)—she might be suspected of having been a previously unrecognized third author here. The alternative is to assume that aristocratic prisoners such as Howard or Douglas were allowed to consult Thynne's weighty volume in confinement or had memorized the lines in question before the arrest.

59. The first stanza sets the tone for Douglas's poem: "I may well say with joyfull harte / As neuer woman myght say beforn / That I haue takyn to my part / The faythfullyst louer that euer was born" (6.1–4).

60. Southall, *Courtly Maker,* 172–73, and "Devonshire Manuscript," 144: "there are only three major hands in the manuscript: A, which is Mary Shelton's . . . [is] responsible for entries on . . . 26–29v [i.e., 29r–32v]."

61. Harrier, *Canon,* 27.

62. Ibid. Harrier adds that the neater of the two distinct hands on this leaf "is by no means a professional hand and makes frequent errors. Perhaps what has been taken as an addition to the poem on f. 3r is simply Mary Shelton lapsing from script into her scrawl before recovering on the next attempt." Examination of the entry in question ("My hert I gave" on fol. 6r [3r]), however, suggests that, rather than an alternation of script by Shelton or anyone else, the change of hands should be associated with pen-failure that occurred during the writing *prima manu* of the word *Vnsacyat* in the eighth (against Harrier's "seventh") line of the poem. Harrier silently contradicts his own claim when he states that the originally incomplete copy of the poem on fol. 6v [3v] (Wyatt's "My hert I gave," for which Egerton is the main witness) was extended "[m]uch later" (37) by reference to a longer—though still defective—copy of the same poem on fol. 91v [75v] of the Devonshire manuscript.

63. Specifically, the attribution finds support in the formation and sequence of strokes of the letters *a, e, n, o, r,* and *u,* which resemble those observed in Shelton's signed autographs. The features of these letters, however, are common in all sixteenth-century secretary script. More striking points of resemblance occur in the form of *b* that predominates in signed autograph and verse, which typically has a rounded rather than a straight-backed stroke as its main descender; in the form of *m,* which bears close comparison with the signatures; *y,* which is made without lifting the pen and shows three distinct changes of direction in its strokes; and certain instances of *p, q, t,* and *w.* The distinctive form of the pronoun *I* observed in the poems also occurs in Shelton's signed work and in her four line doggerel on fol. 73r [65r].

64. Harrier, *Canon,* 25.

65. Ibid. The inscription, however, does not resemble beyond its first three letters the facsimile of Douglas's signature printed in *Letters,* ed. Wood, no. 12 opposite title page.

66. The first two letters, as Harrier recognized, are certainly *ma.* These are followed by several jagged strokes, which Harrier took as an *r* but which may serve to represent a ligature of *r* and some other letter, as in a hastily written signature. The angularity of the strokes, if not the sequence of strokes itself, bears comparison with *ry* sequences in Shelton's signatures. Harrier's supposed *g* is unlike any other example of that letter in the Devonshire manuscript but has the same appearance and sequence of strokes as Shelton's *h.* The letters

immediately preceding and perhaps following this probable *h* appear to be represented by a long oblique stroke that resembles Shelton's regular initial and medial *s*. These are followed by an apparent ligature combining two characters that resemble Shelton's looped *l* and her distinctive *t*, noted above. The rest of the name fails, trailing off to the right with a wavy line, but even this stroke (which according to the hypothesis submitted here would stand for *-on*) can be compared with the ligature *on* appearing in the signature below Shelton's rejoinder on fol. 10r [7r].

67. Thomas Shelton's appointment is mentioned in the Shelton family genealogy; see *Visitacion*, 247. Additional notices of Thomas Shelton occur in *Chancery Patent Rolls, 23–29 Elizabeth I: Index to Grantees*, List and Index Society 141 (London: Public Record Office, 1977), *ex* c. 66/1271–1303 (28–29 Eliz.), 1300, m. 39 and m. 9d; *Chancery Patent Rolls, 30–36 Elizabeth I: Index to Grantees*, List and Index Society 167 (London: Public Record Office, 1980), *ex* c. 66/1304–46 (30–32), 1369, m. 10 (*bis*).

68. It should be stressed, however, that the reconstruction offered here depends on the verification of the previously unidentified signature at the foot of fol. 29v [26v] as Shelton's, which, if my analysis of the handwriting is correct, provides the strongest evidence yet for Shelton's involvement in the Douglas-Howard scandal. There is, moreover, the complicated question of the dating of the entry of this verse on these leaves; I argue below that the most plausible period for the entry of this material is ca. 1536–38, bolstering the view that the material was controversial when Shelton preserved it, but the question is not closed.

69. Southall, *Courtly Maker*, 172, and "Devonshire Manuscript," 144: "It is true that the courtly makers represented in the Devonshire MS. use a diction derived from Chaucer, but . . . Mary Shelton was the only person who 'lifted' poems, if they can be called poems, out of Chaucer"; cf. Zitner, "Truth and Mourning," 513.

70. John E. Stevens, *Music and Poetry in the Early Tudor Court* (London: Methuen, 1961; reprint, New York: Cambridge University Press, 1979), 188 and cf. 13, 119, 207, and 213.

71. The medieval origin of these texts was noted by Ethel Seaton, "'The Devonshire Manuscript' and Its Medieval Fragments" (*Review of English Studies* n.s. 7 [1956], 55–56), more than ten years after their initial publication by Muir, who failed to detect their Chaucerian origins. Their immediate derivation from Thynne was established by Richard C. Harrier, "A Printed Source for 'The Devonshire Manuscript,'" *Review of English Studies* n.s. 11 (1960), 54. In the following discussion, quotations have been taken directly from the first edition of *The Works of Geffray Chaucer*, ed. William Thynne (London: Godfray, 1532); cf. also facs. ed. with introduction by W. W. Skeat (London: Moring, [n.d.]); and facs. ed. with intro. by D. S. Brewer and supplementary material from the editions of 1542, 1561, 1598, and 1602 (Ilkley, Yorks.: Scolar, 1976).

72. For standard references, see Carleton Brown and Rossell Hope Robbins, *The Index of Middle English Verse* (New York: Index Society, 1943), 105 (no. 666), 172 (no. 1086), 306 (no. 1944); cf. Robbins and John L. Cutler, *Supple-*

ment to the Index of Middle English Verse (Lexington: University of Kentucky Press, 1965), 74 (no. 666), 122 (no. 1086), and 226 (nos. 1944–1944.5).

73. See *The Welles Anthology*, ed. Sharon L. Jansen and Kathleen H. Jordan, Medieval and Renaissance Texts and Studies 75 (Binghamton, N.Y.: MRTS, 1991), esp. 166–81 (no. 30) and 303, and *The Findern Manuscript*, facsimile ed., intro. Richard Beadle and A. E. B. Owen (London: Scolar Press, 1977). Jansen is quoted here from a personal communication.

74. Printed by Harrier, *Canon*, 24; cf. Foxwell, *Study*, 125, and Southall, *Courtly Maker*, 17 (who resolves the French expression of good will as "Je voudrais qu'il [en] fût bien").

75. A holographic letter by Margaret Douglas preserved in London, British Library, Cotton Vespasian F.xiii, art. 188, fol. 173, came to my attention too late to be consulted for the present study.

76. Harrier, *Canon*, 27. Harrier offers the following speculative scenario: "[The Devonshire manuscript] was probably purchased in London by Henry Fitzroy about 1533 and was first used by him and his connections, among whom were Mary Howard [later Fitzroy] and her friend Mary Shelton. That the volume remained primarily a Howard family album is shown by its use for the love verses exchanged by Margaret Douglas and Surrey's half uncle, Lord Thomas Howard. Lady Margaret Douglas must have taken the volume with her when she married Matthew Stewart, earl of Lennox, in 1544" (28). None of these statements has so much as a distant claim to historicity.

77. The highest estimate is 122 authentic Wyatt poems, four of which are copied twice; see *Index*, comp. Beal, 589.

78. Bond, "Wyatt's Poems," argued for a much more pervasive presence of Douglas and Howard in the manuscript, finding Howard's poetry or Douglas's copywork in seven poems on fols. 44r [40r]–48r [44r] (arguably Shelton's copywork and in any case followed by one of her four-line poems), four poems on fols. 48v [44v]–51r [47v] copied out by a different scribe from the one responsible for the group immediately preceding, and the medieval extracts that close out the collection, which he presumably associated with Douglas and Harrier because of the *Troilus* borrowings on fol. 32v [29v]. The claims regarding the first two groups are apparently accepted by Harrier, who also would ascribe "That tyme that myrthe" on fol. 20v [17v] to Thomas Howard.

79. See *DNB*, 1151, *s.n.* Knyvet, Edmund. Knyvet supplies poems preserved in the Devonshire manuscript on fols. 67v [59v] and 71v [63v], whose tone is alternately misogynistic and mournful. Knyvet's death in 1546 establishes a previously unremarked terminus ante quem for the composition of these poems. Knyvet is best known for striking Clere and drawing blood in a scuffle on one of the king's personal tennis courts, an offense for which he was formally sentenced on June 10, 1541, to suffer the dismemberment of his right hand, a short-lived English legal innovation promulgated by Henry himself. The execution of the sentence devolved into an extraordinary scenario involving the palace cook and a set of knives, and Knyvet was formally pardoned when he pled to submit his left hand for dismemberment so that he might pledge the right in service to Henry.

80. Lee's bitter lyric on fol. 13v2 [10v] laments the passing of a love that is

no longer "as good as wrytyng"; printed by Muir, "Unpublished Poems," 280 (no. 4); see also Southall, "Devonshire Manuscript," 143, and Harrier, *Canon,* 36, 38, and 40.

81. The Hattfeld contribution begins, "All women have vertues noble and excelent / Who can percyve that / they do offend Dayly"; printed by Muir, "Unpublished Poems," 260–61 (no. 5) from fol. 21v [18v].

82. These include "R.N." (flyleaf monogram), "A.J. [*or* A.I. *or* A.L?]," "Jhon" (*not* "J. Hall," i.e., John Hall, author of *Court of Virtue* [1565]), "Jon K." (perhaps John Clerk, Howard secretary and instructor of Surrey), and "John Holbache" (see Southall, *Courtly Maker,* 18 and 172, and "Devonshire Manuscript," 143; and Harrier, *Canon,* 24, 36, 38–39, and 43–45).

83. The literary activities of Shelton and her companions have never been securely dated. One false lead, tracing back at least to Bond's *Catalogue of Additions,* vol. 1, 23, can be dismissed at once: the poem "My hope is yow for to obtaine" on fol. 61r [57r], which has been claimed as an apparently unique witness to a poem by Lord Darnley (Henry Stewart [1545–67]), father of King James I, which was supposedly copied into the Devonshire manuscript by Darnley himself in the late 1550s or early 1560s. Although Southall and Harrier base their accounts of the later history of the volume almost wholly on this dubious ascription, it should be noted that the poet styles himself "Hary [*not* Henry] Stuart" and, although the alternation of names is relatively common, the poet is more likely to have been the elder Henry Stewart, Darnley's father (ca. 1495–1551), a Shelton contemporary. See Muir, "Unpublished Poems," 272 (no. 28) with discussion at 254 and 281; cf. Southall, *Courtly Maker,* 21, and "Devonshire Manuscript," 147; and Harrier, *Canon,* 24.

84. See *Collected Poems,* ed. Muir and Thomson, 347–50, and *Wyatt: Collected Poems,* ed. Daalder, xviii, who would refine the dating of the satires, with their apparent allusions to Wyatt's imprisonment, the duplicity of Charles V, and their moralization against lust and material things, to June 14, 1536 (Wyatt's release from the Tower), or later, citing a dated letter from Wyatt to his son evincing similar moral concerns; see also *Wyatt: Complete Poems,* ed. Rebholz, 11 and 445–47.

85. See *Collected Poems,* ed. Muir and Thomson, xx and 335–38; Harrier, *Canon,* 4; and also *Wyatt: Complete Poems,* ed. Rebholz, 11 and 390–94. Other items have been dated by correspondences between their thematic content and events in Wyatt's life, e.g., "Alas poore man" and "That tyme that myrthe" on fols. 18v [15v] and 20v [17v] (after 1525–26: allusions to Boleyn) and fol. 42v [38v] "Somtyme I fled" (October 1532: trip to Calais and Wyatt's changing feelings toward Boleyn); and see Harrier, *Canon,* 4. Surviving musical settings of certain Devonshire lyrics confirm the absolute outer termini proposed here for Shelton's work and might, on further exploration, allow some refinement of the dating: "He Robyn" on fols. 25v [22v; fragment] and 27r–v [24r–v], known in Wyatt's day from a setting in the songbook of Henry VIII by Thomas Cornishe (died 1523?; see Harrier, *Canon,* 5; *Collected Poems,* ed. Muir and Thomson, 309; and *Wyatt: Complete Poems,* ed. Rebholz, 432); and "My pen take payn" and "Blame not my lute" on fols. 6v [3v] and 72r–v [64r–

v], set by John Hall in his *Court of Virtue* in 1565; see *Wyatt: Collected Poems,* ed. Daalder, 155; "fforget not yet" (fol. 58v [54v]): musical setting in London, British Library, Royal app. 58, p. 50 (no. 53b), noted in apparatus of *Early Sixteenth Century Lyrics,* ed. Frederick Morgan Padelford, Belles-Lettres Series 2: Middle English Literature (Boston: Heath, 1907), 117.

86. See *Collected Poems,* ed. Muir and Thomson, who set the terminus post quem for the copying of the largest single Wyatt batch in the Devonshire manuscript at 1537–39, remarking that "the majority of the versions in D preceded those in E. . . . It is a reasonable hypothesis that the poems peculiar to D were also written early" (xx–xxv, esp. xxiv). For additional textual analysis, see Harrier, *Canon,* 30–34 and 50.

87. Foxwell states: "The only poem in the D. MS. by Henry Howard is in the hand of Mary Shelton. . . . [It was] certainly written after 1536" (*Study,* 127). Surrey would have been about twenty years old in 1536–37, roughly the same age or slightly younger than Mary Shelton.

88. Zitner, "Truth and Mourning," 514.

89. See the representative passages set out, for example, by Southall, "Devonshire Manuscript," 148–50.

Henry VIII as David: The King's Image and Reformation Politics

JOHN N. KING

A radical revision of Henry VIII's monarchial image followed the outbreak of schism between the newly created Church of England and the See of Rome.[1] Until that time the king's portraiture as a devoutly observant Christian was orthodox in the extreme. Little more than one decade earlier, Pope Leo X conferred upon Henry VIII the title of Defender of the Faith, an honor once granted to his father, Henry VII, and retained to the present day by British monarchs. The declaration of the Reformation Parliament that "this realm of England is an empire,[2] and so hath been accepted in the world, governed by one Supreme Head and King" brought an end to the subordination of "the imperial Crown of the same" to the papal tiara, however, by lodging ecclesiastical and secular authority in Henry VIII.[3] While it is hardly a new development for a politically expedient monarch to adopt a pietistic pose, from this point onward the Henrician image bears the imprint of Protestant ideology even though the king himself rejected change in the official theology and hierarchal structure of church government. We may note this iconographical shift in a variety of works of art and literature that were produced for consumption both inside and outside of the royal court, most notably in the title pages of the Coverdale Bible and the Great Bible.

Hans Holbein the Younger depicted Henry VIII as a powerful Reformation monarch on the title page of the Coverdale Bible (1535); the woodcut border implies that publication of the Bible in the English language had received tacit royal consent (fig. 1). Dissemination of the Bible in the vernacular was a goal that Protestants inherited from Catholic humanists like Erasmus and More. Although the volume was not formally authorized, it circulated under the patronage of Thomas Cromwell, the king's vicegerent in religious affairs.[4] Cromwell presumably sponsored the Holbein image as a publicly available means of validating Henry's claim to govern without clerical intercession as the sole intermediary between temporal society and the divine order, an interpretation supported by Miles Coverdale's preface (sig. +2v).

The intricately carved compartments and emblazoned texts of Holbein's border portray an ideal of evangelical kingship in terms of the transition from the law of Moses to that of Christ. The figures of Adam and Eve at the top left prefigure Christ's resurrection at the opposite side. Henry VIII wields the sword and the book as a worldly instrument of divine revelation at the bottom.[5] His authority is transmitted to him symbolically from the heavens above via the Old and New Testament models for sacred kingship depicted elsewhere on the page. The composite biblical symbol of the sword and the book would play a vital role in a campaign to establish Henry's image as a theocratic ruler capable of unifying ecclesiastical and secular authority. The figures of David and Paul who flank Henry VIII respectively symbolize divine revelation before and after the advent of the Christian dispensation. Whereas the lyre-bearing figure of David serves primarily as a type for Henry VIII's claim to govern by divine sanction, St. Paul's presence denies the papal claim to primacy as an inheritance from St. Peter.[6] Paul's chief attribute of the sword was employed throughout the Middle Ages as a device commemorating his beheading. Protestants revered Paul as the paramount saint for his promulgation of the crucial distinction between faith and works, however, rather than for his martyrdom alone. Reformers aligned the sword in Paul's hands not with the means of his decollation but with "the sword of the Spirit, which is the word of God" (Eph. 6:17).[7] Although the sword in King Henry's hand carries its traditional identification with justice, its proximity to the weapon borne by St. Paul also identifies it with evangelical truth.

The side compartments of Holbein's border align his portrayal of Henry VIII with a sequence of key biblical events. Moses' reception of the Ten Commandments at the left side may be interpreted as a type for divinely inspired leadership capable of delivering God's chosen people out of bondage to the tyrannical pharaoh, whom the reformers interpreted as a figure for the pope. Beneath this scene, Esdras preaches the Mosaic law. In the balanced New Testament scenes at the right, Christ first commissions the apostles to undertake their ministry in the words of Mark 16:15. With tongues of flame upon their heads, St. Peter and his companions then preach the new law at Pentecost (Acts 2:3). The keys borne by the apostles in the inset at the right hand side undermine the papal claim to primacy as the inheritor of the keys of St. Peter.[8] The vertical axis that connects the Tetragrammaton above with the king below establishes a direct line of spiritual authority that descends from heaven to earth without intervention from any ecclesiastical authority.

The prominent quotation of Mark 16:15 suggests that Henry VIII's public image in the Coverdale Bible is connected to the iconography of works designed for the royal court. At the approximate time that Holbein carved the wooden blocks for the title page, a portrait attributed to Joos van Cleve depicted the monarch holding a scroll bearing the Vulgate version of that scriptural text (fig. 2). The iconography of this courtly image corresponds to iconoclastic activity in the outward world by appropriating a text in which the Church of Rome had discovered a precedent for the papal claim of apostolic succession from Christ, thus "demolishing" a key claim to Roman supremacy.[9] The painting presumably refers to Henry's adopted role as a latter-day "apostle" engaged in the evangelical task of propagating the Scriptures; in all likelihood it alludes directly to the publication of the Coverdale Bible. The private self-definition of the monarchial image therefore appears to mirror Henry's woodcut portrait as an embodiment of his permission and control of Bible publication.

The propagandistic title page of the Great Bible (1539; fig. 3) contains a sophisticated variation of Holbein's original portrayal of Henry VIII for the Coverdale Bible. Loosely adapted from the earlier border by a member of the school of Holbein, the Great Bible title page symbolizes royal supremacy over church and state by depicting a graded hierarchy in which the king replaces the pope as the temporal intermediary between heaven and earth. Henry's reception of the divine Word directly from God embodies the reformers' belief that the vertical process of reform is a royal prerogative, for the king alone can transmit the Bible to the bishops and magistrates in the second level. The rigid stratification of the scene exemplifies a conflict between freedom and control, because its orderly ranks reflect Henry's cautious retention of traditional doctrine and ritual during the early stages of the English Reformation. The image ambivalently endorses the Protestant commitment to the priesthood of all believers in a realm where the monarch maintained tight control over religion. Accordingly, the bottom compartment portrays members of a congregation hearing the English Bible from the lectern rather than reading it for themselves, for they are still passive recipients of scriptures that are transmitted by a priestly elite operating under political instructions from the Crown. Even though the text next to this scene is in Latin, the title page as a whole symbolizes publication of this newly authorized vernacular translation of the Bible. The ability of aristocrats to call out the Latin words of homage,

"Vivat Rex," distinguishes them as superiors of the tiny, almost child-like figures of commoners, who shout "God Save the King."

The complicated typology of this woodcut border conveys different scriptural guises of Henry VIII in a heavily layered and overlapping fashion. The most prominent visual allusion is to his instrumental role in the transmission of *verbum Dei*, an apostolic image for the dissemination of the Bible in the post-Pentecostal world of the early church; it offered Protestants a figure for the renewal of the "true" church during the Reformation. The image of the sacred book, as it descends through various levels of the political and social hierarchy, objectifies the utterance emanating from God in the banderole at the top of the border: "So shall my word be that goes forth from my mouth; it shall not return to me empty, but it shall accomplish that which I purpose" (Isa. 55:11). In the Vulgate New Testament, *verbum Dei* refers specifically to the preaching of the divine Word and missionary activity of the apostles (Acts 8:14). The use of the tag phrase *verbum Dei* affords a visual analogue to the inset scenes in the Coverdale Bible showing Christ's delegation of the disciples and the inspiration of the apostles at Pentecost.

Key scriptural texts that are inscribed in sinuous banderoles set forth the iconographical program of the woodcut border. Although Henry VIII's preeminent role is that of David,[10] he also voices King Darius's acknowledgment of the power of Yahweh and speaks to Cromwell in the voice of Moses and to Thomas Cranmer, archbishop of Canterbury, through words uttered by St. Paul. With the exception of Darius, all of these regal prototypes also appear in the border of the Coverdale Bible. The praying figure of the king in the upper right corner utters words attributed to David in celebrating the power of the divine Word as a guide for royal conduct: "Thy word is a lamp to my feet" (Ps. 119:105; Vulg. Ps. 118:105). God reciprocates in his selection of Henry as David to govern over England as a new Israel: "I have found in David the son of Jesse a man after my heart, who will do all my will" (Acts 13:22). The largest banderole attributes to Henry's enthroned figure the response of Darius the Mede to the miraculous survival of Daniel in the lion's den, whereby that ruler proclaimed: "I make a decree, that in all my royal dominion men tremble and fear before the God of Daniel, for he is the living God" (Dan. 6:26). The Bible's presentation of the unhistorical figure of Darius as the conqueror of Babylon may be interpreted as a prefiguration of the English king's rejection of the authority of papal Rome.

The way Henry hands Bibles to figures to his left and right presents him as a figure who unifies the roles of Moses, as one who imparts law to judges, and St. Paul, as a clerical authority who offers counsel to an apostle on the conduct of Christian missions to the Gentiles. In the border's second register, Cranmer's empowerment to "command and teach" religious doctrine (1 Tim. 4:11) casts him in the role of a new Timothy who, as the favored colleague of Pauline Henry, is entrusted with the task of instructing the English in an evangelical religious program. Cromwell in turn receives a Mosaic charge to "judge righteously" and to "hear the small and the great alike" (Deut. 1:16–17). In the third register these servants of the Crown transmit *verbum Dei* respectively to figures representative of the clergy and magistracy. Cranmer instructs the cleric at the left by repeating St. Peter's injunction that pastors fulfil their obligation to "Tend the flock of God" (1 Pet. 5:2); according to Protestant teaching, the Bible is the worldly source of spiritual "feeding." Cromwell outlines the responsibility of civil authorities by quoting from Psalm 34:14 (Vulg. Ps. 33:15): "Depart from evil and do good; seek peace and pursue it." The congregation representative of the English people at the base of the title page hears a biblical text that was interpreted as a foundation of the political doctrine that subjects must obey royal authority. The cleric enjoins them to pray for "kings and all who are in high positions" (1 Tim. 2:1–2).

The iconography of the Coverdale Bible and the Great Bible typified the transformation of Henrician style during the 1530s. Members of court who had reformist sympathies could now appropriate preexisting regal iconography by flattering the king as a new Moses for delivering the English people or as a new David for establishing control over a unified church and state. Henry's apologists and those who sought royal patronage created courtly works of art and literature that contained flattering portrayals of the king that imitated his published images. In some cases these compliments were doubtless designed to encourage the monarch to satisfy expectations for an evangelical government to which the king had a lukewarm commitment if he supported them at all.[11]

Medieval and Renaissance rulers had frequently been envisioned in the image of Moses, but Tudor iconography reinterpreted the Israelite leader as a personal figure for Henry VIII as the initiator of the English Reformation. The association of Henry VIII with Moses on the title pages of the 1535 and 1539 Bibles suggests that the English Reformation is a providential event akin to the Israelites' Exodus out of the land of Egypt. Moses' combined role as both leader of the Chosen People and recipient of the Ten Commandments furnishes a precedent for Henry VIII's reputed deliverance of England out of bondage in papal Egypt and for his authorization of the vernacular Bible. The vignette in the Coverdale Bible that portrays Moses receiving the divine Word from its transcendent author identifies worldly sovereignty with an external and universal source of spiritual power, thus validating its temporal authority.

In line with this view, Catherine Parr, the king's last wife, praises him as a new Moses in *The Lamentacion of a Sinner* (1547), a set of pietistic meditations drawn from the Scriptures. Her complex figure compares the pope to the tyrannical pharaoh from whom the Israelites fled:

> But our Moyses, a moste godly, wise governer and kyng hath delivered us oute of the captivitie and bondage of Pharao. I mene by this Moyses Kyng Henry the eight, my most soverayne favourable lorde and husband. One (If Moyses had figured any mo[re] then Christ) through the excellent grace of god, mete to be an other expressed veritie of Moses conqueste over Pharao. And I mene by this Pharao the bishop of Rome, who hath bene and is a greater persecutor of all true christians, then ever was Pharao, of the children of Israel. (sig. Elr–v)

Catherine Parr's compliment suggests that praise of Henry as a Mosaic king was fashionable at the royal court after the break from Rome, because her works first circulated in manuscript within royal circles before they appeared in print. The continuing currency of the Moses epithet at the Reformation court may be noted in Miles Coverdale's praise of Edward VI as a new Moses in his dedication for the "second tome" of Erasmus's *Paraphrases on the New Testament* (1549).

A different representation of the royal court during this period of religious unrest is provided by miniatures portraying the king as a new David in "Henry VIII's Psalter" (London, British Library, Royal 2.A.xvi), a Latin manuscript written for presentation to him by the French courtier Jean Mallard.[12] Although David had served as a regal prototype throughout the Middle Ages in illustrations for royal psalters and other works, Mallard (or an artist whom he may have commissioned to illustrate the volume) adapts traditional iconography to suit contemporary circumstances by portraying Henry VIII in the guise of David.[13] Both donor and recipient share the prevailing assumption of their time that the Psalms represent an autobiographical collection of lyric songs composed by King David. The portrayal of King Henry playing his lyre in the guise of King David (fig. 4) provides a close analogue to the vignette at the lower left of the Coverdale Bible title page (fig. 1). Holbein's inclusion of David as a type for Reformation kingship may well have derived from Henrician court circles, where volumes like the Mallard psalter circulated, because Cromwell was the effective patron of that Bible translation.

Mallard's miniature fuses type and antitype within a single monarchial image. (Holbein's woodcut border depicts David as a separate figure, on the other hand, albeit one that flanks the central figure of the Tudor king.) The specific image of David with his lyre is associated by convention with David's reputed authorship of the Psalms. Portrayal of the royal fool, Will Somer, at the left of the lyre-playing king provides an amusing illustration for Psalm 53:1 (Vulg. Ps. 52:1): "The fool says in his heart, 'There is no God.'" Mallard's portrait of Henry seated at a table while playing the lyre in a private chamber of a royal palace may also allude to the king's well-known reputation as a musician and composer of both sacred and profane music.[14] According to George Puttenham, the king was fond of hearing English versifications of the Psalms sung by Thomas Sternhold, who received appointment as Groom of the Privy Chamber as a reward for turning out ballad versions of the biblical poems.[15]

Henry appears as both David and one of his lyric subjects in illustrations for two other psalms, whose appeal for deliverance from external enemies and false accusers is altogether appropriate to the self-image of the Reformation king and his court.[16] The manuscript thus identifies the English king as both the subject and the object of a collection of lyrics that was traditionally taken to be an autobiographical work by King David. Henry plays the learned and pious role of "the man who walks not in the counsel of the wicked" in the miniature for Psalm 1 that portrays him reading a book in his bedchamber, with two books on the floor beside him (fol. 3). In this scene Henry has withdrawn from the active world portrayed beyond the portal of the elegantly furnished room into introspective contemplation.[17] A miniature for Psalm 69 (Vulg. Ps. 68) portrays the king praying for deliverance from enemies; with his crown at his feet in a setting of classical ruins, he kneels beneath an angel who has a sword, a skull, and a rod (fol. 79). His plight recalls an outcry attributed to David: "More in number than the hairs of my head are those who hate me without cause; mighty are those who would destroy me, those who attack me with lies" (Ps. 69:4). This verse would have taken on a special meaning during the 1530s and 1540s, when England experienced a sense of encirclement by hostile Catholic powers including the Hapsburg emperor and the French king.

The king evidently received this psalter with approval, because he kept the gift among his private books and accepted Mallard's view that the Psalms constitute a *speculum principis* concerning ideal kingship. Annotations that appear throughout the text in Henry's heavy swashing handwriting designate particular psalms as advice on government and religion. By noting "officiu[m] regi[s]" ("the king's office") beside Psalm 72:4 (Vulg. Ps. 71:4), Henry styles himself as an evangelical king in response to Mallard's view that the hymn was written "De regno christi et gentium vocatione" ("concerning the kingdom of Christ and the calling of the people"). The king indicates his concern with matters of faith by drawing attention to a passage "de idolatria" ("concerning idolatry") in Psalm 44:20 (Vulg. Ps. 43:21). Henry's note "de rege" ("concerning the king") accords with the donor's comment on Psalm 63:11 (Vulg. Ps. 62:12) as an utterance concerning regal piety. The note "de regib[us]" ("about kings") endorses Mallard's view that Psalm 21 (Vulg. Ps. 20) concerns the triumph of Christ through the agency of Christian kings. Henry VIII similarly reads Psalm 20:9 (Vulg. Ps. 19:10) as "pro rege oratorio" ("a prayer for the king").

Jottings independent of Mallard's commentary provide even greater insight into Henry VIII's private interpretation of the Psalms by showing how he applies specific passages to his own conduct as king. Sometimes he merely brackets verses or indicates passages of particular importance with the designations "n[ota] bene" or "bene n[ota]." Many notations indicate that Henry assumes the Davidic role of a righteous man who sings praise to the Lord for delivering him from the hands of his enemies. The 1530s context of the psalter suggests that these perceived threats may have come both from foreign enemies of Henry's policy of religious reform and also from domestic opponents whose hostility to the Cromwellian regime led to the rebellious Pilgrimage of Grace in 1536. The king's annotations furnish a written analogue to the miniature that portrays him as David pleading for divine assistance against enemies (Ps. 69). Thus his "n[ota] bene" beside Psalms 11:6 and 41:11 (Vulg. Pss. 10:7 and 40:12) exults that God will uphold him and direct "fire and brimstone" against the wicked. His annotations on Psalms 18:20–24 and 62:12 (Vulg. Pss. 17:21–25 and 61:13) claim that God will reward him and punish his enemies. Exclamation marks alongside Psalm 34:7, 9 (Vulg. Ps. 33:8, 10) call attention to promises that those who fear the Lord will receive divine protection. Notes on passages in Psalm 37:28, 38, and 39 (Vulg. Ps. 36:28, 38, and 39) that refer to damnation and salvation comment on the meting out of divine penalties "de iniustis et impijs" ("concerning the unjust and impious") and rewards "de iustis" ("concerning the just").

In reading this collection of divine poems as a royal text, Henry VIII joins Jean Mallard in suppressing reference to David's flaws as an adulterer. The king pointedly ignores his Hebrew predecessor's long-standing reputation as an archetype for the repentant sinner in the seven penitential psalms (6, 32, 38, 51, 102, 130, and 143; Vulg. 6, 31, 37, 50, 101, 129, and 142). In contrast to the annotations in which Henry clearly stresses David's status as a model for regal strength rather than personal weakness, avoidance of the psalms of repentance represents a truly significant absence at a time when the king brutally set aside four wives during his search for a legitimate male heir.[18]

Henry's subjects would not so conveniently ignore the negative potential for blame that is inherent within any praise of the king as a latter-day David. Indeed, Miles Coverdale tempers his flattery of Henry VIII in the preliminary matter of the Coverdale Bible by citing Nathan the prophet, who "'spared not to rebuke . . . [David], and that right sharply, when he fell from the word of God into adultery and manslaughter,' offenses for which Henry was already known."[19] (Hugh Latimer was to emulate Nathan's role in his sermons before Edward VI, in which he lodged oblique blame of the late king for setting a bad example for his heir.)[20] When Sir Thomas Wyatt versified the penitential psalms against the contemporary backdrop of Henrician politics, he wrote as one thoroughly familiar with the infidelities and intrigue that permeated the royal court. Although any personal allusions in this poetic sequence would appear to be directed to the circumstances of Wyatt's own life,[21] one may not deny that the poet attaches Protestant associations to a group of psalms that were "essentially and unavoidably controversial" at the time that he versified them (ca. 1534–42). If Wyatt wrote them soon after Anne Boleyn's execution in 1536, he may even "glance, slyly and indirectly, at Henry VIII," who would therefore receive advice that he should imitate the Hebrew king "and repent his own scandalous abuse of power in the service of his lust."[22] The likelihood of critical reference to King Henry is even greater in the sonnet in praise of "Wyates Psalmes" in which the earl of Surrey notes that "Rewlers may se in a myrrour clere / The bitter frewte of false concupiscence." In reading the penitential psalms as a hybridization of a *speculum principis* and a *de remedia amoris*, Surrey discovers a providential warning for lustful monarchs: "In Prynces hartes Goddes scourge yprinted depe / Myght them awake out of their synfull slepe."[23]

In contrast to the private record of Henry VIII's envisagement of himself as David in his manuscript psalter, *The Exposition and declaration of the Psalme, Deus ultionum Dominus* (1539) by Henry Parker, eighth baron Morley, embodies a representation of the king that originated within courtly circles before it was published for popular consumption. The commentator originally prepared his manuscript and dedicated it to the king in 1534, at the approximate time when the Reformation Parliament proclaimed the king to be supreme head of the Church of England. (He had already been declared de facto head of the church by the Act in Restraint of Appeals of the previous year.) Publication of Parker's text by the king's printer, Thomas Berthelet, suggests that Henry VIII favored its dissemination. The patriotic fervor of the baron's interpretation of Psalm 94 (Vulg. Ps. 93) as a Reformation hymn displays the Erastianism that enabled him to survive so many twists and turns in religious policy during the reigns of Henry and his offspring, Edward VI and Mary I. Parker's praise of Henry as a modern version of "the royall kyng David" (sig. A7r) or "the excellente kynge and prophete David" (sig. B8r) is closely aligned with Holbein's juxtaposition of Henry VIII and David in the Coverdale Bible border (fig. 1). By emphasizing the role of David not as the psalmist but as the youthful victor against Goliath, Parker cries out against the violence and arrogance of tyrants and treats Psalm 94 as a prayer to God, the Lord of Vengeance, and as a prophecy of Henry VIII's liberation of England from the pope, the "gre[a]t Golyas [Goliath]" (sig. A7r–v). Complimenting the king as a second Moses leading England as a new Israel out of bondage (sig. A5v), this text also contains hyperbolic appeals for vengeance "ageynst this serpent," the pope, and the liberation of England from its "captivite Babylonical" (sig. A3v and A5r).

Solomon was second only to David as an enduring biblical type for Tudor kingship, one that is rooted in the princely iconography of western Europe and Byzantium. The relationship of the Hebrew monarchs could readily support the Tudor claim to legitimate dynastic descent by tracing out the lineage from Davidic father to Solomonic son. Like his father, Henry VIII received praise as a second Solomon[24] in a doubling of regal prototypes that produced comparisons to both the father and the son who were regarded as paramount among the rulers of ancient Israel. These comparisons were adapted to different purposes, however: David was remembered largely for authorship of the Psalms, slaying Goliath, establishing the united kingdom of Israel and Judah, and governing as the ideal king who was viewed by Christians as a prototype of the Messiah. By tradition, Solomon was the greatest of the Hebrew kings, one whose stature as a sacred ruler was marked by the erection of the Temple in Jerusalem; for Christians the construction of the Temple was a prototype for the foundation of the "true" church during the early Christian period; for Protestants this architectural event betokened the renewal of the church during the Reformation. Solomon's reputation for unparalleled wisdom and prudence was associated with Israel's period of greatest material wealth and well-being. It is important to remember that preexisting iconography of this kind was applied to the particular claims of all the Tudors to govern as Christian monarchs, regardless of whether they embraced orthodox or reformist religious positions.

At about the same time that Holbein juxtaposed Henry and David in the title-page border of the Coverdale Bible, he composed a portrait on vellum showing the king as Solomon receiving the gifts of the queen of Sheba, who kneels at the head of her retinue (fig. 5). The composition of this miniature in the same period as the break with Rome suggests an allusion to the Reformation. After all, the queen of Sheba is a traditional type for the church, and her kneeling homage and submission to an omnicompetent monarch carry every suggestion that the picture commemorates the recent submission of the Church of England to Henry as the head of the church. The opulent attire of the crowded courtiers and the rich offerings borne by the queen's attendants enhance the glory of the king. Although Holbein did not receive royal patronage as king's painter until 1537,[25] this miniature would appear to have been designed as a gift for presentation to the king.[26] The artist, who was known for his Lutheran sympathies, reinterprets the queen's visitation (1 Kings 10:1–13, 2 Chron. 9:1–13) according to the understanding of Solomon's wisdom as a type of divine revelation through Scripture.

Solomon's stance loosely resembles that of King Henry on the Coverdale Bible title page (fig. 1). The full frontal view of the Hebrew king, who sits enthroned, wearing a crown and holding a scepter beneath an arch at the top of a high dais, dominates the scene, in which the queen of Sheba meets him and exclaims: "Happy are these your servants, who continually stand before you and hear your wisdom! Blessed be the LORD your God, who has delighted in you and set you on his throne as king" (2 Chron. 9:7–8). Inscribed on the wall and canopy behind the king, the Latin version of her salutation most likely alludes to the Reformation Parliament's replacement of the pope with Henry as Supreme Head of the Church of England; this text suggests that both Henry and Solomon are responsible to God alone and to no other worldly power. The inscription on the base of the throne articulates the queen's response to their meeting: "VICISTI FAMAM VIRTVTIBVS TVIS" ("By your virtues you have won fame").[27]

Scriptural texts or images of books symbolic of the Bible were widely used as iconographical figures for Reformation kingship after Henry VIII's breach with Rome in the 1530s. Hans Holbein the Younger offered the seminal image for royal supremacy in ecclesiastical and secular affairs when he portrayed the enthroned figure of the English king wielding the sword symbolic of justice and the divine Word as he transmits the book representative of the divine Word on the title page of the Coverdale Bible, the first vernacular translation of the Scriptures to circulate with the tacit permission of the British Crown. This primal scene underwent many variations during the 1530s, notably in the title page for the Great Bible that was modeled upon Holbein's original design, in that artist's miniature portrait of King Henry in the guise of Solomon receiving the queen of Sheba, and in the manuscript psalter in which Henry saw himself portrayed and inscribed marginalia in the manner of a latter-day David. Holbein's image of Henry VIII would undergo transmutation until the end of the Tudor dynasty as an iconographical symbol for governance by a line of "godly" rulers. We may therefore note how praise of a Tudor monarch as a "cult" figure originated during Henry's time rather than that of his daughter, Elizabeth, as schol ars have commonly assumed.[28] The envisionment of Henry VIII as a "sacred" ruler is at one and the same time a conventional means by which an important Renaissance court envisioned itself and a vehicle for public dissemination of a powerful image of regal piety.

Notes

1. This essay incorporates findings presented in John N. King, *Tudor Royal Iconography: Literature and Art in an Age of Religious Crisis* (Princeton: Princeton University Press, 1989), chap. 2. The author has revised and augmented the arguments of that previous work. Unless otherwise noted, scriptural texts are from the Revised Standard Version, including those that are offered without notice in place of the original Vulgate quotations. The Vulgate version of Psalms is cited from *Biblia Sacra iuxta Vulgatam Clementinam Nova Editio,* ed. Alberto Colunga and Laurentio Turrado, 4th ed. (Madrid: Biblioteca de Autores Cristianos, 1965). Figures 2 and 5, *Henry VIII as an Evangelical King* (attr. to Joos van Cleve) and Hans Holbein's *Solomon and the Queen of Sheba,* are reproduced by permission of the Royal Collection, St. James's Palace; copyright 1993 Her Majesty Queen Elizabeth II.

2. That is, a country of which the ruler pays homage to no external overlord.

3. Act in Restraint of Appeals, 24 Hen. VII, c.12, in *The Reformation in England to the Accession of Elizabeth I,* ed. A. G. Dickens and Dorothy Carr (London: Edward Arnold, 1967), 55. Roy C. Strong notes the "far-reaching" impact of this legislation in *Holbein and Henry VIII* (London: Routledge and Kegan Paul, 1967), 6. The present argument is indebted throughout to this pioneering study. See also J. J. Scarisbrick, *Henry VIII* (London: Methuen, 1968), 116–17.

4. Strong, *Holbein and Henry VIII,* 14. See also J. B. Trapp and Hubertus S. Herbrüggen, *"The King's Good Servant": Sir Thomas More, 1477/8–1535,* exhibition catalogue (London: National Portrait Gallery, 1977), no. 144.

5. This "image . . . was to be a definitive one for the Tudor and Stuart Kings" according to Strong, *Holbein and Henry VIII,* 14.

6. On the medieval origins of praising monarchs as recollections of David or Solomon and the relationship of these topoi to the figure of the sword and the book, see King, *Tudor Royal Iconography,* 56–57 and 60. As a variation of

the *tolle lege,* the conventional scene in which Christ confers keys upon Peter and a book symbolic of the scriptures upon Paul, Holbein's image portrays David as an implicit "replacement of Peter, obviously out of favour on account of his association with the Papacy," according to Pamela Tudor-Craig, "Henry VIII and King David," in *Early Tudor England: Proceedings of the 1987 Harlaxton Symposium,* ed. Daniel Williams (Woodbridge, Suffolk: Boydell Press, 1989), 193. Her argument complements that of the present essay, which was published in its original form during the same year as "Henry VIII and King David." On the association of Davidic iconography with reformist or Protestant rulers, see Edward A. Gosselin, *The King's Progress to Jerusalem: Some Interpretations of David during the Reformation Period and Their Patristic and Medieval Background,* Humana Civilitas: Sources and Studies Relating to the Middle Ages and the Renaissance 2 (Malibu: Undena Publications, 1976), 67–68; Anne Lake Prescott, "Musical Strains: Marot's Double Role as Psalmist and Courtier," in *Contending Kingdoms,* ed. Marie-Rose Logan and Peter L. Rudnytsky (Detroit: Wayne State University Press, 1991); and her "Evil Tongues at the Court of Saul: The Renaissance David as a Slandered Courtier," *Journal of Medieval and Renaissance Studies* 21 (1991), 163–86.

7. Although Strong minimizes evangelical iconography by tracing the Henrician sword to the emblem of "The Emperor bearing the book and sword" ("Ex utroque Caesar"), he does acknowledge the "overtly reformist" bias of the Holbein border (*Holbein and Henry VIII,* 14–16).

8. See King, *Tudor Royal Iconography,* 64–70, and Strong, *Holbein and Henry VIII,* 16.

9. Roy C. Strong, *Tudor and Jacobean Portraits,* 2 vols., National Portrait Gallery catalogue (London: HMSO, 1969), vol. 1, 158, and vol. 2, pl. 299. See also Strong, *Holbein and Henry VIII,* 8, and Trapp and Herbrüggen, *"The King's Good Servant,"* no. 202.

10. See Tudor-Craig, "Henry VIII and King David," 193.

11. On a like-minded strategy of Davidic praise under Elizabeth I, see Margaret P. Hannay, *Philip's Phoenix: Mary Sidney, Countess of Pembroke* (Oxford: Oxford University Press, 1990), 91–95.

12. According to King, this manuscript predates the fifth session of the Reformation Parliament (1534), which ratified England's break from the church of Rome with the Act of Supremacy; Henry VIII's marginalia postdate that session (*Tudor Royal Iconography,* 76 with n. 21). Tudor-Craig argues that "Henry VIII's Psalter" is a ca. 1540 manuscript that entered the royal library in early 1542, "two months after he had heard of Queen Catherine Howard's infidelities, and thirty-seven days before her execution" ("Henry VIII and King David," 194). She weakens her case, however, with a questionable identification of this Latin manuscript as the "'psalter in Englishe and Latyne covered w[i]th crimoysyn satyne'" that may be dated by reference to a royal inventory (193). It seems unlikely that the miniature for Psalm 82 (Vulg. Ps. 81; fol. 98v) in Mallard's psalter, a presentation manuscript expressly designed for Henry VIII, would portray God wearing a papal tiara as late as 1540, when that symbolic headpiece would have constituted an insult to the king following his break

with Rome. It remains possible, however, that Henry entered some or all of his marginalia into Royal 2.A.xvi as late as 1542. Tudor-Craig rightly notes that Jean Mallard served in the royal household in 1540–41 as "'orator in the French tongue'" (196). She and I agree that Mallard's styling of Henry VIII as David is aligned with the envisionment of the king that flourished in England between 1534 and 1539.

13. On the earlier portrayal of Francis I as David, see Tudor-Craig, "Henry VIII and King David," 197 with n. 62.

14. Scarisbrick, *Henry VIII*, 15–16.

15. See Puttenham's *The Arte of English Poesie*, in *Elizabethan Critical Essays*, ed. G. G. Smith, 2 vols. (Oxford: Clarendon Press, 1904) vol. 2, 17. On the corresponding, albeit more sophisticated role of Clément Marot at the court of Francis I, see Prescott, "Musical Strains."

16. Yet another miniature, that for Psalm 27 (Vulg. Ps. 26), portrays King Henry as David slaying Goliath according to Tudor-Craig, "Henry VIII and King David," 197. See below for discussion of Henry Parker's application of this figure to the king's conflict with the papacy in a 1534 manuscript dedication.

17. "Henry is himself the Blessed Man" of Psalm 1:1 according to Tudor-Craig, "Henry VIII and King David," 197.

18. Portrayal of "David in penance" in the miniature for Psalm 69 points toward a cleavage between respective portrayals of Henry VIII and Francis I in Mallard's psalter and a French book of hours in the view of Tudor-Craig, "Henry VIII and King David," 198. Although Bathsheba is portrayed in close proximity to Francis in his prayer book, she appears in no illustration for Royal 2.A.xvi because "no touch of Bathsheba was acceptable in Henry's miniature."

19. Hannay, *Philip's Phoenix*, 91.

20. *Select Sermons of Hugh Latimer*, ed. Allan G. Chester (Charlottesville: University Press of Virginia for the Folger Shakespeare Library, 1968), 79. Edward's precoronation pageantry associates Davidic Henry with "hethen rites and detestable idolatrye" when ancient Truth proclaims to Henry's heir: "Then shall England, committed to your gard, / rejoyce in God, which hath geven her nation, / after old David, a yonge kynge Salomon" (quoted from *Literary Remains of King Edward the Sixth*, ed. John Gough Nichols, 2 vols. [London: Roxburghe Club, 1857], vol. 1, ccxci).

21. Alistair Fox, *Politics and Literature in the Reigns of Henry VII and Henry VIII* (Oxford: Basil Blackwell, 1989), 280–85.

22. Stephen Greenblatt, *Renaissance Self-Fashioning: From More to Shakespeare* (Chicago: University of Chicago Press, 1980), 115 and 121. Alexandra Halasz contends that Wyatt's psalms point "toward political allegory" in "Wyatt's David" in this collection, 193–208. On the vexed issue of dating Wyatt's penitential psalms, see *Sir Thomas Wyatt: The Complete Poems*, ed. R. A. Rebholz (New Haven: Yale University Press, 1981), 455–56.

23. Henry Howard, Earl of Surrey, *Poems*, ed. Emrys Jones (Oxford: Clarendon Press, 1964), no. 31 ("The great Macedon that out of Perse chasyd"). The note on ll. 13–14 mentions the possibility of "covert allusion to Henry

VIII." This poem was inserted into London, British Library, Egerton 2711, as a preface to Wyatt's holograph text of his version of the penitential psalms (Halasz, "Wyatt's David," 193 with n. 1).

24. For example, Cambridge, University Library, Dd.7.3, fol. 295v.

25. Strong, *Holbein and Henry VIII*, 13.

26. *Holbein and the Court of Henry VIII*, exhibition catalogue, The Queen's Gallery (London: Buckingham Palace, 1978), no. 88.

27. Michael Levey, *Painting at Court* (New York: New York University Press, 1971), 95 and fig. 77. The Latin text from 2 Chronicles 9:7–8 reads: "Beati viri tui et beati servi hi tui qui assistant coram te omni t[em]p[or]e et avdivnti sapientiam tuam. Sit dominus deus benedictvs, cui complacit in te, ut poneret te super thronvm, vt esses rex constitutvs domino deo tvo." See *Holbein and the Court of Henry VIII*, no. 88. This entry mistakenly claims that this Holbein miniature is "the first known example of Solomon being given a contemporary likeness in such a representation." For discussion of the earlier portrayal of Henry as Solomon in a stained-glass window at King's College Chapel at Cambridge University, see King, *Tudor Royal Iconography*, 85–89.

28. See Frances Yates, "Queen Elizabeth I as Astraea," in *Astraea: The Imperial Theme in the Sixteenth Century* (London: Routledge and Kegan Paul, 1975), 29–87; and Roy C. Strong, *The Cult of Elizabeth: Elizabethan Portraiture and Pageantry* (London: Thames and Hudson, 1977). Late sixteenth-century praise of Elizabeth I as a new David is rooted in the Protestant appropriation of David as a regal prototype during Henry VIII's reign according to Hannay, *Philip's Phoenix*, 91–97. See also Anne Lake Prescott, "King David as a 'Right Poet': Sidney and the Psalmist," *English Literary Renaissance* 19 (1989), 131–51.

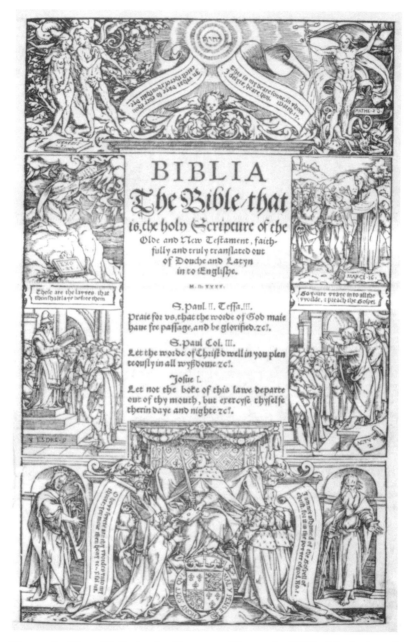

Figure 1. Hans Holbein the Younger. *Henry the VIII with the Sword and the Book*. Woodcut. Title-page border. Coverdale Bible (1535). By permission of the British Library, London.

Figure 2. Attributed to Joos van Cleve. *Henry VIII as an Evangelical King.*
Oil on panel, ca. 1535. Hampton Court.

Figure 3. School of Holbein. *Henry VIII as a Reformation King*. Woodcut. Title-page border, Great Bible (1539). By permission of the Henry E. Huntington Library.

ed sperauit in multitudine diuitiaȝ
suarum: & preualuit in vanitate sua .

go autem sicut oliua fructifera in
domo Dei speraui in misericordia Dei
in eternum, & in seculum seculi .

onfitebor tibi in seculum quia fecisti
& expectabo nomen tuum quoniam bonū est
in conspectu sanctorum tuorum Gloria
patri Sicut erat .

i
xit
insipiēs
in corde
suo nō
est De9
or=
rupti sut

Figure 4. *Henry VIII as David with Lyre.* "Henry VIII's Psalter," ca. 1530–
40. London, British Library, Royal 2.A.xvi, fol. 63v. By permission of the
British Library, London.

Figure 5. Hans Holbein the Younger. *Solomon and the Queen of Sheba*. Miniature, ca. 1535. Royal Library, Windsor Castle.

"The Whole Island like a Single Family": Positioning Women in Utopian Patriarchy

JANEL MUELLER

There are reasons aplenty for interest in how gender roles are construct-ed—and, specifically, how women are positioned—in Thomas More's *Utopia* (1516). Foremost among these is the premise that gender is a foundational category for the analysis of human social identity.[1] Other reasons include More's commitment, unusual in his time, to a human-istic education for his daughters and female wards[2] as well as his title's claim to something like paradigm status for this "little book . . . on the best state of a political order," which is immediately identified with "the new island Utopia."[3] There is no reason, however, to expect easy agree-ment on the representation of gender in this controverted text. J. H. Hexter notes as a "sole point of unanimous agreement" in its reception history that *Utopia* "is a work of social comment."[4] Mindful of its ex-pressly troubled relation to the status quo of European society at the time of its writing, twentieth-century readers continue to dispute the extent to which *Utopia* is visionary or revisionist or playfully or ironi-cally self-qualified. Grounds for such dispute are not far to seek; for an illustration one need not go beyond More's title. The Latin word choice, *optimo* rather than *summo,* carries the sense of the "best possi-ble" rather than simply the "best" state of a commonweal. And the authority for the account of Utopia is the "distinguished man" (*vir ex-imius*) Raphael Hythlodaeus, whose first name is that of an archangel, whose last name is Greek for "expert in nonsense," and whose words are reported by a "citizen and undersheriff of the famous city of Lon-don," a certain Thomas Morus, whose last name means "foolish" in Latin but "appointed share" or "destiny" in Greek. The nested narra-tion thus launched by More's extended title mediates (with who can say what exquisite potential equivocation?) between its two designated is-lands, Utopia and Britain.[5]

Given a text with such features, before I address my interpretive interests I should declare what kind of reading I propose. I aim to read More's text unironically, taking its representations, its rhetoric, and its value judgments at face value, positing a basic correspondence between the authorial More and Morus the reporter of Hythlodaeus. However, I also remain on the alert for possibilities of irony that escape the awareness or control of the text's author—possibilities arising at points where implied meanings or value assignments are at clearly demonstrable odds with those that the text otherwise affirms and articulates. In my unironizing approach to reading (though not in my eye to ironic implications), I align with Quentin Skinner and stake my position on the same generic grounds: the sense that the intertextual relation with Plato's *Republic* is of determinative significance for More's *Utopia*. Both works undertake to model a commonweal; in both, ideation raised to idealization cues tone and themes.[6] Precisely because my reading of *Utopia* is rooted in the link between More's project and Plato's, I want to frame my discussion of gender and women's roles by sketching what I take to be the most notable resemblances between the two.

Utopia works off the *Republic* as an originary text by engaging a lapsed political-ethical discourse that revived with the Renaissance recovery of Plato.[7] This engagement operates not only through overt allusions but, much more largely, through shared objectives and means. More, like Plato, aims to figure a life of assured well-being for all the members of a community. For both authors the city-state is a basic unit of conception and organization. With both authors the primary tactic is to eliminate competing interests by integrating the private and public spheres so thoroughly that everyone will attend to the common good. What Plato devises only for his ruling or guardian class, however, More generalizes across a comprehensive class in Utopia: an equality based negatively on the abolition of money and private property and positively on the application of identical norms for formal education, vocational training, and labor contributions to both sexes.[8] Beyond all such specific features, the radical social rearrangements envisaged by Plato and More ultimately derive their force from a recognition that informs the accounts of *Utopia* and the *Republic* alike. Noting how human identity is shaped by social institutions, Plato and More invest the political order with responsibility for molding character as it assigns and circulates values, primarily through its educational and economic systems.[9]

My discussion of gender relations in *Utopia* requires some further reflection on the recognition just identified, for it not only serves to link More with Plato but also to place More in his own context of Renaissance Christian humanism.[10] Historically, a conviction regarding the constructive potential of human institutions has hinged on a still more basic conviction: that human nature requires control and stabilization.[11] In a study of English utopian writing from 1516 to 1700, J. C. Davis argues that these two premises—native human imperfection and its potential perfectibility through institutional means—are precisely what define the mode of "utopia."[12] More pinned what terrestrial faith he had on the power of a well-wrought polity; *Utopia* everywhere attests the outlook that Davis terms utopian.

Book 2 directly addresses the molding of human nature in the passages on Utopian moral philosophy and religion. These predicate a broadly generic—that is, a degendered and classless—conception of ourselves as experiential and social beings. Utopian moral philosophy sees human beings as naturally and legitimately self interested. Because we fundamentally seek our own pleasure, we might conclude that we should do so at all costs and by all means, but here we are liable to err on three counts. There is a danger of missing out on a truer and greater pleasure by pursuing a lesser one. There is the danger of pain not only from overindulgence but from the insatiable goad of appetite itself. And there is the danger of committing injustice; in our pursuit of pleasure we may deprive or wrong other humans and bring ourselves into enmity with them. Any such enmity is self-defeating, according to Utopian philosophy, because the "humanity" of providing for others' welfare together with our own is "the virtue most proper to human beings."[13] The root paradox of generic human nature, in this representation, is to be at once self-seeking and social. Utopian religion picks up at this point and offers two principles and one corollary for resolving the paradox: (1) the human soul—immortal "and by God's goodness born for happiness"—will enjoy or suffer eternity according to the choice of pleasures that it makes in this life; (2) it is God who creates, guarantees, and administers the moral order to which each human being is subject and finally answerable; hence, (3) we find true happiness when we take pleasure in virtue as the "supreme good" (L & A, *Utopia*, 68, 69). More's vocabulary in these passages on Utopian moral philosophy and religion is peppered with the indefinite personal pronouns in which the Latin language abounds—the *quis*, *quisques*, and *quisquams*, references to "one," "someone," "anyone"—that work from and toward a sense of generic humanity, what it is to be human without specification of age or gender or rank or anything else (Scolar *Utopia*, sigs. H2–J2).

Other Utopian institutions take the undifferentiated, generic notion of human nature a fair distance further. The Utopian order identifies physical needs common to all and ensures that these are met: food, clothing, housing, and health care. To ensure adequate provisions, everyone who is strong enough and of an age to do so—with a very small number of exceptions[14]—must engage in physical labor for six hours a day. Such are the energies of this universal labor program that Utopia emerges as a surplus-producing economy. Yet it maintains the welfare of its people by a series of measures calculated to counterweigh a darker side of human nature. Both individually and collectively, human beings are appetitive, acquisitive, and aggressive—so runs the constant implication and the intermittent articulation of Utopian policy. Hence, measures to protect the state against invaders include conversion of the national surplus into money either to pay foreign mercenaries lavishly to fight on the Utopians' side or to fix outcomes of hostilities with bribes or rewards. Monthly drill at arms for all able-bodied adults provides an additional safeguard.[15]

Utopia's internal defenses against human aggressiveness and acquisitiveness, however, receive much more emphasis from More and attract much more notice from readers. These are the famous measures for uniformity or equity (*aequitas*) which the narration recounts in detail: sameness of clothing in materials and amounts, sameness of housing (so much so that dwellers regularly rotate their units), sameness of city plans and of rural farming complexes, sameness in the directed use of leisure, and sameness in a communitarian life focusing on meals and recreation taken in public halls built for this purpose as well as on rituals in places of worship that accommodate all tolerated expressions of religion.[16] In principle, it is clear, Utopia has been constructed as a society of a single class, all of whose members are equal—firmly equalized. There is neither money nor private property, whether real estate or movables. For extra good measure, gold, silver, and precious stones are put to public uses that attach vile or absurd connotations to them.[17] Yet, given both the variability and the variety in human nature, there are exceptions to Utopian commonality at either end. The ex-citizen slaves embody downward mobility in their harshly punished because scarcely conceivable crimes against Utopian laws; they are disciplined and administered as marginal human beings. Prospective magistrates and priests, however, stand out for their aptitude in the intellectual pursuits that Utopians supremely value among uses of leisure. By the vote of their appreciative fellow citizens, these scholars attain what upward mobility and special status the society affords.[18]

Thus, in *Utopia,* a spectrum of needs, propensities, and attributes is predicated of human nature at large, and the narration specifies correspondingly inclusive ways of dealing with these. Yet it cannot simply be assumed that the indefinite expressions associated with this range of

reference in More's text encompass females. One important consequence of feminism's impact in the academy has been to demonstrate
that general-seeming linguistic and cultural formulations typically encode maleness as their subject and norm.[19] Accordingly I consider it
crucial to attend to junctures where More does not employ indefinite
pronouns but specifies that persons of both genders are in play in the
social system. Here too, however, feminist research has signaled the
likely presence of weighted binary distinctions that operate as cultural
adjuncts of gender—whether in classing males as central and females as
peripheral, or males as bearers of culture and females as extensions of
nature, or in imputing to maleness and masculine roles a categorical
prestige that femaleness and feminine roles do not receive.[20]

It can look at times as if there is no difference between the sexes that
makes any real difference in Utopia. As the basic means of subsistence,
"farming is the one job at which everyone works, men and women
alike. . . . They are trained in it from childhood, [and] not only watch
the work being done, but frequently pitch in and get a workout by
doing the jobs themselves" (L & A, *Utopia,* 50). This equal participation of both sexes in crop cultivation stands in direct material relation
to the need not only for food but also for clothing (which is made only
of flax, wool, and hides) and for shelter (the plastered wattle-and-tim-
ber building frames in which Utopian architecture so much resembles
Tudor).[21] Besides the farming that they all learn and perform on rotating assignments, both men and women become proficient in some
craft. The Utopian crafts are "wool-working, linen-making, masonry,
metal-work, or carpentry." "The women as the weaker sex . . . practise
the lighter crafts, such as working in wool or linen; the heavier jobs are
assigned to the men" (L & A, *Utopia,* 50). Yet, while provision is made
here for a sex-linked biological difference in physical strength, the system of manual occupations does not itself group the women workers in
wool or flax on a conventional distaff side in Utopian society. "Both
men and women carry on vigorous military training," it is noted at another juncture, "so they will be fit to fight should the need arise" (L &
A, *Utopia,* 87). As in the Utopians' formally mandated labor and service to the state, so too in their directed use of other time. The narration here expressly negates sexual difference, registers it only to deny
its relevance to how leisure is employed. "The chief aim of their constitution is that, as far as public needs permit, all citizens should be free to
withdraw as much time as possible from the service of the body and
devote themselves to the freedom and culture of the mind. For that,
they think, is the real happiness of life." The "public lectures" delivered
daily in the hours "before daybreak" are attended by "a great many

people of all kinds, both men and women" who "choose voluntarily to attend" and "devote ... these periods to intellectual activity." The point is later reiterated: "Throughout their lives many people, men and women alike, spend their free time in reading. They study all the branches of learning" (L & A, *Utopia,* 55, 51, 66).

So far, so undifferentiated are the obligations and activities of the gendered persons of Utopia. The provisions for equal education and equal access to intellectual pursuits may seem to spread to a whole citizenry the radically revisionary construction of a ruling elite in the *Republic*—especially since More's narrator, Hythlodaeus, mentions Plato in connection with the Utopians in several places.[22] Sexual difference is precisely the question that Socrates raises and dismisses as he begins detailed discussion of the privileged and powerful guardian class in Book 5 of the *Republic*. Balancing off various complications—that males as a sex seem superior in learning ability and in bodily strength but also that "many women ... are better than many men in many things"—Socrates concludes to Glaucon that women have the same human potential as men for political leadership. They must therefore be offered the identical training: "For the production of a female guardian, then, our education will not be one thing for men and another for women, since the nature which we hand over to it is the same." Glaucon assents: "There will be no difference."[23] Yet the very context given this affirmation of sexual equality now glaringly exposes More's distance from Plato. Is the potential of a woman comparable to that of a man for political leadership? On the evidence of *Utopia,* where the holders of political office from King Utopus onward are uniformly recorded and characterized as male, the answer must be no. To any extent recognized in More's text, the potential of women for political leadership is nonexistent.

As I read and reflect, seeking to account for this prime divergence in More's and Plato's social construction of gender, the explicit terms in which Socrates characterizes the guardians' sexual equality begin to look like stipulations of a necessary condition on such equality. If—that is to say, when—sexual difference is socially negated, all the women will be "common" to all the men, and the relations of the nuclear family unit will be dissolved. "None shall cohabit with any privately," says Socrates; "the children shall be common, and ... no parent shall know its own offspring nor any child its parent." Glaucon retorts that sexual "community" or "possession in common" is a "far bigger paradox" than sexual equality, one that provokes "distrust as to its possibility and its utility." But Socrates will concede only the first of Glaucon's misgivings while stoutly defending against the second. "There would be no debate about its utility," he asserts, "no denial" that sexual community and the splitting off of human reproduction from a family context and roles "would be the greatest good, supposing it possible." Yet the last word is Glaucon's, at least for the duration in the dialogue: "Both . . . would be right sharply debated."[24]

Glaucon's response carries far greater predictive force than do Socrates's assertions where More's social ideology is concerned. Utopia certainly does impose community of property and goods as a universal condition, but just as universally it retains the family and enforces monogamy in the strictest possible fashion. Telling evidence of this society's insistence on defining its members by marking just two differences—one's sex and one's marital status—comes from Utopian clothing, which "is the same everywhere throughout the island, and has always been the same, except for the distinction between the sexes and between married and unmarried persons" (L & A, *Utopia*, 50). Premarital sex disqualifies the parties from ever being able to marry, while adultery and seduction may be punished by enslavement. Divorce is difficult and rare. Such severe measures have been adopted, More's Raphael explains, because the Utopians "suppose few people would join in married love—with confinement to a single partner and all the petty annoyances that married life involves—unless they were strictly restrained from promiscuity," a line of reasoning fully in keeping with the pessimistic bent of commentary on generic human nature in this work (L & A, *Utopia*, 81). From the standpoint of gender construction, however, Utopia's combination of monogamy and community of property is so puzzling a feature that it cries out for explanation. This combination should simply be unattested, according to current anthropological analyses which view monogamy as an institutional concomitant of private property: a wife's body is invested with her husband's proprietary interest as the source of legitimate offspring to inherit the family property and perpetuate the family name.[25]

But inheritance cannot be the rationale for Utopian monogamy. Where, then, does the rationale lie? A step can be taken toward answering this question by noting the structural importance accorded to the household as the elemental unit of Utopian social organization: "Each city . . . consists of households, the households consisting generally of blood-relations" (L & A, *Utopia*, 55). Numerous further details create an image of the Utopian household as an extension of the nuclear family centered on a senior male head. I accordingly trace the Utopian rationale for monogamy to the social necessity of constructing and then identifying bearers of household and familial authority. Even though there is no private property, there is nonetheless in More what Carole Pateman has acutely detected in other early modern authors: a tacit "sexual contract" that shapes the formulations of political theory.[26] This consistently presupposed means of legitimating a male's sexual access to a female constructs male bodies as fathers, and fathers in turn as the citizen body. A variant on the body politic metaphor, with its resonant connotations of naturalness, appears to operate by implication here. A man with a wife and offspring is construed as having dependents, who relate in turn to him as their head. Under its severe enforcement in Utopian society, monogamy certifies that a given male is the father of a given woman's children, investing him with authority and seniority over them (and her).

More's text offers no representation of the nuclear family of husband, wife, and their minor offspring as the discrete economic unit which, under the practice of primogeniture and the pressure of new social attitudes about the requisite independence of married couples, would be a conspicuously emergent social reality in sixteenth-century England.[27] However, the text does provide repeated glimpses of the affective dynamics and hierarchical ordering of the nuclear family encased within the generational layerings of the Utopian great household. The insistence laid by Socrates in the *Republic* on the contingent connection between gender roles and marital and familial arrangements is amply corroborated in More, though altogether differently realized. Bound firmly by Utopian monogamy in the paired roles of husband and wife, father and mother, sexual difference is constructed as a relation of adult male superior to adult female inferior. Both parents are also said to stand as authority figures to their offspring, opening a potential for disruption of the superior-inferior relation of husband to wife that goes unnoticed by More's Raphael and unexemplified in his narration. A typical sixteenth-century European in these regards, he finds nothing to explain or justify as he details the gender hierarchy that is built into family structure in Utopia. Within the household, wives function literally as servants or attendants (*ministri*) "to their husbands, children to their parents, and generally the younger to their elders" (Scolar *Utopia*, sig. G1; L & A, *Utopia*, 57). Again, "husbands chastise their wives, and parents their children, unless the offense is so serious that public punishment is called for" (L & A, *Utopia*, 83). So, additionally, in the household, to prepare for the two-day religious celebrations that mark the turning of the months in Utopia, "wives kneel before their husbands and children before their parents, to confess their various failings and acts of negligence, and beg forgiveness for their offences. Thus if any cloud of anger or resentment has arisen in the family, it is dispersed, and they can attend divine services with clear and untroubled minds" (L & A, *Utopia*, 104). Do husbands and fathers never need chastisement or confession?—to me this seems an obvious question. Yet, unless husbands and fathers become criminals by some means, there is no provision for their chastisement or confession in the Utopian social system. Male heads figure as wholly unconditioned authorities within their families, and the senior male head also heads the great household as its paterfamilias.

The position of a paterfamilias in an extended Utopian household is critical not only with respect to its internal workings. He is also the automatic representative for the household and responsible for it in any dealings beyond its confines. In another twist of gender ideology that More's Raphael fails to clarify or even to perceive, the paterfamilias gains credit as a provider figure in Utopia although housing is publicly furnished, meals purveyed in the public halls, work periods enforced by a public official whose primary duty this is, health care dispensed through a city hospital system, and clothing made at home, mostly by the women. While the dispensing of other necessities of life is just as free and communal, both a power to provide and a proprietary role are ascribed to this figure as he makes his way to the public storehouses: "Here the head of every household looks for what he or his family needs and carries off what he wants without any sort of payment or compensation. Why should anything be refused him? There is plenty of everything, and no reason to fear that anyone will claim more than he needs. Why would anyone be suspected of asking for more than is needed, when everyone knows there will never be any shortage?" (L & A, *Utopia*, 56).

Why, I ask, on reading this description, do the functions of male heads of households accrue a social credit so obviously in excess of their labor contribution or other discernible value? Answering the question requires looking beyond the unit of the extended household while recognizing that its ideological configuration remains intact in the larger sphere. The oscillation of the gender reference implicit in the term "citizen" from point to point in the narration signals—and signifies—an absolutely fundamental asymmetry in the Utopian construction of persons. Where work or leisure or religion are involved, the participating citizens must be male and female, but where voting for local or national offices is concerned, the citizens are male heads of households. Political activity and leadership alike are defined by and confined to these paterfamilias figures. When More's Raphael undertakes to explain what motivates a level of national government in this island of otherwise quite autonomous city-states, the master trope of the Utopian order turns out to be the great household writ greater still. The overall qualification for membership in this system of interlocking communal structures can be specified (in terms transparently not my own) as working according to one's abilities and receiving according to one's needs. Since the exchange and distribution of goods periodically require a comprehensive assessment and coordination of resources, this is the motive for convening a national senate annually for some days at Amaurote, the capital city. Certain heads of households are elected by neighboring heads of households to represent their districts. In Raphael's account of the proceedings, the agenda for those elected involves a simple and straightforward enlargement of the very concerns that exercise their authority back at home. The Utopian senators "survey the island to find out where there are shortages and surpluses, and promptly satisfy one district's shortage with another's surplus. These are outright gifts; those who give get nothing in return from those who receive. Though they give freely to one city, they get freely from another to which they gave nothing; and thus the whole island is like a single family" (L & A, *Utopia*, 61).

"The whole island is like a single family." By a plethora of measures, whether drastic or seemingly paltry, Utopia undertakes to model the political order on the extended family (*familia*) as structured by a gender hierarchy—that is, to realize patriarchy in its fullest etymological sense. Hexter has laid a useful though somewhat extravagant emphasis on the role of the patriarchal family in More's work. He usefully calls attention to how "More magnified the function of the family beyond anything in medieval life" by stripping away from his Utopia the guilds, confraternities, and other associations that continued to structure the corporate economy and society of the early sixteenth century. But Hexter then goes to extremes in characterizing the "lack of corporatism" in More's Utopia as an "absence of all other organs of formal and durable human organization" besides the "greatly enhanced . . . magnitude of the patriarchial family."[28] Actually, as the text itself attests, the ultimate enhancement of patriarchalism in Utopia proceeds not so much through the institution of the family (even as extended in the great households) as through ideological diffusion and religious sanctions. In significant broadenings of patriarchal terminology, we are told that those elected to public office in Utopia, whether civil or religious, "are called fathers and that indeed is the way they behave [*patres appellantur: & exhibent*]." "The people respect them spontaneously, as they should," this passage continues, before closing with references to the "governor [*princeps*]" and the "high priest [*pontifex*]" (L & A, *Utopia*, 84; Scolar *Utopia*, sig. K1). Above all, religion, which is considerably less coercive in Utopia than in More's England or Europe, offers a transcendental anchor for the ideology and force of Utopian patriarchy through the conception of a provider and ruler figure writ greatest of all. "The vast majority of the Utopians," we are told, "and among these all the wisest believe . . . in a single power, unknown, eternal, infinite, inexplicable, far beyond the grasp of the human mind, and diffused throughout the universe, not physically, but in influence. Him they call father [*hunc parentem vocant*—literally, progenitor or parent], and to him alone they attribute the origin, increase, progress, change and end of all visible things; they do not offer divine honours to any other" (L & A, *Utopia*, 96; Scolar *Utopia*, sig. L3). The pronominal references to this figure are consistently masculine.[29]

In due course I will have more to say about this passage, but I want now to pursue the consequences and implications of women's positioning in what is expressly nameable as Utopian patriarchy. Given the concentric enclosures of ideology and social organization that pivot on a fathering figure, no Utopian woman can escape immediate, personal subordination to a male. To begin with, every female is expected to marry. "When the women grow up and are married," says Raphael in a brief and sweeping declaration, "they move into their husbands' households" (L & A, *Utopia*, 55). His much later mention of persons who, from motives of religious service, decide against marrying is distinctly limited in its Latin vocabulary to men. Raphael calls such persons "celibates [*caelebi*]" (L & A, *Utopia*, 101; Scolar *Utopia*, sig. M1)—a term that has no documented application to women. Significantly, the delimitation of women to the category of married persons proceeds linguistically and ideologically, both through the exercise of word choice—and so, presumably, of authorial intent—and through the routine workings of the Utopian social system. Beyond the force of these, there is no legal requirement that a woman marry. By farming and working at her craft to make her labor contribution, she qualifies for continued residence and provision in the great household where she was raised as a dependent daughter. A woman might even stay unmarried as an ordinary consequence of the Utopian system, either because she exercised her right of refusal against every prospective mate on whom she would pass judgment in the nude, or because she herself was rejected for some deformity by the same process of physical inspection which is one of the Utopians' most striking customs. In such an eventuality she could expect either to remain under her father's authority or that of her oldest male relative in a patrilocal household in the city, or to be transferred by public order to fill out the gender ratio in some other male-administered household in the city or country.

Yet it is clearly the prevailing Utopian notion that women will marry and become mothers. Here I discover the corresponding dimension, the necessary female side, of the tacit sexual contract that secures male identity as a patriarchal construction. But if women are necessary to this construction, can the sexual contract be said to serve any interest of theirs? And if so, how does it do so? In the search for answers to these questions, the force of cultural conditioning can be seen to figure markedly in More's text. Certain topics bring Utopian institutions and their accompanying ideology to the fore in the narration; the two main ones involving gender construction are the choice of a mate and the practice of breast-feeding. In both of these cases the narration undertakes to represent the institutions by which the social order exacts what it wants of its women as provisions for the women's own desires. In the first case, which I will examine directly, the casting of female obligation as female desire ends in rhetorical failure—and exposure. Raphael's language veers into an express alignment with male interests that leaves female interests behind. In the case of breast-feeding, to be discussed below, the language ostensibly maintains its equipoise as it works to assimilate female desire to female social necessity. Yet, for all their differences in rhetorical outcome, the treatments of both topics evince the shaping impact of gender ideology on the institutions and persons of Utopia.

The universal expectation that Utopians will marry, and hence must be induced to do so, leads Raphael to describe how they examine their prospective spouses in the nude—a custom which he pretends to ridicule but actually defends on analogy with "buying a colt." A striking fact about this passage—one which it shares with Milton's much later divorce tracts—is how an ostensibly mutual provision for both sexes develops, through phrasing and emphasis, as a safeguard for the man involved. "In the choice of a mate," it is the prospective husband who should not be compelled to "leave . . . the woman's body covered up with clothes and estimate her attractiveness from a mere handsbreadth of her person, the face." "Not all people are so wise as to concern themselves solely with character," the passage resumes with a new gesture at inclusiveness. But again there is an abrupt turn to the male's perspective. "There's no doubt that a deformity may lurk under clothing, serious enough to make a man hate his wife when it's too late to be separated from her" (L & A, *Utopia*, 82). That a man seeking a wife, like a man buying a colt, both needs and wants a breeder recurs as an undertone in the vocabulary of the later passage on celibacy, to which I have already referred in its linguistic limitation to males. In that passage we are told the grounds on which Utopian men decide either to marry or not to marry. Those who opt for "marriage"—*conjugium* in the Latin, with its connotations of yoking—"don't despise its comforts, and think as they owe nature their labour, so they owe children to their country [*patriae*]" (L & A, *Utopia,* 101; Scolar *Utopia,* sig. M1). Startlingly devoid of affect, this wording offers to become revelatory in its reference to sexual gratification (a key sense of "comfort"/*solacium* at this period); I glimpse a possibility here that the masculine covering term might indeed include what both partners, not just the man, expect from marriage. The wording becomes more revelatory and more typical, however, of the asymmetry in Utopian gender ideology as it lays concluding emphasis on the political dimensions of parenthood, which Utopian fathers alone acquire and exercise.[30]

Within this demonstrably masculinist framework, the insistent construction of Utopian females as feeders and breeders culminates in the passage that describes communal meal-taking in the city halls built for this purpose. This is by far the most vividly imagined and developed scene in the whole of Book 2, and it becomes the more focal because it is presented as an emblem of the communitarian life and values of this society.[31] I want to look at it rather closely. The passage is undergirded by an articulation of female roles which, in turn, are shaped and conditioned by the Utopian ideology of gender.

Let me start with the commonsensical observation that it is a big job to purvey what seem to be two substantial meals a day—dinner and supper—in these halls. Each hall accommodates thirty households, each of which by law comprises ten to sixteen adults and however many minor children the married adults have, plus their elected official—a syphogrant—and his family. Not figuring for the children five years of age and older, who in any case stand around the adults' dining area at mealtimes and eat and drink what is handed to them, each Utopian communal meal must at a minimum feed between 300 and 480 adults. Cooking on this scale inevitably demands hard physical work. By the weaker-sex principle enunciated previously in the passage on craft vocations, meal preparation might be expected to count as a labor contribution, and more men than women might be expected to perform it. But any such expectations prove wrong on both counts, laying bare both the untheorized character of female work in Utopia's domestic sphere and the absence of notice given to this work by females in its articulated labor system.[32] Meal preparation does not figure in the six hours of daily work at farming or a craft that are required of all Utopian adults. Yet, although "slaves do all the particularly dirty and heavy chores" in the communal kitchens, "planning the meal, as well as preparing and cooking the food, is carried out by the women alone" on a rotating plan (L & A, *Utopia,* 58). Again, Raphael does not explain but simply asserts this sexual division of culinary tasks, while the marginal gloss pointedly underscores the carryover of roles and connotations from the patriarchal household to the larger community. It reads: "Femine ministre in conviviis [Women are the servants at meals]," re-using the same term—*ministre*—that figured in the detailing of house-hold hierarchy: "Ministri sunt uxores maritis [Wives are the servants of their husbands (or "wait on" them)]" (Scolar *Utopia,* sigs. G1–G2).

But I have only begun to tap the current of gender ideology in this passage on the communal meals of Utopia. Now Raphael describes what the seating (and standing) plan looks like inside a hall at mealtime. The men occupy seats which back against and range all along the walls, with tables of a size to accommodate diners in groups positioned in front of the men's seats. The men's bodies at mealtime, in significant symbolism, are both the encompassing and limiting demarcators of the space of Utopian common life and the fixed points of reference for the women's compulsory ministrations.[33] Whatever the women are called upon to do at mealtime, the men will be settled there for the duration of the meal, the conversation, and the music. Where are the women whose turn it is not to prepare and serve the meal? Raphael tells us where they are, and why. The women sit on the aisle sides of the group tables, so that they can leave their places easily. Again the spatial sym-bolism is significant for its ideological charge in the rationale given for this seating by gender. Here are Raphael's words: "The men sit with their backs to the wall, the women on the outside, so that if a woman has a sudden qualm or pain [*malum*], such as occasionally happens during pregnancy [*quod . . . gerentibus interdum solet accidere*], they may rise without disturbing the arrangements and go to the nurses" (L & A, *Utopia,* 58; Scolar *Utopia,* sig. G2).

This description turns partly on a reference to the nurses—that is, the combination babysitters and sometime wet nurses who tend the chil-dren younger than five in the adjacent public room.[34] I will turn to the nursery and its ideology in a moment, but for now it is significant to note how the seating plan at Utopian common meals assimilates all fe-male adults, whatever their age or status, to the literally "outside" posi-tion and condition of pregnancy or breast-feeding and thence to a con-ception of women as unreliable participants in communal activity. This representation of women as persons who may or may not be there with and for the group certainly exceeds the biology of their gender. The ideology encoded in this scene has implications that carry beyond the setting of communal meals and into the arena of political office and political responsibility. Whether any woman is in fact breeding or breast-feeding a child, or even capable of doing so, her assigned seat is forever one in a contingent position. Utopia categorizes women as always liable to be summoned by a call of nature—from their bodies or the bodies of their offspring—to an elsewhere on a fringe beyond public life. Accordingly, Utopian social dictates also penetrate and prescribe female roles in the elsewhere of the public nursery. Just as women are required to plan, prepare, and serve meals for their thirty-household unit, so too every mother is required to breast-feed her own baby "unless," in Raphael's terse words, "death or illness prevents." However, he quickly adds, finding a woman to suckle an infant is far from being a problem in Utopia. Feminine ideological conditioning runs deep at this point in this shame-and-praise-based society. It runs so deep that a public function connected with breast-feeding has been assigned to the wives of syphogrants—the only function they have besides sitting with their husbands at head tables in the meal halls. When a wet nurse is needed to replace a biological mother, explains Raphael, "the wife of the syphogrant quickly finds a suitable nurse. The problem is not difficult: any woman who can volunteers gladly for the job, since everyone applauds her kindness, and the child itself regards its new nurse as its natural mother" (L & A, *Utopia*, 58; Scolar *Utopia*, sig. G2).

"Everyone applauds her kindness [*misericordia*]"—alternatively, her mercy or pity. This is the sole specific access to public praise for females that Raphael records. But beyond such recognition, which itself is the only reward that anyone can receive for a contribution or achievement of any kind in Utopia, he tells us that the women have internalized their self-validation as mothers. So intense is this internalization that, beyond their own childbearing, they are eager to be adoptive mothers and be credited with more offspring by this means. To be fully realized as a female in Utopia is to embrace an assigned set of serving and ministering functions which are firmly connected to the bearing and nurturing of human life on a concrete, physical level that the society does not acknowledge as a species of its required labor—and to be relegated categorically, as shown by the seating in the dining halls, to a contingent, intermittent position in life beyond the household. In this positioning, as I have noted, the sociopolitics of gender claims a certain grounding in biology—the likelihood that pregnant and nursing women may have to interrupt an extended sitting at table. But what is never explained, because never questioned, is why meals taken in such a hush that readings or music can be heard, followed by carefully monitored, uplifting conversation among adults, comprise the only regular and frequent expression of this society's public life.

In reporting that Utopian women must prepare communal meals in rotation beyond their six hours a day at farming or their crafts of spinning and weaving, and emphasizing too that the women endeavor to increase their contributions as mothers, More's Raphael conveys a fairly precise notion of how much leisure time an adult married female might have during her childbearing years and how she might spend it. In this connection, the broad qualification which he notes on the mandated use of leisure for intellectual pursuits seems especially germane: "But if anyone would rather devote his spare time to his trade, as many do who don't care for the intellectual life, this is not discouraged; in fact, such persons are commended as specially useful to the commonwealth" (L & A, *Utopia*, 51). Here, again, the narration strongly underscores an impetus that draws public praise—this time, what is represented as the personal option of working beyond the required amount in order to be useful to the commonwealth. The loopholes just as much as the exactions of the Utopian labor system conduce effectively to its ideology of femininity: the "choice" of service as the way of spending one's time above and beyond the work demands placed upon one, perhaps even to get done the things, like cooking and childcare, that the system does not register as labor.

Thus, although Raphael, as reported by More, insists more than once on the keen pleasure that women as well as men take in time freed for public lectures and other intellectual pursuits, it becomes by no means equally likely that females will distinguish themselves in learning and be chosen as members of the company of Utopian scholars. This is the highly select company that, on the recommendation of the priests and the vote of the citizens, is excused from the otherwise universal requirement of six hours of physical labor a day to cultivate their wisdom and constitute a talent pool for appointments to the magistracy and priesthood.[35] I have already cited circumstantial indications that women do not hold public office, for if they did, these officials could not be called "fathers"—"parents [*parentes*]," perhaps, but not fathers. No less indicative is the aside inserted in one of Raphael's late pronouncements. Here, to bring out the narrowing effect of More's parenthesis, I translate his Latin more literally than Robert M. Adams has done: "Priests (unless they are women, for this sex is not altogether excluded, but if one is a widow of advanced age, she may be chosen, which happens rather rarely)—priests have the most select women in the population for their wives" (Scolar *Utopia*, sig. M2; cf. L & A, *Utopia*, 102). We can easily supply considerations of fertility, maternity, and scheduling demands to explain this unexplained assertion that only elderly widows are ever (if ever) chosen to the priesthood in Utopia.

But I suspect that this Utopian practice—in its double delimitation to unmarried older women and its emphatic rarity—may encode a masculine repugnance rooted in gender ideology that represents a woman's body as polluting when she is menstruating or has just given birth.[36] Conversely, this ideology, exemplified in patristic writings that More can be assumed to have read on the special holiness of widows, constructs an unmarried woman after menopause as pure, additionally so because she is no longer classed as an object of male sexual desire.[37] Elsewhere in *Utopia* More's Raphael discloses a further aspect of this gender ideology that conditions masculine repugnance toward the fecund female body. The disclosure is the more significant because it occurs quite gratuitously in the section on Utopian philosophy that denounces the perversity of persons who prefer bodily to spiritual satisfaction. Rather than instance a glutton, say, who would be much more germane to his point, Raphael uses the following example, highlighted by the marginal rubric "Morbid tastes of pregnant women," to instance what he means by judgment "depraved by disease or by custom [*aut morbo aut consuetudine depravatum iudicium*]." In such cases, "enjoyment doesn't arise from the experience itself but from . . . the perverse [*perversa*] mind of the individual, . . . just as pregnant women whose taste has been distorted [*corrupto gustu*] . . . think pitch and tallow taste better than honey" (L & A, *Utopia*, 74; Scolar *Utopia*, sig. H4). The meaning in excess of the context here points to the disqualification of breeding adult females from either inclination or access to "higher" concerns of the intellect, religion, and politics because of their unfortunately "morbid" or "distorted" tastes.

A masterly recent study by Peter Brown has provided us with accounts of the ideological construction of the male body in the literature of late antiquity that have demonstrable relevance to the humanistically oriented More in the period when he wrote *Utopia*. In a synthesis of late classical sources that extensively utilizes formulations in a work by a favorite author of More and Erasmus, Plutarch's *Praecepta Conjugalia* (*Advice on Marriage*), Brown offers us the image of the self-controlled citizen householder whose firm yet calm and easy management of his unstable wife and slaves both enacts and validates the superiority of his state of being to theirs.[38] What above all characterizes the social presence of the male body of this citizen-householder is its *aequitas*, its equanimity defined as the sameness of self-containment, which in turn becomes normative in the stability and order identified with his manner and authority. I have already noted the ubiquity of the term *aequitas* in More's descriptions of the sameness that pervades Utopian society and its institutions. I can now proceed to identify that *aequitas* as an aspect of its patriarchy. Compared with the female body that slows its movements and distends in pregnancy, emits blood in menstruation and milk in lactation, and runs the repeated danger of death in childbirth, the relative sameness of the male body is construed by the writers of classical antiquity and their admiring later readers as not simply the emblem but also the source and agent of stability and order in the private domain of the great household and the public domain of politics.[39] Raphael's canard about the morbid tastes of pregnant women extends, through its grounding in their bodies, to implicit aspersions on the quality of their judgments otherwise and, hence, their categorical unfitness for authority and administrative office. Every meal in Utopia has a seating plan that categorizes adult women as—or as if—pregnant. More broadly, women in Utopia are tied to and defined by their marital status and their service roles and functions in the familial, household sphere. Aside from ceremonial inclusion as accompanying spouses on appropriate occasions, women are all but absent from or invisible within the public sphere. Even the women's participation in military exercises, which appears to be an aspect of sexual equality on its first mention in the narration, converts in a later reference into a mainstay of the patriarchal support system for wars that the citizens of Utopia undertake to wage in person. Raphael explains as follows:

> Just as no man is forced into a foreign war against his will, so women are allowed to accompany their men on military service if they want to—not only not forbidden, but encouraged and praised for doing so. Each leaves with her husband, and they stand shoulder to shoulder in the line of battle; in addition, they place around a man all of his children, kinsmen and blood- or marriage-relations, so that those who by nature have most reason to help one another may be closest at hand for mutual support. It is a matter of great reproach for either spouse to come home without the other, or for a son to return after losing his father. The result is that as long as the enemy stands his ground, the hand-to-hand fighting is apt to be long and bitter, ending only when everyone is dead. (L & A, *Utopia*, 92–93)

Thus far, in the specifics of gender construction that I have been amassing in order to locate women in Utopian patriarchy, I do not find much to credit as utopian. I am referring to the kind of thinking and writing which Davis takes to define the genre of "utopia" in sixteenth- and seventeenth-century England: the envisioning of alternative institutions that so mold human nature as to endow it with constructive expressions or possibilities that existing sociopolitical arrangements frustrate or preclude altogether. Patriarchy in Utopia, as a system of roles and relations and connotations, looks instead like a very old, very familiar, very dreary story—at least, to my eyes. I may therefore be expected to conclude by severely faulting the containment, repression, and demeaning of women's work and status in Utopia by comparison with that of the ruling father figures in households, places of worship, syphograncies, cities, and commonweal. But in fact I do not think it possible to draw such a clear-cut conclusion about gender ideology in Utopia.

Utopia is a culture that, for males as well as females, gravitates against the modern Western notions of the self and self-realization that give standard critiques of patriarchy their negative thrust. Judging now by criteria for the development of individuality or individualism, are women in Utopia finally any more controlled and channeled than the men? My answer would be no. All are subject to an almost complete lack of privacy, to constant surveillance at work or in directed leisure, and to incentives for effort that combine praise from others with one's personal satisfaction in a job well done for the common good. It is true that the gender-based difference in a Utopian's prospects of prestige and public recognition does perpetuate male superiority across generations—and may afford some men disproportionately enhanced possibilities for satisfaction. Since statues are erected to the memory of "distinguished men who have served their country well [*viris insignibus & de republica preclare meritis*]," and since most Utopian religions hold that the spirits of the dead are present among the living, watching their conduct and lending moral support, perhaps a dead Utopian steals some moments of posthumous pleasure over his statue (L & A, *Utopia*, 84, 99–100; Scolar *Utopia*, sig. K1). I can find no other concessions to individuality or individualism in the text.

But there is more to say about social recognition, and it gives a deeply paradoxical turn to the implications of patriarchy for gender ideology in Utopia. Certain passages late in the narration articulate this society's norms for ultimate meaning and value, and do so in terms that unsettle or at least complicate the masculinist orientation of earlier passages on the patriarchal social order. One example is Raphael's account of the fundamentals of Utopian philosophy—a brand of humanism that he first introduces in generic rather than gendered vocabulary. But getting to the heart of his subject requires more and more frequent recourse by Raphael to a significantly feminized, normative figure of Nature who initiates, energizes, and rules human life as the Utopians conceive it. Since the compass of this Nature figure manifestly supplies a full rationale for human life, the final, brief entry of God as the transcendental guarantor of her impetus and power has the look of an insertion from Raphael's own religious orthodoxy—and an effect of near irrelevance in the dynamics of the passage:

No one [*Necque . . . quisque*] is placed so far above the rest [*supra generis humani*] that he is nature's sole concern; she cherishes alike all those living beings to whom she has granted the same form [*univer-sos ex aequo fovet quos eiusdem formae communione complectitur*]. . . . Nothing is more humane (and humanity is the virtue most proper to human beings) [*humanum est maxime (qua virtute nulla est homini magis propria)*] than to relieve the misery of others . . . and restore them to enjoyment, that is, pleasure. . . . Thus, they say, nature her-self prescribes for us a joyous life [*finem ipsa nobis natura praescrib-it*], in other words, pleasure, as the goal of our actions; and living according to her rules is to be defined as virtue. And as nature bids mortals to make one another's lives cheerful [*natura mortales invitet ad hilarioris vitae mutuum subsidium*], as far as they can, so she re-peatedly warns you not to seek your own advantage in ways that cause misfortune to others. . . . On the other hand, deliberately to decrease your own pleasure to augment that of others is a work of humanity and benevolence, which never fails to reward the doer over and above the sacrifice [*tibi aliquid ipsi demere: quod addas aliis: id . . . est hu-manitatis ac benignitatis officium, quod ipsum nunque tantum aufert commodi; quantum refert*]. . . . Your mind draws more joy from re-calling the gratitude and good will of those whom you have benefit-ed than your body would have drawn pleasure from the things you forfeited. Finally, they believe . . . that God will recompense us for surrendering a brief and transitory pleasure here with immense and never-ending joy in heaven. (L & A, *Utopia*, 70–71, translation slightly modifed; Scolar *Utopia*, sigs. H2–H3)

In scholarship on *Utopia* that has followed R. W. Chambers's lead, it is standard procedure to assimilate the Utopian philosophy of pleasure to the medieval ideal of imitating Christ in a life of self-sacrificial ser-vice and, then, to equate its realization with the monastic calling that More deliberated so seriously as a young man among the Carthusians and never ceased to venerate. This school of interpretation identifies monastic community as the ultimate value and the figure of the monk as the ultimate human type promoted and institutionalized in Utopia's social relations.[40] There is, certainly, some thematic warrant for thread-ing a connection between the foregoing passage from the philosophy section and the later one on the sect of the "Buthrescas" or "specially holy men" in Utopian religion. These are the "celibates who abstain not only from sex, but also from eating meat. . . . They reject all the plea-sures of this life as harmful, and look forward only to the joys of the life to come, which they hope to merit by hard labour and all-night vigils. As they hope to attain it soon, they are cheerful and active in the here and now" (L & A, *Utopia*, 101). Raphael elaborates as follows on the ethic of subservience in labor for others' welfare to which these specially religious persons devote themselves:

> Only by constant dedication to the offices of charity, they think, can happiness after death be earned; and so they are always busy. Some tend the sick; others repair roads, clean ditches, rebuild bridges, dig turf, sand, or stones; still others fell trees and cut them up, and transport wood, grain or other commodities into the cities by wagon. They work for private citizens as well as for the public, and work even harder than slaves. With cheery good will they undertake any task that is so rough, hard and dirty that most people refuse to tackle it because of the toil, tedium and frustration involved. While constantly engaged in heavy labour themselves, they procure leisure for others, yet claim no credit for it. . . . The more they put themselves in the position of slaves, the more highly they are honored by everyone. (L & A, *Utopia*, 100–101)

I, however, want to argue that an analysis of gender construction in More's work points in a different direction than assimilating the most highly honored form of Utopian life to the model of medieval monasticism.[41] What are the strengths of the case for this assimilation? Certainly, the vow of celibacy is a key similarity. But the lack of personal property and the conformity to a rule for life that correlate, respectively, with monastic vows of poverty and obedience do not differentiate the specially religious men in Utopia, since, as we have seen, these conditions apply to the population at large. Moreover, the contemplative dimension of monastic life is altogether missing from the description of the Buthrescas—surely no insignificant feature in gauging the exactness of fit in a proposed model. Perhaps the strongest claim to be made for medieval monasticism as a supreme norm in *Utopia* is that such an interpretation fits well with what is known of the historical More and hence what can safely be hypothesized about his authorial intent. Yet to say this is to interpret the special prestige accorded to Utopian males who conjointly embrace lives of sexual renunciation and of unwearying, selfless service as resting on partial institutional correspondences alone. What the assimilation to a model of medieval monasticism misses are the final reaches of an internal momentum in More's text that, as I see it, undoes the normative character of patriarchal masculinity on the human plane.

Let me return to the choice of celibacy that renders the Buthrescas unique in Utopian life. Peter Brown has traced an eventually authoritative flesh-spirit cleavage from its origins in the apostle Paul's eschatological yearnings through its systematization in the lives of the so-called desert fathers and then in the writings of the most influential Greek and Latin fathers of the Christian Church. In Brown's representation it is imperative to register the enormous power of a Pauline "synecdoche" that identified "the body's physical frailty, its liability to death and the undeniable penchant of its instincts toward sin" with "the flesh," and "the flesh" in turn with "the state of humankind pitted against the spirit of God."[42] The ascetic reflexes that would be triggered by this view of the body as a site of inherent disorder and inveterate evil led alike to misogyny and to devaluation of marriage. What ensued in the history of Christian spirituality can be termed a contradictory definition of maleness in the vocabulary of gender that I have been using—an affirmation of male superiority in matters of the spirit and a concurrent denial that superior maleness was constructed by heading a household, fathering offspring, and discharging civic functions. This contradiction can be formulated as an elementary subtraction problem: posit a categorical male superiority and take away the conventional social, political, and economic roles of the male. What remains for constructing the religious man who equates the body and, especially, its sexual functions with a self-will and sinfulness that require subjection to the will of God? On the evidence of More's *Utopia*, male superiority minus the patriarchal construction of the male voids recognizable maleness as well. But the remainder is not a generic humanity. The remainder appears recognizably feminine against the backdrop of the patriarchal system that is in full force elsewhere in this society.

A more telling model than monasticism, then, for the most highly honored life of service in Utopia is the position and functions of women as assigned through that society's binary system of gender relations. (The function of slaves might also seem to be a candidate model, except that no one in the position of a slave ever receives honor.) As evidence of the workings of an implicit feminine model, I would cite the feminized Nature of Raphael's philosophy passage, who plays an aetiological part in a sketchy myth of origins for the human genus—a redefinition of human as humane, as finding satisfaction in serving the welfare of others, as, in short, feminized.[43] Again, as evidence of this feminine model, the Buthrescas do not simply forego patriarchal status and authority through their lives of celibacy; they also degender themselves, as gender is defined and shaped in Utopia, because they behave as only dependents and inferiors—women and slaves—otherwise do. Constantly dedicated to the offices of charity, constantly engaged in heavy labor, they claim no credit for it. "The more they put themselves in the position of slaves, the more highly they are honoured by everyone." "They work for private citizens as well as the public, and work even harder than slaves." I read the two passages on the core of Utopian philosophy and religion as signifying the ultimate feminization of the norms for being human in Utopia's ideology and culture.

Even so, this gender ideology—as illuminated by the phenomenon of the Buthrescas—enfolds a savage irony for the position of an actual woman in Utopia. For, simply by virtue of the free individual choice that makes for ethical self-definition, any of the Buthrescas must count as superior to any female in meeting Utopia's femininized moral norms. Clearly, in the women's case, feminization is first a matter of acculturation, and secondarily (with those who throw themselves into the functions of mothering and serving others) a matter of personal ethical choice. To compound the irony of the individual woman's moral position, moreover, there is a further systemic irony in the narration: the contradiction between the patriarchalism of Utopian society and the feminization of its ethics and spirituality is not allowed to take anything like a full toll of the patriarchalism. More's Raphael wrenches his divergent implications into self-consistency with a theological turn. The Utopians—or at least the wisest of them, we are told—believe in a God who, beyond all humanness (for they have not known Christ), anchors humanity in his fatherly authority and provision. Just possibly this God's authority and provision are generically parental, not necessarily paternal and patriarchal. More's Latin permits but does not enforce such a reading. "Unum quoddam numem putant . . . : hunc parentem vocant [They believe in a single power . . . this (literally), they call parent]" (Scolar *Utopia*, sig. L3; L & A, *Utopia*, 96, translation slightly modified). Yet, because this God at other points in the immediate vicinity is explicitly referred to in masculine forms, the phrasing remains no more than a fleeting gesture toward a divinity, a great parent of all, whose being may transcend gender difference. Where then, finally, are women in Utopian patriarchy? Their persons are acculturated, subordinated, and enmeshed in the multiplied ironies of their position. Yet the feminine values that they embody prove central and supreme in what More offers, precisely by means of these values, as a paradigmatic human commonweal.

Notes

This essay developed from a presentation to the Midwest Faculty Seminar on More's *Utopia*, sponsored by the University of Chicago's Office of Continuing Education in January 1989. I am grateful to Elizabeth O'Connor Chandler, the organizer, and to Mark Kishlansky, Thomas Stillinger, Richard Strier, as well as other participating faculty for helpful comments. A presentation to

116 / Janel Mueller

the faculty and graduate students of the Renaissance Workshop at Chicago in February 1990 yielded the benefit of criticisms from Terry Bowers, Amy Mc-Cready, Michael Murrin, and Gavin Witt; they have my thanks. So, especially, do Peter Herman and Katharine Eisaman Maus, who spurred me to some crucial rethinking and revising.

1. See, e.g., Joan Kelly, *Women, History, and Theory* (Chicago: University of Chicago Press, 1983), chaps. 1–4; Joan W. Scott, "Gender: A Useful Category of Historical Analysis," *American Historical Review* 91 (1986), 1053–75.

2. For evidence of More's views on educating females and his encouragement of his daughter Margaret in particular, see the English translations of his Latin letters in *St. Thomas More: Selected Letters,* ed. Elizabeth F. Rogers (New Haven: Yale University Press, 1961), nos. 17, 22–23, 31–33, and 35. More as educator, humanist, and paterfamilias is discussed by R. W. Chambers, *Thomas More* (London: Jonathan Cape, and New York: Harcourt, Brace and Co., 1935), 175–91; Richard Marius, *Thomas More* (New York: Random House, 1985), 221–27; Judith P. Jones and Sherianne Sellers Seibel, "Thomas More's Feminism: To Reform or Re-Form," in *Quincentennial Essays on St. Thomas More,* ed. Michael J. Moore (Boone, N.C.: Albion, 1978), 67–77; Elaine V. Beilin, *Redeeming Eve* (Princeton: Princeton University Press, 1987), 3–28; and Elizabeth McCutcheon, "The Education of Thomas More's Daughters: Concepts and Praxis," in *East Meets West,* ed. Roger L. Hadlich and J. D. Ellsworth (Honolulu: University of Hawaii Press, 1988), 193–207.

3. *Libellus . . . de optimo reip[ublicae] statu, deq[ue] nova Insula Utopia;* cited from the facsimile of Thomas More, *Utopia* (1516; reprint, Leeds: Scolar Press, 1966). The subheadings that introduce both books of the work (sigs. B1r [E3v]) reiterate the phrase "de optimo reipublicae statu." Subsequent quotations of More's Latin are cited from this edition, by page reference, and incorporated in my text.

4. J. H. Hexter, *More's Utopia: The Biography of an Idea* (Princeton: Princeton University Press, 1941; reprint, Westport, Conn.: Greenwood Press, 1976), 11.

5. On equivocation and equivocality, see Elizabeth McCutcheon, "*Mendacium Dicere* and *Mentiri*: A Utopian Crux," in *Acta Conventus Neo-Latini Sanctandreani,* ed. I. D. McFarlane, Proceedings of the 5th International Congress of Neo-Latin Studies (Binghamton, N.Y.: Medieval and Renaissance Texts and Studies, 1986), 449–57. For me, however, the compelling precedent for More's jocoserious mode in *Utopia* remains the *Moriae Encomium* (1509), which Erasmus wrote at More's suggestion. Both works unfold from a shared rhetorical premise: that the deepest truths must be jestingly uttered in an age of moral corruption if they are to gain any quarter at all. In this line, see C. A. Patrides, "Erasmus and More: Dialogues with Reality," *Kentucky Review* 8 (1986), 34–48.

6. On the accumulated period resonances of the theme "optimus status reipublicae," see Quentin Skinner, "Sir Thomas More's *Utopia* and the Lan-

guage of Renaissance Humanism," in *The Languages of Political Theory in Early-Modern Europe,* ed. Anthony Pagden (Cambridge: Cambridge University Press, 1987), 123–57.

7. On the recovery of Plato's works beginning in the fourteenth century, see Paul Oskar Kristeller, *Renaissance Thought and Its Sources,* ed. Michael Mooney (Irvington, N.Y.: Irvington, 1979), 50–65.

8. Although More implies that social equality has produced a single-class state, he is contradicted by the emphatic presence and indispensable functions of slaves in Utopia. Slavery is another feature shared with Plato's republic, though the important difference of its nonhereditary character in More is pointed out by George M. Logan in annotating Robert M. Adams's translation for their collaborative edition of Thomas More, *Utopia* (Cambridge: Cambridge University Press, 1989), 80 n. In implementing their respective conceptualizations of gender equality, Plato sees fit to institutionalize community in sexual relations as well as community of property among his guardians while More emphatically retains and rigorously enforces monogamy throughout his ideal society. More's retention of the married couple as the elemental social unit has eventually pervasive implications for the construction of gender relations in Utopia, as I propose to show.

9. Peter Herman (personal communication) reminds me that this recognition holds only for and within Utopia, that is, in the narration of Book 2. For in Book 1 Hythlodaeus bases his refusal to become a courtier on his conviction that he can only preserve his own moral being by remaining outside of the prince's service.

10. Margo Todd, *Christian Humanism and the Puritan Social Order* (Cambridge: Cambridge University Press, 1987), chaps. 2 and 3, gives an account of this social ideology focused squarely on sixteenth-century England. Of obvious importance for gender relations (and much else in society) is the conviction that the cultural arrangements that humans themselves devise can shape, control, stabilize, and channel human behavior into some desired pattern or patterns; see, variously, Dorothy Dinnerstein's *The Mermaid and the Minotaur: Sexual Arrangements and the Human Malaise* (New York: Harper and Row, 1976) and of Nancy Chodorow's *The Reproduction of Mothering: Psychoanalysis and the Sociology of Gender* (Berkeley and Los Angeles: University of California Press, 1978).

11. Arthur B. Ferguson, in *The Articulate Citizen and the English Renaissance* (Durham, N.C.: Duke University Press, 1965), traces the transformation in political writing that occurs between the fourteenth and the sixteenth centuries in England as authors proceed from emphasis on the God-given order of things to develop a sense of the constructive capacities of government to deal with various social and economic issues.

12. J. C. Davis, *Utopia and the Ideal Society* (Cambridge: Cambridge University Press, 1981), chap. 1.

13. More, *Utopia,* ed. Logan, trans. Adams, 70. The account of Utopian moral philosophy, with annotations on its classical sources and prototypes, oc-

cupies 67–77. Subsequent quotations of More's work in English are taken from this edition, cited as "L & A, *Utopia,*" and incorporated parenthetically with page references in my text.

14. "Barely five hundred . . . in each city and its surrounding countryside" (L & A, *Utopia,* 53); elsewhere we learn that there are fifty-four cities (43) and that the inhabitants of each number "in excess of 100,000" (55, n.). Those excepted from the universal labor scheme thus comprise fewer than one-half of 1 percent of the Utopian population.

15. *Utopia,* 61–62 and 87–91.

16. Ibid., 43–47, 50, 54–55, 57–60, and 104–7.

17. Ibid., 62–65.

18. Ibid., 80, 83, 65–66, and 53. The harshness of the category of "slave" is somewhat mitigated, however, by the foreigners who volunteer for slavery in Utopia in order to improve the destitution which their labor does not relieve elsewhere. I owe this point to Gavin Witt. Regarding the "scholar" category, see Richard A. Lanham's trenchant commentary in "More, Castiglione, and the Humanist Choice of Utopias," in *Acts of Interpretation: The Text in Its Contexts, 700–1600,* ed Mary J. Carruthers and Elizabeth D. Kirk (Norman, Okla.: Pilgrim Books, 1982), 327–43.

19. Perceptive discussions include Robin T. Lakoff, *Language and Woman's Place* (New York: Harper and Row, 1975); Robert Paul Wolff, "There's Nobody Here but Us Persons," in *Women and Philosophy,* ed. Carol C. Gould and Marx W. Wartofsky (New York: Putnam, 1980), 128–44; and Jean Bethke Elshtain, "Feminist Discourse and Its Discontents: Language, Power, and Meaning," in *Feminist Theory: A Critique of Ideology,* ed. Nannerl O. Keohane, Michelle Z. Rosaldo, and Barbara C. Gelpi (Chicago: University of Chicago Press, 1981), 127–45.

20. Foundational discussions on these respective topics include Edwin Ardener, "Belief and the Problem of Women," in *Perceiving Women,* ed. Shirley Ardener (New York: Wiley, 1975), 1–28; Sherry B. Ortner, "Is Female to Male as Nature Is to Culture?" in *Woman, Culture and Society,* ed. Michelle Z. Rosaldo and Louise Lamphere (Stanford: Stanford University Press, 1974), 67–88; Jane F. Collier and Michelle Z. Rosaldo, "Politics and Gender in Simple Societies," in *Sexual Meanings: The Cultural Construction of Gender and Sexuality,* ed. Sherry B. Ortner and Harriet Whitehead (Cambridge: Cambridge University Press, 1981), 275–329.

21. *Utopia,* 54 and 48.

22. Ibid., 36, 38, and 78; cf. the connection drawn between Plato and Hythlodaeus himself on 10. J. H. Hexter, *The Vision of Politics on the Eve of the Reformation: More, Machiavelli, Seyssel* (New York: Basic Books, 1973), remarks on the special status of the *Republic* as a prototype for *Utopia* which does not, however, preclude divergent handling of certain key matters—in particular, More's rejection of Plato's proposals to dissolve family structure (44–45).

23. *Republic* 455d and 456d, trans. Paul Shorey, in *The Collected Dialogues of Plato,* ed. Edith Hamilton and Huntington Cairns (Princeton: Princeton University Press, 1964), 694–95.

24. Plato, *Republic,* 457d–e, in *Collected Dialogues,* ed. Hamilton and

Cairns, 696–97; cf. the opening of discussion at 449c–d on 689. On the contingent connection between gender relations and marital and family arrangements registered in this passage, see Susan Moller Okin, *Women in Western Political Thought* (Princeton: Princeton University Press, 1979), 39–42, 57–60, and 69–70.

25. See Gayle Rubin, "The Traffic in Women: Notes on the 'Political Economy' of Sex," and Karen Sacks, "Engels Revisited: Women, the Organization of Production, and Private Property," both in *Toward an Anthropology of Women,* ed. Rayna Reiter (New York: Monthly Review Press, 1975), at 157–210 and 211–34 respectively.

26. Carole Pateman analyzes Hobbes, Filmer, Locke, and Pufendorf as well as Kant and Rousseau in *The Sexual Contract* (Stanford: Stanford University Press, 1988), chaps. 3–4. Hobbes emerges as exceptional in this context because he undertakes to stipulate the character of sexual relations both prior to and then as bound by the marriage contract.

27. For extensive discussion, see Keith Wrightson, *English Society, 1580–1680* (New Brunswick: Rutgers University Press, 1982).

28. Hexter, *Vision of Politics on the Eve of the Reformation* (cited above, n. 22), 44–45, arguing a key qualification of R. W. Chambers's insistence on More's medievalism in *Thomas More* (above, n. 2), 88, 131–32, and 257–58. For other literalizing uses of the term "patriarchy" to characterize sixteenth-century family structure and domestic life, see Peter Laslett, *The World We Have Lost* (London: Methuen, 1965), 11–21; Lawrence Stone, *The Family, Sex, and Marriage in England, 1500–1800* (London: Weidenfeld and Nicolson, 1977); and Steven Ozment, *When Fathers Ruled: Family Life in Reformation Europe* (Cambridge: Harvard University Press, 1983). Veronica Beechey, among other feminists, has rightly critiqued the diverse conceptions and metaphorical extensions that make "patriarchy" a slippery referent, if not an outright hindrance, that has proved a hindrance in contemporary political theory and analysis ("On Patriarchy," *Feminist Review* 1 [1979], 66–82). I intend only the historical and circumstantial applications of the term that I develop in discussion here.

29. For citations of medieval texts which contrast "lord/ruler" to "mother" but not to "father," see Caroline Walker Bynum, *Jesus as Mother: Studies in the Spirituality of the High Middle Ages* (Berkeley and Los Angeles: University of California Press, 1982), 117–18.

30. For readers steeped in the interpretation offered by Richard Marius in his recent full-length biography, *Thomas More* (cited above, n. 2), this passage from *Utopia* will have a disclosive resonance although Marius himself does not cite it. He identifies as "the ruling drama" of his subject's life and actions the decision to marry rather than enter religious orders: "More always thought he should have been a monk or a priest, and his character was formed by his decision to take a wife, which in turn inexorably drove him to assume a public career" (xxiii). Here, in historical and biographical guise, is the Utopian pattern which constructs maleness politically as paternity legitimated through the medium of marriage.

31. The taking of meals in common by the guardian class is a matter of only

passing reference in the *Republic* (416e), but the wording there evokes the Dorian city-states' practice of *sussitia*—the soldiers' messes that bonded adult males in military training or on campaign (see Plato, *Collected Dialogues*, 661). More may have developed the Utopian communal meal system from suggestions provided in Book 6 of Plato's *Laws* where the Athenian stranger hails the Cretan "public table for men" as "an admirable institution, miraculously originated" and deplores as "a grave error . . . that the position of women has been left unregulated." Women should be compelled to eat with men, he argues, because this "half of the race . . . is generally predisposed by its weakness to undue secrecy and craft" and thence to disorderliness if "allowed to get out of hand" and "left without chastening restraint." It is unclear what the "disorders" are—perhaps overeating or drunkenness?—that the Athenian stranger proposes to remedy by compelling women "to take their meat and drink in public." He stresses, finally, how resolute the male legislator will have to be to overcome the "furious resistance" that can be expected from women. See *Laws*, 780e–781d, in *Collected Dialogues*, ed. Hamilton and Cairns, 1356–57. Surtz's note surveying commentary on the institution of common meals for males written between Plato's time and More's contains no reference to the *Laws;* see *The Complete Works of St. Thomas More*, vol. 4, ed. Edward Surtz and J. H. Hexter (New Haven: Yale University Press, 1965), 419–20.

32. A considerable body of discussion comprises the so-called domestic labor debate, which has sought to analyze the lack of value and lack of recognition accorded women's work within the political economy of the household as a unit, certainly, of capitalist and, possibly, of precapitalist social systems. For overviews of the question, see Eli Zaretsky, *Capitalism, the Family and Personal Life* (New York: Harper and Row, 1976) and Michèle Barrett, *Women's Oppression Today* (London: NLB, 1980), chaps. 5–6; for suggestive discussion of systemic implications of the gendered division of labor in pre- or early capitalist contexts, see Alice Clark, *The Working Life of Women in the Seventeenth Century* (London: Routledge, 1919; reprint, Boston: Routledge and Kegan Paul, 1982) and Margaret Benston, "The Political Economy of Women's Liberation," *Monthly Review* 21.4 (1969), 13–27.

33. Compare Peter Stallybrass's discussion of how later Tudor texts configure male and female bodies in "Patriarchal Territories: The Body Enclosed," in *Rewriting the Renaissance: The Discourses of Sexual Difference in Early Modern Europe*, ed. Margaret W. Ferguson, Maureen Quilligan, and Nancy J. Vickers (Chicago: University of Chicago Press, 1986), 123–42.

34. As Surtz notes (*The Complete Works of St. Thomas More*, vol. 4, 421), Socrates in *Republic* 460b–d alludes to a public nursery and to a professional cadre of wet-nurses from the guardian class who carry out the anonymous breast-feeding of the infants of this class.

35. *Utopia*, 53, 65–66.

36. Jones and Seibel, "More's Feminism" (n. 2), 73, point out that More's later *Confutation of Tyndale's Answer* (1533) gives two reasons for dismissing William Tyndale's proposal that women be allowed to become Christian priests: first, the essential inferiority of women to men, and secondly, the profanation of the sacrament of Christ's body that would be committed if a wom-

an were to celebrate mass. See *The Complete Works of St. Thomas More*, vol. 8, pts. 1–2, ed. Louis A. Schuster, Richard C. Marius, James P. Lusardi, and Richard J. Schoeck (New Haven: Yale University Press, 1973), 92, 190–91, 261, and 594–95. In "The Patrimony of Thomas More," in *History and Imagination*, ed. Hugh Lloyd-Jones, Valerie Pearl, and Blair Worden (New York: Holmes and Meier, 1982), 65, James McConica notes that another of More's texts, close in date to the *Utopia*, lays "emphasis on the worthlessness of all human endeavour apart from the grace of God" by comparing "even the just acts of man to a 'soiled menstrual cloth.'" A footnote records More's allusion to Isaiah 64:6 and cites *The Correspondence of Sir Thomas More*, ed. Elizabeth F. Rogers (Princeton: Princeton University Press, 1947), 203, where no. 83, "To a Monk" (1519–20), reads "sed quoniam omnis iusticia mortalium velut pannus est menstruatae."

37. See Marius on More's steeping in Paul's, Jerome's, and Augustine's negative treatments of sexuality (*Thomas More*, 34–37); also see Marius's suggestion that More's hasty second marriage in 1511 to a wife six years older than himself, one month after his first wife died leaving him a widower with four small children, was contracted in the cognizance that "sexual intercourse after menopause was a questionable act. And it is just possible that More married his second wife with this early Christian abstinence in mind. The doctors of the church had debated the validity of any second marriage, and the debate had gone on for centuries. . . . It is quite unlikely that a man of More's devout and ascetic disposition would have indulged in sexual intercourse with a woman who could not give birth. . . . His marriage with Dame Alice, then, was probably a quiet and unobtrusive way of living a life of sexual abstinence while he remained in the world to do his duty" (42).

38. Peter Brown, *The Body and Society: Men, Women, and Sexual Renunciation in Early Christianity* (New York: Columbia University Press, 1988), 11–17.

39. The powerful ideology encoded in this line of associations has by no means exhausted its hold, as U.S. radio and television newscasts made clear in the summer of 1989 when they suggested that sectarian turmoil in Pakistan had increased during a three-week convalescence by that nation's then prime minister, Benazir Bhutto, after she gave birth to a child.

40. See Chambers, *Thomas More* (cited above, n. 2); P. Albert Duhamel, "The Medievalism of More's *Utopia*," *Studies in Philology* 52 (1955), reprint, in *Essential Articles for the Study of Thomas More*, ed. R. S. Sylvester and G. P. Marc'hadour (Hamden, Conn.: Archon Books, 1977), 234–50, esp. 246; Edward Surtz, *The Praise of Wisdom* (Chicago: Loyola University Press, 1957), *The Praise of Pleasure* (Cambridge: Harvard University Press, 1957), and introduction to *Utopia* in *The Complete Works of St. Thomas More* (above, n. 28), vol. 4, cxxv–cxciv; also D. B. Fenlon, "England and Europe: *Utopia* and Its Aftermath," *Transactions of the Royal Historical Society*, 5th ser., 25 (1975), 115–35, esp. 120–21.

41. As even Quentin Skinner does, to conclude his latest formulation of his view of More's work ("More's *Utopia* and the Language of Renaissance Humanism" [cited above, n. 6], 155–57).

42. Brown, *Body and Society*, 48.

43. Bynum traces the medieval image of the nurturing, "maternal" male to problems of legitimating authority in a Christian society; writers use this image to project alternatives to political rule (*Jesus as Mother*, 146 and 154–58).

Skelton: The Voice of the Mob in Sanctuary

W. SCOTT BLANCHARD

On May 5, 1517, the Venetian ambassador to the court of Henry VIII, Sebastian Giustinian, reported to his state the events in London on May 1, the day of the Evil May Day riot. An estimated two thousand Londoners had stormed through the city's streets, attacking the houses of resident aliens, threatening with death the mayor and aldermen of the city, as well as Cardinal Wolsey and the foreign ambassadors from France and Spain. From what we know of the incident, the citizens' unrest was a reaction to the growing commercial influence of foreigners on the cloth trade in London, though the evidence is somewhat vague concerning the rebels' specific complaints. According to the chronicler Hall, the rioters, incited by the preaching of one "doctor Bele [Bell]," forced the release from prison of several merchants imprisoned on April 28 for striking foreigners and attempted to ruin the house of the French ambassador Meautis, who protected "dyverse Frenchmen that kalendred Worsted, contrarye to the kynges lawes." But the grievances of the rioters must have been motivated by more than economic xenophobia, for Hall tells us that when Wolsey heard of the rioting, he "incontinent strengthened his house with men and ordinaunce." Since the mayor and sheriffs of London had little success containing the "misruled persones"—they "made Proclamacion in the kynges name, but nothynge was obeyed"—the earl of Shrewsbury and other lords were summoned, and by five o'clock in the morning their forces succeeded in quelling the insurrection.[1]

At least twelve and perhaps as many as forty of the rioters were executed, including the incendiary preacher, on charges of high treason rather than riot. Three or four hundred other prisoners were detained until May 19, when they were summoned to appear before Henry VIII. Hall's account tells us that it was through the pleading of Queen Catherine that the prisoners were granted pardon, but the contemporaneous account of Nicholas Sagudino indicates that it was Cardinal Wolsey who pleaded for mercy:

> The King came one day to a place distant half a mile hence, with his court in excellent array, the right reverend Cardinal being there likewise, with a number of lords, both spiritual and temporal, with their followers, in a very gallant trim. And his majesty, being seated on a very lofty platform, surrounded by all those lords, who stood, he caused some four hundred of these delinquents, all in their shirts and barefoot, and each with a halter round his neck, to be brought before him; and on their presenting themselves before his majesty, the Cardinal implored him aloud to pardon them, which the King said he would not by any means do: whereupon said right reverend Cardinal, turning towards the delinquents, announced the royal reply. The criminals, on hearing that the King chose them to be hanged, fell on their knees, shouting, "Mercy!" when the Cardinal again besought his majesty to grant them grace, some of the chief lords doing the like. So at length the King consented to pardon them, which was announced to these delinquents by said right reverend Cardinal with tears in his eyes; and he made them a long discourse, urging them to lead good lives, and comply with the royal will. . . . It was a very fine spectacle, and well arranged, and the crowd of people present was innumerable. As no strangers were killed, the people cannot bear that forty of their countrymen should be so cruelly hanged and quartered. Nothing is to be seen at the city gate but gibbets and quarters.[2]

I shall return to this account in a moment, an account which is quite conscious of the contrived and spectacular nature of this moment of political theater, but first I must follow up this incident through some other sources.

Writing to the earl of Shrewsbury shortly after the riot, Thomas Alen reported that two bills had been set upon the doors of St. Paul's and "our Lady Barkyn's door" by the rioters, demanding redress for the commercial misdeeds of the foreigners who had been monopolizing the wool trade. In response to the appearance of these bills, "in every ward, one of the King's counsel, with the alderman of the same, is commanded to see every man write that can; and, further, hath taken every man's books, and sealed them, and brought them to Guildhall, there to examine them."[3] Hall reports that an initial examination of the prisoners had determined that the rioting had been a rather spontaneous affair and without religious motivation, since "it could never be proved of any metyng, gathering, talking or conventicle at any daye or tyme before that day." Nevertheless, there was apparently enough concern in the minds of officials like Wolsey—who fortified his own residence—to suspect a broader conspiracy, perhaps on the part of a Lollard conventicle. Hence the Privy Council, which discussed the matter during the month of May, carried out an investigation to determine the authors of the bills and their reading habits. We hear no more of the matter, and shortly more than a year later Wolsey boasted to the king that his realm "was never in such peace nor tranquillity; for all this summer I have had nother of reyut [riot], felony, ne forcible entry, but that your laws be in every place indifferently ministered without leaning of any manner."[4] And yet, as the poet John Skelton and Wolsey both knew, the Tudor state could hardly claim, in 1518, either jurisdictional or enforcement powers over *every* place in the realm.

The early reign of Henry VIII was not a period of extensive popular rebellion, though sporadic enclosure riots continued to take place in the countryside. Nevertheless this minor urban riot challenges our understanding of the character of dissent in the early Tudor period, partly because of the nature of the sources, which do not agree on details of the affair, but also because of the role played by Wolsey in his "arranging" of the pardon in such a spectacular manner. Was the riot, as some historians have suggested, merely caused by tensions between Londoners and resident foreigners over their respective commercial interests? If this is so, why did the state authorities subsequently conduct an extensive investigation of the Londoners' reading habits, as had been the case in the notorious Hunne affair of 1514? Why did the authorship of the (presumably) seditious bills matter so much to Wolsey and the Privy Council? Was this a religious, economic, or—given the determination of the Privy Council to discover the authors of the posted bills—a more deeply ideological rebellion in which authorship had become the most sensitive issue for the state authorities?

The Evil May Day riot contains motivations which are difficult to untangle, blurring, as Wolsey did in his own career, the distinction between spiritual and temporal spheres of interest. Although Wolsey's staged appearance on the scaffold of state is an exemplary instance of the management of rebellion—and perhaps a publicity ploy by the Crown's chief minister then in the midst of his ascendancy—it is difficult to determine what role he played. Was he a political mediator, momentarily appropriating to himself the king's decree of pardon, or an ecclesiastic official, pleading for mercy in the people's interest? Would it be more accurate to suggest that he was assuming multiple roles with multiple powers? Finally, to what extent did Wolsey and other ministers of the Crown sense that public order could be maintained in proportion to their ability to control the dissemination of written material?

In 1521 Skelton, writing from the secure confines of the perpetual sanctuary at Westminster, recalled this incident—or one nearly identical to it—when he criticized in the satire *Collyn Clout* bishops who

> . . . lumber forth the lawe
> To herken Jacke and Gyll
> Whan they put up a byll.
> (95–97)[5]

At the time of the May Day insurrection, Skelton had probably already taken rooms at Westminster, a space in which he could enjoy protection from secular authorities.[6] Skelton's allegiances to a specific "estate" or institution, like Wolsey's during the London riot, are difficult to determine with clarity. But during the period when he composed his three anti-Wolsey satires Skelton pursued in his poetry both directly and indirectly his own conflicting attitude toward dissent, a theme which lies beneath his specific complaints against a clergy reticent to enforce its traditional privileges, a nobility which had neglected its responsibilities, and a commons which was experiencing repressive measures under Wolsey. Beneath these more manifest concerns lies a continuous engagement with his own problematic status as an author, a status which, as the May Day riot shows, was undergoing new stresses. The various strategies he deemed necessary in order to empower himself as a dissenting member of the clerical class and to distance himself from his utterances through the construction of provisional authorial personae show him struggling to define his social role. Though many theorists of the "institution" of the author would see its rise in a later period in early modern history—beginning in the late sixteenth century—Skelton's confrontation with this new "institution," an institution still functioning partially under the aegis of the clergy and its traditional liberties, is in many ways exemplary.[7] If, as has been argued, the modern notion of the "author" arose as an institution sanctioning dissent in response to censorship, Skelton's career during an embryonic period in the growth of the early modern state may help to clarify the problems of definition which arose in the development of the "author."

As most investigators of Skelton's poetry have realized, Skelton's style and sensibility resist any comfortable schemes of periodization. Not yet the courtier-poet and yet prepared, on occasion, to write on demand when it served his career, Skelton stands at a critical juncture in early modern history.[8] But he defies our attempts to place him, standing not so much in a place we might call "transitional" as he does in a

territory of his own, a literary bad boy reluctant to assume wholeheart-
edly the social role of either prophet-poet in the tradition of medieval
complaint and satire or a hired pen willing to compose verses aimed at
self-promotion by means of valorizing a political regime. Insofar as it is
possible to generalize about his career, Skelton appears to have en-
dorsed a situation ethics; his poetry is reactive, responsive to specific
historical situations which demanded idiosyncratic strategies. Though
Skelton was steeped in liturgical traditions—including sacred parody—
Arthur Kinney's fine recent study does not fully account for the acute
topicality of some of Skelton's work.[9] And Greg Walker's thorough
study of Skelton in the context of patronage and careerism, while go
ing far toward a revisionist picture of Skelton as an emergent type of the
courtier who frequently turned prodigal, cannot seem to absorb fully
in its argument enough of Skelton's roots in the tradition of popular
dissent.[10] What are we to make of this amphibious poet who defies our
literary taxonomies?

The most recent and provocative student of Skelton, Richard Halpern, has taken a Marxist approach, viewing a number of Skelton's
works as literary enactments of "territorialization," of the definition,
elision, or utter rejection of boundaries of political sovereignty.[11] He
sees among Skelton's typical strategies the creation of "parceled anar
chies" within the totality of the absolutist state, sites for the production
of dissenting discourse beyond the jurisdiction of the emerging and, in
his view, totalizing Tudor polity. I would like to modify Halpern's analysis by examining Skelton's later satires on Wolsey not only through the
trope of "territorialization"—a fruitful poetics for a poet who wrote his
most radical verse while in the confines of sanctuary—but also through
an examination of the more practical means through which such rights
of "territorialization" were asserted—the production and suppression
of writing, both in the form of Wolsey's legitimization of sovereign
authority through legal writ and Skelton's assertion of a form of authorship which sanctioned dissent.

For Skelton, the assertion of authorship demanded strategies which
appear to be contradictory: on the one hand, he often framed his satires with vigorous, even egotistical prefaces and codas indicating his
privileged authorial status as *orator regius* (a title which was especially
misleading by the 1520s, given his inability to secure royal patronage),
while on the other hand, in his three anti-Wolsey satires he frequently
adopted an authorial voice of increasing anonymity and collectivity.
Like his adversary Wolsey, who acted as both clerical intercessor for the
people and conduit of the royal will on the scaffold in 1517, Skelton's
identity as author is ambiguous, lying in a sort of middle ground be-

tween modern notions of "authorship" and older traditions of religious
dissent where the notion of the author is absent, literary production
being constituted in a highly collectivist vox populi capable of claiming,
by its very absence of individuality, authoritative status as an equivalent
of a prophetic vox Dei.

In the satires *Collyn Clout* and *Why Come Ye Nat to Courte?* Skelton
voiced his critique of Wolsey and his complaints about the powerless
conditions of both commoners and clergy in a variety of personae. In
the historical anecdote with which I began, Wolsey's Privy Council carried on its investigation of the sources of the Evil May Day riot with a
special concern for determining the authorship of seditious pasquinades
even after the matter had been publicly brought to a close. By tracing
the growing and nearly obsessive attention Skelton paid to "writing"—
whether negatively, by distancing himself from his own satire through
the device of declaring himself a nearly anonymous vox populi, or positively, by complaining of censorship and criticizing Wolsey for the enor-
mity of his documentary production as a bureaucratic means of asserting jurisdictional authority—I hope to suggest through a more topical
analysis that Skelton was keenly aware of the ambivalent status of authorship in the early Tudor polity and of the pressures which censorship placed on authorial assertiveness.

Skelton's ambivalence can go a long way toward explaining his shifting allegiances in the Wolsey quarrel. As the social categories of clergy
and laity were themselves beginning to blur and overlap—the most
conspicuous example, of course, being Wolsey himself—and as the jurisdictional domains of church and state were experiencing confusion
and conflict, Skelton adopted as a strategy of dissent a variety of improvisational personae, shuttling back and forth between an oral "voice of
the mob," a mock "pen of the bureaucrat," and a prophetic vox Dei,
thereby sanctioning himself as a spokesperson for a commonwealth
conceived as a total structure, despite his traditional understanding of
the three estates as coherent and still meaningful social categories.[12] In
order to reveal the instrumental means of those judicial and political
reforms of Wolsey which most threatened both himself and, by extension, the welfare of a "universal Christendom" (which was arguably already in the process of dissolution), Skelton developed in his later satires on Wolsey a dissenting posture which critiqued the uses of writing
itself. The Evil May Day incident, in light of Skelton's satires composed
three to four years later, emerges with paradigmatic force as one example of how language, rather than "imitating the public riot" (in Jonson's phrase), can have powers of initiation. Such initiatory powers can
explain how Skelton, despite his conservative understanding of class
structure, could at the same time establish a quite independent autho-

rial voice neither fully aligned with the clergy nor with the commons beneath it which found its constituency in an emerging political order which had as yet only a theoretical basis in the secular sphere—the notion of England as a commonwealth comprising a single body politic.

A keen reader of current events, Skelton might more appropriately appear to us as a journalist or even political analyst than as a poet, an astute reader of historical events and their larger meaning. In his attempts at courtly preferment during the years prior to his entry into sanctuary Skelton had learned something of the courtier's need for improvisational techniques—had even, perhaps, learned much from the example of Wolsey himself—and so found a means, later in his career, of playing handy-dandy with several voices, the voice of the mob and the prophetic voice of one crying from the wilderness of perpetual sanctuary in his Westminster rooms. Just as Wolsey could play at the roles of sovereign, minister, and ecclesiastic with theatrical skill (as Sagudino's account quite bluntly admits), so Skelton learned to vary his own authorial voice and tone in counterattacks which mirrored the blurred categories of his historical habitus. When Halpern discusses Skelton's perception, in *Speke, Parott,* of Wolsey as appropriating to himself delegatory powers which more rightly—in a strict construction of absolutism—would be invested solely in the person of the monarch, he points to a concern which became, in Skelton's later satires, a nearly obsessive one.[13] Skelton's counterattack, in the satires *Collyn Clout* and *Why Come Ye Nat to Courte?* was to construct in opposition to Wolsey's bureaucratic machinery of written language (literalized in the punishment known as "wearing of papers" for minor criminals which was among Wolsey's "reforms" and which Skelton had alluded to in the final envoi of *Speke, Parott*) an oral and oracular voice of the mob, a mob which came to include in its composition all of the social classes. Skelton moved away from the dense textual allusiveness of *Speke, Parrot* and also from the more generalizing portrait of Wolsey as an Antichrist fulfilling a role in scriptural history to a quite topical critique spoken in a far less learned voice. This historical specificity emerges in the final envois to *Speke, Parott,* but the strategy of adopting a voice with a more populist resonance, one more deeply rooted in a native tradition of dissent, could not alter the conditions under which Skelton wrote—conditions of explicit censorship. Thus in his last Wolsey satires we see a development in the strategy only implicit at the close of *Speke, Parott*: a continual recurrence to oral formulas such as "Men say" as a distancing strategy to make of Skelton less a poet than a town crier. The refusal of the clergy to engage in quarrels which concern their ecclesiastical privileges, the main concern of Skelton in *Collyn Clout,* becomes even more inclusive in *Why Come Ye Nat to Courte?* as Skelton enlarges his authorial voice to include the points of view of both nobility and commons. In order to counter Wolsey's ever-widening absorption of authority in his use of the written word, whether as actual legal writ or in other bureaucratic forms, Skelton made of his own dissenting voice a more global persona. In Skelton's strident and occasionally hysterical verse, he attacked Wolsey's bureaucratic poaching on spheres of jurisdiction traditionally relegated to common law and canon law, as yet an incipient innovation but one which threatened in Skelton's mind to surround the entire commonwealth in a web of centralized authority. His critique of Wolsey's authority fell especially on that portion of the commonwealth traditionally under separate jurisdictional authority— the church and its distinctive apparatus of canon law—but by the final satire came to include the entire body politic.

Historians of the period have often pointed out the importance of the increased use, in the reigns of Henry VII and Henry VIII, of the statute of *praemunire*.[14] Used as a means of curbing ecclesiastical authority from as early as the mid-fourteenth century, statutes of *praemunire*, which forced clergy in certain cases to submit to the jurisdictional authority of the Crown rather than to Rome, came to have broadened powers under Wolsey, and the underlying agenda behind their use was quite clear to Skelton. These statutes highlight for us the blurring boundaries between civil and canonical power which would eventually give rise to the disappearance of any discrete ecclesiastical power with the 1534 Act of Supremacy. In his later satires Skelton portrays Wolsey as a bloated, Dickensian bureaucrat who has abrogated his putative responsibilities as a legatine authority. Wolsey, Skelton will argue, should resist the use of writs of *praemunire* but instead uses them as an instrument to encroach upon traditionally ecclesiastical jurisdictions which he should, as a prelate, feel obliged to protect. But if Wolsey could play at both Mercy (on the public scaffold) and Justice (in the Privy Council) in the 1517 riot—doing, in T. S. Eliot's phrase, "the police in several voices"—and absorb into civil law issues which had once been decided under canon law, Skelton could also dissent through a form of counter-absorption, writing as a spokesman for all classes in society. Both victim and satirist shared in common a historical situation in which spheres of power were overlapping and blurring. Both in many ways serve as proleptic figures anticipating the antithetical ideologies of Tudor absolutism and the commonwealth sentiments which would emerge more clearly in political theory by the mid-sixteenth century.[15]

In attacking Wolsey in *Speke, Parott,* Skelton achieved largely by indirection what in his later two satires on Wolsey he achieved more directly, though the indirection in the earlier poem, whereby "*metapho-ra, alegoria* withal" was the poet's "protecyon, his pavys [shield] and his wall," may not have seemed so oblique to his contemporaries. Though less appreciative than some scholars of the artistry and wit of *Speke, Parott*, C. S. Lewis clearly saw the poem in a different light from the two subsequent satires, which he dismissed with the remark that in them "Skelton has ceased to be a man and become a mob."[16] Although he clearly disliked much of Skelton's poetry, Lewis correctly identified a radical shift in both poetic strategy and audience in the later two satires. Skelton had begun to fashion a more aggressive voice in the envois to *Speke, Parott*, encouraged by his protectress Galathea at the poem's close to "speke now trew and playne." Skelton's Parott does attack quite specifically certain judicial reforms instituted by Wolsey and his encroachment on clerical privileges. But Skelton's caution and his use of a more courtly persona in the "fayre bird for a lady" diffused what could have been a more thoroughly ideological analysis only hinted at in the final envoi. At the close of *Speke, Parott* we get a glimpse of Skelton's assumption of the voice of the mob, but it is in two less studied poems that Skelton more thoroughly exercised his "lyberte to speke" from sanctuary, finding an audience not only in the more literate court circles of those hostile to Wolsey but in the London merchant class which had rioted in 1517 and had experienced the rough justice of Henry VIII and the duplicitous mercy of his cardinal. The often apocalyptic tenor of *Speke, Parott*, as F. W. Brownlow has convincingly demonstrated, placed Wolsey within a scriptural tradition more removed from the actual historical events of his ascendancy, seeing in his person a Moloch who fulfilled a pattern determined within the arc of salvation history. The two later satires, turning more closely to the domestic sphere of politics, abandon the universal scriptural contexts of *Speke, Parott* for more local concerns, and in so doing sharpen the political analysis of the dimensions of a historical figure such as Wolsey. The Skelton who in *Speke, Parott* presented himself, in Brownlow's words, primarily as a "citizen of Western Christendom,"[17] becomes in the later satires a citizen of England writing from a sanctuary space which had quite recently been under assault. Just as Wolsey had initiated a process by which the space of the *prophanum*, the secular, displaced the *phanum (fanum)* of the universal church (to use terms which, in *Speke, Parott* [124–25], anticipate the ideological concerns of the later satires), Skelton seized upon this territory and wrote from it as if it were a public commons, adopting a more colloquial voice and a more national set of concerns. In so doing his satires became increasingly concerned with deeper, structural changes in the traditional balance of power in

England, while still conveying strong doses of invective aimed at Wolsey's person. From the shrinking space of a territory where the state's authority could not yet reach and the inviolability of which was open to every man or woman in Christendom, Skelton assumed with more conviction the voice of the mob.[18]

It is the voice of a rustic farmer, Colin Clout, that we meet in Skelton's second satire on Wolsey, and the apparent simplicity of his arguments marks an important shift in strategy from *Speke, Parott* and sharpens the focus on structural conflicts in the commonwealth. The persona of Colin Clout is a collective one, garnering his opinions from the chatter that he claims to be in the mouths of all of the common people. Skelton's persona focuses his assaults primarily on the clergy, but early in the poem his purpose is to demonstrate that the distinction between clergy and laity has become blurred, at least insofar as recent developments indicate. Indeed, Colin's reluctance to indict individual ecclesiastics for their failure to perform their social offices responsibly owes as much to Skelton's desire to abstract from recent events their dialectical logic as to Skelton's caution as a satirist. In a curious way, the implicit conditions of censorship enable a *more* disruptive attack on institutions rather than on individuals. Skelton's use of a collective "voice of the mob" to attack an anonymous clergy reinforces his ability to read into the specific signs of the times a larger shift in the social configuration of clergy and laity. In the lines which I quoted earlier, Skelton indicates that the repressive measures against dissidence in England enacted by unnamed bishops are a mark of an even more disturbing and telling phenomenon:

> What trowe ye they say more
> Of the bysshopes lore?
> Howe in matters they ben rawe,
> They lumber forth the lawe
> To herken Jacke and Gyll
> Whan they put up a byll;
> And judge it as they wyll,
> For other mens skyll,
> Expoundyng out theyr clauses,
> And leve theyr owne causes.
> . . . But ire and venyre,
> And so fa so alamyre
> That the premenyre
> Is lyke to be set afyre

> In theyr jurysdictyons,
> Through temporall afflictyons.
> (92–101, 106–11)

Skelton ends this passage with an allusion to the ecclesiastics' use of *praemunire*, an instrument originally intended to establish the preeminence of local, secular authority over formerly ecclesiastical jurisdictions. But in Skelton's verses the topsy-turvy nature of the relationship of the higher clergy to their professional responsibilities, reinforced by the comic intrusion of a disordered musical scale, is revealed by the confusion of the bishops' functions and the misuse of their professional skills. They now "lumber forth" the *civil* law, which would govern a legal matter such as riot or sedition and which should be beyond their ken, using their "lore" (*canon* law) outside of its proper jurisdiction over matters in which they have little or no experience. Conversely, they use a statute of civil law—*praemunire*—as if they were court lawyers, while canon law, which should be used to maintain their own ecclesiastical jurisdictions, is so neglected (inasmuch as they "leve theyr owne causes") that the state will soon swallow up the church's holdings in a wildfire of writs of *praemunire*.

This blurring of jurisdictional domains becomes even more chaotic in *Why Come Ye Nat to Courte?* where Skelton charges Wolsey with reducing to his own "wyll" "lawe canon . . . lawe common . . . [and] lawe cyvyll" (416–19). Although in *Collyn Clout* Wolsey is perhaps the most egregious of newfangled offenders against the church, he is merely the most exemplary instance of the monstrosity which afflicts the realm: clerical servants who, in owing full allegiance to neither church nor state, are de facto not interested in the good of either the commonwealth as a whole or the laity under their care. The vacuum created by such structural confusion in the traditional relationship between ecclesiastical and secular powers compelled Skelton to assert his own autonomy as an author—to invent for himself, however provisionally, a new and independent "classless intelligentsia" (to use Mannheim's phrase) capable of discovering such structural changes. Such an explanation of Skelton's autonomy as a critic helps to explain his own ambivalent class allegiances which he subsequently confronts, however much his persona Colin claims to be a mere spokesperson for "the people."

Knowing as we do the shape religious policy would take in the following decade with the passage of the Act of Supremacy and the dissolution of the monasteries, Skelton's Colin appears to read the signs of the times quite well. The confiscation of properties from church endowments is another matter over which "the people" "rayles lyke re-belles" (412–13) and "Talkes like tytyvylles [tattlers]" (416). Colin's attitude toward the commoners who have grown to lack respect for their prelates is not always one of wholehearted support and sympathy; indeed, he would appear to be ambivalent in these passages, fearing indications of a larger breakdown in the traditional relationship of the three estates.[19] The well-known "prophecy" concerning Wolsey's fall (465–75) allows Skelton's persona momentarily to exorcize his ambivalence, with Wolsey becoming a scapegoat for the failings of the church. But Colin's concerns over the disintegration of the church deepen in the verses devoted to the old and new heresies; the voice of the mob is not necessarily, in Skelton's mind, an equivalent of the vox Dei:

> With language thus poluted
> Holy churche is bruted
> And shamfully confuted.
> . . . For it maketh me sad
> Howe the people are glad
> The church to deprave.
> And some there are that rave
> Presumyng on theyr owne wytte.
> (486–88, 511–15)

While Skelton's general concern is the clergy's abandonment of its responsibilities of sound teaching, allowing an opening for "the people" to assert their own interpretations—potential heresies of a presumably Lutheran cast—the clergy's abrogation of interpretive control is not so much a cause of lay presumption as an effect of a more generalized pollution of "language" which arises from the failure of church and state to maintain their ideological purity.

This pollution of language—literally a desecration (the strongest, and probably intended, connotation for "pollution") and desacralization—derives from the blurring of the formerly coherent and discrete interpretive communities of church and state. This pollution even affects Skelton's own use of language and discomfits him. The referent for the "language" which "pollutes" the church is both ambiguous and manifold: it is Colin's own satiric style mentioned earlier ("I abhorre to wryte / Howe the lay fee [laity] despyte / You prelates" [437–39]), a voice Skelton admits distresses him; it is the logic-chopping language of the reformers, which is discussed subsequently; and it is the liturgical refrains which ironically and inappropriately refer to the bishops' splendor and power and not their God's (442–47). Skelton, as a poet-priest who presumably might represent a member of the spirituality speaking from "pulpyttes autentyke" (696), displays an uneasiness about his assumption of a voice representing either a vox populi or a clerical critic attempting to reform abuses from within. Both personae indicate a disintegration of authority and a blurring of the separation of powers which should maintain between temporal and spiritual members of the commonwealth.

"Authenticity" is here at stake, leading Skelton to an ideological impasse he cannot yet resolve, since authenticity depends upon a reasonably stable and well-defined institution for its validation. Later in the poem Skelton returns to the issue of writs of *praemunire,* urging the clergy to pursue their traditional rights in securing the "estate" of the "holy churche":

> They had lever to please
> And take theyr worldly ease
> Than to take on hande
> And worshypfully withstande
> Suche temporall warre and bate
> As now is made of late
> Agaynst holy churche estate,
> Or to maynteyne good quarelles.
> (909–16)

There are, for Skelton/Colin, "good quarelles" worth engaging in, precisely those which might reinforce the territorial boundaries which separate the clergy from their worldly ministers and thus might return the ecclesiastical estate to some form of authentic and authoritative status. "Autentyke pulpyttes," however, derive their authenticity from their being situated within an institution, and since that institution's territory is contested, Skelton is forced to assert an authorial voice deriving authenticity from the larger constituency of the body politic as a whole.

At its close as the satire sharpens its focus on the unnamed Wolsey, the ambivalence Skelton feels in assuming the voice of the mob diminishes somewhat, but the collective murmur continues to bother his persona:

> By saynt Luke,
> And by swete saynt Mark!
> This is a wondrous warke!
> That the people talke this,
> Somwhat there is amysse!
> The devyll can nat stop theyr mouthes
> But they will talke of such uncouthes,
> All that ever they ken
> Agaynst all spirytuall men.
> (1046–54)

"Whether it be wronge or ryght," concludes the speaker, "Theyr tonges thus do clap" (1055–58). The allegiances of Skelton's speaker are never fully clarified in this satire as Colin ends with this suspension of judgment. Colin's continual reminders of his status as a mere reporter of what "men say," his assumption of the voice of the mob as a provisional means of assuming an authoritative role as spokesman for "the people," serve more than a traditional function as literary strategies of the complaint tradition; all become more understandable when we realize that Skelton did indeed predict from the signs of the times an ideological revolution from which his literary predecessors were more distant, a conceptual revolution in which he stands as yet uncommitted to either side. He may have appeared to sixteenth-century readers as a prophet; to modern readers, he must earn at the very least the status of a political forecaster. He does not and cannot, however, become a fully realized agitator and author; the voice of the mob, though it speaks from sanctuary in this poem (as the final lines make clear), would for the time being remain silenced:

> Nor wyll suffre this boke
> By hoke ne by croke
> Prynted for to be.
> (1237–39)

And yet, like the bills posted in the Evil May Day riot, the voices would be heard, and their cumulative effect would be to assist, in England, in creating a site for dissent in the opening left by the eventual dismantling of the space of sanctuary. As a member of a vanishing "estate," it is understandable that Skelton would hold ambiguous allegiances; his traditional understanding of class structure urged him to anchor himself in the clerical estate, while the very threats to that class moved him in a more radical direction toward the autonomous and secular institution of "authorship."

Why Come Ye Nat to Courte? begins with a refrain which indicates that Skelton now addresses the nobility, but the topical allusions to the forced loans of the early 1520s, which were levied on the commons and which were an especially great hardship to the citizens of London, suggest a larger audience. It is the most historically and politically specific of the three Wolsey satires and speaks in the most colloquial of idioms. The close of the poem, which ends with the repetition of Skelton's Latin phrase "Hec vates ille / De quo loquntur mille" ("This prophet [records] matters about which a thousand speak"), makes explicit Skelton's allegiances to the commoners and the completion of his appropriation of the voice of the mob begun in *Collyn Clout*. Although it is a frantic poem filled with attacks directed almost entirely at Wolsey and his acquisition of wealth at the expense of the commonwealth, the sharpest—and for his adversary, the most threatening—criticism does not, however, lie in Skelton's enumeration of Wolsey's moral failings, but in the pointed analysis of Wolsey's appropriation of sovereign powers and the means by which Wolsey asserted them.

In this satire Skelton makes the most potentially dangerous allegation about Wolsey:

> He dyggeth so in the trenche
> Of the court royall
> That he ruleyth them all.
> So he doth undermynde,
> And suche sleyghtes doth fynde,
> That the kynges mynde
> By him is subverted.
> (434–40)

This passage follows a list of Wolsey's circumventions of the traditional jurisdictions of common law and civil law, his reduction of these bodies of law to his own enormous "will," and his inquisitorial use of the four major prisons in London. It is a picture—quite obviously hyperbolic, unfair to what were in many cases important reforms of the English judiciary—of Wolsey as a tyrant, undermining both the shared customs of the English legal system and the mind of the sovereign himself.[20] A bit later in the satire we read that Wolsey is so arrogant that he "wyll play checke mate / With ryall Majeste / Counte himselfe as good as he" (588–90). Skelton's analysis of Wolsey's appropriation of sovereign authority matches quite well Sagudino's description of the May Day riot, where Wolsey quite literally upstaged Henry VIII:

> He sayth the kynge doth wryte
> And writeth he wottith nat what.
> (678–79)

Wolsey in fact assumed the very pen of his king (we should recall that Wolsey's conveyance of the Great Seal during the Calais conference in the interest of efficiency struck many contemporaries as an important symbol of his arrogation of authority).[21] Skelton has traced the "subversion" of the king's mind to a specific abuse; Wolsey has jeopardized his sovereign's political accountability through his assumption of royal authority, literalized in his appropriation of the instrument which denotes sovereign authorship.

Skelton's recurrent theme in this satire is the status of writing in the commonwealth, both as he experiences it and as it aids Wolsey's ascendancy. The Great Seal (mentioned at 1129) and Wolsey's use of writing in general contrast with Skelton's feelings of impotence as a writer, sentiments which we also saw in the lament over censorship in *Collyn Clout*. In contrast to the unconstrained use of writing by Wolsey, Skelton feels thoroughly constrained, adopting a self-imposed censorship in order to strengthen the contrast with Wolsey's appropriation of the "kynges minde":

> But what his grace doth thinke,
> I have no pen nor inke
> That therwith can mell
>
> . . . .
>
> It were great rewth
> In wrytynge of trewth
> Any man shulde be
> In perplexyte
> Of dyspleasure.
> (683–85, 841–45)

The concern over censorship which had caused anxiety in *Collyn Clout* is even greater in this poem, so that when Skelton speaks as an individuated "I" he is careful to deny any interest in "meddling" with what "his grace" thinks—precisely the mistake Wolsey has made. Skelton's self-censorship compelled him to repeat at two points in the poem that he was acting as a journalist, reporting what a "thousand say." His self-effacement has increased in direct proportion to the Cardinal's assumption of the authorial powers of the sovereign, but it is a self-effacement which paradoxically increases the persuasive force that as an individual author he can claim to be "wrytynge of trewth."

In response to Wolsey's aggrandizement of authority through the appropriation of the sovereign signature, Skelton constructs an authorial voice buttressed by allusions to other authors and strengthened by his own satiric self-deprecation. Wolsey's hyperbolic writ-wielding powers (Skelton mocks him as one who "rolleth in his records" [194]) are contrasted with the unofficial utterances of the poet, who describes his own verses as a "wanton scrowle." Skelton's attack characterizes writing as a two-edged instrument which can serve the uses of dissent as well as political control. He contrasts Wolsey's authority with an allusion to the *auctor* Petrarch, giving a literary exemplum which parallels Wolsey's imminent fall; he uses the trope of meiosis to make his own satirical writings appear improvisational, written under the pressure of a Juvenalian *indignatio* which derives authenticity from a conception of satiric writing as virtually instinctual; and he suggests that others among the intelligentsia ("learned men" [322]) have not written against Wolsey merely out of fear (they "Dare nat set their penne" [323] against him). Finally, in a coup de grace which hoists Wolsey by his own petard, he suggests that the document-wielding Wolsey will find himself perjured if he examines his written oath in the registry records of Archbishop Warham, made upon his assumption of the archbishopric of York, in which he agreed to defer to the superior authority of Canterbury (1125–32).[22] The uses of writing dominate Skelton's analysis of the instruments Wolsey used to assume power: the "newe writ" (939) impelling forced loans in August of 1522, itself an amplification of earlier writs levying financial obligations on the citizenry for Henry's foreign policy, and the continual recurrence to Wolsey's possession of the "king's letter."

Another strategy of attack continues the concern in *Collyn Clout* over Wolsey's confusion of ecclesiastical and secular powers. Skelton complains that Wolsey has abrogated all traditional bodies of law in allowing himself, as a spiritual lord, to preside over cases of murder in a court of civil law. Thus former written laws, both canonical and civil, have been violated ("Decre and decretal, / Constytucyon provincyall, / Nor no lawe canonicall / Shall let the preest pontyficall / To syt in *causa sanguinis*" [1157–61]).[23] In this poem Wolsey figures as a demonic subverter of both "the kynges mynde" and the commonwealth as a whole, including its traditional body of common law or "constytucyon provincyall." His instrument, Skelton says emphatically, is the written word, but given the novel status of language when under Wolsey's self-interested interpretive control, Wolsey himself can easily ignore existing legal traditions ("Decre and decretal") and wrest authority from those institutions which hitherto controlled specific jurisdictional territories. Only the satirist's voice stands against Wolsey's innovative means of governing through bureaucratic writs, a voice presumably much more circumscribed in its ability to command an audience, and possibly relegated to oral recitations during interludes at banquets or, as has been hypothesized, for short-lived posting in public places such as St. Paul's doors or gathering places like the Cheap and the Cross.[24] But despite the limitation in audience and even despite Skelton's cautious countermoves in moments of self-censorship, the degree of authority which the satirist commands increases to the extent to which he can claim to represent the collective body politic. The greater the absorption of sovereign authority in the individual figure of Wolsey, the greater becomes Skelton's ability to fuse his audience with his authorial persona and claim to be writing a "trew text" (261).

Greg Walker has suggested that there are many conventional elements in the portrait of Wolsey, and Skelton's most recent editor, Scattergood, offers at a number of places parallel complaints about Wolsey from nearly contemporary satires such as *Rede Me and Be Not Wroth*. But what is striking in this satire in particular is the specificity of the charges which Skelton makes about Wolsey, and even his use of proper names of citizens and nobles who have suffered from the Wolsey regime. Not only do individuals like Lord Dacre, the ambassador Meautis, and the merchant Thomas Spring receive specific attention (a departure from one convention of satire by which individuals are alluded to in code), but Wolsey's career is itself given a detailed analysis. He is an impostor as a prelate. Skelton abusively enumerates his lack of academic credentials, even in the "new learning" Wolsey pretends to further—"Tullis faculte / Called humanyte" (528–29). Thus the conventional and moralizing elements, though certainly present, give way to a more pointed and topical critique which has important consequences for our understanding of Skelton's innovative analysis. For though Skelton enumerates the details of specific contemporary events, he never loses sight of the larger implications of his details, extracting from them deeper structural changes. That Wolsey, for instance, has no credentials by which to claim an understanding of canon law—a criticism which on its surface seems patently ad hominem—has paradigmatic force for Skelton, since it is another example of a more global confusion of secular and ecclesiastical authority in the realm as a whole. And by recurring to a central instrument in Wolsey's arsenal, his use of writing, and contrasting to it his own less "authoritative" satire ("wanton scrowle," "paper I thinke to blot"), Skelton elicits from his details an argument which points to a significant feature of the Henrician regime—its mastery of legal procedure achieved through the use of skillful chancellors whose main tool is that of the legal writ. Against that, Skelton's "voice of the mob," which can exclaim that it is voicing a satire which has the status of a "trew text," is hardly powerless, for though it speaks from a sanctuary space which would not long survive the Henrician reformation, it claims for itself collective representation.

In the May Day riot of 1517 Giustinian recorded that the mayors and sheriffs of London "made Proclamation in the kynges name, but nothynge was obeyed." A year later Wolsey gloated over his successful imposition of law and order in London, and we now know, thanks to the studies of J. A. Guy, precisely what sorts of measures were enacted to constrain the "misruled persons" of the Henrician regime.[25] The wearing of papers, the use of public pillories, and even the cutting off of ears were among some of the measures employed by Wolsey in his role as head of both the Privy Council and Star Chamber, but the recurring motif in Skelton's analysis of Wolsey's instrumentality is the "polluted language" of *Collyn Clout* and the Great Seal of the "kynges owne hande" appropriated by Wolsey. In the thematic organization of what is sometimes diffuse invective Skelton traced the lineaments of an important moment in early modern history, a moment when the institution of authorship was fitfully emerging in response to the increasingly repressive judicial apparatus of the early modern state. Wolsey, of course, was not the servile minister of a totalitarian—and Skelton never launched attacks at Henry himself—and the growing implementation of his judicial reforms was in no way global in its reach nor always repressive. The most recent scholar of the Tudor proclamations has warned us of taking too seriously a view of the Henrician regime as a period in which authority was radically centralized. He cites an interesting case from quite late in the reign when a commoner simply ignored a government official who had invoked a royal proclamation to restrain him.[26] Similarly, Skelton had many strategies by which to preserve his right to dissent—the medium of satire, the privilege of sanctuary, and the surreptitious circulation of his work, however constrained that was by a state which still lacked a fully centralized judiciary and a means to enforce ubiquitously its various restrictive measures. But such a system was emerging, and Skelton felt its force acutely, responding to the pressures of an emergent absolutism with perceptive criticism of a highly specific nature.

Rather than the last medieval author, Skelton may instead appear as a writer who struggled to define the modern institution of "the author" as it emerged as a dissenting and prodigal force in response to censorship. Just as Skelton's career stands at a critical juncture in the history of early modern Europe, a juncture where older structures of legitimization and authenticity were vanishing or becoming elided with newer ones, so his character and political allegiances resist easy categorization under modern terms like "radical" and "conservative." His was a highly adaptive and various career, continuing and modifying an anticlerical tradition of complaint while at the same time upholding fiercely the privileges of the clerical class. Skelton's allegiance probably remained ultimately attached to a notion of universal "Christendom" which was becoming anachronistic, as was the shrinking territory from which he wrote his most powerful satires against Wolsey. The narrowing verge of sanctuary quite neatly symbolizes this gradual secularization of the commonwealth, and Skelton's more frantic style in the later satires may even seem to approach claustrophobic shouting. Yet his analysis of the apparatus of Wolsey's regime is remarkably sophisticated, giving at least a measure of credence to the notion that poets can,

indeed, read the signs of the times in a manner which, if not quite prophetic, may at least be proleptic. Viewed in hindsight, Skelton's poetry
singled out with remarkable accuracy changes in the institutions surrounding him. Perhaps in the root sense of the word "radical" he was a
radical author: he could sense beneath the flux of events a fundamental
shift in the site of political authority, away from the sanctuary (or what
he had termed the *phanum* in *Speke, Parott*) to the public scaffold, from
the workings of the private conscience in confession to the theatrical
display of justice and punishment. He will continue to challenge our
modern understanding of the relations between political life and literary works, even as he anticipates them.

Notes

1. On the May Day riot, see *Calendar of State Papers . . . Venice*, ed. Raw-
don Brown et al., 38 vols. (London: Longman, Green, 1864–1940), vol. 2
(1509–19), 381–86 (nos. 879, 881, 883, and 887); *Letters and Papers, Foreign
and Domestic, of the Reign of Henry VIII*, ed. John Sherren Brewer, James
Gairdner, and Robert Henry Brodie, 21 vols. (1862–1910; reprint, London:
HMSO, 1920 [hereafter cited as *LP*]), vol. 2 (1515–18), pt. 2, 1031 (no.
3204) and 1045 (no. 3259); *Hall's Chronicle, Containing the History of England during the Reign of Henry the Fourth and the Succeeding Monarchs to the
End of the Reign of Henry the Eighth*, ed. Henry Ellis (London: Johnson, 1809;
reprint, 1904), 588–91; J. J. Scarisbrick, *Henry VIII* (Berkeley and Los Ange-
les: University of California Press, 1968), 67; Roger B. Manning, *Village Re-
volts: Social Protest and Popular Disturbances in England 1509–1640* (Oxford:
Clarendon Press, 1988), 196–98; Martin Holmes, "Evil May-Day, 1517,"
History Today 15 (1965), 642–50; and Peter Gwyn, *The King's Cardinal: The
Rise and Fall of Thomas Wolsey* (London: Barrie and Jenkins, 1990), 442–46.
See also John A. Guy, *The Cardinal's Court: The Impact of Thomas Wolsey in
Star Chamber* (Hassocks: Harvester Press, 1977), for the use of Star Chamber
in dealing with riot (15–16 and 30–32).
2. *LP*, vol. 2 (1515–18), 3259.
3. Edmund Lodge, *Illustrations of British History, Biography, and Manner*,
3 vols. (London: Nicol, 1791; reprint, London: J. Chidley, 1838), vol. 1, 9–
11 (Letter of Thomas Alen to the earl of Shrewsbury). Guy, *Cardinal's Court*,
30, notes that the records of Star Chamber mention these "slanderous bills."
4. *LP*, vol. 2 (1515–18), appendix, 38.
5. All references will be to *John Skelton: The Complete English Poems*, ed.
John Scattergood (New Haven: Yale University Press, 1983).
6. The dating of Skelton's entry into sanctuary has not been completely
resolved; I follow here the conjectures of F. W. Brownlow, "*Speke, Parrot*: Skelton's Allegorical Denunciation of Cardinal Wolsey," *Studies in Philology* 65
(1968), 124–39, and Greg Walker, *John Skelton and the Politics of the 1520s*
(Cambridge: Cambridge University Press, 1988), 88, who both think that *Spe-*

ke, Parott was written from the security of Skelton's Westminster lodgings. Walker convincingly suggests a shift in Skelton's allegiances by the 1520s; he was no longer a "Court poet" but a "Westminster or London poet" appealing to the merchant class for his audience (51). For details of his lease, see H. L. R. Edwards, *Skelton: The Life and Times of an Early Tudor Poet* (London: Cape, 1949; reprint, Freeport, N.Y.: Books for Libraries Press, 1971), 178–81.

7. The somewhat unresolved issue of the birth of the author was first broached by Michel Foucault; Annabel Patterson, *Censorship and Interpretation: The Conditions of Writing and Reading in Early Modern England* (Madison: University of Wisconsin Press, 1984), argues that "it is to censorship that we in part owe our very concept of 'literature'" (4), and that a tacit and somewhat "fragile relationship" existed between writers and state authorities in the early modern period (7). The degree of Skelton's engagement with censorship is problematic; it appears that his satires were allowed to circulate within the court but not to be published. See Walker's discussion cited below, n. 24.

8. Richard Halpern, *The Poetics of Primitive Accumulation: English Renaissance Culture and the Genealogy of Capital* (Ithaca: Cornell University Press, 1991), indicates that Skelton "tried to write himself out of literary history" and displays a "seemingly perverse refusal to act like a 'transitional' figure" (104–5).

9. Arthur F. Kinney, *John Skelton, Priest as Poet: Seasons of Discovery* (Chapel Hill: University of North Carolina Press, 1987).

10. Walker, *John Skelton and the Politics*. Though less directly interested in the historical background, Stanley Eugene Fish, *John Skelton's Poetry* (New Haven: Yale University Press, 1965), notes in discussing the persona of *Collyn Cloute* that it is inappropriate to identify Colin's interests with any particular class; he is instead a "quester" who "stands apart from the various systems of value he meets" (194–96). In this formulation, Skelton's status would seem to be anticipatory of the modern intellectual, a point I develop later.

11. Halpern, *Poetics*, 117. Halpern sees Skelton enacting in *Phyllyp Sparowe* a "flight from absolutism" (249) which would later become a more difficult manoeuvre as the "autonomy" of the church as a "holy estate" had more thoroughly eroded by later poems like *Speke, Parott*.

12. Skelton would seem to be expressing in his various personae both the "emergent" notion of the state as a commonwealth, which developed later in the century in thinkers like Thomas Starkey, and the "residual" ordering of the polity into three estates in feudal political theory. Compare this idea with Halpern's suggestion (with whose terminology I disagree) that Skelton's conceptualization of the social order is both "anarchic" *and* "totalitarian" (*Poetics*, 135). For the terms "residual" and "emergent," see Raymond Williams, *Marxism and Literature* (Oxford: Oxford University Press, 1977), 121–27. On Skelton's adoption of a vox populi in the two later satires, see Robert Kinsman, "The Voices of Dissonance: Pattern in Skelton's *Collyn Cloute*," *Huntington Library Quarterly* 26 (1963), 291–313.

13. See Halpern for Skelton's fascination with Wolsey's "delegatory" appropriation of authority, and for Wolsey as one who "mysteriously becomes a *source* of speech and authority" (*Poetics*, 130–33, italics in original).

14. On *praemunire*, see Albert F. Pollard, *Wolsey* (London: Longman,

Green, 1953), 31–33; on the galvanizing effect the Hunne affair had on the jurisdictional dispute between church and state which writs of *praemunire* reflect, see A. G. Dickens, T*he English Reformation* (New York: Schocken Books, 1964), 86–90 and 103–4. Gwyn, *King's Cardinal,* is a good account of both *praemunire* and the more global question of religious and lay spheres of interest (33–57).

15. On commonwealth theories, see Thomas F. Mayer, *Thomas Starkey and the Commonweal* (Cambridge: Cambridge University Press, 1989). Interestingly, Mayer argues for a more radical picture of Skelton as an early proponent of so-called commonwealth sentiments, at least as regards the responsibilities of the aristocracy to the body politic (160–67). For mid-century commonwealth theory, see the treatise now thought to have been composed by Sir Thomas Smith, *The Discourse of the Commonweal* (1549), where Henry VIII's councillors are criticized quite directly for causing economic privation.

16. C. S. Lewis, *English Literature in the Sixteenth Century, Excluding Drama* (London: Oxford University Press, 1954), 140.

17. Brownlow, "*Speke, Parott,*" 124.

18. It should be noted that even the "perpetual sanctuary" of Westminster was not immune from the state's reach in cases of treason—perhaps one reason for the charges of treason rather than riot in the May Day Riot. See Halpern, who suggests that the "distinction between 'sacred' and 'profane' ground provided an ideological undergirding for the entire feudal system" (*Poetics,* 108).

19. As Fish notes, "Colin seems to . . . attack his own attack" (*John Skelton's Poetry,* 178).

20. Gwyn, *King's Cardinal,* is a revisionist attempt to retrieve Wolsey from beneath the thick patina of moral invective which overlays virtually every sixteenth-century account of him other than Cavendish's *Life.* Certainly, as Walker notes, there are conventional elements in Skelton's portrayal of Wolsey, but Gwyn does not fully account for why so much vituperation became attached to Wolsey, as opposed to, say, Cromwell.

21. See Scarisbrick, *Henry VIII,* 88, and Scattergood, *Complete English Poems,* 462.

22. Scattergood, *Complete English Poems,* 493 (notes for ll. 1115–26).

23. As Scattergood notes (ibid., 493), the clergy were forbidden to sit in judgment on cases which might result in the death sentence.

24. Walker has some interesting speculations on the circulation of Skelton's satires and on the possibility that some of them may have been performed in public, possibly in the pulpit or in the street in the manner of a balladeer (*John Skelton and the Politics,* 119–23).

25. See Guy, *Cardinal's Court,* 115–17.

26. R. W. Heinze, *The Proclamations of the Tudor Kings* (Cambridge: Cambridge University Press, 1976), 295.

Leaky Ladies and Droopy Dames:
The Grotesque Realism of Skelton's
The Tunnynge of Elynour Rummynge

PETER C. HERMAN

Despite John Skelton's consistent presence in modern anthologies of sixteenth-century literature, he occupies the margins of the canon rather than a central position.[1] Erasmus's praise for Skelton's abilities notwithstanding, the majority of Skelton's contemporaries considered him more of an embarrassment than an adornment to English letters.[2] Indeed, his antics were so bizarre that they became the subject of a jest book, making Skelton the only major poet, let alone priest, so honored. While he was alive, Skelton enjoyed a modicum of fame as the class clown of English literature, and after his death his already dubious reputation managed to plummet even further. Pope, for example, called the man "beastly," and as we shall see, few have dissented from this opinion. Skelton's ill repute among the elite did not prevent his works from enjoying a certain popularity in the Renaissance or his style (if not his life) from serving as a model for other writers; however, his work endured in spite of the disparagement of such influential tastemakers as George Puttenham, who found both the man and his works "ridiculous," and Sir Philip Sidney, who omits him altogether from the canon set out in his *Apology for Poetry*.[3]

Not insignificantly, critics have singled out Skelton's most popular work, *The Tunnynge of Elynour Rummynge*, as the prime target for abuse. In *The Plaine Man's Pathway to Heaven* (1590), for example, the Elizabethan divine Arthur Dent linked "Ellen of Rumming" with other "vaine and frivolous bookes of Tales, Iestes, and lies," which he dismissed as "so much trashe and rubbish."[4] Nor do modern critics depart all that much from their Renaissance counterparts. John Berdan set the tone by describing *Elynour Rummynge* as "a poem rather notorious than known," and evidently most critics concur, which helps explain the rather amazing silence about this text.[5] Susan Staub's "Recent Studies in Skelton (1970–1988)" does not contain even one article devoted to Elynour and her crew,[6] and the rare critic who does grant the poem's existence usually does so only to condemn it. Like Berdan, C. S. Lewis calls the poem a "shapeless volley of rhymes," granting it a legitimate place in the canon but only barely so: "it works, but we cannot forget that art has much better cards in its hand."[7] And Stanley E. Fish, doubtless for the first and last time, agrees with Lewis: "The *Tunning of Eleanor Rumming* [*sic*] is a picture, a verbal painting—and designedly nothing more. . . . As one of the few really abstract poems in the language, *Eleanor Rumming* pleases (if it pleases at all) because of its virtuosity. One doesn't think about the poem, one only takes it in."[8]

The distaste, if not outright disgust, of both Renaissance and modern critics originates in the poem's unsparing physicality, especially its treatment of the female body. Lewis sums up the poem thus: "We have noisome details about Elinor's methods of brewing, and there are foul words, foul breath, and foul sights in plenty. The merit of the thing lies in its speed: guests are arriving hotfoot, ordering, quarrelling, succumbing to the liquor, every moment. We get a vivid impression of riotous bustle, chatter, and crazy disorder."[9] The poem is meaningless and gross, meaningless *because* it is gross. Such Christian interpreters as Arthur F. Kinney and Robert D. Newman agree that the poem's treatment of the body is vile, but they try to rescue *Elynour Rummynge* by reading it as an orthodox condemnation of sin.[10] Feminist critics also condemn the poem, but in place of a description of vice, a topers' Mass, or a mindless series of images, Elizabeth Fowler, Gail K. Paster, and Linda Woodbridge interpret *Elynour Rummynge*'s descriptions of the female body as a rehearsal of either clerical antifeminist satire or more generalized masculine fears of women meeting together.[11]

Now, to our sensibilities, Skelton's treatment of women *does* seem repulsive:[12]

> Her lewde lyppes twayne,
> They slaver, men sayne,
> Lyke a ropy rayne,
> A gummy glayre
> She is ugly fayre:
> Her nose somdele hoked
> And camously croked,
> Never stoppynge
> But ever droppynge;
> Her skynne lose and slacke,

> Greuyned lyke a sacke;
> With a croked backe.
>
> (22–33)

Only a mother could love such a face. But how to interpret Elynour's ugliness remains less obvious than critics have assumed. On the one hand, Elynour's looks can be interpreted as sign of evil. Deborah Wyrick, for example, notes that Elynour's features correspond to "the archetype of the *maleficus*." Along these lines, Kinney also suggests that the poem describes a witch's sabbath that burlesques the Resurrection, the Crucifixion, and other church rituals.[13]

However, it is exactly Elynour's physical appearance that provides the key to a more sympathetic, more complex view of this work. Rather than interpreting Elynour's visage using the conventional standards of beauty or orthodox Christianity, I want to argue that Elynour's startling appearance begs to be interpreted through the lens of what Mikhail Bakhtin, in *Rabelais and His World*, terms "grotesque realism."[14] In other words, instead of judging Skelton's representations of the female body as evidence of personal or cultural misogyny, I suggest we consider that he challenges conventional expectations by turning Elynour and her customers into vessels, albeit leaky ones, for the festive values of transgression, contestation, and inversion. The alehouse itself clearly constitutes a festive marketplace writ small, a delimited area where holiday license rules amid the noise and confusion. But at the same time, Skelton's text is far from monological, and just as one strand valorizes Elynour, another draws us away from unqualified sympathy with the denizens of the alehouse, making *Elynour Rummynge* a much more difficult, much more *dialogical*, to invoke another of Bakhtin's terms, work whose thematic range comprehends both gender and the nature of interpretation.[15] However, we first need to locate *Elynour Rummynge* within the discourse of grotesque realism. Although the general outlines of Bakhtin's theories are by now quite familiar, I shall briefly rehearse his morphology, partially for the sake of clarity, but also because in recent years the linguistic Bakhtin has displaced the Bakhtin of *Rabelais and His World*.

Bakhtin defines carnival as "the suspension of all hierarchical rank, privileges, norms and prohibitions" (10). Not only suspension but also inversion of power relationships mark carnival: the woman rules the man, the student whips the teacher, the ass drives the man, the mouse chases the cat, and so on.[16] Festive transgressions include the disruptions of physical as well as political or social boundaries, and the bodily images in Rabelais illustrate what Bakhtin calls "the concept of grotesque realism" (18). Just as carnival challenges the social order, the grotesque body, Bakhtin writes, "is not a closed, completed unit; it is unfinished, outgrows itself, transgresses its own limits" (26).[17] More precisely, if one can be precise about something whose essence lies in mutability: "The grotesque body . . . is a body in the act of becoming. It is never finished, never completed; it is continually built, created, and builds and creates another body. . . . [I]t outgrows its own self, transgressing its own body" (317). The classical body, on the other hand, is constructed in the opposite fashion. Where the grotesque body emphasizes and celebrates its porousness, "[a]ll orifices of the [classical] body are closed"; where perpetual flux marks the grotesque body, "[the classical body] presents an entirely finished, completed, strictly limited body." And where the ideology underlying the classical body privileges the upper body, the mind, the head, to the denigration of the lower strata (i.e., the genitalia and the anus), the grotesque body privileges "the material acts and eliminations of the body—eating, drinking, defecation, sexual life" because the body finds renewal in these activites. The grotesque foregrounds and exaggerates the anus and the phallus because dung is recycled as fertilizer, eating restores life, sex creates life, and so on (336). Consequently, the activities of the grotesque body center on the areas of "interchange." The classical body, on the other hand, is constructed as "opaque," denying and hiding the seepages that distinguish the grotesque body (320).

Bakhtin's theories of carnival and the grotesque have not gone unchallenged, and Peter Stallybrass's modifications are particularly relevant to my argument. Stallybrass rightly points out that even though Bakhtin concentrates on class, not gender, he nonetheless leaves himself open to be critiqued for not bothering to "gender" the body described above, for assuming that the ungendered body will of course be a male body.[18] Stallybrass then argues that the distinction between the grotesque and the classical body very much concerns gender because of the widespread assumption that the female body is ipso facto grotesque, that "[i]t must be subjected to constant surveillance precisely because, as Bakhtin says of the grotesque body, it is 'unfinished, outgrows itself, transgresses its own limits.'"[19] Now, both Bakhtin and Stallybrass focus on post-1530 texts, assuming that the cultural discourses they talk about come after the early Henrician era. Stallybrass, for example, cites Norbert Elias, who documents in *The History of Manners* the creations of new kinds of behavior that will go under the rubric of *civilité*. According to Elias, these developments will follow in the wake of Erasmus's *De civilitate morum puerilium* (1530; first published in English, 1531).[20] In other words, critics appear to have assumed that Skelton predates the transformation of the body into a locus of class and gender conflict, thereby ruling out the possibility of analyzing his texts using the same theoretical paradigms. However, even though Bakhtin defeminizes, as it were, the grotesque body through his masculinist assumptions, his analysis contains two salient points. First, the tradition of grotesque realism vastly predates the 1530s, and Bakhtin cites many examples taken from late antiquity and the Middle Ages. Second, the earliest expression of this tradition uses the female body as its vehicle. Bakhtin found the principle of grotesque realism first embodied in the Kerch terracotta figurines of naked, laughing, senile hags. To understand the full complexity of Skelton's treatment of women, we need to recognize the validity of the misogynist traditions brought to bear by Kinney or Wyrick *and* to reinscribe these women back into the discourse of feminine grotesque realism that begins at least as far back as the Kerch terracottas, a discourse that for Skelton had not yet faded into obscurity.

The Tunnynge of Elynour Rummynge so perfectly fits Bakhtin's descriptions of grotesque realism that it seems as if Skelton magically used *Rabelais and His World* as a blueprint for his poem. The treatment of the body, says Bakhtin, constitutes the most important aspect of grotesque realism, and so let us begin there.

The proprietress of Skelton's imaginary tippling house establishes the standard that her customers will follow. As per Bakhtin's morphology, Elynour's body continuously overflows its limits. Her lips slaver, "lyke a ropy rayne," her nose never stops dripping, and her skin hangs loosely about her like a sack. Even though "her youth is farre past," yet she still "wyll jet, / Lyke a joyly fet" (51–52) about the town in an ancient, threadbare coat, which is of course green, the color of life. And her brew so rejuvenates her and her mate that:

> Ich am not cast away,
> That can my husband say,
> Whan we kys and play
> In lust and in lyking.
> He calleth me his whytyng,
> His mullyng and his mytyng.
> (219–24)

Like the Kerch terracottas that sparked Bakhtin's thinking, Elynour combines physical decrepitude with a sense of life, of renewal, and of joyful sexuality. As we have seen, her body refuses stability, various fluids (sweat, drool, nasal mucous) are perpetually seeping out of it and are reintroduced in the form of ale.

The bodies of Elynour's customers similarly refuse closure. Indeed, it seems that the abandonment of all corporeal boundaries acts as the price of admission into the tavern. The first group enters having thrown off the conventional means of restraining their breasts and their hair:

> Some wenches come unlased,
> Some huswyves come unbrased,
> Wyth theyr naked pappes,
> That flyppes and flappes
> It wygges and it wagges
> Lyke tawny saffron bagges.
> (133–38)

Others arrive without "herelace, / Theyr lockes aboute theyr face / Theyr tresses untrust, / All full of unlust" (145–48) or "Unbrased and unlast" (320). Or if they come suitably reined in, upon entering this restraint quickly disappears:

> There came an old rybybe;
> She halted of a kybe,
> And had broken her shyn
> At the threshold comyng in,
> And fell so wyde open
> That one might see her token.
> (492–97)

Nearly all are so ugly that they scarcely seem human. One Maude Ruggy "was ugly hypped, / And ugly thycke-lypped / Lyke an onyon syded, / Lyke tan ledder hyded" (467–71). Another anonymous patron has a neck "lyke an olyfant; / It was a bullyfant, / A gredy cormerant" (519–21). Margery Mylkeducke tucks her kirtel about an inch above her knee, so that:

> Her legges that ye might se;
> But they were sturdy and stubbed,
> Myghty pestels and clubbed
> As fayre and as whyte
> As the fote of a kyte.
> She was somwhat foule,
> Crokenebbed lyke an oule.
> (421–27)

And just as Elynour is always leaking one fluid or another, so do their bodies transgress their limits at every opportunity. Some "renne tyll they swete" (266) to the alehouse; one's "mouth fomed / And her bely groned" (341–42). Another manages to combine nearly every form of physical and verbal seepage into one visit. She arrives "full of tales," which she gladly shares with the accompaniment of "snevelyng in her nose" (364). Then, as Gail K. Paster neatly puts it, "having overflowed at one end, she proceeds to flow at the other."[21] After taking a long swig of ale, "She pyst where she stood. / Than began she to wepe" (373–74). Like the anonymous tale-teller, the open pores are matched by open mouths. Elynour yells and swears at her customers and her customers yell and swear right back:

> Jone sayd she had eten a fyest.
> "By Chryst," sayde she, "thou lyest.
> I have as swete a breath
> As though, wyth shamefull deth!"
>
> Then Elynour sayde, "Ye calettes,
> I shall breke your palettes,
> Wythout ye now cease!"
> And so was made the peace.
> (343–50)

In his analysis of the Kerch terracottas, Bakhtin isolates how these figures intertwine life and death: "It is pregnant death, a death that gives birth. . . . Life is shown its two-fold contradictory process; it is the epitome of incompleteness" (25–26). Elynour herself, as we have seen, constantly transgresses the barrier between youth and old age. And the food brought to her establishment also straddles the border between ripeness and rottenness. To pay for her ale, Margery Mylkeducke totes along "A cantell of Essex chese [that] / Was well a fote thycke, / Full of magottes" (429–31). Skelton depicts the cheese as grotesquely large (one foot thick), but more importantly, it is simultaneously wholesome and decaying, life-giving and poisonous. And Skelton concludes this section with the food singled out by Bakhtin as the most emblematic of grotesque realism: "trypes that stynkes" (444). Tripes are so resonant (or redolent) because they combine the ambivalence of life's processes: intake and elimination, nutrition and excrement. In addition, tripes represents the near erasure of the boundary separating the swallower from the swallowed: "the belly does not only eat and swallow, it is also eaten, as tripe" (163). Finally, tripes represent both death, because the animal had to be disembowelled, and life, because its consumption leads to regeneration: "Thus, in the image of tripe life and death, birth, excrement, and food are all drawn together and tied in one grotesque knot; this is the center of bodily topography in which the upper and lower stratum penetrate each other" (163).

The same applies to the composition of Elynour's ale. On the one hand, Elynour touts her ale as a fountain of youth:

> Drinke now whyle it is new;
> And ye may it broke,
> It shall make you loke
> Yonger than ye be
> Yeres two or thre,
> For ye may prove it by me.
> (211–16)

And she proves its virtues by providing scenes from her connubial erotic life. Now, the image of a sexually active Elynour appears grotesque in precisely the same way that the Kerch terracottas are grotesque; what I want to note here is that Skelton depicts Elynour's restorative ale as a carnivalesque food. Like tripes, her ale ties together rebirth and decay in a "grotesque knot" because Elynour's secret ingredient is chicken shit:

> But let us turne playne,
> There we lefte agayne.
> For, as yll a patch as that,
> The hennes ron in the mashfat;
> For they go to roust,
> Streyght over the ale-joust,
> And donge, whan it commes,
> In the ale tunnes.
> Than Elynour taketh
> The mashe bolle, and shaketh
> The hennes donge awaye,
> And skommeth it into a tray
> Where as the yeest is,
> With her maungy fystis.
> And sometyme she blennes
> The donge of her hennes
> And the tale togyder.
> . . . .
> For I may tell you,

> I lerned it of a Jewe,
> Whan I began to brewe,
> And I have found it trew.
> (187 203, 207 10)

If one chooses to interpret this poem solely from the standpoint of orthodoxy, the source of this recipe only further condemns both Jews and Elynour. However, its Jewish origin only increases the complexity, the ambivalence, of the "grotesque knot." Jews were commonly associated with the death of the spirit, but Elynour's brew reinvigorates. Furthermore, the alliance between Elynour and her anonymous teacher is particularly apposite since the dominant powers marginalize and demonize both (the former for religious reasons, the latter because she is an unruly woman), and much of carnival's point lies in the reevaluation of the rigorously opposed and excluded.

Pigs function in this text in much the same way. At every opportunity, Skelton associates Elynour with swine. In his opening description, for example, Skelton compares Elynour's face to "a rost pygges eare, / Brystled with here" (20–21), and her customers must compete with them for her brew:

> With, "Hey, dogge, hay,
> Have these hogges away!"
> With, "Get me a staffe,
> The swyne eat my draffe!
> Stryke the hogges with a clubbe,
> They have dronke up my swyllyng tubbe!"
> (168–73)

If one opts to read the poem through the template of orthodoxy, the pigs, long a symbol of everything low and bestial, suggest Elynour's own depravity. But as Stallybrass and White pointed out, "the pig . . . occupied a focal symbolic place at the fair (and in the carnival)."[22] Simultaneously demonized and praised for their ability to ingest offal, for their skin's similarity to human skin, for the closeness of their food to human food, they are both among the most essential of barnyard animals and the most hated.[23] Ironically, given the traditional Jewish view of pigs, the two occupy the same ideological position as both represent the socially peripheral, if not outrightly demonized, that in a carnivalesque universe becomes symbolically central—the Jew, because he gave Elynour his (or her) "grotesque" recipe, pigs, because they challenge the binary opposition between the human and the nonhuman.

It should be clear that all the elements of grotesque realism are not only copiously present in Skelton's text but that each overlaps and reinforces the other. The drinking and the physical coarseness suggest the pigs, whose carnivalesque overtones point us back toward the leaky, droopy female bodies; the ale again brings us back to the pigs, whose defecations (178–87) remind us of the hens's, the tripe, Elynour's Jewish teacher, and so on. In sum, nearly every detail in this poem joins in the "grotesque knot" that firmly holds *The Tunnynge of Elynour Rummynge* within the carnivalesque tradition. But when we have ascertained that Skelton scrupulously inscribes Elynour and her customers within this discourse, the question arises as to what sort of intervention, what sort of cultural work, this inscription performs.

Critics and anthropologists have pointed out that carnival and carnivalesque texts can serve to reinforce rather than subvert the dominant social structures.[24] Festivity and festive texts, to simplify the argument greatly, provide a "safety-valve" for the release of tensions or resentments that might otherwise build into an effective oppositional social movement, and so carnival preserves and strengthens the culture or the values that it ostensibly opposes. This interpretation has found recent support in the later work of Michel Foucault, who in such works as *Discipline and Punish* and *The History of Sexuality* argued that power operates not so much by repressing opposition as by organizing and producing it, and in Stephen Greenblatt's earlier model (much indebted to Foucault) of an authority which produces subversions only to contain them. Thus, using this mode of analysis, whatever challenges *Elynour Rummynge* delivers are contained by the degradation of women's bodies, the reader's laughter, and by the reauthorization of misogyny at the end of the text. But if the relationship between carnival and contestation is more complicated than Bakhtin initially allows, to assume that carnival is *always* contained also oversimplifies the matter. Sometimes the critiques are contained, sometimes not, and a considerable body of evidence has been collected illustrating how carnival and carnivalesque texts can function effectively as social critiques. As Michael D. Bristol writes, "Carnival misrule is overt and deliberate, but, by accurately mimicking the pretensions of ruling families, the covert and possibly willful misrule of constituted authority is exposed."[25] Natalie Z. Davis and Emmanuel Le Roy Ladurie have both shown how carnivals have led to genuine political upheavals, and Peter Stallybrass has written on the complicated relations between the carnivalesque Robin Hood ballads and the dominant authorities.[26] I propose that Skelton's *The Tunnynge of Elynour Rummynge* also constitutes a similarly complicated, similarly festive intervention into the gender politics of the Henrician era.

Elynour Rummynge's most obvious target would be the discourse of the closed, classical body soon to be codified in such texts as Erasmus's *De civilitate*.[27] The leaky, droopy bodies of the alehouse women, like their Jonsonian progeny, Ursula the pig-woman, not only destabilize the boundaries separating the body from the outer world, they privilege exactly those aspects of the body that Erasmus *et alii* wish most to suppress.[28] Furthermore, their carnivalesque bodies uncover the nexus where the construction of gender roles and the rules of politeness intersect. Thus, the refusal of breast and hair restraints in the initial description of Elynour's customers suggests that *from the start* these women are declaring their independence from the cultural imperative to bind up, hide, and control the emblematically feminine parts of their bodies. Similarly, their crude, loud (impolite) speech defies the patriarchal attempt to silence women.[29]

However, the text's grotesque realism also has a less obvious and more subtle focus: the place of women within a dominantly male economy. First, Skelton transforms Elynour's establishment into an exclusively female club. Although the narrator initially describes the alehouse as open to all kinds of people, so long as they are "all good ale-drynkers" (106), all of Elynour's customers are women, a fact that would have appeared quite remarkable to Skelton's original audience since there were no alehouses serving only women.[30] Moreover, the popular ballads and carols that made up Skelton's sources place at least some men, if only waiters and bartenders, in the tavern.[31] None exclude men altogether, as Skelton does. The first to enter are "Kate, / Cysly and Sare" (118–19), then come "wenches" and "huswyves" (133–34), then a host of anonymous female patrons, "haltyng Jone" (326), the sniveling, urinating, tale-teller, Margery Mylkeducke, with her huge Essex cheese, and Maude Ruggy. Furthermore, going to the alehouse, according to the women in the poem, constitutes an act of defiance against male domination:

> Some go streyght thyder,
> Be it slaty or slyder;
> They holde the hye waye,
> They care not what men saye!
> (257–60)

Elynour's husband remains the only male allowed to enter the poem's narrative, but even he constitutes an "absent presence" since

Elynour only *talks* about him: he never actually sets foot in the ale-house. And since the spirit of carnival informs nearly every detail of this poem, Elynour's treatment of her husband suggests that she has become a "woman on top" insofar as she reverses the customary hierarchy by reducing her husband to a sexual object whose purpose is to service his wife and to praise her unstintingly. In other words, she casts him as the ideal wife.

Having created a women-only alehouse, Skelton then proceeds to feminize the alehouse's legal tender. In place of utilizing a money economy, Elynour's customers prefer to barter for their ale:

> In stede of coyne and monny
> Some brynge her a conny,
> And some a pot with honny,
> Some a salt, and some a spone,
> Some their hose, some their shone;
> Some ranne a good trot
> With a skellet or a pot.
> (244–50)

The goods brought to the alehouse can be divided into roughly three categories, all of which emblematize the mandated and subservient roles of women within patriarchy. The first group consists of culinary items, foodstuffs and such cooking utensils as pots, frying pans, and cutlery. The next category consists of items that symbolize women's labor in general, but especially weaving and spinning:

> And some went so narrowe
> They layde to pledge theyr wharrowe,
> Theyr rybskyn and theyr spyndell,
> Theyr nedell and theyr thymbell.
> (297–300)

Another group brings in a "sylke lace," a pincase, a "pyllowe of downe" and "some of the nappery" (525–32), while other women enter with "a skeyne of threde, / And . . . skeyne of yarne" (310–11). Finally, a number of women bring their husbands' property and even the symbols of their marriages for swapping. One women offers "Her hernest gyrdle, her weddynge rynge" (280), while "some bryngeth her husbandis hood . . . / Another brought her his cap / To offer to the ale tap" (280–86).

True, Elynour's customers appear to take whatever they can lay their hands on to satisfy their dipsomania, but they are also challenging patriarchy in a number of very interesting ways. First, the women are fashioning a precapitalist economy in which goods circulate through bartering rather than money. By deliberately ("In stede of coyne and monny") returning to an older form of economy in which women had more opportunities for empowerment than in the later money-based economy, the text's women seem to be undoing the economic process by which they were increasingly marginalized.[32] In addition, the bartering system itself has contestatory overtones because the women trade in symbols of female labor and subjugation. In an analogous fashion to how the grotesque realism of their bodies challenges women's subservient role, bringing these symbols within the festive confines of the alehouse/marketplace allows these women the freedom to *invert* these emblems of female disempowerment, to first metamorphose them into a currency of their own and then utilize it to buy a product made by a woman for women. In sum, the pins, pans, and wedding rings that Elynour's customers barter for their drinks are more than simple domestic items, they are the constitutive elements of an autonomous, exclusively female economy that challenges the increasing marginalization of women.

Skelton's use of grotesque realism in his depiction of female bodies and his invention of a contestatory female economy takes on further point when one situates them within the history of women's labor. The historicizing of *Elynour Rummynge* conventionally begins and ends with the identification of Elynour with one "Alianora Romyng," a "common tippellar of ale" who was fined in 1525 for selling her product at "at excessive price by small measures," the ruling interpretation being that Elynour is as criminal as her real-life counterpart.[33] The identification of Elynour with a dishonest woman remains significant (we shall return to it below), but we need to complicate the easy interpretation by looking at the position of women ale-brewers circa 1520.

From the twelfth to about the end of the fifteenth century, the production of ale was (given a certain amount of regional fluctuation) a predominantly female activity. According to Peter Clark, in the early thirteenth century almost all of Wallingford's fifty or sixty brewers were women, and a century later the proportions had not significantly altered, the records showing only four male brewers as compared to over fifty women. And Wallingford does not represent an atypical example.[34] Judith M. Bennett, in her study of the role of women in medieval Brigstock's industries, confirms that in the fourteenth century women made up the majority of those involved in the brewing and selling of ale.[35] By the end of the 1400s, the alewife had started to become a stock figure in literature, as evidenced by the appearance of the dishonest brewster in the Chester mystery cycle lamenting her lot from hell:[36]

> Of cans I kept no true measure
> My cups I sold at my pleasure
> Deceiving many a creature
> Though my ale was nought

The pronouns employed in the various bylaws regulating the cost and quality of ale testify to the degree to which women dominated the brewing industry. Whereas the laws pertaining to other industries (e.g., textiles or baking) assume that they will apply to men, the laws directed at the brewing industry consistently employ feminine pronouns (i.e., brewster, not brewer).[37]

How much the feminization of brewing contributed to the empowerment of women remains in dispute. Bennett, for example, argues that the preponderance of female brewers did not contribute significantly to the betterment of their situation because the complexity and the expense of this enterprise necessitated marriage and a full household. Single women could not raise the capital to buy the necessary ingredients or do all the work brewing required. Consequently, "Ale-wives were classic female workers: their work changed with shifts in marital status, their work was relatively low-skilled, their work was unpredictable and unsteady, and their work was highly sensitive to male economic priorities (and susceptible to male incursions)."[38] However, others suggest that the female near-monopoly on brewing did contribute materially to female empowerment. Alice Clark asserts that the later exclusion of women from the trade "seriously reduced [the] opportunities [open to women] for earning an independence."[39] And Rodney Hilton argues that marriage notwithstanding, brewing allowed women to enjoy a not insignificant amount of independence, even legal standing. Hilton cites manorial court records indicating that "a considerable body of pleadings . . . seems to have been conducted by women in their own names and only rarely through attorneys." Furthermore, despite the political marginalization of women during the Middle Ages (and the Renaissance), women were allowed to become official ale-tasters.[40]

The crucial event that led to the defeminization of the ale trade was the introduction of hops into the brewing process in the late fourteenth century, which allowed beer (as the drink was now called) to last much longer without souring.[41] The exact relationship between this innovation and the professionalization of the industry remains unclear; nonetheless, the two developments coincide with each other, and it seems likely that the discovery of beer's commercial viability resulted in women's being pushed out of this suddenly more profitable enterprise.[42]

Alice Clark has suggested that the seventeenth century witnessed the exclusion of women from brewing, but one can see this movement starting to begin within the late fifteenth century as well. The establishment of guilds and monopoly usually meant the exclusion of women from profitable trades, a process especially evident in the beer industry.[43] In 1464, for example, a group approached the mayor and aldermen of London with a petition asking for more official recognition of their trade; significantly, they refer to themselves as "bruers of Bere," using the masculine term, not the feminine "brewster."[44] On September 24, 1493, the brewers were officially recognized as a guild, and their request assumes that the master brewers would be men, not women (e.g., "That no member take into his service any one who had been proved by the Fellowship to be an 'untrue or a deceyvable servaunt in myscarying or mystailling' between his master and his customers").[45]

Even though the brewing industry underwent considerable growth throughout Henry's reign, the independent female producer began to die out.[46] Women were not banned from the industry, but because the guilds allowed only men to become masters, they tended to be relegated to positions of inferiority. For example, the records of a late-fifteenth-century guild feast record that "2 women [were] engaged to draw the ale in the buttery for 2 days and 2 others . . . were kept busy washing and cleaning dishes." A century earlier, those women might have been paid to produce the ale; now, however, they hold the same position as dishwashers.[47] In sum, the actual position of women within the trade steadily deteriorated as the industry became more formalized, more professionalized, a trend which only accelerated during the later Tudor and Stuart eras.[48]

By situating *Elynour Rummynge* within the shift from a female-dominated to a male-dominated beer industry, we can see that the poem's cultural work goes beyond mere satire or misogyny. Elynour represents a type that by Skelton's time was already an endangered species—the independent female producer of ale and beer. In all probability, the text's first audience would have recognized Skelton's originality because his sources always present women as consumers, never as producers, a convention that will obtain well into the seventeeth century.[49] In sum, notwithstanding the popularity of the literary topos of the alewife, Skelton's poem intervenes in the gradual exclusion of women from this industry by representing activities that sound for all the world like an early modern economic self-help group. By setting up a business run by a woman only for women, a business not dependent upon masculine capital or patronage, Elynour keeps herself in business while the other women of the beer industry were being pushed out.

The text's protofeminism exhibits itself, then, in two complementary ways. Just as the carnivalesque representation of female bodies contests patriarchal attempts at enclosure and control, the precapitalist barter system of the alehouse resists women's economic disempowerment. The combination of the two suggests that Elynour's alehouse performs roughly the same function as the women's clubs described by the anthropologist Ernest Crawley in *The Mystic Rose*. After enumerating several primitive male associations designed to keep women in subjection, Crawley then shows how the opposite side returned the favor: "Women in their turn form such organisations amongst themselves, in which, for instance, they discuss their wrongs and form plans of revenge. Mpongwe women have an institution of this kind which is really feared by the men. Similarly amongst the Bakalais and other African tribes."[50] Like these clubs, Elynour's alehouse forms a kind of society of consolation, but instead of plotting physical retributions for wrongs done, this "club" supports women's business ventures as well as translates symbols of female oppression into a currency supporting female independence.[51]

However, if there are many elements of this text that valorize female autonomy, it contains important qualifying elements as well. Most obviously, Skelton uses the name of a woman who was hauled into court and fined for dishonesty, which strongly suggests that the poem's immediate audience would catch the reference and judge Skelton's Elynour accordingly. Also, the life-affirming aspects of grotesque realism are balanced, if not subverted, by the narrator's repeated assertions that these women are sexually repulsive. Elynour's face, all "Scurvey and lowsy" would "aswage / A mannes courage" (10–11). Maude Ruggy is so "ugly hypped, / And ugly thycke-lypped" (468–69) that "Ones hed wold have aked / To se her naked" (478–79). And a third anonymous "dant" "was nothynge plesant; / Necked lyke an olyfant; / It was a bullyfant, / A gredy cormerant" (519–21). Furthermore, the narrator makes his disgust with these ladies apparent at every opportunity. At one point he describes them as a "rabell" (382), frequently calls them foul sluts (340, 426, 436), and associates them with the devil. For example, the narrator says that "The devyll and she [Elynour] be syb" (100), a customer "could make a charme / To helpe withall a stytch; / She semed to be a wytch" (456–58), and when another customer stumbles, exposing her "token," the narrator exclaims "The devyll thereon be wroken!" (498). Finally, Skelton's Latin colophon interprets the poem as a tirade against the wicked and invites the guilty to listen and learn: "All women who are either very fond of drinking, or who bear the dirty stain of filth, or who have the sordid blemish of squalor, or who are marked out by garrulous loquacity, the poet invites to listen to this little satire. Drunken, filthy, sordid, gossiping woman, let her run here, let her hasten, let her come; this little satire will willingly record her deeds: Apollo, sounding his lyre, will sing the theme of laughter in a hoarse song" (Scattergood trans.).

The narrative stance of this text, a masculine "I" reporting on an exclusively feminine gathering and then turning to the reader at the end with an antifeminist moralization, is a common motif of this genre. William Dunbar, for example, uses this technique in his roughly contemporary *Tretis of the tua mariit Wemen and the Wedo,* and one also finds it in the late-fifteenth-century ballad, *A Talk of Ten Wives on their Husbands Ware.*[52] As Linda Woodbridge suggests, the eavesdropping motif implies, at the very least, male curiosity about what women do when they are alone, and more probably, considerable anxiety at the thought of autonomous women.[53] Critics have tended to assume that Skelton's text follows this convention to the letter, that the voice of the colophon represents a misogynist authorial intention. In other words, the narrative "I" and the Latinate voice are coterminous and meant to be taken as authoritative. This view, however, needs complicating because Skelton's text repeatedly calls attention to the role gender plays in the formulation of the "I"'s and the audience's views.

Elynour's looks would "aswage / A *Mannes* courage" (11), "A *man* wolde have pytty" to see her gums (39), "As *men* say," Elynour lives in Surrey (95; my emphasis). Having established at the start that the "I"'s reactions are not neutral but masculine, Skelton then masculinizes the audience. What women say about Elynour, we may assume, does not count because women do not make up this poem's audience. They are not part of the "one" whose heads would have ached to see Maude Ruggy naked (478–79). And the invitation to listen and learn (although the colophon sounds more like an invitation to abuse) would perforce fall on uncomprehending female ears because Elynour and her customers, on account of their relative poverty and their gender, were barred from having an education. In general, only men had access to the "universal" language, Latin.

Now, the gendering of audience and narrator cuts two ways. Certainly, one could argue that the text shows no sign of irony, that Skelton intended his audience to regard Elynour and company with contempt. However, another view also presents itself as equally plausible—by rendering explicit the gender of both audience and narrator, Skelton also renders explicit the conditions of interpretation by forcing us to recognize that both the narrative "I"'s and the implied reader's reactions are grounded in their masculinity, not objective reality. The question implied, then, by the opening emphasis on what men say or think is

whether or not *women* might agree. By raising the possibility of difference, Skelton reminds us that interpretations are not universally valid
but contingent upon any number of factors, not the least of course being gender. Given that the few critics who have looked seriously at
Elynour Rummynge all agree on its misogyny, my own interpretation
may sound more fanciful than plausible, but this process also occurs in
Elynour Rummynge's companion poem.

Susan Schibanoff has cogently argued that in *Phyllyp Sparrowe* Skelton involves us "in the conscious examination of how we are actually
reading," and I would argue that the same project informs *Elynour
Rummynge*.[54] In *Phyllyp Sparrowe*, Jane illustrates how gender can govern reading through her (re)readings of medieval and liturgical texts.[55]

Rewriting in her own image, an important part of which is her sex,
Jane models her grief on that of two female mourners, Thisbe and Mary.
As a reading woman, she has, in other words, rewritten the placebo, the
psalm subtitled "the prayer of the just man in affliction," to give herself
the role of a female mourner. And Skelton has enormously empowered
this fictional female reader to make a place for herself in the predominantly male world of textuality. In her text she can even transform Gyb, the
familiar tomcat of earlier vernacular literature, into a female.

But having given with one hand, Skelton then takes away with the
other by reclaiming ownership of Jane's text "and arrogates to himself
the exclusive control of her body."[56] In *The Tunnynge of Elynour Rummynge*, Skelton applies analogous strategies. He first valorizes the alehouse's women by situating them within a contestatory tradition but
then condemns them for their transgressiveness.[57] He inscribes numerous testimonials to the women's sexual and moral repulsiveness, but
then he brackets these testimonials by ascribing them to the masculine
gender, suggesting at least the possibility that a feminine interpretation
of Elynour, like Jane's interpretation of the tradition, might be different. Finally, just as *Phyllyp Sparrowe* moves in the end to comment upon
reading, *Elynour Rummynge* follows suit by suggesting how the text's
use of grotesque realism parallels a concern with the text's interpretations of itself and of narrative in general.

To conclude, then, *The Tunnynge of Elynour Rummynge* moves in
two directions simultaneously, and the trick in reading this poem is not
to totalize it into either an expression of misogyny *or* a carnivalesque
challenge to male hegemony. To claim that the text belongs exclusively
to either discourse, the reader would have to repress necessary evidence,
and so *Elynour Rummynge* privileges neither reading while insisting
upon the partiality of any interpretation. Thus Skelton's text works in a
fundamentally different manner than other examples of grotesque real-

ism but rather similarly to *Elynour Rummynge*'s companion poem, *Phyllyp Sparrowe*.[58] The carnivalesque construction of female bodies is undeniably qualified by the disgusting physical details of the poem and the misogyny of both the narrator's asides and the colophon, in which Skelton's "I" re-presents the alehouse's women as objects of ridicule. But at the same time, the "I"'s judgments are not objectively valid either, since they stem from a masculine perspective. Furthermore, the narrator, or even the reader, may not much like or be attracted to the alehouse's women, but the very act of representing independent women, especially, given the conditions of the beer industry circa 1520, an independent producer of ale, grants them a legitimacy that cannot be entirely contained. *The Tunnynge of Elynour Rummynge*, then, should not be considered a purely carnivalesque or a purely antifeminist text but rather an unstable, complex mixture of both.

Notes

1. Although the editors of the *Norton Anthology* grant that Skelton is a "major" poet, they are among the few who mention him without condescension. For example, Roy Lamson and Hallett Smith cite Skelton's "roughness, his vulgarity, and his mediaeval prolixity" as reasons for his obscurity over the ages (*The Golden Hind* [New York: Norton, 1956], 16). John Williams damns Skelton with faint praise. He is a "primitive" poet, but "within the limits of that primitivism . . . [his poetry is] always skillful and frequently moving" (*English Renaissance Poetry: A Collection of Shorter Poems from Skelton to Jonson* [Garden City: Anchor Books, 1963], 1).

2. As Greg Walker reminds us, at the time that Erasmus penned his eulogy he could not read English and probably had never heard of Skelton before. Furthermore, in 1519, Erasmus created a list of the distinguished scholars who graced the court of Henry VIII, and Skelton is not among them (*John Skelton and the Politics of the 1520s* [Cambridge: Cambridge University Press, 1988], 40–41).

3. Quoted in Anthony S. G. Edwards, *Skelton: The Critical Heritage* (London: Routledge and Kegan Paul, 1981), 61.

4. Quoted in ibid., 16–17.

5. John M. Berdan, *Early Tudor Poetry: 1485–1547* (New York: Macmillan, 1931), 215.

6. Susan Staub, "Recent Studies in Skelton (1970–1988)," *English Literary Renaissance* 20 (1990), 505–16. Actually, Staub omits the solitary (albeit very short) publication on *The Tunnynge of Elynour Rummynge*: Robert D. Newman, "The Visual Nature of Skelton's 'The Tunnynge of Elynour Rummyng,'" *College Literature* 12 (1985), 135–40.

7. C. S. Lewis, *English Literature in the Sixteenth Century, Excluding Drama* (London: Oxford University Press, 1954), 138.

8. Stanley E. Fish, *John Skelton's Poetry* (New Haven: Yale University Press, 1965), 251 and 255.

9. Lewis, *English Literature in the Sixteenth Century*, 138.

10. Arthur F. Kinney, *John Skelton, Priest as Poet: Seasons of Discovery* (Chapel Hill: University of North Carolina Press, 1987), 172.

11. Elizabeth Fowler, "Elynour Rummynge and Lady Mede: The Sexual Conduct of the Money Economy" (paper presented at the International Congress on Medieval Studies, Kalamazoo, Mich., 1989), 2; Linda Woodbridge, *Women and the English Renaissance: Literature and the Nature of Womankind, 1540–1620* (Urbana: University of Illinois Press, 1984), 225; Gail Kern Paster, "The Incontinent Women of City Comedy," *Renaissance Drama* 18 (1987), 51. I am grateful to Fowler for allowing me to read her paper and to make use of it.

12. All references to Skelton's poems are to *John Skelton: The Complete English Poems,* ed. John Scattergood (New Haven: Yale University Press, 1983).

13. Deborah B. Wyrick, "'Within that Develes Temple': An Examination of Skelton's *The Tunnynge of Elynour Rummynge,*" *Journal of Medieval and Renaissance Studies* 10 (1980), 249–50; Kinney, *John Skelton,* 177–79.

14. Using Bakhtin to analyze Skelton seems anachronistic until one realizes that "grotesque realism" is a tradition that stretches back to antiquity and to which Skelton belongs (Mikhail Bakhtin, *Rabelais and His World,* trans. Michael Holquist [Bloomington: Indiana University Press, 1984]; all further references will be given parenthetically).

15. By *dialogical,* I mean to apply Bakhtin's sense that each utterance contains within it competing definitions for the same things. In this case, the competing definitions that defy a centralized, unitary meaning would apply to the different interpretations of Elynour and her customers. See Mikhail Bakhtin, *The Dialogic Imagination: Four Essays,* trans. Caryl Emerson and Michael Holquist (Austin: University of Texas Press, 1981), 272, and the editors' definition of *dialogical* in the accompanying glossary (426–27).

16. I have in mind the illustrations of the *mundus inversus* reproduced and analyzed by David Kunzle in "World Upside Down: The Iconography of a European Broadsheet Type," in *The Reversible World,* ed. Barbara Babcock (Ithaca: Cornell University Press, 1978), 39–94.

17. I am assuming here that the subversions of licensed misrule are not either necessarily or completely contained by the dominant culture.

18. Peter Stallybrass, "Patriarchal Territories: The Body Enclosed," in *Rewriting the Renaissance: The Discourses of Sexual Difference in Early Modern Europe,* ed. Margaret W. Ferguson, Maureen Quilligan, and Nancy J. Vickers (Chicago: University of Chicago Press, 1986), 125. For a very different view of the grotesque, see Geoffrey G. Harpham, *On the Grotesque: Strategies in Art and Literature* (Princeton: Princeton University Press, 1982). Harpham understands the grotesque as occupying the margins, neither inside nor outside, neither art nor non-art; it is, as Harpham says, "a species of confusion" (xxi). Although I find Harpham's arguments provocative, he is more concerned with the aesthetics of the grotesque than with their social and political implications.

19. Stallybrass, "Patriarchal Territories," 126, and Bakhtin, *Rabelais*, 26.

20. Stallybrass, "Patriarchal Territories," 124–25.

21. Paster, "Incontinent Women of City Comedy," 51.

22. Peter Stallybrass and Allon White, *The Politics and Poetics of Transgression* (Ithaca: Cornell University Press, 1986), 44.

23. Ibid., 46–47.

24. See, for example, C. L. Barber, *Shakespeare's Festive Comedies: A Study of Dramatic Form* (New York: Meridian Books, 1963); Emile Durkheim, *The Elementary Forms of the Religious Life*, trans. J. Swain (London: George Allen and Unwin, 1982); Victor Turner, *Dramas, Fields, and Metaphors: Symbolic Action in Human Society* (Ithaca: Cornell University Press, 1974) and *The Ritual Process: Structure and Anti-Structure* (Ithaca: Cornell University Press, 1977).

25. Michael D. Bristol, *Carnival and Theater: Plebeian Culture and the Structure of Authority in Renaissance England* (New York: Routledge, 1985). The same paradigm also applies to the exposure of rule as role in Shakespeare's history plays. See, for example, David Scott Kastan, "Proud Majesty Made a Subject: Shakespeare and the Spectacle of Rule," *Shakespeare Quarterly* 37 (1986), 459–75, and Peter C. Herman, "'O, 'tis a Gallant King': Shakespeare's *Henry V* and the Crisis of the 1590s," in *Tudor Political Culture: Ideas, Images and Action*, ed. Dale Hoak (Cambridge: Cambridge University Press, forthcoming).

26. Natalie Z. Davis, *Society and Culture in Early Modern France* (1975; reprint, Stanford: Stanford University Press, 1987), 97–151; Emmanuel Le Roy Ladurie, *Carnival in Romans*, trans. Mary Feeney (New York: G. Braziller, 1979); Peter Stallybrass, "'Drunk with the Cup of Liberty': Robin Hood, the Carnivalesque, and the Rhetoric of Violence in Early Modern England," in *The Violence of Representation: Literature and the History of Violence* (London: Routledge, 1989), 45–76.

27. Stallybrass and White, *Politics and Poetics of Transgression*, 64.

28. On Ursula as the embodiment of the material bodily principle, see ibid., 64–66, and Jonathan Haynes, "Festivity and the Dramatic Economy of Jonson's *Bartholomew Fair*," *ELH* 51 (1984), 647.

29. In this sense, *The Tunnynge of Elynour Rummynge* is a protofeminist text rather than solely an expression of cultural misogyny. On the justifications for calling Renaissance literature feminist (or even protofeminist) long before the term actually existed, see Constance Jordan, *Renaissance Feminism: Literary Texts and Political Models* (Ithaca: Cornell University Press, 1990), 1–10.

30. Peter Clark, *The English Alehouse: A Social History* (London: Longman, 1983), 131–32.

31. R. H. Robbins, "John Crophill's Ale-Pots," *Review of English Studies* 20 (1969), 182–89; "How Gossip myne," in *The Early English Carols*, ed. Richard I. Greene (Oxford: Clarendon Press, 1935), 280–84; and "Four Witty Gossips," *The Pepys Ballads*, ed. H. E. Rollins (Cambridge: Harvard University Press, 1929), 174–79. The only critical survey of alewife literature remains Woodbridge, *Women and the English Renaissance*, 224–43.

32. On the increasing exclusion of women from the European and English

work force throughout the 1400s and early 1500s, see David Herlihy, *Opera Mulieria: Women and Work in Medieval Europe* (New York: McGraw-Hill, 1990), 178–80. Although the barter economy dominated the rural areas until much later in the century, the towns (like Leatherhead, Surrey) and cities had a money economy (W. G. Hoskins, *The Age of Plunder: King Henry's England 1500–1547* [London: Longman, 1976], 225).

33. See Fowler, "Elynour Rummynge and Lady Mede," 4–5, and Kinney, *John Skelton,* 167. The citation is quoted in Edwards, *Critical Heritage,* 115; in Kinney, *John Skelton,* 167; and in Scattergood's notes for this poem.

34. Peter Clark, *English Alehouse,* 21.

35. Judith M. Bennett, "The Village Ale-Wife: Women and Brewing in Fourteenth-Century England," in *Women and Work in Preindustrial Europe,* ed. Barbarba A. Hanawalt (Bloomington: Indiana University Press, 1986), 22–23.

36. Quoted in Peter Clark, *English Alehouse,* 30.

37. Alice Clark, *The Working Life of Women in the Seventeenth Century* (London: George Routledge, 1919), 221–22.

38. Bennett, "Village Ale-Wife," 24–25 and 30. See also Herlihy, *Opera Mulieria,* 190.

39. Alice Clark, *Working Life of Women,* 228.

40. H. Hilton, *The English Peasantry in the Later Middle Ages* (Oxford: Clarendon Press, 1975), 104–5.

41. Bennett, "The Village Ale-Wife," 35, n. 32.

42. On the reduction of the numbers of brewers in the fifteenth century and the gradual professionalization of the industry, see Christopher Dyer, *Lords and Peasants in a Changing Society: The Estates of the Bishopric of Worcester, 680–1540* (Cambridge: Cambridge University Press, 1980), 347.

43. Herlihy, *Opera Mulieria,* 196–87.

44. Quoted in Herbert A. Monckton, *A History of English Ale and Beer* (London: Bodley Head, 1966), 68. Cf. Alice Clark, *Working Life of Women,* 225–33.

45. Quoted in Monckton, *History of English Ale,* 70–71.

46. Hoskins, *Age of Plunder,* 231.

47. Monckton, *History of English Ale,* 81.

48. On the professionalization of the beer industry, see Peter Clark, *English Alehouse,* 14.

49. E.g., Samuel Rowlands, *'Tis Merry When Gossips Meet* (London, 1602).

50. Ernest Crawley, *The Mystic Rose: A Study of Primitive Marrriage and of Primitive Thought in Its Bearing on Marriage,* ed. Theodore Besterman, 2 vols. (New York: Boni and Liveright, 1927), vol. 1, 55. Woodbridge, citing this passage, thinks that *Elynour Rummynge* and all the other Good Gossip poems suggest "male apprehensiveness that women, intractable enough as individuals, might begin making a habit of banding together to improve their lot" (*Women and the English Renaissance,* 241–42).

51. Perhaps because he found himself marginalized during his life, in his poetry Skelton repeatedly and sympathetically deals with liminal characters who trangress boundaries. Susan Schibanoff, for example, persuasively reads *Phyllyp*

Sparrowe, which is commonly taken as a companion poem to *Elynour Rummynge* (e.g., H. L. R. Edwards, *Skelton: The Life and Times of an Early Tudor Poet* [London: Cape, 1949], 212), as a text that empowers the female reader by presenting Jane, whose marginality rests in her gender and her age, rewriting the canon so as to privilege the feminine ("Taking Jane's Cue: *Phyllyp Sparrowe* as a Primer for Women Readers," *PMLA* 101 [1986], 835 and 834). The same paradigm functions in the satires as well. Richard Halpern notes that even though *Ware the Hawk* directs its anger at the falconer who violates the Church's boundaries, the poem's "gay destructiveness delights in the violation of boundaries and in the consequent evaporation of the authority constituted by them" (*The Poetics of Primitive Accumulation: English Renaissance Culture and the Genealogy of Capital* [Ithaca: Cornell University Press, 1991], 112). On Skelton's rocky political career, see Walker's important revisionary work, *John Skelton and the Politics of the 1520s,* cited above, n. 2.

52. *A Talk of Ten Wives on their Husbunds' Ware,* in *Jyl of Brentford's Testament,* ed. F. J. Furnivall (London: Taylor, 1871); William Dunbar, *Poems,* ed. James Kinsley (Oxford: Clarendon Press, 1958).

53. Woodbridge, *Women and the English Renaissance,* 236.

54. Schibanoff, "Taking Jane's Cue," 835.

55. Ibid., 834.

56. Ibid., 841.

57. Ibid., 841.

58. One could argue that by setting the "protofeminist" and "misogynist" strands in the text against each other, I have created a false dichotomy because such double-edged treatment is typical of the carnivalesque tradition, that it always degrades while it celebrates. Although this paradigm may accurately describe (and I am not sure that it does) such other examples as Chaucer's Wife of Bath, Rabelais, and Jonson's Ursula, these texts lack *Elynour Rummynge*'s overtly misogynist narrator and the most uncarnivalesque Latinate voice in the colophon. In this text, Skelton departs from the tradition by separating the two edges, as it were, and then pitting one against the other.

Surrey's Wyatt: Autumn 1542 and the New Poet

W. A. SESSIONS

The relationship of Sir Thomas Wyatt and Henry Howard, the earl of Surrey, has never been satisfactorily understood or interpreted. In standard estimations, more often than not, Wyatt and Surrey have been pitted against each other. At first, Surrey was assumed the better poet, from the title page of *Tottel's Miscellany* to Sidney's *Defense* (where Wyatt is not even mentioned) to Nott in his Romantic editions of both. The overwhelming opinion in the twentieth century, however, has been so firmly on the side of Wyatt that Surrey has been virtually ignored as a poet of any consequence.[1] In fact, the whole question of the relationship (as opposed to the competition) of the poets in whose texts modern English poetry originated has been marginalized, as have so many other aspects of the Henrician period.

It was hardly so in the later Renaissance. The Elizabethan Puttenham made them "courtly makers," and they were considered to have given to their native language a special authority. For the revisionist Puttenham, and for all Elizabethan and Jacobean poets and dramatists who imitated Wyatt and Surrey, these Henrician "courtly makers" had invented poetic forms in English that carried with them more than originating metrical strategies. It was not merely that the later Renaissance could predicate the positive endurance of these forms through their own cultural experience and so would not have been surprised that Surrey's blank verse has defined heroic moments in Western literature, not least in something as contemporary as Wallace Stevens's "Sunday Morning," or that both poets textualized the English sonnet in ways that over four centuries of poets writing in English have drawn upon. It was primarily that the later Renaissance sense of historicity recognized in the two poets (viewed as one and, more often than not, under the name of Surrey) a special moment of origin. For them, a new inscription of the poet writing in English arose from the legends of their lives and their own political and social roles, some of the highest order, at the court of Henry VIII, as well as from their self-defining texts.[2]

In this essay I argue that the special authority for both poets that Puttenham names explicitly, and that the later Renaissance implicitly understood as crucial, originates in what may be seen, at least culturally, as a particular interventionist act. As a result of this act in the autumn of 1542, the role of the poet in society changed. The Vergilian and Horatian figure both humanist poets inherited became a newly inscribed English model involved in a new georgics or concept of labor that took mastery of language into the fashioning of a new social order. More specifically, this theorized authority originates when the new idea of the English poet (embodied in both courtiers) crosses Tudor paradigms of honor and nobility, essentially historical structures of cultural leadership, and inverts both the inherited paradigms and the new ideologies, such as that of Henry as Supreme Head. It is Surrey who makes this act of subversion and intervention with his elegy on Wyatt, identifying Wyatt as the new representation for English society of a specially powerful honor, as a master of language in the classical tradition of Vergil and Horace. He intends to establish a new cultural hegemony, and it was this the later Renaissance understood, blurring fiction and historical fact but seeing clearly in the hegemony the exalted place of the poet.

Because of the courtly terror that finally destroyed both poets, Surrey's act of intervention had to be carefully orchestrated in order to subvert the old model of honor and then inscribe the new in Wyatt. Two events define this intervention: Surrey permits his elegy on Wyatt to be printed for the general public in the autumn of 1542 and, in the same weeks, he supports (and probably finances) Leland's *Naeniae,* which virtually canonized Wyatt and named Surrey as his "phoenix." These events came as close to an active historical intervention as a man of Surrey's eminent social rank could make without total risk, and it is clear he acted quite consciously and even programmatically in his ideologizing the new poet. Wyatt had no such consciousness of himself as poet, that is, as a Horace or Vergil, although his texts recapitulate social and court experience and have their own new ritualizations of courtly honor. Surrey's elegies on Wyatt go a step further; out of Wyatt's life and texts, Surrey defines the ideological terms for the new poet of honor and nobility. That is, in their own transtextuality (to use Genette's term), Wyatt and Surrey, viewed as modern and new, would generate another set of texts and, if not a revolution, then a *renovatio* in that Ciceronian sense both humanist poets understood.[3]

The terms *honor* and *nobility* carry, of course, notorious ideological baggage, with class and gender discriminations, and a complexity of usage, often negative. It is difficult, if not impossible, to posit any transcendent or transhistorical meaning for these terms without reverting to the kind of dogmatism that obviates any complex historical analysis. Yet it is equally impossible to analyze, with any complexity, the early Renaissance without taking these terms seriously. As specific studies of honor in the English Renaissance, such as those by Council and James, and the more inclusive definitions by Stone and others have graphically shown, this ideology of honor dominated the political and social codes of the Tudor world and demonstrated, as Council notes, an "immediate relevance of the system to the day-by-day thoughts and actions of sixteenth-century Englishmen." Council is concerned with Elizabethan audiences and the usages of honor-representations, but the terms debated and held as truth by an Henrician court were still inscribed by Burgundian ceremony, at the center of which stood the concept of *gloire*. Ironically, when in the 1530s Henry VIII sought to revise radically the very basis for that systemized honor, the College of Arms, he intended to make it not more democratic but less, as James has illustrated, with all honor emanating from the Supreme Head rather than any collective group. Indeed, in the same years as the Reformation Parliaments declared him Supreme Head, Henry VIII began to reshape the whole basis for nobility in England, as Helen Miller's incisive study details.[4] New definitions of honor marked this shaping, but the larger point cannot be missed: the conception of honor, whatever the definition, still dominates modes of social action.

Thus, in the ferment of a fluctuating cultural scene, Surrey asserts his own interventionist act (as he will once more before his beheading) that he sees producing a new form of honor. His elegiac texts on Wyatt in 1542 will define a nobility and honor outside the normal systems. Surrey will inaugurate in effect his own new College of Arms by inscribing a clear archetype for a collectivity of language-makers that the later Renaissance and the neoclassical satirists would increasingly recognize as authoritative, if unacknowledged, "legislators" of the political body. In 1542, in an act of personal and social humility, Surrey locates his intervention and the new cultural paradigm in the person, in the honored body, of Wyatt himself. This is the structure and intention of his elegy, as we shall see.

In this sense, the sanction for the later Renaissance of Surrey's and Wyatt's texts, as these texts were disseminated and defined by Tottel and Puttenham and others, generated the idea of the poet. Wyatt and Surrey became a plural voice of honor for all of the nation in a way that, for example, neither Chaucer, Gower, nor Lydgate were seen as national voices (at least until Thynne's edition). The self-reflexive texts of Wyatt and Surrey thus demonstrated how nobility could be centered in the new emerging English language and the fashioning of it. They reveal, self-consciously, not only the process of writing but the moral ethos the good poet can reveal through, to use Surrey's word for Wyatt, the "labor" of his making. A result of this courtly georgics, inscribed at the same time Surrey is translating Vergil into his newly invented English blank verse, is the new poet. He carries an authority that Puttenham and others understood correctly as an historically original English reinscription in England of honor and nobility. Nobility may move now from its definition as a social class (although it may still include that older definition) to its new definition of "courtly makers." The English poet as noble communal hero may be figured forth precisely because of the very Orphean shaping of society (as Sidney defines it in his *Defense*) implicit in the poet's diachronic power of language as well as his synchronic "fashioning."

The newly inscribed poet has become the "courtly maker" of society who remains, in Roland Barthes's definition, "on the blind spot of systems, adrift" with "his place, his (exchange) *value*" varying "according to the movements of history, the tactical blows of the struggle" and "desiring nothing but the perverse bliss of words" that itself cannot be separated, however, from loss, such as imprisonment and beheading. At the same time, in the dialectic that Surrey textualizes in his elegy, the "courtly maker" labors in both the Vergilian and Marcusian sense of limited historical space or in Marcuse's cave image: "Waking up from sleep, finding the way out of the cave is work within the cave: slow, painful work with and *against* the prisoners in the cave."[5]

In this essay, I want to show how this process of the new georgics-poet began. For that, I focus on three sets of texts: John Leland's epigrammatic elegies for Wyatt dedicated to Surrey and delineating their relationship; Wyatt's single rather unnoticed poem to Surrey, possibly dedicatory to a psalm translation; and Surrey's own elegiac epigrams in his new sonnet form and then his longer elegy on Wyatt in his new heroic quatrain. All of these texts, but more consciously Surrey's, inscribe, quite early, the poet as a communal voice of honor and nobility in an innovative fashion that the later Elizabethan age recognized, in Peter C. Herman's terms, as "transformative" and "not alchemical."[6] For the later Renaissance, Surrey is, of course, the chief survivor of the Henrician period. In his elegiac poems he reflects on, and reconfigures, Wyatt's innovative texts that parallel his own, especially in the five previous years. Indeed, a radically political and social shift in roles for Henry Howard, the earl of Surrey, namely, from aristocrat to aristocrat/poet, signifies all three sets of texts. In my argument I shall turn to these texts after analyzing the significance of these poets after their deaths, particularly in definitions by Tottel, Puttenham, and Sidney, because the poems of Wyatt and Surrey themselves carry best this new inscription of the poet.

The autumn of 1542 marks the moment of origin. Although Wyatt probably wrote his poem to Surrey not too long before, both Leland and Surrey composed their elegies within weeks after Wyatt's death on October 11. His death followed an exhausting ride to Falmouth to greet the new Spanish ambassador, Dr. Corrierez, who had also been court orator for the Holy Roman Emperor, Charles. Henry VIII had specifically sent Wyatt, whom both the court orator and the emperor himself knew well (and whose diplomacy Charles admired, however obliquely). Wyatt's death had ended a friendship with Surrey that may have begun through family connections (Anne Boleyn was the first cousin of Henry Howard) but developed through a natural affinity as the two Henrician courtiers most interested in writing poetry. Indeed their personal ties could have begun as early as 1532 when both were in Calais with Anne Boleyn and Henry VIII, but probably flourished after 1540 when Wyatt returned from his duties on the Continent. Despite almost fifteen years' difference in age and the looming social disparity in their ranks, the friendship appears to have been constant. It was probably on the basis of this earlier relationship that the close friendship of Surrey with Thomas Wyatt Junior developed, especially as the son served under Surrey at Boulogne in 1545–46 when the Howard heir was Henry VIII's "Lieutenant General of the King on Sea and Land."

In March 1541 Surrey had a chance to rescue his friend and did. It is probably his intercession with his first cousin Queen Catherine Howard that secured Wyatt's release from the Tower, this second imprisonment a bitter experience for him. Surrey may have been a special adviser to his young cousin. Records of her gifts show how close she was to the countess of Surrey (and also to their little Howard cousin, Princess Elizabeth);[7] it would have been logical that the twenty-year-old queen sought the counsel of a twenty-five-year-old stylish cousin in a very close-knit clan. In any case, as the imperial ambassador relates it, on the royal barge to Greenwich one afternoon during that March, the young queen turned to her fifty-year-old husband and manipulated Wyatt's release, Henry's only stipulation being the pious warning that Wyatt cease his adultery and return to his wife.[8] This final imprisonment had considerably weakened Wyatt, and Surrey had dared to use all his influence to gain freedom for England's leading poet. Wyatt's deep respect for, if not gratitude to, the younger poet underpins his one poem to Surrey, and the interaction of the whole event demonstrates, once more, the friendship of the two poets just before Wyatt's death.

Wyatt's death gave Surrey, himself only twenty-five, a moment to reflect on the older poet's career, on his own growing conception of the poet, and on his own role as poet and courtier. Inevitably as Henry Surrey translated Vergil in these years, he considered the symbolic role of the poet in the new Henrician world that had committed, as J. J. Scarisbrick notes, "a remarkable act of amnesis" in its rapid destruction of ancient forms and institutions of human existence.[9] As Leland's own *Naeniae* on Wyatt suggest, such reflection on the life of Wyatt was not singular; it had probably occurred throughout the court and university circles dominating intellectual life in England. Certainly for Surrey, Wyatt's death helped to focus what was latent in the culture. The fact that both Leland's and Surrey's responses to the death were so immediate proves how much their ideology had already been worked out. It appears that the death of Wyatt had simply released what had been "transformative" for them in Wyatt's life and career. Wyatt's death focused and symbolized their own solutions to the cultural crisis of their time, as that death also prefigured ironically their own demises—Surrey's beheading, less than five years later, as Henry VIII's last execution, and the antiquarian Leland's breakdown and total insanity shortly after Surrey's execution.[10]

These acts of poetic intervention would have had little social result without three encapsulating critical judgments. Revising history for their own purposes, Tottel, Sidney, and Puttenham may have had different audiences or written with quite different intentions, but the effect of canonizing was the same: the "courtly maker" in each text provided a new way of interpreting society. In fact, Sir Philip Sidney's brief inscription of the nobility of the earl of Surrey in his *Defense of Poesie* may be as close as anything Sidney ever composed to an archetype for himself as poet and courtier as well as for his generation. Tottel's dedication and preface to his *Miscellany* in 1557 and Puttenham's remarks on both poets in his *Arte of English Poesie* in 1589 had more practical roles to play within the courts of the Tudor queens, Mary and Elizabeth. Tottel could find, for example, positive economic advantage in authorizing and elaborating the legend of these two Henrician poets. Wyatt and Surrey had made English competitive with other European languages, and Puttenham could represent, in one combined figure for both poets, the power of this new language that was interpreting, in quite original forms, the new superior age he felt had arrived. Furthermore, such an invented plural poet could give an ambitious critic like Puttenham, if not social advancement and a position, at least a promise for his audience in the same way that Tottel had predicated a future source of power for Tudor society in the new English language.

The texts of the autumn of 1542 can thus be seen, at least through the perspectives of Tottel, Puttenham, and Sidney, as the transforming "events" they were. For Tottel's editorial or Puttenham's critical purposes, Wyatt and Surrey could be constructed as mythic inventors of courtly language, new humanist heroes, Horace's Amphion and Orpheus redivivus (in the sense that Sidney had appropriated the ancient poets for the *Defense*). Wyatt and Surrey could be officially launched as the first poets in English to reshape their time with a special consciousness of their own place in it as "courtly makers." In fact, although his survey may be inaccurate, Puttenham stresses the specific role of the earlier poets as heroic. Wyatt and Surrey had originated new forms of language at the moment of *renovatio* that was the later Henrician court when ideological documents from the past were either being rewritten or inscribed anew. New texts, like those of the English Bible and Cranmer's Book of Common Prayer (finished just as Surrey was being beheaded), had sought, through their newly imprinted language, the old iconic bases of power, formerly centered in the building or body of the church, and won them.

There was a difference in the origination of new poetic language from that of other public languages. Its base of power could never be as strictly iconic or static as other social texts. Built into the very dialectic that had marked Wyatt and Surrey in their own texts and in the encapsulating texts was a destabilizing element. It rose from the original dual perception: honor and nobility as embodied in a person and then as generated in a poetic text by a person who, by virtue of mastery of language, represented honor. The line was never clear, and from the empowering perspectives of Tottel, Puttenham, and Sidney, there was no intention that it should ever be. Once combined by Tottel and Puttenham, the single-figure poet led to the blurred nobility of the poet-"maker," whose fashioning of language transcended the limits of any social class. However canonized therefore, in his time or after death, the plural poet wrote texts both diachronic as well as synchronic. The plural poet represented, from the empowering three later perspectives, transcendent values that could inform new generations of language-makers.

Beginning with a courtly base in the earl of Surrey, the descendant of both Edward I and Edward III, Tottel and Puttenham took the whole enterprise of the new English language in another direction. They reconfigured a paradox implicit in the georgic emphasis of Surrey's elegy on Wyatt. That is, at the same time they reached higher (in 1557, for example, Tottel suggested that most of the poems in his *Miscellany* were Surrey's), their printed books extended, in reverse, this language of nobility that had originated, at least for Tottel and Sidney, with Surrey. If such public language emanated from the highest rank in English society outside the royal family, concomitantly honor from the highest nobility could authorize language for *every* class of the kingdom through forms of printed communication that all of society could appropriate and engage and imitate, with the sanction of blood nobility. It may be very easy to forget the rigorous stratification of class in the English Renaissance, especially in the Henrician era, but almost any document from the hand of Henry VIII is a quick reminder. Ironically, at the same time that the lower classes reached upwards, the chivalric class ideals of the nobility permeated the lower ranks of society.[11]

Thus the origin of the new kind of poet had a clear ideological frame. What Brian Tuke had indicated in his preface to Thynne's 1532 edition of Chaucer—as obvious a place as any to locate the inception of the idea of a new language—the later Tottel and Puttenham knew absolutely: the power of language was nothing if it did not center primarily on that source of all power and finance, the court. The act of honoring the nation through elevating language and its "courtly makers" and nationalizing poetic language and vocation could only originate in the court. The court could create reform, as it did in 1529 and 1532, or alter it, as in the Six Articles of 1539, whatever the wishes of the people, bourgeois or proletariat. But for 1532 (Thynne's Chaucer) or 1557 (*Tottel's Miscellany*) or 1579 (Sidney's *Defense*) or 1589 (Puttenham's *Arte of English Poesie*), the court was only one part of the equation. That is, if, in the dialectic of these later texts, only courtiers could be important poets, they could also be more than courtiers. They could perform as the Orphean makers of language that humanists had envisioned. It was thus the great achievement of Tottel, Sidney, and Puttenham to shift the emphasis in this dialectic from "courtly" to "maker." They were, after all, presenting or discussing literary texts, including Surrey's original English translation of the master poet Vergil, who had authorized in his text Roman honor itself. Of course, at the same time, Tottel and Puttenham did not abandon the first term or the dialectic of the two terms, because, as the middle term of such a dialectic, an entrepreneur of printing or criticism might considerably advance his career.

Quite naturally, the earl of Surrey presented the best paradigm for such a paradox. Very early in 1548, a year after Surrey's beheading at twenty-nine, Sir John Cheke had spotted and praised this dialectic of honor in Surrey. The noblest courtier could also be the greatest poet of his time; the most honored imitations of Petrarch and Vergil could spring from England's most stylish aristocrat, who had ranked so high in August 1546, at the reception at Hampton Court for the French admiral, as to stand with his father, the duke of Norfolk (England's leading peer), Cranmer, and Henry VIII himself, or, in the receiving line, just after the princesses Mary and Elizabeth. Cheke himself was powerfully placed, both in his own time and in future Tudor society, as a model (and a cultural hero for Milton in the revolution); he was the tutor of Edward VI, teacher of Ascham, and beloved brother-in-law of the young William Cecil, the future Lord Burleigh. In Cheke's elegy on Surrey (the first and itself imitating Surrey's invention of English hexameters) Henry Howard as poet bears the two honors of birth and virtue and acts as

> natures device, so fyne in sute to molde
> and plentifull to make one kynde with shifted sorte
> thie headd she made of witt, a paragon, of tongue
> a subtill toole to fyle the rowghe hewen to the best,
> of style a Streame to flowe.[12]

Such poets of the later sixteenth century as Turbervile, Gascoigne, Harvey, and Churchyard (who actually lived at Surrey House in Norwich in the 1540s) understood Cheke's dialectic of honor, which their contemporaries Tottel and Puttenham were also expounding.[13] In the texts of these later poets, praise of Surrey embodies precisely this dual definition of honor. Writing in 1567, George Turbervile builds on, and simplistically borrows from, the poems he has read in *Tottel's Miscellany*, not least Surrey's elegy on Wyatt:

> What should I speake in praise of Surreys skil
> Unlesse I had a thousand tongues at will?
> No one is able to depaint at full,
> The flowing fountaine of his sacred skull. . . .
> Eche worde in place with such a sleight is coucht,
> Eche thing whereof he treates so firmely toucht. . . .
> Our mother tongue by him hath got such light,
> As ruder speach thereby is banisht quight . . .
> Yet was his honours life a Lampe of light.
> A myrrour he the simple sort to traine,
> That euer beate his brayne for Britains gaine.
> By him the Nobles had their vertues blazde,

When spiteful death their honors liues had razde. . . .
I write of him whose fame for aye endures,
A worthie Wight, a Noble for his race,
A learned Lord that had an Earles place.

And in his letter-book, just before writing Spenser, Gabriel Harvey fantasizes how, after Gascoigne's death, the older poet will meet in heaven the great poets including Skelton, More, and Surrey (but not Wyatt):

And loa my lorde of Surrey tooe
     What countenaunce he shows to the

O happye and thrise happye man
     that fyndes sutch heavenlye curtesye [14]

Such dialectical reinscriptions of the original poet—the laboring maker of language who is at the same time an exemplar of "curtesye" or the highest nobility—had their own sequence. These texts by later poets actualized a process of linguistic and social mythmaking that did more than make Surrey a cult figure of honor in the 1590s in, among others, the hagiographical texts of Nashe and Drayton. By moving language up to the rank of the highest nobility, these texts that reconfigured "courtly makers" as heroes of language also lifted the power of the new English language as an "honorable stile," in Tottel's phrase, as a vernacular instrument for all of society. Through the new English language, exemplified in this plural composite figure of Wyatt and Surrey, the power of authoritative discourse could come not only to the nobility but also to any other point of the social spectrum, including the marginalized. The effect in the language would be permanent. When, for example, the self-conscious Thomas Gray in the eighteenth century seeks a form to inscribe the honor of the proletariat dead in a country churchyard, he turns to Surrey's invention of the heroic quatrain out of the courtly Petrarchan *strambotto*. Surrey had first used this form in his elegy on his beloved friend Fitzroy, the bastard son of Henry VIII and at one time considered an heir to the throne. Then he had used it for his elegy on the socially lower Wyatt, in his own evolution of the concept of honor from prince to poet. Gray took the dialectic a step further. Even the socially marginalized, through the poet and his forms, might be honored.

A closer look at the three encapsulating critical texts on Wyatt and Surrey will demonstrate the evolution of this dialectic of the poet and the dependence of the later Tudor era on their Henrician forebears. In

1557 Tottel is particularly proud to proclaim the English achievement of both Wyatt and Surrey. The Latins and Italians "and other" have gained great praise "to haue wel written in verse," especially, he says, with an eye toward the Petrarchans, "in small parcelles." Now "our tong is able in that kynde to do as praiseworthely as the rest" and this because of "the honorable stile of the noble earle of Surrey, and the weightinesse of the depewitted sir Thomas Wyat the elders verse" that have now been published "to the honor of the Englishe tong, and for the profit of the studious of Englishe eloquence."[15] In 1589 Puttenham goes a step further. He sees in this achievement of language another reformation. Like Bacon in the *Advancement of Learning* sixteen years later, Puttenham makes his own history of style, one equally distorted (Surrey was never in Italy, for example) and revisionary, an inverted Protestant polemic that would also have strong middle-class appeal. Puttenham thus invents a positive narration that will lead, among other things, directly into the cult of the earl of Surrey in the 1590s that Nash and Drayton, among others, will propagate.

For Puttenham, the English language developed, with Wyatt and Surrey, to serve what he saw as the inevitable forces of history. Against the darkness of the early reign of Henry VIII (and what Puttenham sees as the linguistic absurdities of John Skelton), a reformation of light and language appeared: "In the latter end of the same kings raigne sprong vp a new company of courtly makers, of whom Sir *Thomas Wyatt* th'elder & *Henry* Earle of Surrey were the two chieftaines, who hauing trauailed into Italie, and there tasted the sweete and stately measures and stile of the Italian Poesie as nouices newly crept out of the schooles of *Dante Arioste* and *Petrarch,* they greatly pollished our rude & homely maner of vulgar Poesie, from that it had bene before, and for that cause may iustly be sayd the first reformers of our English meetre and stile." Continuing to draw his sharp historical lines, Puttenham finally conflates the two poets, in a general synthesizing fiction, for his own purposes: "*Henry* Earle of Surrey and Sir *Thomas Wyat,* betweene whom I finde very litle difference, I repute them (as before) for the two chief lanternes of light of all others that haue since employed their pennes vpon English Poesie, their conceits were loftie, their stiles stately, their conueyance cleanely, their terms proper, their meetre sweet and well proportioned, in all imitating very naturally and studiously their Maister *Francis Petrarcha*."[16]

The third crucial text in this incremental evolution of the poet's nobility completely ignores Wyatt. Written probably by the early 1580s, Sir Philip Sidney's *Defense* may or may not have been read by Puttenham. Sidney does name Surrey, however, as one of only four authors in the entire history of English literature whose works have "poetical sinews in them." The significance would not have been missed, if read by the aspiring Puttenham, and would certainly have given him authority and impetus for his own historicizing. Sidney's oration in defense of the poet appeared in print within months of the publication of Puttenham's text.

It is precisely the nobility of Surrey that Sidney authorizes, and nobility as nowhere else in English literature, either in Chaucer, Sackville, or Spenser, or, for that matter, in the English court. In fact, in such an inscription, Sidney makes a decisive turn from honor or nobility as defined by the "bastard feudalism" of the late Middle Ages and most extravagantly fossilized in 1580 by the earl of Oxford, Surrey's nephew, who had feuded, at the time of the composition of the *Defense*, with Sidney on the tennis court precisely on a question of honor.[17] Sidney's text on Surrey embodies, as we shall see, in the universal minor premise that ends his enthymemic syllogism about Surrey, a sign of the living future beyond such fossilized honor:[18] Surrey's art, his "many things," emanate from true nobility, are "worthy of a noble mind." Although Sidney was likely building in his *Defense* from Tottel's prefatory language (and in the Sidney library, *Tottel's Miscellany* was catalogued under the title *Epigrames &c by the Earle of Surrey, London Anno 1574. 8.[octavo]*),[19] nobility does receive in the *Defense* not only a new context but also a surprisingly full inscription.

This fullness rises from the ambiguity in Sidney's language, his dialectical shifting between Surrey as noble lord—considerably higher in rank than Sidney—and Surrey as a noble poet in himself. The dialectic allows Sidney to position his terms. It offers, as Sidney has said he intends his entire digression in the *Defense* to offer, models for a sick English literary scene. In Surrey, Sidney inscribes terms for an archetypical model English poet in the 1580s. These terms will add to Sidney's mounting argument of the nobility of the English poet in the structure of his *Defense*. Such a true poet is an Orphean legislator for society, whether unacknowledged or not. "And in the Earl of Surrey's *Lyrics*," says Sidney, there are "many things tasting of a noble birth, and worthy of a noble mind."[20]

Sidney's dialectic of honor, in which virtue of "mind" balances virtue of "birth," emerges in a text by Richard Mulcaster. Although he describes a new Elizabethan gentleman and not a poet, its terms build on the dialectic of honor already revealed in a contemporary text like Turbervile's, itself composed at least in part from an intermediary text like Richard Tottel's book. Indeed, for Spenser, Sidney, and all of that generation, Richard Tottel's crucially influential text (an influence attested as late as the gravedigger's song in *Hamlet* [V.i] and Slender's remark in the *Merry Wives of Windsor* [V.i]) had universally announced itself on its title page as the poems of "the ryght honorable Henry Haward, late Earle of Surrey, and other." The projected ideal of the poet on this title page, a native English paradigm of honor, was soon picked up by Richard Mulcaster, probably in his teaching but certainly in his printed definition of a new gentleman's honor.

In the decade after the *Miscellany*'s first printing, Mulcaster taught the young Edmund Spenser at the Merchants Taylors' School and probably prepared him for his first publication in 1569, so soon after the *Miscellany*. In a work on the education of children, published in 1581 but obviously drawn from earlier ideas, Mulcaster specifically accepted the new pluralism from which honor could arise. He felt, however, the ideal gentleman should still be able to boast of both noble lineage as well as virtue. In his definition, the legacy and heraldic symbol of Surrey (beheaded for his coat of arms) would seem to be present because, even if Mulcaster's model has "desert in his own person," still his ideal gentleman or courtier (and no one could be a poet who was not either) must "well deserve double honour among men, as bearing the true coate of right and best nobilitie, where desert for vertue is quartered with discent in blood, seeing aunciencie of linage, and derivation of nobilitie is in such credit among us and alwaye hath bene."[21]

Surrey's nobility in descent and desert mark the one text Wyatt wrote to Henry Howard. Written around 1540, the text orginated certainly after the disastrous experiences of 1536 when Wyatt was in the Tower. There he may have seen Surrey's cousin, his friend Anne Boleyn, executed on Tower Hill, a sight visible from his cell window that Fitzroy and possibly Surrey may also have watched as official court observers (the king himself never attended any of his executions). Wyatt's famous poem to all those executed with the Howard queen shows his deep commitment to the whole event, and its horror may indeed have occasioned another poem with its choral refrain from Senecan drama: "These bloody days have broken my heart." In any case, the violence of the court of Henry VIII dominates Wyatt's surprisingly personal lyric to Surrey:

> Somtyme the pryde of mye assured trothe
> Contemned all helpp of god and eke of man:
> But when I saw man blyndlye how he goi'the
> In demyng hartes, whiche none but god there can,

And his domes hyd wheareby mans Malyce growth;
Myne Earle, this doute my hart did humble than,
FFor errour so might murder Innocence.
Then sang I thus in god my Confydence.[22]

In the form of a Petrarchan *strambotto* that he and Surrey introduced into English, this conversational poem hinges, for all its tone of familiarity, on the word "doute." In an earlier meaning closer to Dame Julian of Norwich's "for doubte of death" and Chaucer's "doute of Jesus Christ," the term carries not only fear but also a sense of profound awe.[23] In Wyatt's text, the word signifies, after directly invoking the noble Surrey, the twofold act that is the performance of the poem: a doubting and then a singing in confidence. This dual structure results from two syllogisms, the conclusion of one being the major premise of the next in the same sixth line, the turning point of the poem. The double effect here defines the place of Surrey as catalyst. He has been a witness to the same political and social violences as Wyatt and to Wyatt's own intimate conversion that the poem describes.

The first syllogism rises from Wyatt's intensely held new Christian vision of an inscrutable God with hidden judgments. Such a God appears before the pride of human beings with their judging hearts, and the resultant dichotomy allows (at least in the logic of Wyatt's text) evil to grow. In such a fearful dilemma, community and humility are necessary. Only then can the murderous potentiality of error not destroy the necessary condition for all life (again, in the logic of the text): innocence. As Wyatt's own life-shattering imprisonments in both 1536 and 1541 could attest, a world without innocence could only lead to greater terror (and, as Wyatt could not know, to the beheading of Surrey in 1547 as the final execution in Henry VIII's thirty-eight-year reign). In such a world of terror and breakdown—the social actualization of Luther's and Calvin's basic human condition of original sin—Wyatt's solution is a community of language and humility. Wyatt simply recapitulates in his poetic text what would—and indeed had already—become the humble Calvinist *ecclesia* with its emphasis on the Word. And so the poet's confidence springs from his double syllogism: in true noble community and humility—virtues of a social dignity "Myne Earle" clearly would understand—a poet may sing and praise the reality of a genuine innocence such as the contrite David sought.[24]

In the Arundel Harrington manuscript, Wyatt's text comes after his translation of Psalm 37 and may have introduced another psalm paraphrase of the type Surrey himself made in his last days in the Tower in

1547. The connection between Wyatt's Psalm 37 and the incidental lyric to Surrey, with its call for a stoic control at court, appears in Wyatt's first lines of the psalm:

> Altho thow se th'owtragius clime aloft,
> Envie not thowe his blinde prosperitye;
> The welth of wretches tho it semith soft,
> Move not thy hert by theyre felicity.

If Surrey echoes this stoic control before false felicity throughout his Ecclesiastes paraphrases,[25] Wyatt's poem has taught the younger poet the way. Wyatt's own lyric to Surrey embodies the calm and control needed if "Innocence" is to survive in the murderous Henrician court: "Let vprightnes be still thie stedfast grownde."[26]

Within weeks of Wyatt's death in October 1542, John Leland published under his name the *Naeniae in mortem Thomae Viati equitis incomparabilis.*[27] At the same time, as Thomson surmises,[28] Surrey had written and printed his elegy on Wyatt, although, as would befit a nobleman of his rank, anonymously with a title obviously given by the printer: "An excellent Epitaffe of syr Thomas Wyat." Surrey's appearance in print signified a daring move. The fact that Surrey would deign to have his poem so circulated reveals his deep friendship for the older dead poet. In allowing an epideictic poem on a person of considerably lower rank to be published for a common audience, Surrey ran the terrible risk of court shame and thereby the serious loss of prestige and power at a moment of crisis.

At this time—soon after the beheading of Catherine Howard—the factions of Seymour (in five years to be the Lord Protector, duke of Somerset, and virtual ruler of England in the first years of Edward VI), of Dudley (Sidney's grandfather soon to be the duke of Northumberland and virtual ruler of the kingdom in the last years of the boy king), and of the new queen Catherine Parr could use any inappropriate gesture as one more weapon to defeat the more conservative Howards and their circle. Protocol marked survival. That is, a Leland could write on a Wyatt, but the earl of Surrey, the heir of the duke of Norfolk, the Earl Marshal of the kingdom, could write an elegy on a prince like Henry Fitzroy but hardly anyone else without danger of ridicule. Furthermore in 1542, such a *printed* poem might be viewed as one more proof of Surrey's failure of nobility, his mental instability, and social, even effeminate, inadequacy.[29] Above all, it would show the arrogant Surrey's inappropriateness as a male aristocrat to have power at court, especially as protector for a boy king. Public poetry-writing was simply no part of the "bastard-feudal" model of nobility nor of the other models for the factions in closer control of the king in 1542. Of course, the whole court, including the Seymour, Dudley, and Parr factions and even the powerful Sir Antony Denny of the King's Privy Chamber, admired Surrey as master of a humanist language. Language was, after all, their own most vital technology for the reformation and control of the state. That admiration proved part of the problem, of course: Surrey's immense talent could be used for the wrong political purposes. It could not be trusted, and so if the Howard heir slipped and looked absurd, the better for everyone.

Given this social perspective, Surrey's gesture toward Wyatt appears as quite a generous act. To the public gesture of this elegy, Surrey added three more poems in manuscript that members of court and university circles could read, if not the general public. They are written in Surrey's English sonnet form, used by Henry Howard in 1537 for his almost suicidal outburst on the death of his beloved friend, the duke of Richmond and Somerset, Henry Fitzroy, and for other texts of love. Because these elegiac sonnets carry a destabilizing thesis, that mastery of language reveals a source of true nobility in a society, these short epigrammatic lyrics must be read in conjunction with Surrey's longer elegy on Wyatt. In these sonnets particularly, the loss of the poet and his language, as evidenced in Wyatt's most famous work in his lifetime, his translation of the penitential psalms, is a communal loss of the highest order. Such a maker of language was needed: "In Prynces hartes goddes scourge yprynted depe / Myght them awake out of their synfull slepe." Wyatt's death is also a moral loss for the entire community as well as a clear personal loss. It ranks (at least in Surrey's sonnet form) with the death of his friend Richmond and like the loss of a lover, in the manner in which the erotic, the political, and the historical are coterminous elsewhere in Surrey's texts and in Wyatt's own "Tagus, fare well, that westward with thy stremes."[30] The tragedy is that Henry Howard knew this man (so Surrey argues in his text) and what personal and social loss the slander of court had brought about:

> But I that knowe what harbourd in that hedd,
> what vertues rare were tempred in that brest,
> honour the place that such a iewell bredd
> and kysse the ground where as thy coorse doth rest
> with vaporde eyes from whence such streames avayle
> As Pyramus did on Thisbes brest bewayle.
>
> (28)

In Surrey's longer elegy, the full definition of Wyatt as beloved man and as beloved poet is made. This elegy also inscribes a new definition of nobility and honor in English society. Toward the obviously public statement of this poem—Surrey's only published work in his lifetime—Leland's elegies are a fitting prolegomena. Both the very title Leland gives his texts and the Roman origin of the genre he names in the title provide, for the reader in 1542, the depth of the occasion. Although the epigrammatic brevity of Leland's elegies plainly shows Martial as one source, Leland fittingly derives, for a larger social inscription, his form from an elegiac genre defined by Cicero in *De legibus* 2.24: "honoratorum virorum laudes cantu ad tibicinem prosequantur, cui nomen *naenia* [the praises of honorable men sung by a flute-player follow, to which (we give) the name *naenia*]." The actual Latin form could thus suggest in 1542 the model of Ciceronian political virtue and eloquence. In an era of increasingly Roman imitation at court, as illustrated by the *naenia*-like inscription on Holbein's monumental mural of Henry VIII and his family looming above the Privy Chamber at Whitehall, Leland deliberately chooses this Ciceronian form. Leland's original Latin texts will sing the praises of a very honorable member of the Henrician court who has just died. In another *naenia* in the sequence, he will sing of another courtier still living, the heir not only to the greatest aristocratic title in England after that of the king himself but to the poetic mantle of Wyatt, England's premier poet.

In the staging of his elegies, Leland deliberately makes the earl of Surrey a major figure. In the 1520s Leland had been tutor to Surrey's younger brother Thomas at the East Anglia Howard palace at Kenninghall and obviously knew the family well. He would later go on to make the first antiquarian studies in England, lamenting, for example, at the very moment of dissolution, the loss of monastic centers of learning, especially of their manuscripts (they were, so said Leland's fervent admirer and disciple John Bale, often used as toilet paper).[31] In his elegies, Leland names no other eminent member of court except Surrey, whom Leland calls, in his *Itinerary,* "elegantis litteraturae plane studiossimus [clearly most devoted to elegant literature]."[32] It is to this twenty-five-year-old Henry Howard that the whole sequence is dedicated, who likely both encouraged and financed the series of *naenia.*

In the dedication, Leland honors Surrey as his patron for the Latin encomia on the heroic Wyatt: "The Song of John Leland, the Antiquary, dedicated to the most learned and most noble young Earl of Surrey" (262). The dedication further spells out the relationship of the two poets with a realism that could only have come from firsthand knowledge and direct observation by Leland himself:

Accept, illustrious Earl, this mournful song
Wherein I praised your Wyatt, whom in brief space
Death brought beneath the earth. He greatly loved
Your name. You revered him while he was alive,
And since his death, have given him due praise
In such a song as Chaucer had approved
As sweet, and worthy of his mother-tongue.
Continue, Howard, his virtues to revive,
And you'll confirm it by your honoured race.

(262)

It should be noted that Surrey could not possibly be considered a close friend of Wyatt, as these lines show and as the sixth *naenia* demonstrates with its naming of Poynings, Blage, and Mason as Wyatt's close friends: "three, above all, he chose for himself" (263–64). Wyatt's only son was, of course, Henry Howard's major lieutenant when Surrey was general in France in the next years (1545–46), and Surrey's dispatches and letters make clear the genuine rapport between him and Thomas Wyatt, Junior, later defeated by Surrey's father in his rebellion against Mary Tudor. In the eyes of Leland, however, Henry Howard, the earl of Surrey, was something more than a friend to the older Wyatt, as his elegiac *naenia* entitled "The Sole Phoenix" reveals:

The world a single Phoenix can contain.
And when one dies, another one is born.
When Wyatt, that rare bird, was taken away
By death, he gave us Howard as his heir.

(265)

Surrey's famous elegy on Wyatt proves how quickly the new phoenix was reborn. The poem was both composed and published between October 11, the date of Wyatt's death, and the end of the year 1542, probably while Surrey was at the war front in Scotland. For it, Surrey used, for the second time, his new invention of the heroic quatrain created earlier for his elegy on Fitzroy. His text thus recapitulates the implicit strategy of an epideictic oration but now more obviously designed for a public audience with gestures social and political that make the personal public. In this choice of form, Surrey explicitly relates the exalted natures of both Fitzroy and Wyatt, and his love for both. During a period when he would have a drawing of himself modeled on the bust of a Roman emperor and have Holbein, the king's official artist, paint him in full panoply as a new Vergilian poet,[33] the analogy allows Surrey to make another remarkable gesture toward self-reflection, if not a kind of self-iconization. The poem he would now write will mark one more transformation of Henry Howard himself into a new laureate poet in a new Rome, following the language-maker whom Surrey will now announce as worthy of a laureate.[34] Yet the transformation begins and ends in humility: Wyatt sets the model that all later poets, including Surrey, would follow. In his elegy, Surrey thus fashions a dialectical text to define the nature—the literal body—of this new communal poet that Surrey would become and that, at least as refigured in Surrey's text, Wyatt became.

The essential gesture of the poet's transfiguration lies in Surrey's actualized thesis: a poet who was a communal voice of honor has died. The substructure of blame in the poem expresses bitterness at the loss of this noble voice, a bitterness more developed in the sharper satiric invective of the sonnets on Wyatt, but the subtext finds its positive antithesis in the elegy in the dominant motif of Wyatt as laborer. The model outweighs the loss and bitterness because this archetypical poet-worker actively labors in society by personifying Castiglione's noble courtier for whom, as Signior Ottaviano argues, virtue is action and, beyond that, by personifying the Vergilian georgic hero who will redeem and build society.[35] Wyatt is thus the opposite of the idle royal Sardanapalus, whom Surrey's recent sonnet had probably modeled on Henry VIII:

> Who scace the name of manhode dyd retayne,
> Drenched in slouthe and womanishe delight,
> Feble of sprete, unpacyent of payne,
> When he hadd lost his honor and hys right.
>
> (J32)

Wyatt's nobility can only be understood by action and *labor,* one of the three key words in the *Aeneid* (with *fatum* and *pietas*). It is quite probable that during these last months of 1542 Surrey was translating Vergil, especially Book 4. In fact, two crucial passages in this book (the second repeating the first) recapitulate Vergil's georgics theme that the Roman poet had used from the *Eclogues* on. The key passage is spoken by none other than Jupiter himself, who declares to Mercury that Aeneas must abandon Dido for the greater social and political good of founding Rome. In this injunction, the Father of the Gods balances the dialectic of "laude" and "laborem." Surrey translates this divine dialectic as "honour" and "pain" ("Ne that he listes seke honour by som paine") and then, when Mercury repeats to Aeneas Jupiter's dialectic of "laude" and "laborem," Surrey balances the two in "Ne list by travaile honour to pursue" (J42; 298, 352). The fact that Surrey chose this special diction (both Latin words were open to other perhaps more natural translations) demonstrates his special emphasis on the divine relationship of true honor and painful labor. Thus, Vergilian *labor* as textualized in Surrey's elegy carried the very mark of the thirty-nine-year-old Wyatt, the product of his young body stretched out before Surrey with Erasmian realism.

In his first quatrain, Surrey uses the communal and liturgical *hic requiescit* formula to set his scene. Surrey is literally leaning over the dead body of Wyatt, as in his Windsor sonnet on Fitzroy he leans over the parapet near suicide. Wyatt's body carries honor Surrey's text will inscribe (as later Surrey will inscribe, in a sonnet literally affixed to his tomb, another model of nobility in his dead squire Thomas Clere). Surrey thus structures, in its very opening language, the resolution and confidence that had ended Wyatt's earlier text to Surrey:

> W. resteth here, that quick could never rest;
> Whose heavenly giftes encreased by disdayn
> And vertue sank the deper in his brest:
> Such profit he by envy could obtain.
> (J27)

The labor and action of this text are not merely humanist answers to monastic idleness, a polemic reformed Christians from Tyndale to Milton would utilize, but the first statements of what would be a new social anthropology, redemption by work. This rubric of noble labor subsumes the communal *hic requiescit* formula. If the poem evokes the Roman *epicedium* in which the mourner stands over the corpse of the beloved, looking at the beauties of body that reveal deeper glories of virtue, here the catalogue of the poem centers on the work of that body. Thus, in the first line, with its paradox and polyptoton, the ironizing by which the poem will progress becomes focused. Here was a poet who knew how to take the political disdain and vilification and turn it into action. Here is a true and quite literal Vergilian georgics that built (and builds) virtue to redeem community, as did Aeneas himself. Wyatt's enduring labor could redeem the language of the nation through his own text-making:

> A hand that taught what might be sayd in ryme;
> That reft Chaucer the glory of his wit;
> A mark the which, unparfited for time,
> Some may approche, but never none shall hit.

> A toung that served in forein realmes his king;
> Whose courteous talke to vertue did enflame
> Eche noble hart; a worthy guide to bring
> Our English youth by travail unto fame.
>
> (J27)

As I have shown elsewhere in more detail,[36] the final stanzas of this blazon of the body sum up Wyatt's nature. He has become the model new poet, the image of a true community of nobility, humility, and honor—a prophetic human being rejected by a court viewed here as an earlier Tudor Blatant Beast.

As an example of Wyatt's textual metamorphosis into a positive soteriological figure—a martyr for the new honor of language-making—one stanza particularly recapitulates Surrey's catalogue and *epicedium*. It also provides a spectacular instance of transtextuality, with a single line as literally transfigured as the body before the weeping Henry Howard. Thus, for his transfiguration of Wyatt's body, Surrey takes a Vergilian passage in which the beautiful and noble Dido sums up her own life just before her suicide and disappearance in Book 4 of the *Aeneid:* "Vixi, et, quem dederat cursum fortuna, peregi" and "Felix, heu nimium felix" (653, 657). Likely, during this same period, Surrey was translating these same lines: "I lived and ranne the course fortune did graunt / And under earth my great gost now shall wende" and "Happy, alas to happy" (J86; 873–74, 876).

Surrey now combines the Vergilian lines in a fusion of texts suited to the character of Wyatt. Vergil joins Saint Paul's passages on the strong athlete and the purposeful body from the letters to the Ephesians and Corinthians. Wyatt then becomes a newly transtextualized and transfigured shape that will be an appropriate model, like a classical statue, for all to view. As concentrated model, Wyatt had epitomized the paradigm of honor for future communities. His (and Surrey's) precise self-conscious language embodies and teaches nobility:

> A valiant corps, where force and beawty met;
> Happy, alas, to happy, but for foes;
> Lived and ran the race that nature set;
> Of manhodes shape, where she the molde did lose.
>
> (J27)

The final stanza and coda of Surrey's elegy show that the mold of the man, the mold of this new poet, is not lost. In fact, Surrey inscribes anew the genre of prophecy, as he would the next year with his *capitolo* "London how hast thow."[37] The dead body then, like his language, may have been "Sent for our helth, but not received so," yet both live on—in a surviving text with a brilliant new meter that generations will imitate. Conflating both ideas of the new Christianity Wyatt espoused and its language, Surrey boldly announces that, in spite of the death-dealing politics around him, Wyatt knew that only labor like that of Aeneas could set it right and, in Saint Paul's Ephesian phrase, redeem the time.

This labor meant the right English language. Wyatt's labor is thus poetic as well as courtly and political; and only the two labors of text and court, language and politics in dialectic, could build new communities, Orphean societies that will function with genuine language and truly precise communication. Furthermore, within the community of transtextuality now literally renewed in Surrey's 1542 elegy (as Tottel, Puttenham, Sidney, and others would attest), the new English poet, continually phoenixlike, would be "Witnesse of faith that never shall be ded." The survival of texts and the communities of honor and nobility (and humility) that produced both poets would continue. The community of living language would generate other hero-poets who would invent new texts in their own new times, however martyred and marginalized. The idea of a new poet, both singular and plural, had originated in autumn 1542 with texts that would themselves embody, and, phoenixlike, originate, the living poet.

Notes

1. Patricia Thomson's remarks in her survey of Wyatt and his background are incisive about the relationship of the two poets, though often limited to Surrey's imitations of Petrarch vis-à-vis Wyatt's own (*Sir Thomas Wyatt and His Background* [Stanford: Stanford University Press, 1964], 166–68). The most perceptive evaluation of the relationship is by Frederic B. Tromly, "Surrey's Fidelity to Wyatt in 'Wyatt Resteth Here,'" *Studies in Philology* 77 (1980), 376–87. Tromly focuses on the elegy on Wyatt, showing, with excellent analysis, Surrey's own role and the careful inscription of his elegy that obviates the presence of self (as in the other Wyatt poems and his elegy on Fitzroy) or any imitation of Wyatt's style, as the genre of an elegy might require, but "rather to capture the deeper moral concerns" of Wyatt the man and his verse (385).

2. These roles make the poetry of Wyatt and Surrey as particularly suited for the kind of recent critical analysis of the last fifteen years implicit in my discussion. For a general touchstone of such criticism, see Gary Waller, *English Poetry of the Sixteenth Century* (1986; rev. ed., London: Longman, 1992) and in the general bibliography there, especially Waller's own "Author, Text, Reading, Ideology: Towards a Revisionist Literary History of the Renaissance," *Dalhousie Review* 61 (1981), 405–25.

3. For one example of Surrey's pervasive influence, see Jonathan V. Crewe,

Unredeemed Rhetoric: Thomas Nashe and the Scandal of Authorship (Baltimore: The Johns Hopkins University Press, 1982), 79: "Surrey rather than Wyatt or Sidney epitomized for Elizabethans the phase of Petrarchan sonneteering." For the concept of transtextuality, see Gérard Genette, *Palimpsestes: la littérature au second degré* (Paris: Seuil, 1982), 7–13; and for the term "renovatio," see Cicero, *De officiis,* a work widely read at the Henrician court and throughout the English Renaissance (frequently cited by Sidney). See my discussion of *renovatio* and how the term fits the Henrician era better than revolution in "'Enough Survives'" in *History Today* 11 (June 1991), 49.

4. Helen Miller, *Henry VIII and the English Nobility* (Oxford: Basil Blackwell, 1986); Lawrence Stone, *The Family, Sex, and Marriage in England 1500–1800* (New York: Harper and Row, 1977), 90 (Stone sees honor as "the third highly prized value" of this society); Norman Council, *When Honour's at the Stake* (London: George Allen and Unwin, 1973), 24; and Mervyn James, *English Politics and the Concept of Honour 1485–1642,* Past and Present Supplement 3 (Oxford: Past and Present Society, 1978).

5. Roland Barthes, *The Pleasure of the Text,* trans. Richard Miller, with a note on the text by Richard Howard (New York: Hill and Wang, 1975), 35; Herbert Marcuse, *Negations: Essays in Critical Theory,* trans. Jeremy J. Shapiro (Boston: Beacon Press, 1968), 241. See Marcuse's key introduction to the cave image and his own call to action in the midst of cultural collapse, a breakdown and call Wyatt and Surrey would have understood, although with utterly different categories of analysis: "But the Uroboros has busted a long time ago; the distinctions and divisions are our reality—real with all its symbols" (239).

6. See Herman's introduction to this volume.

7. *Letters and Papers, Foreign and Domestic, of the Reign of Henry VIII,* ed. John Sherren Brewer, James Gairdner, and Robert Henry Brodie, 21 vols. (1862–1910; reprint, London: HMSO, 1920 [hereafter cited as *LP*]), vol. 16 (1540–41), 636–37 (no. 1389).

8. *LP,* vol. 16, 391, grant 18.

9. J. J. Scarisbrick, *Henry VIII* (Berkeley and Los Angeles: University of California Press, 1968), 241.

10. See the *DNB* entry on Leland.

11. For a clear example of how such class ideals remained, see the dialectic in Milton's prologue to Book 9 of *Paradise Lost.* For this cultural transference among classes in European society in general, always with the ideals of nobility directing the transference, see, among many studies, Fernand Braudel, *The Mediterranean and the Mediterranean World in the Age of Phillip II,* trans. Sian Reynolds, 2 vols. to date (New York: Harper and Row, 1972–), vol. 2, 725–33. Also, for the same phenomenon in another context, see Georges Duby, *The Chivalrous Society,* trans. Cynthia Postan (Berkeley and Los Angeles: University of California Press, 1977).

12. *The Arundel Harrington Manuscript of Tudor Poetry,* ed. Ruth Hughey, 2 vols. (Columbus: Ohio State University Press, 1960), vol. 1, 332.

13. *Tottel's Miscellany (1557–1587),* ed. Hyder Edward Rollins, 2 vols. (Cambridge: Harvard University Press, 1928–29), vol. 2, 108–10.

14. George Turberville, "Verse in Prayse of Lorde Henrie Howarde Erle of Surrey" in *The Works of the English Poets from Chaucer to Cowper,* ed. Alexander Chalmers, 21 vols. (1810; reprint, New York: Johnson Reprint Corporation, 1970), vol. 2, 588. For Turbervile's indebtedness to Tottel (more than two-thirds of his poetry influenced by the *Miscellany*) and especially his acceptance of Surrey as its sole author, see John Erskine Hankins, *The Life and Works of George Turbervile* (1940; reprint, New York: Folcroft Library Editions, 1971), 72. For the Harvey passage, *Letter-Book of Gabriel Harvey A. D. 1573–1580,* ed. Edward John Long Scott (New York: Johnson Reprint Corp., 1965), 57.

15. *Tottel's Miscellany,* vol. 1, 2.

16. George Puttenham, *The Arte of English Poesie,* ed. Gladys Doidge Willcock and Alice Walker (1936; reprint, Cambridge: Cambridge University Press, 1970), 60.

17. For a discussion of this term, cf. K. B. McFarlane, *England in the Fifteenth Century: Collected Essays,* ed. G. L. Harriss (London: Hambeldon Press, 1981), chaps. 1–2; and James, *English Politics and the Concept of Honour,* passim.

18. For a discussion of the use of this kind of syllogism in Renaissance poetry, see S. L. Bethell, "The Nature of Metaphysical Wit," *Northern Miscellany of Literary Criticism* 1 (1953), 19–40.

19. MS. KAO U147/5/2. I am indebted to Professor Germaine Warkentin, Victoria College, the University of Toronto, for this information.

20. Philip Sidney, *The Defense of Poesie* in *Literary Criticism: Plato to Dryden,* ed. Allan H. Gilbert (Detroit: Wayne State University Press, 1962), 448. To see the difference in the role of the poet and of poetry-reading in Sidney's *Defense* and in his public letters, see Peter C. Herman, "'Do as I Say, Not as I Do': The *Apology for Poetry* and Sir Philip Sidney's Letters to Edward Denny and Robert Sidney," *Sidney Newsletter* 10.1 (1989), 13–24.

21. Richard Mulcaster, *Positions wherein Circumstance be examined necessarie for the training up of children* (1581), ed. R. H. Quick (London: Longmans, Green, 1888), 200.

22. *Collected Poems of Sir Thomas Wyatt,* ed. Kenneth Muir and Patricia Thomson (Liverpool: Liverpool University Press, 1969), 240.

23. See the uses listed in the *OED* definitions of "doubt."

24. Cf. the essay on Wyatt by Alexandra Halasz in this same volume.

25. See, for example, the ending of the fourth paraphrase in Henry Howard, Earl of Surrey, *Poems,* ed. Emrys Jones (Oxford: Clarendon Press, 1964), 46 (ll. 50–58); hereafter all references to poems are given by page number in text.

26. Wyatt, *Collected Poems,* 75–77.

27. John Leland, *Naeniae in mortem Thomae Viati equitis incomparabilis,* STC 15446, translated by Kenneth Muir in his *Life and Letters of Sir Thomas Wyatt* (Liverpool: Liverpool University Press, 1952), hereafter noted in text by page number in Muir.

28. Thomson, *Sir Thomas Wyatt and His Background,* 30.

29. See the strictures by Sir Thomas Elyot against even a gentleman

"plainge or singing in a commune audience" in *The Boke named The Gouernour*, ed. H. H. S. Croft, 2 vols. (1883; reprint, New York: Burt Franklin, 1967), vol. 1, 42.

30. Cf. the introduction to the present volume by Peter Herman and the essay "Mary Shelton and Her Tudor Literary Milieu" by Paul Remley.

31. Jesse W. Harris, *John Bale: A Study in the Minor Literature of the Reformation* (Urbana: University of Illinois Press, 1940), 111. The quotation is from Bale's *Preface to Leland's New Year Gift* (1549).

32. Quoted in Edmond Bapst, *Deux gentilshommes-poètes de la cour de Henry VIII* (Paris: Librairie Plon, 1891), 161. Leland's *Itinerary* was an account of his journey throughout England when he tabulated what remained from the older world. There is no adequate modern study of Leland, an important figure in the Henrician era.

33. See my analysis of these portraits in "'Enough Survives.'"

34. This gesture of self-laureation Surrey may have learned from the close family friend, John Skelton, who may have been his tutor.

35. Baldesar Castiglione, *The Book of the Courtier*, trans. Charles S. Singleton (Garden City: Doubleday, 1959), 329, and my article "Spenser's Georgics," *English Literary Renaissance* 10 (1980), 202–38.

36. William A. Sessions, *Henry Howard, Earl of Surrey* (Boston: G. K. Hall, 1986), 116–22.

37. Ibid., 83–87.

Wyatt's David

ALEXANDRA HALASZ

Era intagliato lì nel marmo stesso
lo carro e' buoi traendo l'arca santa
per che si teme officio non commesso.
                    —*Purgatorio* 10.55–57

Sir Thomas Wyatt's *Paraphrase of the Penitential Psalms* consists of the seven penitential psalms set into a narrative drawn from the biblical story of David. In a sonnet inserted as a preface to the *Paraphrase,* Henry Howard, earl of Surrey, raised the question of where or how to place Wyatt's poem:[1]

> The great Macedon that out of Perse chasyd
> Darius of whose huge power all Asy Rang,
> In the riche arke if Homers rymes he placyd,
> Who fayned gestes of hethen Prynces sang,
>
> What holly grave, what wourthy sepulture
> To Wyates Psalmes shulde Christians purchace?
>
>   (1–6)

Surrey's opening stanza rehearses a poetic desire to address, if not surpass, political concerns: to speak of Alexander's devotion to Homer's verse is to envision a world in which the greatest princes accord poetry a sacred place. The matter is complicated by the question that follows. Heathen poems may be valorized by princes, but the value of Wyatt's poem depends on "Christians purchace." On the one hand, Surrey's question suggests that the allocation of sacred place is not a courtly concern, while on the other, it is posed in a courtly manuscript and in relation to a princely exemplar. The effect of Surrey's question is to suspend Wyatt's poem between the political and the religious, between princely and Christian determinations of value, as if their congruence would not be assumed. Overtly offering a consoling fantasy of poetic accomplishment, Surrey also tacitly positions Wyatt's poem squarely in the central debate of Henry VIII's reign.

Surrey does not answer his question; rather, he goes on to call attention to the figure of David and to the exemplum contained in the narrative links:

> Wher he [Wyatt] dothe paynte the lyvely faythe and pure,
> The stedfast hoope, the swete returne to grace
>
> Of iust Davyd by parfit penytence,
> Where Rewlers may se in a myrrour clere
> The bitter frewte of false concupyscence,
> How Jewry bought Vryas death full dere.
> (7–12)

The story of David turns out be divided: on the one hand, it is the story of "the swete returne to grace / of iust Davyd by parfit penytence," on the other, of "the bitter frewte of false concupyscence" and wasteful death. The two aspects of David are at odds with each other, and the final couplet implies that the story is not ended, but awaits resolution: "In Prynces hartes goddes scourge yprynted depe / Myght them awake out of their synfull slepe." Surrey substitutes the divided story of David for an answer to his question about the place of Wyatt's *Paraphrase;* the substitution exposes a fault line between the traditional idealization of a penitential David and the negative political example of his story. The sonnet progresses from question to fault line to the equivocation of the final couplet: the question remains posed but not answered. Yet the progress suggests that we need to examine the figure of David in Wyatt's narrative if we are to understand the political, religious, and poetic implications of Wyatt's poem.

It may seem tendentious to make a fault line out of what is an obvious seam in the extrabiblical composition of David's story. The association of psalms and story was by no means unique to Wyatt. David was traditionally idealized as the author of the Psalms and his biblical story often used to concretize the more abstract meditations of the prayers. Wyatt's poem is derived from a similar work by Pietro Aretino that presents David as a penitential exemplar. In the final narrative prologue, Aretino's David has a vision of the Redemption; his biblical story has been left behind; and he is the David of the early Christian exegetes, the progenitor of Christ, a figure to be fulfilled by the Incarnation and a guarantor of the providential order. Aretino's poem is typical of the extrabiblical development of David's story in which the penitential example of the psalms provides concrete evidence that David merits redemption and is therefore an appropriate model for (Catholic) Christian conduct. Wyatt's narrative follows Aretino's closely, but the final stanzas of his story continue beyond the vision of redemption.[2] They present David speaking to himself:

> Whereby he frames this reason in his heart:
> "That goodness which doth not forbear his son
> From death for me and can thereby convert
> My death to life, my sin to salvation,
> Both can and will a smaller grace depart
> To him that sueth by humble supplication.
> And since I have his larger grace assayed,
> To ask this thing why am I then afraid?
>
> "He granteth most to them that most do crave
> And he delights in suit without respect.
> Alas, my son pursues me to the grave,
> Suffered by God my sin for to correct.
> But of my sin since I my pardon have,
> My son's pursuit shall shortly be reject.
> Then will I crave with sured confidence."
> And thus begins the suit of his pretence.
>
> (711–26)

David's request recalls his biblical story yet again. Absalom's rebellion and death are the return of David's sin, its visitation on him in the form of loss, as prophesied by Nathan in the Bathsheba episode.[3] But Wyatt's David construes his sin as already expiated ("But of my sin since I my pardon have") and foresees the end of Absalom's rebellion not as a loss but as the occasion of future benefit ("Then will I crave with sured confidence"). David's words cannot be made to fit either the logic of his biblical story or the tradition of his idealization as the repentant psalmist. The "reason" David frames in his heart is a parodic allusion to the promise of redemption. Because redemption has been secured, David reasons, he can ask a small favor from God: first, the preservation of his earthly power ("My son's pursuit shall shortly be reject") and, then, whatever else he might crave. Against the predisposition to read David as an idealized figure, as a surrogate in penitential prayer, his words belatedly present an unregenerate David. Both the belatedness and the indirection of David's unmasking raise the question of his status, as well as the poem's. The final stanza of the narrative recalls the divided characterization of David that Surrey substitutes for an answer to his question about the place of the *Paraphrase*. The logic of Surrey's displacement of his question is affirmed by Wyatt's final stanza: we must place the problematic figure of David before we can place the poem.

The perspicuous agent of David's unmasking is the narrator of the *Paraphrase*, who has ventriloquized David's speech/prayer since the first psalm. For most of the *Paraphrase*, the narrator respects the boundary between the story, which is his to tell, and the prayer, the sacred text he is paraphrasing.[4] But in the final stanzas of his narrative, he gives words to David within his story and makes those words resonate against the sacred words associated with the psalms. He crosses the boundary between his text and the psalmic text and shows David's ostensibly sacred words to be shaped by another moment of David's private discourse, not his discourse with God, but with himself and his own interests. The David unmasked by his own final words in the narrative is at odds with his biblical original and with the singer-self of the psalms. Placing him requires that we place the narrator as well if we are to understand how this David, created within the context of the traditional association of biblical narrative and psalm sequence, is made to appear as the knowing user of the cultural values attached to and expressed by the psalm sequence.

Modern critics have understood the *Paraphrase* as a devotional work and identified it as a powerful, anguished, and Protestant voice in the theological discourse of its time. Their attention to the religious issues in the poem necessarily places their readings within a penitential interpretation. The psalm sequence has its own, long-established implied teleology, a gradual reconciliation to a forgiving God, that even a critic like Stephen Greenblatt, committed to widening the context of interpretation, acknowledges: "Each of the psalms thus expresses a version of the whole, but in graded degrees of intensity and elaboration; the movement is at once repetitive and linear. . . . The poems express a single, unified process which we may describe in religious terms as penitence or in psychological terms as loving submission to domination."[5] As we have seen, however, Wyatt's narrative frame finally presents an unregenerate David. In other words, the teleology of Wyatt's representation of David opposes the implied teleology of the psalm sequence. Critics reading the *Paraphrase* have, in fact, been sensitive to a certain tension in the poem. H. A. Mason formulated the tension in terms of the figure of David: "anything put into the mouth of such a pictorially conceived puppet as the David of this [the opening] prologue would only sound insincere if not blasphemous."[6] Mason recuperates the tension by making it dramatic and by making the drama work in the interest of David's repentance, in short, by calling on the traditional hegemony of the penitential interpretation when story and psalms are presented together. Robert G. Twombly investigates the theological issues and sources of the paraphrase of the psalms and locates David within the existential complexity of proto-Protestant belief. Thus, while he too is bothered by moments that seem parodic, he can read them, following and correcting Mason as the dramatic example of the felt need for grace, for what he calls "moral rehabilitation."[7] What is interesting about this critical history is that both Mason and Twombly freely acknowledge their discomfort with the figure of David and then, perhaps in response to that discomfort and the moral ambiguity it implies, proceed, counterintuitively, to redeem David. Greenblatt refocuses the Protestant "inwardness" of the *Paraphrase* by considering it in the context of Wyatt's other poems and his participation in the courtly milieu. He suggests that "the invocation of David may glance, slyly and indirectly, at Henry VIII himself" (121), but does not pursue the implication of his remark because of his larger argument: "I would suggest that there is no privileged sphere of individuality in Wyatt, set off from linguistic convention, from the social pressure, from the shaping force of religious and political power. Wyatt may complain about the abuses of the court, he may declare his independence from a tempting sexual or political entanglement, but he always does so from within a context governed by the essential values of a system of power that has an absolute monarch as head of both church and state" (120). Within this larger argument, neither David nor the narrator are important. Indeed, though Greenblatt asserts that "the voice seems unmistakably Wyatt's" (122), he is primarily interested in the "speaker of the psalms" to whom he often refers as "the psalmist." What is important for his argument are the circumstances that shape the psalmic voice and allow Greenblatt to make the descriptive equation I quoted earlier between a religious and psychological understanding of the psalm sequence. Perhaps the most telling consequence of this critical move is the restriction of poetic space to a psychologized inwardness: not only are Wyatt, the narrator, and David collapsed into "the psalmist" anxiously petitioning his powerful God but the figure of determining power can be indifferently filled by God, Henry VIII, the Reformation, or the generalized system of power. In a circular system there is only "inward" room. While I find Greenblatt's argument provocative, I think his reduction of the voice of the *Paraphrase* to that of "the psalmist" does both the poem and his argument a disservice. While I grant the interpenetration of various cultural forces in Wyatt's production, I think Wyatt creates a perspective in his poem from which "the values of a system that has an absolute monarch as head of both church and state" can be judged, the power of the monarch notwithstanding. His ability to do so depends on the initial distinctions he establishes between himself, the narrator, and David. I will demonstrate that Wyatt inscribes not only this "privileged" perspective in his poem but also its cost. As a poet, he addresses the king with a consciousness of loss. He can call the king to account, but he cannot do so from a position of innocence or spiritual purity.

The *Paraphrase* was written between 1534 and 1542, a period that encompasses the deaths by execution of Thomas More, John Fisher, Anne Boleyn, and Thomas Cromwell.[8] An episode from Wyatt's life illustrates the complexity of determining the place of Wyatt's poem. In 1541, imprisoned and accused, among other things of sympathy with Reginald Pole, Wyatt defended himself by specifying his religious opinion: "ye bring in now that I shulde have this intelligens with Pole by cawse of our opinions that are lyke and that I am papyste. I thynke I shulde have much more adoe with a greate sorte in Inglonde to purge my selfe of suspecte of a Lutherane than of a Papyst."[9] The self-characterization, more Lutheran than Catholic but not definitively either, indicates discretion and, perhaps more important, suggests the difficulty of specifying precise ideological affiliations among the many-voiced disputations of the Reformation, Henrician and European. Wyatt's circumlocution is noteworthy on other counts as well. It not only serves as a defense but as a protection of Wyatt's private opinion. He will not, as Pole did, publicly oppose the king's position, yet he does not denounce Pole. He is a faithful servant of his king: "God be thanked, he is no tyrant. He woll no such thynges agaynst mens consciens. He will but his lawes and his lawes with mercie." Such a statement from a former intimate of Thomas Cromwell (and possibly of Anne Boleyn) testifies to a marked discretion as well as an ability to survive and remain effective in spite of the confusion around him. It also underscores the fact that Wyatt's opinion, religious or otherwise, is not a simple matter. Similarly, the decision to imitate Aretino's poem is not a simple matter; it can be aptly characterized as overdetermined. The literary work of psalmic paraphrase, drawn out of both Catholic and Protestant sources and set into the tacitly, if not explicitly, politicized narrative of David's kingship, mimics Wyatt's diplomatic work of negotiating the political interests of Protestant, Catholic, and vacillating kings (Henry VIII, Charles V, and Francis I).[10] In the discourse of reformation, David's figuration as the political and religious leader of the chosen people was obviously useful and appropriated by all sides.[11] In the Henrician context, the story of his lust and its effect on his kingdom were, to say the least, apposite. Finally, David's extrabiblical identification as the psalmist suited Wyatt's purposes, as we will see. With this overdetermination and complexity in mind, we can return to the *Paraphrase* and trace its operation against the ground of David's biblical story.

The *Paraphrase* opens with a rendition of the story of adultery and murder. In the biblical story David sees Bathsheba bathing, sends for her, has sexual intercourse with her, and then sends her away. Later, when he learns that she is pregnant, he sends for Uriah that he might come home, sleep with his wife, and be the putative father of Bathsheba's child. Uriah comes, but on his soldier's honor and for the glory of Israel and Judah, he refuses to sleep in his wife's house. Angered at the failure of his scheme, David sends Uriah back to battle with the letter that is, in effect, his death warrant. Uriah is killed in battle, and David takes Bathsheba as one of his wives. God sends Nathan to indicate David's sin and punishment. The first child of David and Bathsheba, conceived in adultery and fathered by murder, dies. The rest of Nathan's prophecies, the visitation of David's sin upon other member of his house and its return to him in the form of loss, await fulfillment in the history of David's reign.[12] The initial sin emerges out of sexual desire; compounded by murder, it becomes unavoidable tragedy for David and his people.

Wyatt's opening line suggests the cause of David's adultery with Bathsheba: "Love, to give law unto his subject hearts, / Stood in the eyes of Barsabe the bright" (1–2). It is not clear, however, whether this Love should be read as a first cause, a divine Love upon which a moral order could be predicated, or simply as a force that imposes its control on "subject hearts." The first reading is consonant with the later psalmic voice that tells us that "God seeks love" and suggests a testing situation typical of the Old Testament. The second reading anticipates the compulsion of David's adultery with Bathsheba, suggesting not only an already determined outcome but also a Petrarchan tradition. The succeeding lines push us toward and beyond the second reading; this is the tyrant Cupid imposing himself:

> And in a look anon himself converts
> Cruelly pleasant before King David sight;
> First dazed his eyes, and furtherforth he starts
> With venomed breath, as softly as he might
> Touched his senses, and overruns his bones
> With creeping fire sparpled for the nonce.
>
> (3–8)

200 / Alexandra Halasz

Love's action, "with venomed breath" and "creeping fire," recalls Satan's story in a radically compressed form: initially at one with divinity, by a willful act he becomes opposed and by a second willful act, he transforms himself into the serpent who tempts. The syntax of line 3 leaves the question of agency unresolved. Is it David's look that converts love? Or Bathsheba's? Or is Love a Manichaean God who converts himself into his opposite? Once the satanic allusions are made, however, it is clear that David takes this "converted" love as his own: "The form that Love had printed in his breast / He honour'th it as thing of things best" (15–16). The first reading of the opening is displaced by the accumulating force of the second, and our sense of both a predetermined outcome and David's willfulness is reinforced by the precipitousness of the murder: it is accomplished not, as in the biblical story, after the adultery but before, in order to facilitate the adultery.

> So that forgot the wisdom and forecast
> (Which woe to realms when that these kings doth lack)
> Forgetting eke God's majesty as fast,
> Yea, and his own, forthwith he doth to make
> Urie to go into the field in haste—
> Urie I say, that was his idol's make—
> Under pretence of certain victory,
> For en'mies' swords a ready prey to die,
>
> Whereby he may enjoy her out of doubt
> Whom more than God or himself he mindeth.
> (17–26)

Repeating Uriah's name, the narrator individuates himself out of the impersonal voice that opened the poem; he calls out the name of the victim as he narrates the murder. His narration of the murder is framed by terms that reintroduce the perspective of a moral order. This order of "wisdom," "forecast," and "God's majesty" enlarges and alters our sense of the predetermined outcome by providing for the extrabiblical development of David's story: here is the divine order to which David returns by the penitential work of the psalms, the Love to which the opening line momentarily seemed to allude. As if enabled by the establishment of a fuller, more authoritative frame of interpretation, the narrator now calls David's act by its unequivocal name:

> And of that lust possessed himself he findeth
> That hath and doth reverse and clean turn out
> Kings from kingdoms and cities undermindeth,

> He, blinded, thinks this train so blind and close
> To blind all thing, that naught may it disclose.
>
> (28–32)

Though David is blinded, the narrator implies that he is also aware he has something to hide, that he is conscious of his sin as sin.

Nathan comes not only, as in the biblical story, to tell David that he has sinned but to tell him that he has been found out:

> But Nathan hath spied out this treachery
> With rueful cheer and sets afore his face
> The great offence, outrage, and injury
> That he hath done to God as in this case—
> By murder for to cloak adultery.
>
> (35–37)

Nathan's words are unspoken in the narrative. Instead of an agent of God who foresees the future, we have a man who investigates David's secrets and before whom David throws himself to the ground when the treachery is brought into the open. Confronted by Nathan, David is converted into the penitent. Both Nathan's normalized status, that is, his appearance as some sort of peer, and David's quick conversion from the arrogance of thinking he can act with impunity ("so blind and close . . . that naught may it disclose") to the abject posture of a penitent ("His purple pall, his sceptre he lets fall / And to the ground he throw'th himself withal" [47–48]) foreground David's story as one being played out in the temporal world, that is, without divine intercession. The urgency of the narrative, emphatically indicated in Uriah's precipitate murder, here is directed away from the events of David's biblical story and toward close scrutiny of the penitential process that he enacts. The stanza that accomplishes this transition establishes a double perspective on the figure of David:

> The pompous pride of state and dignity
> Forthwith rebates repentant humbleness.
> Thinner vile cloth than clotheth poverty
> Doth scantily hide and clad his nakedness,
>
> . . . .
>
> More like was he the selfsame repentance
> Than stately prince of worldly governance.
>
> (49–52, 55–56)

David adopts the penitential posture "forthwith," as quickly as he sends Uriah to his death. This David, the narrator implies, not only knows how to get what he wants but also knows his part in a penitential performance. The stanza, at any rate, clearly establishes the extremes of David's position: repentance versus worldly power.

Nathan sees what David had thought "so blind and close . . . that naught may it disclose"; David therefore converts and Nathan presumably sees "repentant humbleness" before he disappears from the poem. From the reader's point of view, however, the vision is less clear. Grammatically, the subject and object of "The pompous pride of state and dignity / Forthwith rebates repentant humbleness" are interchangeable or reversible. Indeed, the latest edition of Wyatt's poems glosses the meaning of these lines by the reversed order: humbleness brings down pride. The stanza continues with a description of David in the dress of humility and so seems to support the meaning generated by the reversed syntax, a meaning that is also consonant with the traditional association between David and the psalm sequence. While Aretino's "humiliando la superbia de la sua dignita con l'humilitade del pentimiento" leaves no question as to how David's action is to be read, Wyatt's sentence renders that reading difficult. In the syntax of Wyatt's sentence "pride" and "humbleness" are placed in a determinate relation to each other. If "rebates" is read as a diminishment or lessening, as the sentence unfolds, pride acts upon humility, lessening it. Then, realizing the discrepancy between the syntactical unfolding of the sentence and the continuation of the stanza, we must read the sentence again, backward, to fit it to the ostensible meaning of the stanza. Why is this labor made necessary? If "rebates" is read as a hawking metaphor, the reversed reading is telling.[13] As the sentence unfolds, pride is the falconer, calling humility back and forth as it pleases. In the reversed reading, humility is the falconer, but its action of calling the falcon back and forth as it pleases is one that belongs to pride, to the desire to control and not to be subjugated. Reading "rebates" as a hawking metaphor underscores the primacy of pride and suggests that the sentence provides us with a syntactical model for the difficulty of subordinating pride to humility, one that simultaneously points to the ease with which pride dominates. Moreover, Wyatt's presentation clearly places "pompous pride" at the beginning not only of the sentence but of the stanza. Humility appears in David's dress; then, appropriately clothed, he appears to be like "self-same repentance" rather than "stately prince of worldly governance." Pride initiates the stanza, and the embodiment of pride, the stately prince, closes it. David's appearance as a humble man is syntactically contained between the pride of state and dignity and the stately prince of worldly governance. There is no question as to David's appearance, but the arrangement of the stanza suggests that the appearance is generated and contained by a proud prince. David's will-fulness before Nathan is of a piece with the willfulness of the murder and adultery.

In the second narrative link, the narrator again draws attention to himself. To lines that derive from Aretino and describe David's relief after singing the first psalm, he adds his signature, "I say":

> Whoso hath seen the sick in his fever,
> After truce taken with the heat or cold
> And that the fit is passed of his fervour,
> Draw fainting sighs, let him, I say, behold
> Sorrowful David after his langour.
> (185–89)

After an intervening stanza, which I will discuss momentarily, the nar-rator returns to the place where he left David at the end of the first link: a dark cave to which David had withdrawn to pray. There, he repeats the invitation to behold:

> For who had seen so kneel within the grave
> The chief pastor of th'Hebrews' assemble
> Would judge it made, by tears of penitence,
> A sacred place worthy of reverence.
> (205–8)

The commentary calls attention to a contradiction at work in the nar-rative, a contradiction that ultimately has its root in the story of David. David's sin is personal or private, but it unfolds itself through, and has consequences for, his princely or public power. The first invitation to behold ("whoso hath seen . . . let him, I say, behold") is predicated on David's extrabiblical status as an exemplary penitent, a surrogate for anyone "whoso hath seen" or felt the discomfort of sin; the second depends on and contradicts David's biblical story. In the biblical story David's personal sorrow and contrition, though publicly displayed, were of no avail in protecting his kin or his kingdom from the conse-quences of his sin; yet the personal sorrow and public avowal secured the promise of redemption for future generations. In Wyatt's narrative David's penitence is private, even secret. It is indeed of interest to "th'Hebrews' assemble" if their chief pastor repents, but the narrator's conditional statement emphasizes that the assembly does not see. Here Wyatt departs again from Aretino's narrative, which has David judging the appropriateness of the cave as a penitential place, in order to intro-duce the hypothetical perspective of an onlooker ("for who had seen"). The conditional "would" does double service: it indicates that the conditions enabling sight, and therefore judgment, do not exist, while at the same time, it offers a perspective and posits a judgment. By the perspective he opens, the narrator acknowledges the reader and places him or her in a position similar to Nathan's in the first link. We presumably see penitence. At the same time the perspective complicates rather than clarifies the narrative: the hypothetical onlooker is at once present, as the reader, and absent, as the Hebrew assembly. The effect of this complication, however, is not to underscore David's willfulness but the narrator's. By his signed and repeated invitation to behold, he does not simply indicate the secrecy of David's penitence, he also supplies publication. He offers his effort in the place of David's. In his first emergence, calling out Uriah's name, the narrator opened a space between himself and David. Here, by suggesting the inadequacy of David's penitence, he begins to dislodge David from the penitential position and to offer his effort in the place of David's. In so doing he becomes fully implicated in the princely David's world. In order to analyze how the narrator dislodges the princely David from his idealized penitential status, however, we must proceed as if the narrator could be distinguished clearly from David.

In the stanza that separates the invitation to behold from its problematizing repetition, the narrator suggests that David is thinking tactically rather than penitently: "Till he had willed to seek for his succour, / Himself accusing, beknowing his case, / Thinking so best his Lord for to appease" (197–99). David's "will" to present "his case" finds psalmic rhetoric congenial. The language of the psalms is dominated by metaphors of economic, legal, and emotional power; the psalmic voice is now abject and pleading, now assured, if not arrogant. When the psalms are understood as David's words and contextualized in terms of his life, they are, furthermore, the words of a man accustomed to the exercise of power. In the amplification of Psalm 6, for example, the dread accompanying David's awareness of his sin alternates with presumption: "Of thee this thing [I] require" (80), he sings and then later suggests that his need or requirement ought to find its complement in God's need to maintain his reputation.

> Return, O Lord, O Lord I thee beseech
> Unto thine old wonted benignity.
> . . . .
> For if thy righteous hand that is so just
> Suffer no sin or strike with damnation,
> Thy infinite mercy want needs it must

> Subject matter for his operation.
> For that in death there is no memory
> Among the damned, nor yet no mention
> Of thy great name, ground of all glory,
> Then if I die and go whereas I fear
> To think thereon, how shall thy great mercy
> Sound in my mouth unto the world's ear?
> (116–17, 127–36)

What is, in the psalmic original, a plea for mercy and an offer of praise ("Return, O Lord, deliver my soul: Oh save me for thy mercies sake. For in death there is no remembrance of thee: in the grave who shall give thee thanks?") becomes, in the paraphrase, a negotiation involving two parties in the operation of justice. The basic plot, "making a deal with God," is present in the psalmic original, but the amplification, by developing at length why it is in God's interest to forgive David, emphasizes David's presumption. The suitor in this court speaks familiarly of the presiding judge ("thine old wonted benignity") and presumes to offer him a deal (the glorification of his name and mercy). The deal is made in chambers, as it were, away from the place where David is threatened, that is, away from the center of his princely power, his court. In itself, the amplification does not vitiate the meaning of the psalmic original, but in the context of the narrator's representation of David, it reinforces David's willfulness. The alteration of a single word can align the represented presumption of David and a psalm. In Psalm 51, for example, the biblical half-verse "restore unto me the joy of thy salvation" (verse 12) becomes "render to me joy of thy help and rest" (483). The sense of the passage in the psalm clearly calls for some notion of giving back, of regaining. "Render" allows that meaning but also suggests a sense of obligation, of duty, as in the meaning associated with Christ's words in Mark 12:17: "render to Caesar the things that are Caesar's, and to God the things that are God's."[14] The distinction between the tribute due worldly power and the tribute due heavenly power is precisely the distinction that eludes Wyatt's David. He not only conflates the worldly and the transcendent but demands both as his due: "render to me."

David's negotiations are not confined to the psalms. His "case" becomes, not the argument within the psalms, but the use of the psalms to settle his account with God. In the fifth narrative link, the narrator stages a rhetorical crisis in the presentation of David's "case"; David surprises even himself:

> Of deep secrets that David here did sing,
> Of mercy, of faith, of frailty, of grace,
> Of God's goodness, and of justifying,
> The greatness did so astone himself a space,
> As who might say: "Who hath expressed this thing?
> I, sinner, I! What have I said, alas?
> That God's goodness would within my song entreat
> Let me again consider and repeat."
>   (509–16)

The narrator imagines David speaking to himself and acknowledging that the song is not his own, but God's working within him. "As who might say" recalls the "whoso hath seen" and "for who had seen" of the second link, which, by emphasizing the secrecy of David's penitence, suggested that it might be inadequate. The "who" of David's surprise and the stanza in which it appears, evenly split between the catalog of secrets in David's song and the surprise, suggest a separation between the prayer and the "case." In describing David's reconsideration of the psalmic voice, the narrator emphasizes his appraisal of what that voice does:

> And so he doth, but not expressed by word.
> But in his heart he turneth and poiseth
> Each word that erst his lips might forth afford.
> He points, he pauseth, he wonders, he praiseth
> The mercy that hides of justice the sword,
> The justice that so his promise complisheth
> For his words' sake to worthiless desert
> That gratis his graces to men doth depart.
>   (517–24)

David's appreciation of the power of the psalmic voice results in the renewal of his plea: "He dare importune the Lord on every side / (For he know'th well to mercy is ascribed / Respectless labour), importune, cry and call" (537–39). The prayer that follows appears inseparable from David's presumption, as though the issues raised by the first stanza had been resolved by David's reconsideration. But in the stanza that links David's appraisal to his renewed plea, the narrator carefully indicates how David resolved his surprise:

> Here hath he comfort when he doth measure
> Measureless mercies to measureless fault,

To prodigal sinners infinite treasure,
Treasure termless that never shall default.
(525–28)

The formulation builds on lines added to Psalm 51, which David has just sung, lines referring to measurement ("And for thy mercies' number without end" [431], and "For unto thee no number can be laid / For to prescribe remissions of offence" [439–40]). Within the psalm these additions can be read as the commonplace expression of the contrast between the finitude of earthly conceptions and the infinitude of heaven, but in the link, the narrator tells us that David is measuring what the psalmic argument insists cannot be measured. He is calculating the value of the prayer. We also should be reminded of the story of David in 2 Samuel 24. There David counts the people of Israel and Judah, a sin of numbering that God punishes by killing twenty thousand people "from Dan to Beersheba." Unlike the biblical David, this David does not repent; rather he continues to press his "case."

In the penultimate narrative link, David enacts a final conversion: "And all the glory of his forgiven fault / To God alone he doth it whole convert. / His own merit he findeth in default" (658–60). His "case" has come to its conclusion. Should the forgiveness or remedy be found lacking, the error will rest with the party in possession, God. David knows he is in default and so petitions anew: "Thee have I called, O Lord, to be my borrow" (667). "Borrow" is Wyatt's addition; the psalmic original calls upon the Lord without specifying in what capacity. The word choice in the psalmic paraphrase concludes an argument elaborated in the narrative link. In the settlement between David and God, David's power is secured by his deal with God according to David's use of psalmic rhetoric. What David lacks, God will provide. Confident, David specifies the last favor, "frames this reason in his heart." But the narrator, by making us privy to David's reason, has framed David. David's words betray as mere appearance the repentance he has been so concerned to enact. His last request reveals that this David still operates within the train of lust; the order of Love and divine justice is beyond him, though he wishes to subordinate it to contract, to the needs of his power. In asking the final favor, David condemns himself and dispels the ambiguity of his presentation by suggesting his necessary separation from the spiritual content of his prayer.

The final unmasking necessitates a revision in our reading of the narrative not only to accommodate an unregenerate David but also to accommodate that knowledge to our understanding of the spiritual issues of the psalm sequence. The narrator may expose David's "case," but in order to make his case against David, the narrator mimics him; he too appropriates the rhetoric of prayer. The historical context of the *Paraphrase* suggests that the narrator's case against David is, in fact, Wyatt's case against Henry VIII. The association of Henry's lust with David's is obvious; perhaps more important to Wyatt's poem is the Act of Supremacy (1534) in which Henry claimed absolute spiritual and temporal jurisdiction and in protest of which More and Fisher lost their lives. It is no accident that the narrator's "I" emerges by calling out Uriah's name: that murder can be analogized to any number of incidents in which servants or soldiers of the English king went to their deaths in the interest of achieving Henry's desire or protecting his power. Wyatt suggests but does not draw those analogies. The allusion to David's sin of measurement in the fifth link similarly points toward, but does not draw, the analogy to Henry's appropriation of ecclesiastical revenues. The biblical incident is telling. To stop the plague that God has visited on the kingdom in punishment of David's sin, the prophet Gad tells David that he must build an altar on Araunah the Jebusite's threshing floor. Araunah offers to give David the threshing floor as well as sacrificial oxen, but David refuses the gift, saying, "Nay, but surely I will buy it of thee at a price, neither will I offer burnt offerings unto the Lord my God of that which doth cost me nothing" (2 Samuel 24:24). Though Henry's appropriation of ecclesiastical revenues, managed by Cromwell, included payoffs to the church functionaries who ceded those revenues to him, such moneys were not for purchase, but to facilitate appropriation. Working under the patronage of Cromwell, Wyatt was fully implicated in Henry's actions, as his narrator is in David's. The poem's allusiveness does not depend on its date. The execution of More and Fisher (1535) provides a basis for a critique of Henry's power moves, and emotional impetus (as well as sympathy for the Uriah position) can be seen in the execution of Anne Boleyn (1536) if we accept the tradition of Wyatt's involvement with her, but it is in the period between Boleyn's execution and Cromwell's (1540) that the extent of Henry's intention to appropriate religious power and wealth becomes obvious to an observer of courtly affairs. Luther's comment after the executions in 1540 offers an explicit judgment: "Junker Heintz will be God and does whatever he lusts."[15]

The historical context clarifies several aspects of the relation between the narrator and David. First, the narrator's appropriation of the rhetoric of prayer is a reappropriation, an attempt to take back what has been compromised by David's appropriation. Yet the penitential anguish present in the psalmic paraphrase registers the problem of complicity, both the possibility that the narrator also has no claim to spiritual authority or legitimacy and the possibility that his situation is a penitential one. The narrator manipulates his representation of David in order to expose the temporal and spiritual issues caught up in David's position. Yet the arrogant position of the narrator is also questioned, and so is that of the poet, for whom the narrator is a surrogate. Wyatt destabilizes both the narrator and David in order to expose the temporal, spiritual, and poetic issues that the figuration of David allows. In order to trace the poet's effort, we must return to the poem.

Many of the passages I have discussed in setting out the political concerns of the poem can also be read in terms of their poetic concerns. The willfulness shared by David and the narrator is also the poet's as he sets out the claim of his song. David's act of measuring, for example, alludes to the rendering of the psalms in English verse as well as to the biblical story. The ongoing tension between alternate readings invests the poem with its sense of poetic and moral urgency. The figure of David is split across the fault line that Surrey exposed: on the one side, there is a David valorized by the traditional idealization and by Wyatt's desire for sacred song, and, on the other, a negative David whose story testifies to Wyatt's anxious recognition that his desire cannot find fulfillment. In the third narrative link, the poet calls particular attention to the representation of David: "A marble image carved of singular reverence / Carved in the rock with eyes and hands on high, / Made as by craft to plain, to sob, to sigh" (306–8). This particular figure evokes one in Dante's *Purgatorio,* another David in another penitential context. The allusion to Dante's David has a double resonance. First, as in Aretino's poem, it inscribes the poet's activity within the poem by recalling that David is a figure for the poet. But Aretino's "man de l'arte" becomes Wyatt's "made as by craft." "Craft" indicates the problematic nature of Wyatt's effort: the word carries the possibility of deceit even as the lines make a poetic as well as a sacred claim for the songs. As we have seen, David craftily subverts the psalms in order to gain material ends, and the narrator craftily subverts David in the hope of separating the songs from their tainted use. Dante's David informs Wyatt's and will allow us to understand not only the poet's relation to his figure but also, finally, the place of his poem.

In *Purgatorio* 10, Dante sees David carved in a marble frieze:[16]

> Lì precedeva al benedetto vaso
> trescando alzato, l'umile salmista,
> e più e men che re era in quel caso.
> Di contra, effigïata ad una vista

> d'un gran palazzo, Micòl ammirava
> Sì come donna dispettosa e trista.
> (*Purgatorio* 10.64–69)

(There the humble psalmist went before the blessed vessel girt up and dancing, and that time he was both more and less than king; opposite, figured at the window of a great palace, Michal looked on, like a woman vexed and scornful.)

This David is an exemplary figure in the first and weightiest of Purgatory's circles, that which purges pride. He is portrayed as he brings the ark of the covenant into Jerusalem, the central figure in a representation of the ark narrative of 2 Samuel. As Dante presents the frieze, the ark comes first:

> Era intagliato lì nel marmo stesso
> lo carro e' buoi traendo l'arca santa
> per che si teme officio non commesso.
> (*Purgatorio* 10.55–57)

(There, carved in the same marble, were the cart and the oxen drawing the sacred ark on account of which men fear an office not committed to them.)

The allusion to Uzzah, struck by God for his presumption in touching the ark when the oxen pulling the cart stumbled (2 Samuel 6–7), reminds us that David had recently been impressed by God's power. He dances before "the sacred ark on account of which men fear an office not committed to them" in order to demonstrate his subordination and devotion to God. The frieze ends with the contemptuous Michal, reminding us of David's defense of his action in 2 Samuel 6:21–22: "It was done before the Lord which chose me before thy father, and before all his house, to appoint me ruler over the people of the Lord, over Israel: therefore will I play before the Lord and I will yet be more vile than this and will be base in mine own sight; and of the maidservants which thou hast spoken of, of them shall I be had in honor." These are words of a good king, one who knows his power is the gift of and subject to a higher authority. They are also the words of a good king, one who knows that his power and effect will be enhanced if he presents himself in devout subordinate relation to the universal law and power of the God of the covenant. David accompanies the ark into Jerusalem in awe of God's power and conscious of his own as well as their necessary differentiation. The ark narrative precedes the adultery with Bathsheba in 2 Samuel; David does not yet presume, though Michal's angry presence recalls the difficulties of David's reign. Dante also marks the rest of his biblical story by the curt description "that time [quel caso] he was both more and less than a king." Dante's narrative presents only "quel caso" displayed in the frieze; in *Purgatorio*, Dante provides the fixed positive exemplum lacking in Wyatt's narrative.

The figure of David in the center of the frieze is also the center of Dante's rendition of David's story. He is mentioned twice before and twice after the circle of pride, but nowhere else is his biblical story represented. Dante's first reference to David (*Inferno* 4.58) announces unequivocally that he was saved: Christ took "King David, of Israel" when he harrowed hell. Near the end of the *Inferno*, David's biblical story surfaces in Bertran de Born's explanation of his treachery: "I made rebellion between the father and the son; Achitophel did no worse for Absolom and David with his wicked goadings" (28.136–37). Here David is presented as the victim of another's evil design, not the perpetrator of his own. In fact, David's sin and his culpability in the losses to himself and his people is suppressed in Dante's narrative until the final reference to him. Only when David is recalled among the community of the Celestial Rose does the sin surface: "the singer, who, in grief for his sin, cried, 'Miserere Mei'" (*Paradiso* 32.11–12). The sin is excluded until the penitential efficacy of the psalms can testify to David's worthiness. Dante's use of the figure, in accord with the extrabiblical development of David's story, provides concrete evidence of his merit. But in Dante's rendition of David's story, the argument for his merit arises first from the ark narrative, from his kingly devotion.

The frieze depicting David dancing before the ark is the center of the three friezes which, as a group, are framed by two comments addressing the nature of artistic representation. In the fiction of *Purgatorio* 10, God figures David as an exemplar of perfect worship and as an example of perfect art. Upon seeing the carvings, Dante tells us they were "such that not only Polycletus but nature would be put to shame there" ("esser di marmo candido e adorno / d'intagli sì che non pur Policleto, / ma la natura lì avrebbe scorno" [30–33]). In the narrative of the circle of pride, Dante uses the figure of David, a paradoxical exemplar of humility, to thematize the status of Dante's own art, as the comment closing the frieze indicates:

> Colui che mai non vide cosa nova
> produsse eso visibile parlare
> novello a noi perchè qui non si trova.
> (*Purgatorio* 10.94–96)

(He for whose sight nothing was ever new wrought this visible speech, new to us because it is not found here.)

The only "visible speech" "here" is Dante's own text. The figure of David at the center of the center panel of this carefully framed ekphrasis suggests an analogy between Dante and David that might be stated as follows: Dante is a good artist in the same double manner that David is a good king: he knows his art is less than God's, and he knows his art will be enhanced if he presents it in relation to the creative power of God.

In *Paradiso* 20, David "shines in the middle for pupil" of the eyes of the eagle of Divine Justice. The eagle says of David to Dante:

> Colui che luce in mezzo per pupilla,
> fu il cantor dello Spirito Santo,
> che l'arca traslatò di villa in villa:
> ora conosce il merto del suo canto,
> in quanto effecto fu del suo consiglio,
> per lo renumerar ch'è altrettanto.
> (*Paradiso* 20.37–42)

(He that shines in the middle for pupil was the singer of the Holy Ghost, who carried the ark from house to house; now he knows the merit of his song so far as it was the fruit of his own counsel, by the reward that is proportioned to it.)

Here David is refigured as an exemplar of the poet. His historical existence is of no importance in Paradise; rather Dante describes the value of poetic activity and particularly the importance of the poet in creating that value. Dante redeems David by separating him from most of the events of his temporal existence and making him into a figure of the poet, by grace of God. When Dante acknowledges the singer of "Miserere Mei," he not only makes David an exemplary penitent and a figure of the transcendent power of human artistic activity, he also recalls the opening of his poem, his cry as Vergil appears in the desert: "Miserere di me" (*Inferno* 1.65). Both David's and Dante's songs are valorized by the divine order, the representation of which has been the project of Dante's poem. The final reference to David completes a circular defense of the poet's position.

In Dante's poem, David's temporal authority is explicitly subordinate to his devotion. He dances before the ark he fears to touch because it embodies the spiritual authority of God. He is exemplary because his devotion is transformed into sacred song, but he acquires that status and spiritual authority only after his temporal existence is finished: "*now he knows* the merit of his song." While Dante redeems the figure of David in accord with tradition, he also indicates the problematic nature of the figure by defensively (and aggressively) marking the redemption. Dante meets the difficulty of reconciling David's biblical story to his reputation as the psalmist by disassociating David from those events usually associated with the psalms and foregrounding his kingly devotion; he joins the biblical story to David's idealization as the singer of sacred song so that no seams are visible, no dissonance evident. At the same time, he makes David an example of humility in the place of pride; David's presumption surfaces only indirectly in order that Dante may acknowledge his own. Dante's song, like David's, is the fruit of his own counsel, he rewrites David's story from the vantage of a Christian re-demptive history. From that vantage the events of David's story in the books of Samuel are not central except insofar as they prefigure Christ's redemption. For Dante, David's biblical story is important because his kingly devotion in the ark narrative adumbrates Dante's desire for a unified religious and political *imperium,* but his real interest is in David as a poet. Writing after the Redemption, unlike David, Dante knows the value of his song: it inscribes his redemption.

Wyatt's *Paraphrase* also makes David's song the fruit of his own counsel, but his own counsel is finally revealed to be at odds with his song. When Wyatt separates the princely David from the authority of his song, he joins Dante in the insistence that temporal concerns be subject to spiritual authority, but he cannot redeem the figure of David, who functions in his poem as an object lesson in the unrepentant transgression of the limits of princely power. Like Dante, Wyatt is acutely conscious of the contradictions within the received figure of David; unlike Dante, he does not suppress them. While Wyatt's poem recalls and depends on the shift that Dante traces in the *Divine Comedy* from David the king to David the poet, his alteration of Aretino's "man de l'arte" to his own "made as by craft" suggests a critique of Dante's, and incidentally Aretino's, use of the figure. Both the dependence and the critique can be seen in Wyatt's paraphrase of Psalm 102.

The penitential anxiety that should be David's is the poet's, and in its expression the poet speaks for the community of which he would be a member, the community of Zion. But he asserts neither the positive existence of the community nor his membership. In the paraphrase of Psalm 102, Zion is defined as "the people that live under thy law" (584), terms that recall the opening of the poem:

> In this Zion his holy name to stand
> And in Jerusalem his lauds, lasting ay,
> When in one church the people of the land
> And realms been gathered to serve, to laud, to pray
> The Lord above so just and merciful.
>
> (607–11)

The poet not only doubts his membership ("But to this sembly running in the way / My strength faileth to reach it at the full" [12–13]), he indicates that the community is also a matter of doubt, desire, and prayer:

> The greatest comfort I can pretend
> Is that the children of my servants dear,
> That in thy word are got, shall without end
> Before thy face be stablished all in fere.
>
> (628–31)

The theological bases of this doubt are quintessentially Protestant: only out of a profound anxiety is faith born. But Wyatt's description of the desired community, "in one church," indicates the gap between Zion and the England in which he writes and suggests that the theological issues ought not be divided among partisan positions. When Wyatt imagines the community of Zion "before thy face be stablished all in fere," he takes his cue not from any of the Protestant translations of the Psalms but from Dante's vision in *Paradiso*.[17] Dante saw the face of God, he tells us, "painted with our likeness." He also witnesses the community of the saved and notes that not many seats remain for new members. Wyatt's "before thy face be stablished all in fere" is not a vision but a stated hope, "the greatest comfort I can pretend." "Fere" is a pun, playing on the archaic meaning of "company" and the modern meaning of "fear." "Face" recalls Dante's vision, while "fere" at once recalls the community of the celestial rose and the possibility that no seats remain. For Dante, spiritual authority is clear: he is witness to the community of the saved, and his David is among them. Dante's clarity is an act of will, a presumption he marks by his strategic use of the figure of David. For Wyatt, spiritual authority is suspended, as it were, between David's attempt to subordinate it to his temporal interests and the narrator's attempt to reclaim its separateness and its transcendent relation to the temporal world. Wyatt does not presume; he does not bear witness to the community of the saved. He bears witness instead to a profound and anxious concern that a place be found for his song. In so doing, he at once aligns himself with Dante's poetic project and distances himself from it. He too wishes to sing a sacred song, but his song is not triumphant, as Dante's is. Rather, by creating the tension in his poem between the narrator and David or, put alternately, between the narrative, which works to dislodge David, and the psalm sequence, which works to redeem David, he suggests that redemption cannot be inscribed except by a willful act that refuses to acknowledge the complicity of temporal desire in an utterance that wishes to be spiritually pure. We may retrospectively identify Wyatt's concerns as Protestant, but we must also acknowledge their historicity. Wyatt's strategic use of the figure marks a crisis, not a solution. Here again, the comparison to Dante is instructive: it is in Wyatt's poetic interest to destabilize the figure of David and to reveal the issues behind its putative coherence. To use David as Dante did, as a figure for a poetic task conceived within a (desired) redemptive history is to use David's idealization as a touchstone for one's own. To destabilize David is to raise the questions that were once David's and to show that they are David's no longer. In Wyatt's poem the pointing toward political allegory reveals that David's example can be enacted in bad faith, his voice assumed for interested purposes. What is true for the princely David is also true for the singer-self of the psalms. The possibility of bad faith results in the loss of the idealized figure; it necessitates a severance of the figural connection between David and the psalmic voice. If the identity between David and the psalmic voice enabled the inscription of a redemptive history (for the Church Fathers as for Dante), then the disjunction ironizes the figural interpretation that underwrites that redemptive history. David may have once sinned, sung his penitence, and even thereby earned his redemption, but that concrete event does not, in the logic of Wyatt's poem, implicate the future.

The irony resulting from Wyatt's dislocation of David returns the issues of his poem to their own history; the voice that ends the *Paraphrase* is a voice without a figure, a voice that knows only the urgency of its own problematic historical position. In using the psalmic voice as his ground, Wyatt claims the position of poet as sacred singer, as the one who can call kings to account, counsel kingdoms away from their errors, and articulate the temporal and spiritual desires of a people as well as his own. We have returned to the issues that Surrey identified in the opening stanzas of his sonnet. Yet we would have to conclude that Surrey's invocation of the Homeric precedent was a consoling fantasy; Wyatt's poem has not been accorded the place Surrey suggests it ought to have. Its publication in 1549, for "Christians purchace" ("very pleasaunt & profetable to the godly reader") removed it from the historical and courtly circumstances of its production and assigned it to the realm of devotional verse.[18] For Wyatt, however, there can be no spiritually pure, simply devotional song, only a song aware of its implication in the temporal world. The poet is also, finally, unregenerate.

Notes

Reprinted from *Texas Studies in Language and Literature* 30:3 (1988), by permission of the author and the University of Texas Press.

I am indebted to Jonathan Crewe, Elizabeth Hanson, Joseph Harrison, and Karen Sanchez-Eppler for their comments on this essay.

1. Surrey's poem appears as a preface to the *Paraphrase* in the Egerton manuscript (London, British Library, MS. Egerton 2711); the *Paraphrase* is in Wyatt's hand, together with autograph revisions. For a brief account of the Egerton manuscript, see Muir and Thomson (n. 2, below), xii. I have used the text of Surrey's poem found in *Wyatt: The Critical Heritage,* ed. Patricia Thomson (London: Routledge and Kegan Paul, 1974), 28.

2. Aretino's poem is *I Sette Salmi de la Penitentia di David* (1534). Two modern editions of Wyatt's poems contain bibliographic information and offer passages from Aretino's poem in their commentary: *Collected Poems of Sir Thomas Wyatt,* ed. Kenneth Muir and Patricia Thomson (Liverpool: Liverpool University Press, 1969; hereafter cited as Muir and Thomson); and *Sir Thomas Wyatt: The Complete Poems,* ed. R. A. Rebholz (New Haven: Yale University Press, 1981). My citations from the *Paraphrase* are from the Rebholz edition. The Muir and Thomson edition includes the Italian original of each narrative prologue. Most of the cruxes in my reading of the *Paraphrase* involve passages in which Wyatt departs, often dramatically, from Aretino's text. Nevertheless, my reading of the *Paraphrase* suggests that a critical reexamination of Aretino's text might yield equally interesting, though different, results.

3. Muir and Thomson annotate this passage as a reference to the death of the first child (as an infant; see 2 Samuel 12:14–19). Rebholz correctly refers the lines to Absalom's rebellion: the use of "pursues" and "pursuit" does not allow otherwise.

4. See below, n. 18.

5. Stephen Greenblatt, *Renaissance Self-Fashioning: From More to Shakespeare* (Chicago: University of Chicago Press, 1980), 117 and 126. Further citations are included parenthetically in the text.

6. H. A. Mason, *Humanism and Poetry in the Early Tudor Period* (London: Routledge and Kegan Paul, 1959), 202–21, esp. 209.

7. Robert G. Twombly, "Wyatt's Paraphrase of the Penitential Psalms of David," *Texas Studies in Language and Literature* 12 (1970), 346–80, esp. 346.

8. More and Fisher were executed in 1535, Boleyn in 1536, and Cromwell in 1540. Cromwell's execution was followed two days later by that of three Lutherans and three Catholics, signaling then as it does now that any opinion

on religious authority contrary to the royal opinion could be fatal. See James Kelsey McMonica, *English Humanists and Reformation Politics* (Oxford: Oxford University Press, 1965), esp. 106–99.

9. Pole published an opinion against the royal supremacy, *Pro ecclesiasticae unitatis defensione,* in 1536. See McMonica for a discussion of his career. See *Life and Letters of Sir Thomas Wyatt,* ed. Kenneth Muir (Liverpool: Liverpool University Press, 1963). The citations from Wyatt's defense are from Muir's text, pages 195–96 and 208 respectively.

10. See the commentary in Muir and Thomson as well as Rebholz for Wyatt's sources. Twombly's discussion of Wyatt's use of his sources is particularly acute. For Wyatt's diplomatic work, see *Life and Letters.* For a general discussion of Renaissance diplomacy, see Garrett Mattingly, *Renaissance Diplomacy* (Baltimore: Penguin Books, 1964).

11. See, for example, the essays collected in *The David Myth in Western Literature,* ed. Raymond Jean Frontain and Jan Wojcik (West Lafayette: Purdue University Press, 1980).

12. David's story begins at 1 Samuel 16 and ends at 1 Kings 2. Nathan's prophecies are contained in 2 Samuel 12:11–14; he specifies only the death of the first child. The story of Absalom, beginning with Ammon's incest with Tamar and ending with Absalom's death, is considered to be the fulfillment of Nathan's general prophecy: "Your family shall never again rest from the sword. I will bring trouble upon you from within your own family." For general purposes of citation, I have used the Authorized Version (1611). In the case of psalmic material, I have checked the Authorized Version against the Coverdale Bible (1535) and the Great Bible (1539) as well as the commentary in Muir and Thomson and Rebholz.

13. See *OED,* rebate, v 1. The use of "rebate" as a hawking term is the oldest use cited in the *OED.*

14. As Rebholz notes in his commentary on l. 483, Wyatt originally used "restore," as did all of his sources, and then revised it to "render."

15. Among those executed following Cromwell was the Lutheran preacher Robert Barnes, who had been prominent in Henry's negotiations with Wittenburg. Luther's comment is quoted by J. J. Scarisbrick in his biography of Henry (*Henry VIII* [Berkeley and Los Angeles: University of California Press, 1968], 526) from the *Letters and Papers, Foreign and Domestic, of the Reign of Henry VIII,* ed. John Sherren Brewer, James Gairdner, and Robert Henry Brodie, 21 vols. (1862–1910; reprint, London: HMSO, 1920), vol. 16 (1540–41), 106.

16. All citations of the *Divine Comedy* are from the edition and translation by John Sinclair (Oxford: Oxford University Press, 1970).

17. Both the Coverdale Bible and the Great Bible have "in thy sight." The Authorized Version has simply "before thee."

18. The *Paraphrase* was the first of Wyatt's poems to appear in print. For further information and the text of the dedicatory epistle, see Muir and Thomson, xviii and xix. The promise of profit to the godly reader appears on the title page. The printed version emphasizes the boundary between the narrative and

the psalms not only by providing the Vulgate titles to each of the psalms (which had been entered in the Egerton manuscript as well), but also by labeling each prologue as belonging to "the auctor."

Wyatt's Unlikely Likenesses: Or, Has the Lady Read Petrarch?

BARBARA L. ESTRIN

Desire does not speak. It does violence to the order of utterance.
— Jean-François Lyotard,
"The Dream Work Does Not Think"

Judith Butler locates "gender trouble" in the destabilizing, parodic, decentering force of the woman that promotes a "radical critique of the categories of [cultural] identity."[1] *Genre* trouble, the subversions of society, sexuality, and form inherent to the lyric, might similarly be connected to the critical presence of the woman in certain poems that critique the hierarchical binarisms of the Petrarchan dyad. In its challenge to the Italianate conventions so appealing to Henrician England, Wyatt's "They flee from me" is such a pivotal poem. In this text, the sexually aggressive and verbally threatening woman of the second stanza amplifies the "characteristic nervousness"[2] critics have noted about Petrarch into the serious angst of impasse. The woman's linguistic powers unseat the poet's confidence in his ability to make the comparisons that engender poetry. Her sexual comparisons unravel the lover's confidence in his ability to retain the physical excitement that sustains relationships. If readers know one Wyatt poem, they know this one. If readers remember one Henrician woman, they continue to be both titillated and repelled by this one. Her effect on Wyatt himself is devastating. Her "trouble" within the poem parodies the poetic process and unsettles the self Wyatt invents. In the last lines, she completely depletes his sexual and verbal energy. She attacks. He withdraws. She is articulate. He babbles. The poem ends in a bullying and vague threat figured by the poet's inability to find the words to say or the form to express his rage: "I would fain know what she doth deserve."

Her "trouble" outside the poem seems to serve as catalytic agent to Wyatt's reluctant Petrarchism. In his translations, Wyatt knows exactly what to do—giving Laura less than she "deserves" by withholding Petrarchan idealization or by withdrawing from Petrarchan poetics altogether. If the woman of "They flee from me" upsets the lyric balance by imposing her real body on the imagined body of the poem, the retaliative Wyatt disrupts the balance by rendering either the sexual situation of some poems too graphic or the poetic occasion of still other alleged tributes too semiotic. When he issues a series of indictments against the threatening woman, as he does in the dark future of "My lute, awake" or the eviscerated past of "When first mine eyes" and "Process of time," Wyatt sets the idealized Laura into a body that might feel some of the poet's pain. When he projects a sequence of appropriations that write the woman out of the poem, as he does in the involuted craft and art of "Go, burning sighs," the self-sufficient answer of "What word is that" and the self-induced reproductivity of "Will ye see what wonders," Wyatt internalizes poetic energy and invents a mythology that renders creation exclusively male. In the first set of poems, Wyatt attempts to manipulate the imagined lady into malleability, offering the hope that, if she modifies the behavior he identifies, she might still be laurelized in future poems. In the second, he positions himself independently so that he can function without her entirely. But the woman of "They flee from me" instigates Wyatt's anti-Petrarchism even as the poems written in the shadow of her threat recast, in Henrician terms, the Petrarch he imitates.

When the woman of "They flee from me" mixes the vocabulary of desire with the desire for vocabulary, she links the semiotic occasion of the poem to its romantic setting. Her intrusion invades the chambers of the speaker's mind. The second stanza presents a rare occasion where the Henrician lady speaks. Her voice shatters the structures she interrogates:

> Thanked be fortune it hath been otherwise
> Twenty times better, but once in special,
> In thin array after a pleasant guise,
> When her loose gown from her shoulders did fall
> And she me caught in her arms long and small,
> Therewithal sweetly did me kiss
> And softly said, "Dear heart, how like you this?"
> (117)[3]

In its hints at physical, female, detail—the loose gown, the bare shoulders, the long, small arms, the sweetness—the poem fuses the visual and the tactile to arrive at the question which throws everything into confusion. What is the *this*? What is the woman showing? What is she telling? What is she exposing, what withholding? Confirming her sexual prowess in the likeness, the lady also insists on her verbal power to make likenesses. But does she defend her femaleness in that power or indict his maleness in the prowess? Is the kiss she mouths in the linguistic tactile *this* an inversion of the kissing vulva she exposes in the visually naked this? Is she saying with the inversion "I do with this what you do with words: create replicas?" Or does she mean the aggression she replicates in imitating him? Is her sexuality male? Or does her reproductive power as a woman lend her verbal primacy as well? Is she defending, or denying, her sex? Is she mimicking, or seizing, his power? As her deer/hart, "he" is "she." As his dear/heart, "she" is "he." Her question heightens the male fear of dissolving into the woman that inhibits sexual release by turning it into an anxiety of being replaced by the woman that cancels poetic discourse. As woman, she flaunts her procreative power, inverting vulva and mouth. As man, she flaunts her creative power, her "catching" a turn of phrase whose ambiguous enactment challenges male linguistic authority. The more the man dissolves physically in the satisfaction she promises, the more the lady—now watching him—is empowered linguistically by the description she withholds and empowered visually by the gaze she identifies. Though she exposes herself in her nakedness, she actually exposes him, her "how like you this" something he thinks is indeterminate and private but actually is something she knows and reveals. In identifying her resemblance to the man, she duplicates—and so halves—his power. In articulating the pleasure she gives to the man, she reads—and so doubles—his weakness.

Thomas Greene argues that "for males at any rate, the habit of transforming the object of desire and especially [the woman's] body into a symbol seems virtually irresistible."[4] But what happens when the symbol talks, declaring both her refusal to be what the man wants (the pin-up girl seductively—but conventionally—beckoning) and her insistence on representing what he represses (the pent-up poet who calls his sexual ambivalence the lady's conventional reluctance)? When she conflates power and pleasure, this woman repels the self she attracts. Her mirror objectifies and so names his narcissism, pulling the symbol of her body into the fact of his body and mixing the mysterious with the threatening in her *this*. If she has already mirrored him in act, she has only next to usurp him in word. Her use of her body as a metaphor (her resemblance to the poet in the likeness) and her use of her metaphor as a body (her tantalizing the poet with this) defines lyric anxiety as the extent to

222 / Barbara L. Estrin

which its sexuality obscures the difference between real and imagined power.

To Fredric Jameson's lament, "how will we ever learn not to confuse the penis as an organ of the body with the phallus as signifier,"[5] "They flee from me" gives Andrew Parker's answer: "the phallus cannot *not* be confused with the penis."[6] In "They flee from me," the body's intrusion is measured by the lady's inclusion of male desire in her female voice. Her power derives from her knowledge of the poet's overt, but private, actions, his intimate, and therefore vulnerable, thoughts. If she knows how to give the man pleasure, then she knows his tricks and weaknesses, her *this* a manifestation in promised act of a that still inchoate in thought. Her *this* says what he thinks without specifying it even as it promises release without giving it. Wyatt's excitability and vulnerability compete; his "likeness" hangs in suspension, achieved as imitation, deferred as pleasure, the lady's *this,* a retrospective accomplishment and delayed disclosure. In its visual specificity, the *this* threatens the man. She shows what he thinks. In its semiotic vagueness, the *this* undermines the poem; it veils—in tantalizing obscurity—what poems usually represent in concrete resemblances. Poems tell; the lady shows. Her question troubles and interferes with what should be an absolutely pleasurable moment.

Spenser describes Calidore's entrapment in *The Faerie Queene* (6.9.10) in terms of a similar suspension of male power. Calidore is "caught like the bird, which gazing still on others stands." Calidore's moment of sexual curiosity—his gazing in wonder—merges with the moment of his visual trap—his standing in impasse. Seen seeing, he becomes what he sees and something else. Caught as observer, he is left "standing" in desire—not moving toward fulfillment. Immobilized in what he objectifies, Calidore relinquishes agency. His visual pleasure becomes his emotional ineffectuality. Wyatt's "I" is similarly caught with his pants down. At the very juncture that he is most the viewer (watching the striptease), he discovers that he is most on show (teased by stripping). Wyatt's "she" privileges for herself the metamorphic power of release, promising Wyatt the very thing (in the anticipatory *this*) he most wants but compromising him (in the retrospective *this*) by revealing her power to catch and—hence—reflect him. She holds a mirror (in the likeness) the "I" wants both to deny and to watch. Her question, "how like you this," is anticipatory (referring to what she is about to do) and congratulatory (referring to what she has just done). The woman exults in her accomplished transference but withholds her final thrust.

Anticipating the "I'"s pleasure, her "this"—the mysteriously provocative something—comes from experiencing the "I"'s psyche—the transferable shared identity. As the "this" becomes retrospective, Wyatt's "she" emerges menacing;[7] if she knows the "I," then he has no privacy, nothing to withhold. Because she possesses what Terry Eagleton calls "the real object which signs designate,"[8] the woman of "They flee from me" almost gives what she keeps in reserve. Her *this* not yet a *that,* her phallus not yet a penis, she defines her power to deliver in terms of the man's desire for deliverance. Petrarch's elusive Daphne becomes his obvious Narcissus. When the woman enters the poet's chamber, she entertains the form of the poem. When she enters the poem's language, she unhinges its means of representation. Trapped in her assumption of his linguistic identity and by her knowledge of his sexual proclivities, the "I" is caught in her arms and wrought by her "hand." She has the words to inscribe him and the tool to release him. But at the same time that she is *like* the man in the mirror of her identity, she is *unlike* him in her refusal to be specific. Her *this* remains deliberately vague. She evades the precision of poetic representation and opens up the arena of speculative abstraction. Her question remains a question; its being is resistance.

In overturning the established hierarchies of gender, the woman of "They flee from me" threatens the balance the lyric struggles to maintain between the biology of sexuality and the semiotics of representation. Wyatt's reaction in other poems is to mythologize poetry, to pull it out of the realm of Petrarchan mutuality and even out of the realm of love: to make it all text and no context. Petrarch retaliates by giving, his "stance," as Michael McCanles maintains, "one of unremitting respect and idealization."[9] Wyatt retaliates by withholding. If the woman of "They flee from me" suspends the final act that would ensure the man's sexual release, the Wyatt who appears in other poems retracts the final art that would facilitate the lady's Petrarchan idealization. The process of deconstruction begins in the songs, proceeds through the poems where he demands a "no," and evolves into the vision of "Will ye see what wonders." The phoenix image of "Will ye see what wonders" internalizes the inspirational flame[10] and mythologizes the body. It frees the "I," as it will Milton's Samson, from the burden of the woman who, in the doubling of likeness, knows too much. Wyatt's appropriation of the woman in the hermaphroditic emergence of "Will ye see what wonders" seems a logical consequence of his distortion of the woman in his Petrarchan songs, his immolation of the woman in "Process of time" and "Go, burning sighs," and his excision of the woman in a series of poems where he calls *her* "no" *his* answer. Reforming one side or another of the Petrarchan equation offers Wyatt myriad possibilities for such revisions. What if he stops the song, as he does in "My lute, awake," and imposes his Petrarch on her? What if he stops memory, as he does in "When first mine eyes," to shift the indifferent Laura on to his undifferentiating self?

In "My lute, awake," Wyatt withholds the signification through which the idealized "you" is materialized in the first place. When he urges the lute to be *still* at the end of the first and last stanzas, he points in the direction of his intention to cut short the supply of Petrarchan praise. His "stilling" command enjoins the instrument both to continue a previously held position and to remain silent. Jonathan Crewe defines the poem's deliberately self-defeating syntax: "The poem not only keeps on repeating its own wish to end, but the desire to end is paradoxically what causes the poem to start in the first place."[11] The poem perpetuates its own negations and, in the lute's distilled image, finds an expression for the deadening impact of love. The condition of stillness depends on the meaning of "I have done." In the first stanza, the speaker urges the lute to retain its past resonances and repeat all that he has "done" (experienced) in the name of love:

> My lute, awake! Perform the last
> Labour that thou and I shall waste,
> And end that I have now begun;
> For when this song is sung and past,
> My lute, be still for I have done.
>
> (144)

At the conclusion of the poem, he urges it to be quiet because he has "done" (outlived) the name of lover. There is a third dimension to the equation between stillness and experience that transfers the burden to the woman who will herself both bear the sting of the poet's refrain and sing the "burden" of her own misery. The poet refrains from singing at the very moment the woman sings the refrain, the "stillness" of his silence instilled by her lapsing into imagined song.

If the plaint is the instrument for registering the absence in desire (the wish and want of Petrarchan stasis), to end the complaint is to proclaim the absence of desire (the quieting of the Petrarchan lover). The "stillness" suggests a remembered vacant past and an anticipated future silence. At the very moment the woman becomes the man, the "I" ceases to be the self who sings the song. His revenge is to make her what he was so that he can be something else. In stanza 6, the lady will inherit the man's emptiness:

May chance thee lie withered and old
The winter nights that are so cold,
Plaining in vain unto the moon.
Thy wishes then dare not be told.
Care then who list for I have done.

And then may chance thee to repent
The time that thou hast lost and spent
To cause thy lovers sigh and swoon.
Then shalt thou know beauty but lent
And wish and want as I have done.

(145)

Her future will repeat his history as it relates to her unavailability. When she lives his past, she will, like the lute to the "I," reflect the state of absence the "I" already hollowed out (wishing and wanting) and feel the effects of rejection she had previously issued forth (lost and spent). When she reaches into the hollow, she enters the abyss. The "I" multiplies her punishment by making her future his past. She sees her past for what it was and lives his past as what he suffered. Her punishment is both to repent her past and to become her own victim.

If, in the future, she feels what he is feeling now, then she will understand the unrequited desire (wish and want) that provokes swooning songs and the knowledge that the songs come to nothing (are in "vain"). In the premature old age the "I" has invented for her, she is robbed of her spoils (denied his songs because he has stopped singing) and despoiled (denied the self he defined for her). She is left with both the barrenness of her unsung self and the nothingness of his philosophical awareness. No longer the idealized and fully formed beloved of the song, she instead acquires the deprived and always hollowed-out psyche of the lover. As the "you" is personalized, she is literally depersonalized, transplanted unto the dying body of the "I" and therefore denied both the exalted prominence of his idealization and the comforting music of his expressiveness. Spoiled, she is besmirched by his reality.

Her third emergence, however, provides yet another torture. When the "I" announces, as he does in the three last words of each stanza, "I have done," he speaks both to his past experience and his present escape. "Done," he is dead to the self she must continue to live. Finally, his lute can be "still" in both senses. As *his* lute, it is silent; now that "she" is "he," it becomes hers, playing out the past as a sepulchral chorus and endlessly repeating the "wishing and wanting" the speaker has transferred to the lady. Even in "stillness" (quiet), the lute represents the love situation; it is the abandoned instrument of love, from which the lover, having conferred his identity on the lady and hers on the instrument, is released. *His* lute can rest, since her lute will stand—still—as a reminder of the lady's cruelty. In "Ma Jolie," and in the endless Petrarchan collages Picasso and Braque invented for cubism, the lady appears as Wyatt's lute. The male instrument emerges the woman's "still" life, her being represented as the projection of lapsed male desire. Her image contracted to the form she enables the "I" to manipulate, the woman assumes his phallus, at the moment when it remains—in stillness—a representation of lost desire. In "My lute, awake," as in "She sat and sewed" (another poem where Wyatt projects his poetic and sexual ambivalence onto the woman), the lady is meant to feel "if pricking were so good in deed" (92). Through the male tool she acquires, she repeats (in stilling song) the history of male pain. Like the colorless modernist cubes, her gray, aged, image reflects—in its physical attenuation—the poet's presently depressed emptiness. In its stillness, the lute is sterile, the lady's reproductive potential remanded to the instrument's wooden immobility. Wyatt triply spoils the woman: first, he effaces her idealized self; then he cancels her maternal self; finally, in stillness, he dries up her desiring self. The lute's repetitions are hollow, its song having no future potential. Rendering the dead end of Petrarchism as the woman's future, the Wyatt of "My lute, awake" perpetuates the death wish of its own distillations.

If "My lute, awake" cancels the future, "When first mine eyes" annihilates the past and thereby reverses Petrarch's revitalization of history. As Petrarch celebrates the feelings of love's first assault by retracing the steps of the beloved and transplanting Laura's body everywhere, Wyatt's "I" begins by wishing away the body, sucking the earless other of "My lute, awake" into the deaf self, decorporealizing where Petrarch *in*corporates. The body that felt the pain washes away:

> And when in mind I did consent
> To follow this my fancy's will
> And when my heart did first relent
> To taste such bait my life to spill
> I would my heart had been as thine
> Or else thy heart had been as mine.
>
> (140)

The heart exchange the "I" proposes decomposes the self to create a scenario that re-creates the original love situation. Such a transposition repeats, without changing it, the nothing that was. "My lute, awake" is about the demise of the Petrarchan lover. When the "I" stops singing, his complex of feelings is sustained by the woman who, in becoming him, retains his desperation. "When first mine eyes" is about the beginning of love viewed from that sour end; when the "I" stops singing here, all feeling disappears. In following fancy, he tastes the bait that "spills" his life. In Shakespeare's Sonnet 129, the swallowed bait of sexual consummation drives the taster mad. Here, the bait is tasted but never consumed. It consumes the speaker. The stillness of "My lute, awake"'s immobility—stasis prolonged—reverts to a spilling—looseness dissolved—here. "My lute" turns the woman into an instrument that records pain in *still life*. "When first mine eyes" creates a vacuum that is numb to pain and therefore speaks of *no life*. As he opens his self to love, the poet actually ejects his inner self, a loss which, in the process of the poem, he attempts to generalize by wishing away the Petrarchan organs (eyes and ears) that perceived the beloved and the Petrarchan instruments that recorded the love (lips and tongue):

> I would as then I had been free
> From ears to hear and eyes to see.
>
> I would my lips and tongue also
> Had then been dumb, no deal to go.
> (140)

The "I" does to himself what he wishes for the beloved in the vindictive future of "My lute, awake." First, he presides over his own dismemberment. He commands his dissolution and so does away with the body. Then he transfers the pain he felt to the lady, testifying to the waste that was by calling its initiation a spilling, an outpouring that cannot be returned in the clarity of metaphor.

"My lute, awake" turns the instrument of love into a reminder of death. "When first mine eyes" turns organs of love (the senses) into origins of absence (senselessness). "My lute, awake" retains feelings and so consolidates pain. "When first mine eyes" dispels feeling and celebrates nothingness:

> And when my hands have handled aught
> That thee hath kept in memory
> And when my feet have gone and sought
> To find and get thy company,
> I would each hand a foot had been
> And I each foot a hand had seen.
> (140)

Wishing away the elements of poetry (the imagistic *hand* of invention, the musical *foot* of meter), Wyatt washes away the song which immortalized ("kept in memory") the lady. If hand becomes foot, the poem is all music. If foot becomes hand, music dissolves altogether. In the first case, the excess robs the poem of its body. It ceases to be plastic. In the second case, the poem is deprived of its movement. It ceases to commemorate because, without the rhythmic element, it goes nowhere in memory. What for Petrarch is a change from one solid form to another—a metamorphosis—becomes in Wyatt simply a return to formlessness—an annihilation. The spoiling of "My lute, awake" cancels future songs. The spilling of "When first mine eyes" repudiates songs already sung. They evaporate, having neither form to record them nor body to receive them. What is articulated in the sublimated Laura of Petrarchan memory vanishes in the hazy past of Wyatt's undifferentiated waste.

In these poems, Wyatt cancels the idealized Laura of the Petrarchan dyad and replaces her with: (1) his instrument in "My lute, awake"; and (2) his vacant history in "When first mine eyes." In other poems, Wyatt sets to work on Petrarch. First, he turns him into the ferocious and therefore unpoetic woman in "Process of time." Then, he silences him in the new poetic of "Go, burning sighs." In "They flee from me," the physical violence of the woman's takeover mimics male aggression even as it anticipates male pleasure. When Wyatt imitates the woman in "Process of time," the pleasure is in breaking bounds not in encircling them, the imitation an excess of violence not a containment or return of it. The "scant" help of the lady's denial revokes the "scanning" life of the poem. Wyatt begins "Process of time" where Petrarch concludes in *Rime sparse* 265: "I live only on hope, remembering that I have seen a little water by always trying finally wear away marble and solid rock: there is no heart so hard that by weeping, praying loving, it may not sometime be moved, no will so cold that it cannot be warmed."[12]

Working within contraries, Petrarch posits a process that lends him hope. If nature can change art (rain soften marble), then art (weeping, praying, loving) can soften nature (move hard hearts, warm cold wills). Like the steady stream of rain, the steady flow of the Petrarchan arsenal (weeping, praying, loving) will work. Petrarch keeps producing poems in order to "soften" Laura's resistance. Wyatt's revenge in "Process of time" is to cease being the poet the Petrarchan tradition has lead the imagined lady to expect. When he establishes a philosophical equivalent to her psychological ferocity, he produces a poem the lady would rather not get. The revenge follows two stages. In stanza 2, he accuses her of upsetting the Petrarchan balance in her pretence. In stanza 6, he moves with her out of the Petrarchan arena and pits his exaggerated vindictiveness against her excessive bestiality. Outside the frame of Petrarchan gentility and gentleness, "he" becomes "she." Beginning with a Petrarchan premise, the "I" undermines the purpose of Petrarchan persuasion on which it is based. In stanza 2, the lady seems too persuaded (already where Petrarch would have Laura, already tender); in stanza 6, she is unpersuadable, so monstrous and unnatural that art is pointless. "Process of time" violates the Petrarchan patience it seems (in the opening imitation of Petrarch and subsequent allusions to Isaiah) to be rigorously following. In his "seeming," Wyatt matches the lady's pretence. In his abandonment of art, he avenges her unnaturalness. In both sections of the poem, he undermines her expectations and thereby retracts the poetic spoils his opening pretends to deliver.

Starting with the Petrarchan assumption, Wyatt heightens its sexuality. He stiffens the soft water into the phallus that pierces the marble:

> Process of time worketh such wonder
> That water which is of kind so soft
> Doth pierce the marble stone asunder
> By little drops falling from aloft.
>
> (136)

Like *Canterbury*-Chaucer's gentle showers and *Merchant*-Portia's forgiving cloudbursts, Wyatt's rain starts the natural growth cycle that depends on making different qualities similar (water softening marble)[13] and similar qualities multiple (water inseminating the earth). Poetic power is thereby linked to procreative power, as rain prepares the earth for what Chaucer calls "engenderings." To render likenesses is to be engaged in the poetic process, a process Wyatt seems to enter in the act of translation. Moreover, in speaking of working wonders, the "I" situates the poetic act in the natural order of the universe, which will evolve into the supernatural era of biblical revelation. In its repetitious invocations, his rhetoric alludes to the Christian millennium and further heightens the imagined lady's expectations. The persuasion of the poetic word anticipates the realization of the biblical promise where opposites merge in a union of understanding:

> And it shall come to pass that before they call, I will answer;
> And while they are yet speaking, I will hear
> (Isaiah 65:24, AV)

The constant repetition of "it shall come to pass" in the biblical sequence parallels the "process of time" in Wyatt's poem. In Isaiah, the softening of the world proves the mercy of the divine word; in Petrarch, the future yielding of the woman in the millennium of love will prove the ultimate power of the persuasive plaint. Both the biblical passage and the Petrarchan complaint are premised on an initial hardness that melts. Time works not only to soften the hard nature of things but also to allow a realization of the complete nature of things: marble is not fully marble until it is battered by rain; a heart is not fully a heart until it is sounded by love; a woman is not fully a woman until she responds to a man.

In the second stanza, Wyatt short-circuits the biblical and Petrarchan imperative by demonstrating how his woman violates the construct of process:

> And yet an heart that seems so tender
> Receiveth no drop of the stilling tears
> That always still cause me to render
> The vain plaint that sounds not in her ears.
>
> (136)

In Isaiah, all things evolve into a compression where speech is answered even before it is articulated and eventuality becomes simultaneity ("while they are yet speaking, I will hear"). But in her seeming tenderness, Wyatt's "she" has condensed the eventuality. She renders the tears vain. They cannot sound in her ears because their work has already been done. His "she" is a "he." She plays his part. She seems "tender"; she hides "under so humble a face"; she pretends to be what he already is. The idealized Laura of *Rime sparse* 265 permits the Petrarchan opposites to occur by resisting. The biblical lion begins in opposition to the lamb. But Wyatt's woman disrupts the formula by an initial pliancy that inverts the order, both of poetry and of miracle. Already tender, this Laura threatens the lyric dyad by being too like the Petrarch who pursues her. In "They flee from me," the woman's resemblance to the poet causes him to question the metaphoric process through which she mirrors him. Here the "process" of rhyming—dependent on the progression of timing—is undermined: first by the lady's seeming tenderness in stanza 2, and then by her actual excessiveness in stanza 3:

> So cruel alas, is naught alive,
> So fierce so froward, so out of frame.
>
> (136)

Her pretence renders the persuasive process of poetry unnecessary. She is already persuaded. Her violence breaks the order of idealizing progress. She is already inflamed. In her initial "seeming," she erodes the difference that structures metaphor. In her subsequent extreme, she breaks the metaphor that contains desire.

Imitating Petrarch, the "I" sculpts a marble statue of entreating poet and denying mistress, a configuration which the "she" undermines. If she is what she seems, then she isn't Laura. She is Petrarch to the poet's Petrarch. She renders the plaint pointless because, in her pretense, she has already been mollified, the marble of the original statue corroded into the miasma of her pliability. The subversion of her seeming tenderness leads to the perversion of the third stanza. Wyatt's "she" exceeds Laura and puts his Petrarchism "out of frame." If the woman of "They flee from me" invades the chambers of poetic origination by entering the poet, the woman of "Process of time" shatters the boundaries of poetic discourse by emerging incomparable. She is like "naught alive." That perversion explodes, rather than forms, metaphor. Her fierceness here is too "froward" to be contained. If the lady's likeness in "They flee from me" embodies the concision of male metaphor, the lady's excessive behavior in "Process of time" removes her from the frame of the poem. The poet retaliates in inverse ratio to her behavior. If she is out of bounds in her excessiveness, he is out of words in his withdrawal. With the third stanza, Wyatt changes the mode of discourse. Since he cannot negotiate with the troubling woman, his revenge is to become her.

No longer philosophically imitating Petrarch and no longer posing as Petrarchan lover to an already subdued mistress, he goes beyond the formula. What begins as a definition of poetry ends as a deconstruction of its premises:

> Each fierce thing, how thou dost exceed
> And hides it under so humble a face
> And yet the humble to help at need
> Naught helpeth time, humbleness nor place.
>
> (136)

When the "I" defines the "you"'s bestiality, he links the falsity of her initial pose to the fierceness of her ultimate deformations. Her monstrosity lies in her seeming lowness and consequential short-circuiting of the natural cycle. But when he eliminates her from the range of the possible, the poet kills off the lover who lives in the "process"; instead he develops an acrimonious self who comes into being as the "beseecher" ends his plaint. In the identification of the lady's monstrosity, he assumes it and emerges as menacing in his estimation of her as the special "she" of "They flee from me" was disquieting in her imitation of him. Initially used, the Petrarchan frame is dismantled: first by the lady's playing Petrarch to his Petrarch and equaling his tenderness; then by the poet's playing tiger to her tiger, matching her extremes.

The contagion of her ferocity transfers her violence to him. Petrarchism is undermined in the first half of the poem because there seems to be no reluctant Laura. In the second half, the persuasive Petrarch disappears. The "you" spreads her influence, like fire, to the "I." Masked by humbleness, her fierceness breaks the frame of metaphor. The conflagration of her "process" renders "time" and "place" (the loci of poetic likenesses) unrecognizable. She has effaced the materials. As a consequence, he materializes her effacement and wipes out the poem. In "When first mine eyes," the poet pulls out the bottom of the poem, undoing the boundaries of metaphoric identity; the past is vacant. In "Process of time," the lady breaks the frame, shattering the construct of patient formulation; the present is savage. Language has no form to hinge a metaphor on in "When first mine eyes." In "Process of time," language tears the form, its containing utterances collapsed by the ferocious things contained. The final contrast between fierceness—an excess of self—and humbleness—a denial of self—derides Petrarchan modesty. The "I" wears the lady's mask. His refusal to be the meek lamb leaves room only for the poem-eating tiger. Petrarch retaliates against Laura's cruelty by pretending to ignore her deconstructions. He continues to contain her body in the poem. Wyatt reacts by retracting the body of the poem. When his lady exceeds, he recedes. But it is the lady who starts the cycle the poet cancels. Ultimately, she is the agent of her poetic delaurelization. She instigates the "excess" that inspires the poet's recess from the idealizing "process."

In "Go, burning sighs," the poet seems wiser. He himself stifles the art the lady has come to expect. As it burns itself out, some other art is born. In "Process of time," the poet is reduced by the lady's indifference to naming and so assuming her monstrosity; in "Go, burning sighs," he is similarly at first motivated by her coldness to calling her icy and heartless.[14] But in the course of pointing to her villainy, he finds another source for his poem. He splits from the Petrarchan model:

> Go, burning sighs
> I must go work, I see, by craft and art
> For truth and faith in her is laid apart,
> Alas I cannot therefore assail her
> With pitiful plaint and scalding fire
> That out of my breath doth strainably start.
> Go, burning sighs.
> (72)

Wyatt turns the optimistic Petrarch of *Rime sparse* 153, one who believes cruel fortune may end, into one who sees no end to his end. Whereas Petrarch contrasts his anxiety and darkness to Laura's peace and light, Wyatt questions the lady's "truth and faith." If, in "Process of time," the "I" defines how the woman breaks the frame of Petrarchan discourse, here the "I" defines a new art.

When he commands the "burning sighs" to "go" in the refrain, he no longer sends them back to the lady who inflamed him. He asks them to wither away. Having no fuel to fan them, they become extinct. Since neither pitiful plaint nor scalding fire can get the lady to yield, the speaker must use other means. Once more, she is out of range. Truth and faith (pitiful plaints and burning sighs) are useless with her. When the speaker dismisses the burning sighs as ineffectual and abandons his spontaneous songs, he finds inspiration from a source that "worketh" independently of the Petrarchan dyad. That artifice depends on something in the self which the speaker calls craft. Allowing the "burning sighs" to extinguish themselves, he acknowledges the powerful center of his art. Aimed at a Laura who one day will be accessible, Petrarch's flaming sighs are fueled by expectancy. Wyatt's flames die with the resting "I" of stanza 1 and burn out with the absent "I" of stanza 2. Canceling the Petrarchan lover, the "I" negates the Petrarchan "you." She is neither a Laura who might one day succumb nor a lady whose ego may be inflamed by his ardency. This time she goes with the sighs, banished from his art.

When he detaches himself from Petrarch and announces his intention to write in a different vein, Wyatt heralds a self-contained doubling. He uses his anger at the imagined woman to justify his dismissal of her as source of his poem. He will work with "craft and art." The practiced accomplishment of craft suggests experience. The elusive mystery of art premises privacy. Wyatt's new art is self-sustaining. In "Go, burning sighs," it comes into being against the futility of Petrarchism, the tears of the Petrarchan plaint dried by the annihilative fire of the Petrarchan flame. The poem goes, banished by a poet whose muse has run dry. But the inward turning suggests the possibility of a doubleness in the self which counters the woman's indifference and is independent of it. Petrarchan sighs have their origin in the single-mindedd obsessiveness of the lover, but an "I" who begins in doubleness, in craft and art, speaks to ambiguity and mystery. His art implies the craftiness of a secret expertise which he will ply not in the flame of the beloved's eye but in the darkness of something personally fostered.

Wyatt annexes the doubleness of the lady's duplicity and turns it into the complexity of his many-layered (and hence partly secretive) self. Jonathan Crewe emphasizes the various meanings of "craft" in Wyatt as a combination of technical skill and ethical doubleness. From that premise, Crewe argues that the discovery of the woman's duplicity "makes no difference in the end since the movement of the poem culminates in an anticlimactic repetition of 'Go, burning sighs.'"[15] But it is possible to see the difference Wyatt insists on by reading the sighs not as emissaries to the woman but as poetic swan songs. "Go, burning sighs" heralds the end of Petrarchan negotiations. As self-immolative commands, the burning sighs stop the discourse before it starts. If the "I" of "Process of time" is outward bound, the "I" of "Go, burning sighs" is inward bound. He seeks an art whose origin lies in his privileged arena. That exclusivity becomes clear in the "no" poems—like "What word is that" (96) and "Madam withouten many words" (132)—where Wyatt turns Laura's refusal into something other than a poetics centering on the woman.

In "What word is that," Wyatt calls the lady's refusal "mine answer," identifying her "no" as his initiative. No longer a sign of the woman's leverage, the "no" empowers him. Anthony Low suggests that the answer is not, as most critics agree, the elusive "Ann, sir" (Anne Boleyn) but the exclusionary "an na" ("a no" in the Renaissance spelling):[16]

> What word is that that changeth not
> Though it be turned and made in twain?
> It is mine answer, God it wot,
> And eke the causer of my pain.
> It love rewardeth with disdain,
> Yet is it loved. What would ye more?
> It is my health eke and my sore.
>
> (96)

The lady's "no" becomes an expression of the poet's negativity. Wyatt assimilates the lady's denial. He calls her "no" the poet's "own" answer. If the sexual or external rebuff rewards desire with pain, the internal answer dissolves desire and so obviates disdain. A "no" may be the lady's response. But in making it "mine answer," the "I" posits a resistance in the self, a private resource merely matched by the lady's refusal, "loved" because it ascribes to the other a reluctance already existing in the self. The double possessive of the "no" establishes in the self the resources Petrarchan poetics locate in the other. The lady's evasions become his health as, assimilated, the soreness of her denial emerges the source of his acerbity. The humbled Petrarch keeps petitioning the sorely denying Laura, finding the health of his poem in her refusals. The sharpened Wyatt ends the petition, locating his strength in his own craft. Word, not woman, sparks the poem.

In "Will ye see what wonders," the woman's absorbed energy is transmuted into a mythological—and hence safely semiotic—status. If

female sexual denial becomes the poet's resource in the "no" poems,
female biological reproductivity becomes his strength here:

> Will ye see what wonders love hath wrought?
> Then come and look at me.
> There need nowhere else to be sought,
> In me ye may them see.
>
> For unto that that men may see
> Most monstrous thing of kind,
> Myself may best compared be;
> Love hath me so assigned.
>
> A bird there flieth, and that but one;
> Of her this thing ensueth:
> That when her days be spent and gone
> With fire she reneweth.
>
> And I with her may well compare
> My love that is alone,
> The flame whereof doth ay repair
> My life when it is gone.
>   (234)

In *Rime sparse* 135, Petrarch begins with the phoenix, uses the magnet
metaphor and then proceeds with transformation myths that continue
the magnet effect: the catablepa, the African springs that annihilate the
self, the Epirean springs which burn the self, the Fortune Island springs
which torture the self, until he returns to the spring near Sorgue which
started the process of his misery. In Petrarch, the self is always extract-
ed. The lady becomes the powerful magnet who slights the ever-slight-
ed and abject lover. Wyatt reverses the journey so that he rests not with
unending Petrarchan depletion but with a continued vision of growth.
The "I" begins as "the most monstrous thing of kind," having become
what, in "Process of time," he accused the woman of being. If, in the
first stanza, the "I" combines with the most monstrous "she" the lady
often was elsewhere, he also emerges the hermaphrodite. He assumes
the bisexuality, the monstrosity of kind, implied in the figure he evokes.
But while Petrarch survives that annihilation only to resurface as the
continuously unmanned self, Wyatt returns to remasculinize the hermaphrodite as he becomes the self-engendering phoenix of the last
metaphor. Twice comparing himself, Wyatt doubles female reproductive powers. In the hermaphrodite, he is the male/femaled. In the
phoenix, he is the female/remaled, propagated as a figure that perpetuates itself through language. Petrarch begins his poem with a desire

236 / Barbara L. Estrin

that keeps fueling itself. Wyatt ends his with the doubling of "mine own," now tripled in its insularity. When he speaks of "My love that is alone," he refers to "repairing" as an energy independent of desire. To "re-pair" the self is to find the other in the self, that "most monstrous thing of kind" whose being in the regendered private arena contains the flame of its own regenerative resources.[17] To "re-pair" the self is, then, to pull the woman back inside: to double by retracting. Finally, to compare himself with the "she" that is the phoenix is to find in the monstrosity of the hermaphrodite all the othering one needs. Anticipating Marvell's variously plumed bird in "The Garden," Wyatt's self is mother and lover to the poem. When the flame becomes a light guiding the self onward instead of a cinder returning the self to the other, the concentrated and concentric "I" kindles in himself the inspiration Petrarch claimed came only from Laura's eternal spark.

When the woman of "They flee from me" (1) imitates in likeness what the man does; (2) presents in likable acts what the man wants; (3) alludes in vagueness to what the man says; and (4) eludes, by mystifying it, what language specifies, she speaks to the poet's sexual and verbal impotence. Eliot's Prufrock blames a similar ineffectuality on the woman's aura, reducing her to a vague, disembodied essence. ("Is it perfume from a dress that makes me so digress?") But his irresolution simply reverses Petrarchan revenge: scattered woman; scatterbrained poet. Wyatt retaliates against the lady's intrusions by changing his poetics: conferring his future or past onto her (in "My lute, awake" or "When first mine eyes"); equaling rather than worshiping her (in "Process of time"); or dropping her altogether (in "Go, burning sighs"). The woman of "They flee from me" undermines his representational authority, as she prods him into the further reclusiveness of the "no" poems and the inverted reproductivity of "Will ye see what wonders." Faced with a "she" who could become "he," Wyatt dismisses the woman and, instead, chooses an art that is his "own." But the dismissal of the woman is a response to her poetic and reproductive agency. Imagining his troublesome woman, Wyatt undermines the categories of cultural identity on which Petrarchism is based.

That the imaginer of a woman worth imitating is a man who feels compelled to unimagine her heightens the spiral of revenge even as it deepens the involutions of privacy. The distancing accounts for the restraint in Wyatt's "refrain," an abstinence he repeats each time he hesitates to impersonate the Petrarchan "I" or to laurelize the difficult "she." Wyatt's "love that is alone"—a withdrawal that defies the invasive woman—answers her challenge to the male privileging of the figu-

rative by invading her territory. It patterns its creativity on her enclosures and locates its mystery in her evasiveness. In firing the woman out
of his poems (matching her ferocity in "Process of time" and extin-
guishing his own embers in "Go, burning sighs"), Wyatt immolates the
Petrarch who idealized the lady. But in "Will ye see what wonders,"
Wyatt incorporates the womanly flame. Sexually neutral, he wipes out
Petrarch. Absorbing her myths, he neutralizes Laura. Attaching himself
to the Ovidian bird, he circumvents the dangers of the physical woman, his muse now exclusively his own. Yet the self-sufficiency of Wyatt's
reparation imitates the encircling powers of the woman he sought to
escape. The signification of his phoenix (and restored phallus) is partly
hers, the revitalization of his visual space with her duplicated image synchronous to the autoeroticism of his linguistic self-homage. In the "no"
poems, Wyatt obviates the woman by making her denial an answer that
liberates him sexually to turn elsewhere for satisfaction and poetically
to look inward for inspiration. In "Will ye see what wonders," Wyatt
avoids the woman by rendering her affirmations his premise. The "yes"
of her reproductive courage becomes the source of his metaphysical
renewal.

If, as Patricia Parker argues, the sequence of Genesis 2 gives man
"the hierarchical superiority of his coming before [the woman],"[18] in
"They flee from me," all precedence is the woman's, a precedence
Wyatt acknowledges in the "it was no dream" of the last stanza. The
poem restructures the situation of Adam's Genesis 2 sleep. The aggressive woman is a reality. When she catches him in her arms, she contains
him. Her imagination refocuses the mirrors of identity. The reversal—
her replication of his initiative—doubles her hold. If sexuality is her
idea, if she asks him what he likes but knows the answer, then textuality
is her invention. She images forth the terms of his pleasure. That nightmare is the sexual and linguistic trap. The woman of "They flee from
me" enters the man's chamber and controls his vision, casting him back
into her chamber: the womb of female biological and poetic origination. Wyatt's reaction to this *mise-en-abyme* is to distort his Petrarch
beyond recognition, as if he felt compelled to redouble the self in other
poems to undo the doubling woman he imagines in "They flee from
me." He disarms Laura by banishing her from the retaliatory poems
and rearms the self by calling the semiotic "no" of "What word is that"
his answer and the replicative body of "Will ye see what wonders" *his*
production. If the woman of "They flee from me" is the nightmare other, the woman of "Will ye see what wonders" is absorbed by the dream-
ing self: the self re-paired in the "monstrosity" of its own aggrandizing
capacity. Doing without the woman Petrarch imagines as ideal means

reimagining the man as retaliatory. But it is the imagined agency of the "troubling woman" that opens up the "alternative domains of cultural intelligibility"[19] manifest in Wyatt's transformations of the Petrarch he Englishes.

Notes

1. Judith Butler, *Gender Trouble* (New York: Methuen, 1990), ix.

2. Joel Fineman, *Shakespeare's Perjured Eye: The Invention of Poetic Subjectivity in the Sonnets* (Berkeley and Los Angeles: University of California Press, 1986), 194.

3. *Sir Thomas Wyatt: The Complete Poems,* ed. R. A. Rebholz (New Haven: Yale University Press, 1978). All references are from this edition and are cited by page number in the text.

4. Thomas Greene, "The Poetics of Discovery: A Reading of Donne's Elegy 19," *Yale Journal of Criticism* 2 (1989), 132.

5. Fredric Jameson, "Imaginary and Symbolic in Lacan," *Yale French Studies* 55–56 (1977), 352–53.

6. Andrew Parker, "Mom," *Oxford Literary Review* 8 (1986), 101. See also Jane Gallop, "Phallus/Penis: Same Difference," *Men by Women,* ed. Janet Todd (New York: Holmes and Meier, 1981), 243–51.

7. Shormishtha Panja sees the question as "lace[d] with menace." See "Ranging and Returning: The Mood-Voice Dichotomy in Wyatt," *English Literary Renaissance* 18 (1989), 353.

8. Terry Eagleton, *Literary Theory: An Introduction* (Minneapolis: University of Minnesota Press, 1983), 167–68.

9. Michael McCanles, "Love and Power in the Poetry of Sir Thomas Wyatt," *Modern Language Quarterly* 29 (1968), 145.

10. For a brief critical history of the identification of Wyatt's "inwardness," see Nancy Leonard, "The Speaker in Wyatt's Lyric Poetry," *Huntington Library Quarterly* 41 (1977), 1–8; John Kerrigan, "Wyatt's Selfish Style," *Essays and Studies* 34 (1981), 1–18; Anne Ferry, *The "Inward" Language: Sonnets of Wyatt, Sidney, Shakespeare, Donne* (Chicago: University of Chicago Press, 1983); Stephen J. Greenblatt, *Renaissance Self-Fashioning: From More to Shakespeare* (Chicago: University of Chicago Press, 1980); and Panja, "Ranging and Returning," 347–68.

11. Jonathan Crewe, *Trials of Authorship: Anterior Forms and Poetic Reconstruction from Wyatt to Shakespeare* (Berkeley and Los Angeles: University of California Press, 1990), 39.

12. *Petrarch's Lyric Poems,* trans. Robert Durling (Cambridge: Harvard University Press, 1976), 434.

13. Natalie Angier (*New York Times,* Jan. 14, 1992, C, 1) contemporizes and problematizes the Petrarchan "process of time," as she applies the poetic commonplace to real statues, specifically to the Lincoln and Jefferson memorials:

The monuments are suffering, not so much because they have been battered by grit, grime and acid rain or even because pigeons shamelessly roost on the heads of the Presidential statues within, but because, in the half century since the monuments were built, they have been kept so meticulously clean.

Partly as a result of the constant washing, the marble has eroded so badly in spots that last year a chunk of one 42-foot column at the Jefferson Memorial crashed to the ground and other columns were found to be teetering dangerously.

14. Donald Guss maintains that it is "the lady's falsity [that] makes it impossible to assail her with pitiful plaint. . . . Wyatt's personification of his sighs reflects his alienation from love and his sense that he has been imposed on." See "Wyatt's Petrarchism: An Instance of Creative Imitation in the Renaissance," *Huntington Library Quarterly* 29 (1965), 12.

15. Greene, *The Light of Troy*[?], 34.

16. Anthony Low, "Wyatt's 'What Word Is That,'" *English Language Notes* 10 (1972), 89–90.

17. Of the positive, infusive, rather than exhaustive nature of the hermaphrodite, Lauren Silberman writes: "From our wider perspective, we can see Hermaphrodite as a biform sign in which arbitrary semiological difference plays against sexual difference. The 'he-she' hermaphrodite is neither genuinely androgynous nor genuinely a boundary figure; it is arbitrarily classed with 'she.'" See "The Hermaphrodite and the Metamorphosis of Spenserian Allegory," *English Literary Renaissance* 17 (1987), 212. When Wyatt reclassifies the hermaphrodite as the self-perpetuating phoenix, he doubly consolidates his gains.

18. Patricia Parker, *Literary Fat Ladies* (London: Methuen, 1987), 179.

19. Butler, *Gender Trouble*, 145.

The Colonial Wyatt:
Contexts and Openings

ROLAND GREENE

One critical factor in the European understanding of the Americas—
perhaps the most urgent development for the provision of a common
literary medium to hold post-Columbian responses to the New
World—is the sixteenth-century, multinational project of renovating
Petrarchism for lyric poetry. Anyone who studies the colonial period in
European-American history or literature continually runs across historical figures that work in two spheres of activity, imperialism and Petrarchism, that we now think of as discrete: some are political figures
who turn out to be accomplished Petrarchan poets, such as the legitimate son of the conqueror of Mexico, Martín Cortés; others are poets,
such as Philip Sidney, who have more extensive international contacts
and ambitions than many literary scholars take into account.[1] Why is the
divided commitment to these particular occupations found so often in
this period? Where personal careers give way to the common enterprises of circles, classes, and societies—for instance, the movement of a giv-
en poem out of Petrarch's *Canzoniere* through translations in several
languages and cultural situations, where it often attracts different political associations—the mutual incursions of the Petrarchan and colonial
projects are still more evident, though perhaps harder to trace and explain than in the lives of persons.[2]

In view of its importance as a cultural transaction, however, Petrarchism has been treated as scarcely having a real-world political dimension—and still less, a relevance to contemporaneous events in the
New World. Twenty-five years ago Elizabeth Armstrong's *Ronsard and
the Age of Gold* (1968) considered the intersections of received myths
of the Golden Age and the mid-century ethnography of the Americas
in the works of poets such as Pierre de Ronsard (1524–85) and Joachim
Du Bellay (1522–60). Settling on anticipations of the so-called noble

savage for its New World element, and refusing to approach Ronsard's poetry through Petrarchism, Armstrong's monograph vitiates both the Petrarchan and the American factors as though to keep them apart. The book steps back from issues and questions that would make a connection manifest: for example, Armstrong declines to treat the import, for both intellectual history and poetic imagery, of the gold recovered in Mexico and Peru during the first wave of the sixteenth-century Petrarchan revival.[3] Despite some obvious points of entry, the line of her argument runs between the adjacent histories of colonial exploitation and amatory lyric without explicitly engaging either, let alone both.

More recently, an issue of *Representations* assembled around the topic of the New World exemplifies some current versions of the same critical disengagement.[4] In successive essays, Mary C. Fuller and Louis Adrian Montrose propose to describe the workings of endlessly deferred desire and the politics of gender difference, respectively, in Walter Ralegh's *The Discoverie of the large, rich, and beautifull Empire of Guiana* (1596).[5] Both Fuller and Montrose demonstrate certain problems that seem to shadow scholars who treat the writing of European colonialism from the limited view of sixteenth-century English literature. Perhaps the most common of these, the lack of a deep store of source material to connect with that of Europe, appears in Montrose's awkward attempt to pass off the *Discoverie,* with its specific history, qualities, and agenda, as representative of an entire European "discourse of discovery" he leaves practically uninterrogated. Fuller and Montrose alike react passively to Ralegh's own sleight of portraying the *Discoverie,* anachronistically, as an originary text about a new site: while Ralegh produces a nearly parodic version of the sort of account that was more appropriate in 1496 than in 1596, Fuller and Montrose obligingly accept his work as "early [writing] about America," part of "an emergent colonialist discourse."[6] More to the immediate point, both Fuller and Montrose observe in Ralegh's text—but only implicitly—something that amounts to a Petrarchan aesthetic and ideological program. Whether citing instances of "affinity between the *discovery* and the *blazon*" as "two Renaissance rhetorical forms that organize and control their subjects," seeking in vain "the material body" at the end of a chain of signifiers, or characterizing the prototypical Spanish imperialist as a "specular figure of desiring European Man," both critics describe that program as though for the first time instead of giving Petrarchism its due, which would mean acknowledging it as a widely adopted template in the discourse of discovery and moving forward from there.[7]

All of these motions make Ralegh's text seem unique, and perhaps more important than it is. But when *The Discoverie of Guiana* is put back into the colonial literature to which it belongs as a late instance, and restored to the decade of Petrarchan lyric writing in English in which it occurs, one sees its participation in a widely distributed discursive complex. Ralegh's text insists on a fully informed commentary, while Fuller's and Montrose's essays, like Armstrong's monograph, are limited by the consensuses of their moments. To go further, one might ask what the Petrarchisms in Ralegh's text would show as antecedents in earlier entrepreneurial, ethnographic, or historical writing about the New World; how Petrarchism gets into such writing, and whether the vitality of Italianate love poetry during one hundred years of discoveries and colonizations is somehow affiliated with those events; and finally whether the category of American-oriented writing in which Fuller and Montrose situate *The Discoverie of Guiana* might properly include lyric poems, and with what implications. If early modern Petrarchism was widely understood as an internationally sanctioned medium for the deliberation of both kinds of issues—if, in fact, its usages were taken to indicate that sixteenth-century poets, explorers, and readers knew these as in effect the same issues of desire, conquest, and exploitation—then imperialist discourse would seem to emerge through many more openings than recent work on colonial history, law, and politics has found for it. A text such as Ralegh's *Discoverie of Guiana* would have, after all, a much broader historical and contemporary context than even carefully reasoned accounts like those in *Representations* allow.

On a continental scale, the occurrences of Petrarchan discourse are less potential than manifest across three generations of early modern lyric writing. As conceived by the generation of European poets born around 1500, Petrarchism absorbs the impact of many particular events of the era while maintaining its own slightly anachronistic character. Following the Mexican conquest of 1521 and contemporaneous with the intra-European imperialist wars of the earlier sixteenth century, the Petrarchism of such poets as Thomas Wyatt (1503–42) and Garcilaso de la Vega (1503–36), and their younger contemporaries Gutierre de Cetina (?1520–57), Louise Labé (1520–66), and Luís de Camões (?1524–80), produces a lyric poetry attentive to the immediate political and cultural applications of unrequited desire—some of which concern the continuing European experience in knowing and governing the recently conquered societies in the New World. With weighted terms, transcultural imprints, and thematic equivocalities, these poets effectively widen the import of love to take in the problems of exploration, conquest, and rule as exemplary cases; extending what I describe elsewhere as the Columbian invention of an emotional prototype for the discoverer or entrepreneur, their work posits attitudes that can be modulated and reassembled in a virtually endless array of texts.[8] More-over, the lyrics fashioned by these poets, including some of the most influential of the period in their languages, deliver imperialist questions to a readership that may otherwise have only a distant relation to the mid-century American enterprises of Spain, Portugal, and France. The poems I have in mind take their investments in the Americas directly from the shared concerns of their authors, many of whom are explorers, diplomats, and administrators, and their audiences—although these persons and societies often have been treated by literary history as though their travels, embassies, and enterprises were matters of inert fact.

The Henrician regime with which this volume is concerned, though lacking an American policy, witnesses the entry of the contemporaneous, international discussion of imperialism into English literature—the beginning of what will become, by Ralegh's time, a speculative debate of considerable urgency. This essay proposes a colonial approach to a first-generation English Petrarchist poet, Thomas Wyatt. Though Wyatt's work has been claimed—and properly so—by the newly revived historical criticism of sixteenth-century literature, it has largely been seen as political in the courtly sense alone: in the case of his Petrarchan lyrics, to simplify the consensus only a little, as either light entertainments or disillusioned reports on the hazards of the court.[9] On the contrary, I would insist that Wyatt's concerns run well beyond the stock courtly situations with which criticism has been occupied. Like many of his contemporaries, Wyatt has at least a speculative interest in certain transcultural, American-oriented questions that belong to the intellectual and emotional agenda of the period: these properly include such issues as the moral obligations of entrenched mastery, the costs of submission, and the practical correlations of race and power. When this interest shows up in his lyrics in perspectival—not unequivocal—fashion, it may seem to occur only subjectively or in trace amounts, or to vie with courtly matters for control of the poems' historical or topical dimensions. In fact, Wyatt's consciousness of America is neither subjective nor all-important. In its sixteenth-century revivals, Petrarchan lyric writing has the capacity to bring many concerns together in the compass of a single amatory fiction. The modulations of personal, national, and ideological accents, after all, are much of what keeps off redundancy among manifestly similar works by poets such as Wyatt, Du Bellay, and Garcilaso. Where blanks or openings in the texts seem to mitigate a strict historical or allegorical relation to colonial events, or where less topical models intervene, these poems simply operate like lyrics of any time and place—widening their reach, diversifying their precedents, and inviting the reader to realize a personal and cultural connection to the text. If such a poem is "about" colonial experience in some sense, it is no less about other relevant models. But its colonial aspect can often be the factor that ensures the lyric's contemporaneity in a political register; where Henrician and later audiences recognize it, as they amply did, this topical dimension reinvents Petrarchism as well, producing a channel through which some of the most searching and difficult questions of the time engage what was, at least for the literate classes, a sixteenth-century mass medium.[10]

Surely there is nothing obvious about the relevance of colonial events to Thomas Wyatt's poetry. Where his work accommodates the uncertainties of contemporary developments in the Americas, it does so in some large part because Wyatt is attracted to instabilities in all things, social and political as much as romantic. His lyrics tend to collapse investigations of deceit, illusion, and powerlessness in multiple settings—between persons, in the court, and in the geopolitical world—into compact, haunting statements that wobble because they are so full. In this sense, it is surprising that little has been said about his late career in connection with the poetry.[11] Wyatt was sent by Henry VIII to the Holy Roman Court in the spring of 1537, mainly with the purpose of reporting on the incipient alliance of Charles V and Francis I of France.[12] Beginning in 1538, Wyatt participated in the negotiations for Henry's proposed marriage with Charles's niece, the duchess of Milan. Later that year, Wyatt conveyed Henry's unsought advice to the emperor concerning his son Philip of Spain's chances for succession not only to the Spanish crown but to the elective "Imperial dignity," and sent back Charles's polite reply: "As touching his Spains, he now, at these Courtes, entendeth to stablish his son among them, with their oaths, for his successor. . . . The Empire [however] he intended not to his son, [but to] his brother, being king of Romans."[13] An uncommonly curious and talkative ambassador, Wyatt was even brought before the Inquisition at Toledo on charges of heresy, but let go with a "most severe admonition" from the emperor that "he ought to be careful how he spoke."[14] In all of these occupations, Wyatt was in contact with his exact contemporary Diego Hurtado de Mendoza (1504–75), a Petrarchan poet of considerable distinction who at different times was the emperor's envoy to Venice, attended the Council of Trent as imperial legate, and served as ambassador to Rome. A friend of the prolific Italian poet Pietro Aretino (1492–1556), whose recent paraphrase of the penitential psalms (1534) Wyatt had probably begun to use for his own version, Mendoza was Wyatt's counterpart, having been dispatched to England in 1537 for the same marital negotiations that concerned

Wyatt.[15] The envoy was the great-grandson of Iñigo López de Mendoza (1398–1458), the marquis of Santillana, who in the 1440s had introduced Italianate models into Spanish poetry. Mendoza's elder brother Antonio (1491?–1552) served contemporaneously as the first viceroy of New Spain, and was near the turbulent start of his fifteen-year administration in Mexico City while "Don Thomas Wiet" observed the emperor's court.[16]

Moreover, the term of Wyatt's ambassadorship coincided with a critical moment in the empire's relations with its territories in the New World. The late 1530s and early 1540s saw a more urgent theoretical discussion of cultural difference and its political and religious consequences, and a greater number of attempts to fashion policy according to such a discussion, than any time since Columbus's discovery. The *encomienda* system, for instance, which had been modeled on peninsular Spanish administration and transplanted to the Caribbean in 1503 as a system of forced Indian labor for the gain of designated Spanish *encomenderos*, was under terrific strain in this period as the question of reciprocal obligations between the Spaniards and the Indians of New Spain came into open debate. Among the issues in play were the accumulating, near-feudal powers of the encomenderos, their harsh treatment of the Indians whose labor they exploited, and the rising international challenge to Spanish control of the Indies.[17] The system had been initially modified in 1536 by limiting ownership of any encomienda to two lifetimes.[18] In 1537 Pope Paul III issued the bull *Sublimis Deus*, which agitated the discussion by asserting the capacity of the Indians for Christian conversion, their well-founded claims to freedom, and their rights to hold property even when they remained unconverted.[19] At the same time, Fray Bartolomé de Las Casas was undertaking his closely watched experiment at Tuzutlán in Guatemala, in which he proposed to convert the Indians to Christianity and imperial subjection through strictly peaceful means.[20] In this climate of aggravated legal and moral sensibilities, Antonio de Mendoza and Fray Juan de Zumárraga established a humanist academy for the Indians of New Spain, the Colegio de Santiago de Tlaltelolco, and Viceroy Mendoza authorized the publication of books for Indian readers; the earliest surviving New World book, *Breve y mas compendiosa doctrina christiana en lengua mexicana y castellana* (1539), was printed under this initiative in Mexico City.[21] In 1539 the Dominican jurist Francisco de Vitoria delivered his lecture entitled *De indis recenter inventis*, which went as far as to undermine not only the emperor's but the pope's authority on matters of Indian dominion.[22] Meanwhile, "letter after letter" came from America over these years—from Mendoza and many other correspondents—indicting the encomenderos for their abuses of the emperor's Indian subjects and recording the shortcomings of the system as it stood, was modified, and stood again.[23] Shortly after the end of Wyatt's embassy, the New Laws of 1542–43—I will discuss them below as a provisional context for the discussion of rights and obligations in the poem "They fle from me"—represented an opportunity to quell the debate and reform the system, but instead generated further dissensions and modifications. Placed where he must have noticed the continuing issues between Old and New Spain, and often "in such credit with the Emperor that no man is so meet to fill that room," Wyatt is probably the first important English participant in the international convention of rendering a common language for personal and political matters in the medium of Petrarchism.[24] The situation in the imperial court and abroad, where diplomats and administrators who happened to be accomplished Italianate poets found themselves conversing over intractable issues of law and policy, implies a concrete instance, but only one, of how such a transposition occurred. As a foreign observer of the issues of Charles's government, Wyatt was probably less compelled to see these questions resolved than intrigued by them, obliged to register their assumptions in his own thinking about the politics of romantic love and courtly aspiration.

Accordingly, these concerns appear around certain lyrics as a loose context—a scrim through which a set of fresh questions becomes visible even in familiar poems. "They fle from me," for example, is such a poem. In it, an inconstant woman is figured as a prey who becomes a hunter, a conceit that trades on any number of stylized hunting scenes in the early modern stock of images.[25] Of these, the encounters between imperialist hunters and hunted indigenes in the literature of discovery are particularly immediate and available in the 1530s and 1540s. The motif of Europeans chasing Indians or Indians stalking Europeans— there are literally dozens of relevant instances in first- and second-generation European texts about the Caribbean, Mexico, Peru, and Brazil—draws on the authority of classical, Christian, and courtly hunt scenes, lending them contemporary urgency and receiving cultural sanction in turn.[26] Some texts report approaches followed by flights, some tell of the reverse: Columbus's Cuban diary, for example, contains several paradigmatic descriptions of encounters in which the Indians first approach his men ("the women [were] kissing their hands and feet, feeling them"), then suddenly withdraw ("today of the six young men he took . . . the two eldest ones fled").[27] There is, of course, no single authoritative instance of this traditional-turned-colonial motif. Early modern poets and readers know it in various outlets, as a particular of the (mutual but scarcely synchronous) attractions and resistances felt by Europeans and Americans alike in their first negotiations. Wyatt's poem, I maintain, is one more such outlet:

They fle from me / that sometyme did me seke
    with naked fote stalking in my chambre
    I have sene theim gentill tame and meke
    that nowe are wyld and do not remembre
    that sometyme they put theimself in daunger
    to take bred at my hand & nowe they raunge
    besely seking with a continuell chaunge
Thancked be fortune it hath ben othrewise
    twenty tymes better but ons in speciall
    in thyn arraye after a pleasaunt gyse
    when her lose gowne from her shoulders did fall
    and she me caught in her armes long & small
    therewithall swetely did me kysse
    and softely said dere hert howe like you this
It was no dreme I lay brode waking
    but all is torned thorough my gentilnes
    into a straunge fasshion of forsaking
    and I have leve to goo of her goodenes
    and she also to vse new fangilnes
    but syns that I so kyndely ame served
    I would fain knowe what she hath deserved.[28]

In the several places where the woman-as-deer conceit comes apart and the speaker's presumably human experience shows through, the physical descriptions, the contrast between civilized and barbaric behavior, and the climactic switch in political roles (the speaker hunter becoming a "dere hert") allow a New World orientation.[29] To expand the potential colonial reading of the poem still further, one might ask: why are we sure "they" are deer? Could they be Indians? Or to insist on a common mid-century motif, could they be Indians described as deer? On a journey to Florida in 1565, the English slaver John Hawkins notes of the Indians the "Colours both red, blacke, yellow, & russet, very perfect, wherewith they so paint their bodies, and Deere skinnes which they weare about them, that with water it neither fadeth away, nor altereth colour."[30] The Jesuit José de Acosta moralizes a similar scene in 1590 when he looks back on the several conquests and admits that "we entered by the sword without hearing or understanding them, their affairs seemed not to deserve any credit, but they were like game caught in the wilds and fetched for our service and desire."[31] Even the pronominal crux, in which "they" becomes "she" after line 11, can be seen to put the woman's former compliance in terms of a conquered population and to restore her individual agency when she turns loose from his conquest.[32] If transcultural encounters may participate in a received motif such as the Renaissance hunt, one might speculate that "They fle from me" refers to such episodes at least as much as it engages the guesswork and anecdotes, largely about Anne Boleyn, that are often treated as its intersection with history.[33]

Moreover, the late 1530s and the early 1540s, the era of "They fle from me," see a continual discussion by *conquistadores*, ecclesiastics, and jurists of the ethnic character and legal and moral rights of the Indians—of who they are and what they deserve, to paraphrase several documents issued through the ecclesiastical juntas convened by the emperor in this period. In these years, during which the New Laws of 1542–43 proscribing the perpetuation of the encomienda system through inheritance were announced and debated, many internationally minded Spaniards and others were openly concerned with the mutual obligations between a colonizing society and a colonized people, with making "the rights of the Indians . . . as secure as possible."[34] The *pareceres* elicited by three legislative visits to New Spain between 1532 and 1544—the second of which, in 1539, is contemporaneous with Wyatt's embassy to Charles's court—are saturated with comment on how the Indians (called "los naturales"), although given to "novelties" and "infidelity," should be "humanly treated."[35] The *relación sumaria* of the junta of 1544 tells how the continuing dissolution of the encomienda system through changes in the inheritance laws has turned the Indians "wild," encouraging them to kill Spaniards, while the reestablishment of hereditary encomiendas would ensure that "the Indians would be better treated."[36] Further, in a continuing symptom of the idealist critique to which the Spanish put their own imperialism in this period, a widely pitched debate over "service," with the Indians as servants but also recipients of Spanish attentions, appears throughout these texts. For decades the matter of "personal service" rendered to encomenderos by Indians had troubled the moral agenda of Spanish imperialism: in 1529, the Consejo Real had recommended to the emperor that encomiendas be abolished because "it seems that the Indians by all rights . . . are obliged to personal service no more than other free persons of these kingdoms."[37] Several informants of Wyatt's era testify that everyone involved, from God to the emperor to the naturales themselves, is "disserved" by the current arrangements, that all "deserve" better.[38] What emerges in "They fle from me" as a rhetoric of service ("I . . . ame served" / "what she hath deserved") and a more fundamental questioning of the woman's nature is rooted in one of the most important discussions of its time.

None of this is to suggest that Wyatt's "They fle from me" directly allegorizes either Columbus's frustration or the more advanced imperialist dilemma of the 1530s and 1540s. No single matrix really works for most poems in the Wyatt corpus, even if this one has achieved a tenuous critical equilibrium as a fiction of amatory frustration in a courtly setting. Rather, I mean to argue that the mutuality of colonial and Petrarchan discourses at mid-century produces texts of each mode that manifestly register the concerns and emphases of the other. In this case, a sizable ecclesiastical and juridical literature, which records so-called infidelities and ingratitudes committed against the Europeans, and treats the religious, ethical, and pragmatic question of what the Indians deserve, comes to bear on the twenty-one lines of Wyatt's lyric: the immediacy and availability of this literature allow Wyatt to accommodate his poem to the stresses of the moment, which makes it no less Petrarchan but vastly more urgent even as a statement about interpersonal love. At the same time, poems such as "They fle from me" cannot be separated from the collective thinking and rethinking of colonial questions that sweep across many boundaries—national, linguistic, discursive—in mid-sixteenth-century Europe. Like *relaciones,* like treatises of many sorts, Petrarchan lyrics are often implicated in the raising and deliberation of issues we would retrospectively classify as social or political; unlike other contemporary texts, these poems operate as an apparatus that puts individual readers into seemingly direct relation with the relevant issues and questions—that brings them into complicity with the colonial project, and into immediacy with its ideological matters, and thus disseminates its purposes and contradictions for a collective consideration. The usual readings of this poem, as treating courtly deceptions or rehearsing the literary tradition itself, are not wrong. But most of the interpretations in these reflex modes depend on unexamined assumptions about the prevalence of court-oriented questions, or on the dramatization of thematic patterns that lift the poem almost entirely out of its contemporary site.[39] Against motions of these sorts, a reading that finds "They fle from me" in the rhetorical thick of an immediate moral and political problem, not merely a hazy setting or a tradition, must enter the discussion with a certain sufficiency, perhaps even primacy.[40] There are many roughly contemporaneous poems, equally charged with the ideology of their moments, that avoid mentioning the American enterprise—but cannot lose their political investment, with its speculative but privileged relation to the poems' semantics, only on that account. I think of Camões's "Amor é um fogo que arde sem se ver" ("Love is a fire that burns without being seen"), a seemingly received list of comparisons for amatory experience, in which two or three lines break the psychic logic to put the speaker back into history ("it's serving the one that conquers, the conqueror / it's having loyalty for those that slay us").[41] As the contemporary, topical dimension of such an overwhelmingly conventional poem can be fugitive, one is obliged to read probatively, often against the assumed trend of the fiction, often for voices that answer other voices across national and linguistic borders, across genres and texts.

"The longe love," one of these poems that draws in voices from a distance, revises the landscape of *Canzoniere* 140 ("Amor, che nel penser mio vive et regna") to contain two commonplaces of the European landfalls such as those of Columbus, Vespucci, and Cabral, namely the harbor and the forest. The sites are scarcely political in themselves, but become so when put into relation in this peculiarly compact and expansive poem, which seems to condense the atmospheres of the early discovery narratives while it rehearses issues with which contemporary *relaciones* and debates are concerned. The earl of Surrey's equally famous version of 140, which has no colonial overtones, involves no such places.[42]

> The longe love that in my thought doeth harbar
>   and in myn hert doeth kepe his residence
>   into my face preseth with bold pretence
>   and therin campeth spreding his baner
> She that me lerneth to love & suffre
>   and will that my trust & lust negligence
>   be rayned by reason shame & reverence
>   with his hardines taketh displeasur
> Wherewithall vnto the herts forrest he fleith
>   leving his entreprise with payn & cry
>   and ther him hideth & not appereth
> What may I do when my maister fereth
>   but in the feld with him to lyve & dye
>   for goode is the liff ending faithfully.[43]

In his canon-making anthology of mid-century English lyrics, Richard Tottel's printing of "The longe love" typically reinforces the poem's interpersonal dimension through his gloss: "The louer for shamefast-nesse hideth his desire within his faithfull hart."[44] Read with some attention to colonial contexts, however, Wyatt's poem tells a miniature narrative of overzealous conquest, like that for which Cortés was notorious, and directly confronts an urgent emotional and ideological problem of this period with which Las Casas, Vitoria, and other speculative thinkers are concerned: the need to restrain collective and individual "lust" or "hardines" (which is called cruelty or inhumanity when it is practiced by the Indians) with "reason shame & reverence." The conqueror's position dissolves in an instant with the disapproval of the queenly woman, and he becomes an inarticulate figure running through the forest. But in this instance, the conqueror is not the speaker but the catalytic emotion of love itself, while the speaker plays the role of the Indian, or perhaps a personification of the conquered land itself. The sonnet moves through these changes in a swift, almost disorienting fashion, until the conqueror's disappearance at line 11, which presents a kind of dramatic and political crisis. How can the enterprise continue when its agents and its idealist principles are in open conflict? How can the Crown exploit the cupidity of a Cortés or a Pizarro without losing control to them or abandoning its supposed goals?

This poem's provisional response, as I see it, is a stunning shift that is almost always naturalized and underplayed by Wyatt's critics. The speaker, who was landed and encamped on at the first, joins the other side. Like a Moctezuma, he identifies with his cupidinous conqueror and vows to die at his side. Where the theoretical and practical problem of the present day delivers the crisis in line 11, however, Wyatt papers it over with an appeal to something that sounds very much like the ideal of *comitatus,* an earlier English notion of reciprocal obligation that is arguably anachronistic in this poem's artfully constructed context of sixteenth-century internationalism.[45] A provisional idealism, articulated by the indigene himself, stands in awkwardly for "reason shame & reverence": what do these principles avail in contemporary imperialism, with its emotions and conflicts that go unanticipated in received codes of conduct?

It is as though no one, least of all Wyatt, can answer the present-day problems posed in the sonnet; instead of answering, he redistributes sentience, agency, and authority away from their objective sites, and chronicles the amatory-colonial plot in an especially fluid and baffling rendition. Its fiction worked through, the poem discloses the woman, nominally a monarch, as its least empowered standpoint; her willed ideals are quickly set aside in favor of the speaker's "faith" for conqueror over sovereign. The experiences of conquest and love, Wyatt insists, manifest a moral logic of their own that will countervail the imposed orders of kings, ladies, and societies watching from a distance—and yet, affirmed, that logic is certain to ring hollow. With the final sentence, the speaker is seen to reach for a justification that will cover an ideological gap without quite fitting over it. Inasmuch as they rhyme with the preceding line-end only conjecturally and hang off the extremity of "The longe love," the last three syllables alone—"faithfully"—indict the factitiously idealist conclusion. The latter is portrayed as the product of an imperialism, inseparably amatory and colonial, that moves everything it touches. It makes lovers solicitous rather of Love than of a beloved, and conquered persons faithful more to their conquerors than to themselves.

Another lyric, less often treated than the two poems I have mentioned so far, evokes the savagery of the colonial project by maintaining a deliberately ambiguous application to the two principal standpoints.

> What rage is this? What furor of what kind?
> What pow'r, what plague doth weary thus my mind?
> Within my bones to rankle is assigned
>   What poison pleasant sweet?
>
> Lo, see mine eyes swell with continual tears
> The body still away sleepless it wears.
> My food nothing my fainting strength repairs
>   Nor doth my limbs sustain.
>
> In deep wide wound the deadly stroke doth turn,
> To cured scar that never shall return.
> Go to, triumph, rejoice thy goodly turn.
>   Thy friend thou dost oppress.
>
> Oppress thou dost, and hast of him no cure,
> Nor yet my plaint no pity can procure.
> Fierce tiger fell, hard rock without recure,
>   Cruel rebel to love!
>
> Once mayst thou love, never be loved again:
> So love thou still and not thy love obtain.
> So wrathful Love with spites of just disdain
>   May threat thy cruel heart.[46]

One notices how quickly the poem makes the neo-Platonic idiolect of the first line obsolete: it charges directly into the real world of "power," "plague," and "poison" as though to contend that the prevailing intellectual paradigms have run out of force in this situation. Hence the rhetorical emphasis of the first clause: "What rage is *this?*" In fact, the poem probably makes more sense in view of contemporary history—including the several key terms that drive Wyatt's argument—than in the context of Petrarchan emotions and conventions. Certainly it has been little discussed in that context, a prime example of the sort of lyric that loses visibility because it fits poorly with the consensus about Wyatt's largely national interests and courtly values.

At the start, the woman's arsenal of oppressions against the speaker seems to put her in the position of European colonist—powerful and victorious, bearing a steel sword and strange diseases—and him in the role of native American.[47] The first stanza, like many lyrics of the so-called plain style, conspicuously imitates a natural utterance—here, that of a conquered and infected subject seeking after the causes of his affliction. Wyatt's poetic career, of course, occurs near the midpoint of a century of plagues that the biohistorian Alfred W. Crosby, Jr., calls "the most spectacular period of mortality among the American Indians"; that span saw perhaps fourteen epidemics in Mexico and seventeen in Peru between 1520 and 1600.[48] Shortly before Wyatt's embassy, writing in a book that the inquisitive Englishman may well have read, the *Historia general y natural de las Indias* (1535), Gonzalo Fernández de Oviedo looks back to the Columbian landfalls and observes that of about a million inhabitants on Hispaniola in 1492, all of whom were conscripted into *repartimientos* and encomiendas, "and of those born afterwards, it is believed that at present there are no more than five hundred persons, children and adults, who are natives descended from those originals."[49] He claims that in Panama, in the sixteen years after the arrival of Pedrarias Dávila at Darién in 1514, two million people died "without [the Spaniards'] giving them to understand the *requerimiento* that His Catholic Majesty ordered them to observe before war broke out."[50] Crosby fills out Oviedo's account by observing that the first post-Columbian pandemic "began in 1519 in the Greater Antilles and swept through Mexico, Central America, and—probably—Peru," killing perhaps more native Americans than any later epidemic.[51] Of course, as Paul Slack has shown, there was a regular incidence of plague and other diseases in Tudor England as well as the Americas, but for this lyric it is exactly the opening question by a plaintive victim—as though speaking of something really transcultural and unfamiliar—and the joining of disease to other forms of oppression that imply the American connection, and for that matter give the complaint its force.[52]

Plague, it might be argued moreover, is not simply a contemporary event tossed among sixteenth-century amatory tropes: Petrarchism and contagious disease are often the results of the same events, and are involved in a shared repertory of assumptions and constructions by a small cast of contemporary recorders. One of the most influential historians of the conquest era, Oviedo had been a friend early in the century of Jacopo Sannazaro (1458–1530) and Serafino dell'Aquila (1466–1500) in Naples, and was a tireless Italianate poet himself. To the end of his life, as his intermittently autobiographical *Quinquagenas* attests, Oviedo oriented himself according to the convictions, values, and dicta of his humanist youth.[53] In 1514 he traveled in Dávila's transatlantic expedition, and in enacting the transit from Italy to Spain to America, Oviedo anticipated by perhaps ten years a movement of Spaniards that was to have the most drastic results for political, cultural, and biological exchange. Recent historians speculate that the Spanish occupation of Italy between 1510 and 1513, one of the indispensable events leading to the cultivation of sixteenth-century Hispanic Petrarchism, exposed the future conquistadores of Mexico and Central America to malaria, with disastrous results for the American population, especially the coastal Indians in the first quarter of the century.[54]

Further, in the intensely polemical atmosphere of the 1530s and 1540s, words such as "plague" and "pestilence" acquire a certain semantic extensibility. This range notably includes a political sense that takes in the Spanish exploitation of the native population, as in Fray Toribio de Benavente Motolinía's account, written in the early 1540s, of the "ten plagues" that ravaged New Spain during the early colonial period:

> This first plague [of measles] was quite similar to that of Egypt, of which one reads that the waters were wounded and turned to blood, the rivers as much as the springs and creeks. . . .
>
> The second plague was the many that died in the conquest of New Spain, especially in Mexico City. . . .
>
> The third plague was a very great famine that followed the conquest of Mexico, as they could not plant with all the wars. . . .
>
> The fourth plague was the calpixques or farmers and blacks; for after the land was distributed, the conquistadores put in the repartimientos and towns that were encomendados to them, servants or negros to cover the tributes and to comprehend the farming business. . . .
>
> The fifth plague was the great tributes and services that the Indians made.[55]

Motolinía's conclusion, popularized by the *oidor* Alonso de Zorita in his *Breve y sumaria relación de los señores de la Nueva España* (written between 1566 and 1570), joins an indictment of the Indians' forced labor with a description of their Petrarchan but literal affects and the result for public health: "Suffering these toils, hungers, colds, wearinesses, heats, winds, sleeping on the ground, in the wilderness, in the cold and the dew, is thought to bring on pestilences and infirmities, for with great breakdowns comes pestilence or *cámaras* [diarrhea]: the natives have no cure or relief, and die on the fourth or fifth day, and have death as their only cure and alleviation of their labors, because as long as they live they are never free of these."[56]

Meanwhile, one of the common characterizations of sixteenth-century Petrarchism is as an epidemic: probably the most memorable formulation is Thomas Campion's sanitary caution, toward the end of a decade of Petrarchan contagion, that "the facilitie and popularitie of

Rime [out of 'barbarized *Italy*'] creates as many Poets as a hot sommer flies."[57] "What rage is this?" and many other mid-century Petrarchan lyrics that invoke the analogy of plague are exploiting something that amounts to an empirical, authorless trope: the transcultural thinking about love in a certain way, and the social experience of plague, can be products of the same movements of soldiers, administrators, and entrepreneurs, sharing a material relation to European imperialism before they meet again in lyric poetry. The conceit of romantic love as plague does not appear in the *Canzoniere*, being largely unimagined by Petrarch's program of highly individual experience that seldom acknowledges its condition as mass culture of any sort. It is, however, a distinctly sixteenth-century intuition, written across the personal and collective histories of the generation of Wyatt—for instance, not only in the diagnosis of "What rage is this?" but in the ambiguous term "disease" in the ballade "That time that mirth did steer my ship."[58]

The political situation between the lovers in "What rage is this?" is shot through with inconsistencies. The most evident interruptions in its logic occur in the final lines of the last three stanzas. In line 12, the implicit analogy is broken by the speaker's insistence to the woman: "thy friend thou dost oppress." Asserting their old acquaintance beneath the analogy, as no Indian would, the speaker breaks open the lyric's terms to disclose a prior situation or relation—to allow, in other words, that a real-world analogy, including a borrowed history and a figurative politics of identity, has been imposed on their relations. The next line moves to restore the political conceit ("oppress thou dost, and hast of him no cure"), recalling indictments like Motolinía's and Zorita's. But something in the poem's controlling analogy has given out, and what shows through the cracks here and there is an already existing situation that perhaps seems less political than personal—but that, as a personal situation, is as coercive and frustrating as the imperialist conceit. Unrequited love, it seems, admits the complexities of imperialism even when that analogy has fallen or been set aside. In the fourth stanza the speaker, infected again, touches a Petrarchan commonplace ("my plaint no pity can procure"), resorts to what seem some standard-issue amatory metaphors ("tiger" and "rock"), and then issues his central and most urgent characterization: "Cruel rebel to love!" Does a confused speaker scramble the hierarchy of this relationship, senselessly calling the woman he has worked to cast as his oppressor, his oppressed? Or does he reveal the politics around, and in control of, the horizons of the poem to this line, identifying his Petrarchan notion of "love" as the hegemony against which the woman stands out as rebel, other, American?

Without quite saying so, the last stanza restages these questions. The seeming redundancy of the two lines

Once mayst thou love, never be loved again:
So love thou still and not thy love obtain

properly fashions two versions of unrequitedness: that of the subject in society whose love is never returned, and that of an intersubjective desire that cannot hold its object. In the first of these lines, the subject is singled out by the Petrarchan trope that treats temporality as constitutive of identity (recall Petrarch's "che son! che fui!" in Canzone 23, where the duration of love implies the fragmentation of identity). Here, loving "once" in the active voice set against an impersonal, continual rejection evokes a clash between an oppressed subject and a structure that enforces his or her frustration. The next line, however, calls up a continual, perhaps systematic loving with the design of possessing more than being loved in return, which seems somehow impersonal and acquisitive compared to the other line's hypothesis, but is every way as frustrated. The woman, then, is put in the emotional double bind that runs across both Petrarchism and imperialism in this period—of being the oppressor in love and oppressed by love—and if the speaker seems to know her position well, it is because he occupies it himself, or they inhabit it together, in mutual relation. The last line poses the dilemma again, in the delicate oxymoron of her "cruel heart." One notices, retrospectively, that the woman became a physical presence only in the sentence that ended with the name-calling of "cruel rebel"—in other words, where she herself became a potential victim. For this lyric, "the body" belongs to the oppressed; the oppressor can be embodied only when the double-edged political situation is revealed. For this mid-century conception of Petrarchism, versus (for example) Petrarch's own work, it will not do to represent the woman as heartless, because she must have the longings of an oppressor, and must be able to register her own oppression. With the discovery of these interchangeable standpoints for the two persons, the poem's original questions become more arresting: what rage is this after all? Is it the speaker's reaction to going unloved, or the woman's response to love's tyranny over her? What power wearies the speaker, his own, or the power that triumphs over him? The conceit of plague proves its force in such highly equivocal readings, where the diagnostic drift of these questions is genuine and the sheer communicability of amatory and imperialist "poison" confronts us in every line.

Cetina draws on the same intuition of love as plague in one of the most striking and elliptical sonnets of this era. His "Amor, ¿qué es ésto?" is a poem of exile and jealousy, not of the "continuell chaunge" between lovers. But in announcing that it aims to circumvent present love and its problems, Cetina's sonnet, spoken in two voices, corroborates several of the conceits developed by Wyatt and other contemporaries:

"Amor, ¿qué es ésto?" "Amor." "Mayor mal siento
Que Amor." "¿Pues qué es?" "No sé." "¿Dónde te ofende?"
"En el alma." "¿Con qué fuego lo enciende?"
"¡Fuego sí! ¿Quién lo enciende?" "El pensamiento.
    ¿Arde?" "Abrasa que parte el sentimiento."
"¿Cómo de imaginar no te defiende
La causa?" "Nó." "¿Por qué?" "Porque desciende
Muy alta." "¿A buscar qué?" "Mi perdimiento."
    "¿Luego no es fuego?" "Nó, que será rabia."
"¿Huyes del agua?" "Nó." "¿Cómo?" "Llorando."
"Descanso es desear." "Nó." "¿Es pestilencia?"
"¡Pluguiera á Dios!" "¿Por qué?" "Que á quien me agravia
Se pegara." "¿Es recelo?" "Recelando
Muero." "¡Ya sé lo que es!" "¿Qué es pues?" "Ausencia."[59]

    ("What is this love?" "Love." "I feel a greater sickness
Than Love." "But what is it?" "I do not know." "Where does it hurt?"
"In the soul." "What fire ignites it?"
"Yes, fire! Who ignites it?" "Thought.
    Does it blaze?" "It burns my feelings apart."
"How does the cause not preserve you
From imagining?" "No." "Why not?" "Because it descends
From high." "Looking for what?" "My perdition."
    "So it is not fire?" "No, more like rabies."
"Do you run from water?" "No." "How so?" "Weeping."
"Relief it is to desire." "No." "Is it pestilence?"
"Would to God it were!" "Why?" "So that the person offending me
Would be infected." "Is it suspicion?" "Suspecting
I die." "Now I know what it is!" "What then?" "Absence.")

The diagnostic mode of Wyatt's "What rage is this?" is intensified, as the speaker's two voices conduct a more urgent self-interrogation, and actually name "cause[s]" and diseases: Wyatt's "rage" and "furor," for instance, are transposed from colloquial "rage" to literal "rabies" (both appropriate to "rabia") by the question about hydrophobia, and the poem itself is symptomatic of the divided feelings mentioned as the result of mental "fire" in line 5. Where Wyatt's poem breaks apart the received situation to show its controls at work—and to imply that his "plague" is highly contagious to the woman, who has desires of her own—Cetina here maintains a complete separation (for which "absence" is a kind of standard) between his lovers. The sick voice wishes his suffering were caused by pestilence, which might broach the oblivion that surrounds him, and would imply that distance was not an issue. But the most profound cause of this lyric's affliction, the clinical voice decides, is that the woman is absent to the speaker, literally or otherwise or both; and that this condition occurs in a world of international, transcultural possibilities that sees separation, unrequitedness, and even pestilence as superficially unlike but cognate elements of the same political order. The symptoms of the speaker's disease are coextensive with the political culture around Cetina's sonnet; and as in Wyatt's "What rage is this?" there is no imaginable cure that can be separated from, let alone opposed to, that plague.

Such a revisionary reading of "What rage is this?," not to mention the other poems I have addressed here, forces one to realize that there is much about such lyrics that we only think we know, through conventional (perhaps even unquestioned) habits of observation; and at the same time, that many of these poems are held in reverence by scholars and readers who cannot be easily moved to rethink the terms of their investment. In fact, because of the weak particulars of that investment, our notions of the poems themselves need no thorough reworking. "The longe love" and the rest have always been concerned with the slippages between personal identity and political power, with loyalty and betrayal, above all with conquest—of one sort or another—as a continuing problem for persons and societies. A recent general history of the Tudor period blandly states that "poetry, too, became politicized in the hands of Skelton, Sir Thomas Wyatt, and Henry Howard, earl of Surrey," and goes on to assert that "when Wyatt translated Petrarch, the result was a poetry of protest."[60] If one accepts this much, there is no reason that such a politics should be exclusively national, or that the textual and historical evidence of the poet's wider interests should be minimized where it qualifies particular poems. This call for renewal puts nothing indispensable in danger. The few lyrics that respond principally to courtly, national readings will continue to do so, and other poems will gain their own contexts. At the least, I believe, Wyatt's love poetry and that of his European contemporaries should have the multiple contexts contributed by each other—their Petrarchisms are hardly as unmediated, and their historical settings as vague, as some accounts indicate.[61] More threatening to the present order of sixteenth-century literary studies, however, is the recognition that the overly familiar history we now apply to these poems is one we have built ourselves: that having asked too few questions of the period and the poetic material, we are unable to contest the predictable interpretations that result. A recent commentary on Wyatt's lyrics by H. A. Mason that explicitly hypostatizes the poet's roles—the poems are grouped as pertaining to "The Lover," "The Christian," and "The Courtier"—should warn of the suspicious convenience between history and poetics that has taken over certain texts and made others too hard to handle.[62] (Significantly, the poems I choose here as having a feasible international or colonial dimension, except "They fle from me," are left out of Mason's arrangement.) Interrogating the static places in Wyatt's background, recasting him as diplomat and entrepreneur as well as courtier, registering the overlapping discourses that go into his lyrics—in all of these ways we can widen the import of the poems, and shake them loose from certainties. To do so would not only disclose a larger Wyatt, but find early modern poetry newly located in its historical world.

Notes

1. Margarita Peña, ed., *Flores de varia poesía* (Mexico City: Secretaría de Educación Pública, 1987), summarizes the life and literary career of Cortés (1532?–89), the second Marqués del Valle de Oaxaca (32–34).

2. In my forthcoming book *Unrequited Conquests: Love and Empire in the Colonial Americas,* I consider some of the family, class, and social dimensions of these projects, which fall outside the scope of the present essay.

3. Elizabeth Armstrong, *Ronsard and the Age of Gold* (Cambridge: Cambridge University Press, 1968), esp. 134–41 and 171–79.

4. *Representations* 33 (Winter 1991), ed. Stephen Greenblatt. The issue is a tribute to the late French cultural historian Michel de Certeau.

5. Louis Adrian Montrose, "The Work of Gender in the Discourse of Discovery," ibid., 1–41, and Mary C. Fuller, "Ralegh's Fugitive Gold: Reference and Deferral in *The Discoverie of Guiana,*" ibid., 42–64.

6. Fuller, "Ralegh's Fugitive Gold," 46; and Montrose, "Work of Gender," 8.

7. Montrose, "Work of Gender," 13; Fuller, "Ralegh's Fugitive Gold," 60; and Montrose, "Work of Gender," 30. Recent work by Petrarchists that seems to inform the Renaissance paradigms with which Montrose and Fuller work includes John Freccero, "The Fig Tree and the Laurel: Petrarch's Poetics" (1975; reprinted in *Literary Theory/Renaissance Texts,* ed. Patricia Parker and David Quint [Baltimore: The Johns Hopkins University Press, 1987], 20–32); Nancy J. Vickers, "Diana Described: Scattered Woman and Scattered Rhyme," in *Writing and Sexual Difference,* ed. Elizabeth Abel (Chicago: University of Chicago Press, 1982), 95–109; Thomas M. Greene, *The Light in Troy: Imitation and Discovery in Renaissance Poetry* (New Haven: Yale University Press, 1982), 81–146; and an essay by Vickers cited by Montrose, "'The blazon of sweet beauty's best': Shakespeare's *Lucrece,*" in *Shakespeare and the Question of*

Theory, ed. Patricia Parker and Geoffrey Hartman (New York: Methuen, 1985), 95–115.

8. My account of Columbus's first-person construction appears in the first chapter of *Unrequited Conquests.*

9. Among the many examples of this perspective on Wyatt's poetry are C. S. Lewis, *English Literature in the Sixteenth Century, Excluding Drama,* Oxford History of English Literature 3 (Oxford: Clarendon Press, 1954), 222–30; Raymond Southall, *The Courtly Maker: An Essay on the Poetry of Wyatt and His Contemporaries* (Oxford: Basil Blackwell, 1964); Douglas L. Peterson, *The English Lyric from Wyatt to Donne* (Princeton: Princeton University Press, 1967), 87–119; A. M. Kinghorn, *The Chorus of History: Literary-Historical Relations in Renaissance Britain* (London: Blandford Press, 1971), 250–58; Jonathan Kamholtz, "Thomas Wyatt's Poetry: The Politics of Love," *Criticism* 20 (1978), 349–65; Stephen Greenblatt, *Renaissance Self-Fashioning: From More to Shakespeare* (Chicago: University of Chicago Press, 1980), 115–56 (where even "a discussion of Wyatt's psalms will be drawn irresistibly from the presentation of the self in the court of God to the presentation of the self in the court of Henry VIII, that is, to the court lyrics" [116]); A. C. Spearing, *Medieval to Renaissance in English Poetry* (Cambridge: Cambridge University Press, 1985), 278–300; and Jonathan Crewe, *Trials of Authorship: Anterior Forms and Poetic Reconstruction from Wyatt to Shakespeare,* The New Historicism 9 (Berkeley and Los Angeles: University of California Press, 1990), 23–47. For a general study of the courtly context in early modern literature, see Daniel Javitch, *Poetry and Courtliness in Renaissance England* (Princeton: Princeton University Press, 1978). Ellen C. Caldwell, "Recent Studies in Sir Thomas Wyatt (1970–1987)" (*English Literary Renaissance* 19 [1989], 226–46), is a useful survey of the present-day consensus about what matters in Wyatt and his background.

10. Several recent critics seem to recognize the issues relevant to, if not the substance of, a colonial interpretation of some of Wyatt's poems. Besides Kamholtz's "Wyatt's Poetry: The Politics of Love" (cited in preceding note), see Michael McCanles, "Love and Power in the Poetry of Sir Thomas Wyatt," *Modern Language Quarterly* 29 (1968), 145–60, and Barbara L. Estrin, "Becoming the Other/The Other Becoming in Wyatt's Poetry," *ELH* 51 (1984), 431–45. The sixteenth-century recognition of amatory and colonial experiences as correspondents appears in a number of texts. In the third chapter of *Unrequited Conquests,* I treat two of these: anthologies of lyric poetry, assembled in Mexico City (1577) and published in Madrid (1591), respectively, that openly address the problems of love and conquest in terms of each other.

11. An incurious but widely shared view is expressed by Kinghorn in *The Chorus of History:* "one or two of [Wyatt's] poems may be linked with his movements in other countries between 1537 and 1539" (256). He goes on to cite "Tagus, farewell." Patricia Thomson, *Sir Thomas Wyatt and His Background* (Stanford: Stanford University Press, 1964), narrates what is known of Wyatt's diplomatic years ("if posterity remembers only the courtly love poet, Wyatt's contemporaries regarded also, and more keenly, the servant of the

state, his father's [Sir Henry Wyatt's] heir" [quotation 4, see also 61–70]). Greenblatt acknowledges the significance of Wyatt's ambassadorial experience for his poems, especially the translations, but limits this experience to "French and Italian culture" (*Renaissance Self-Fashioning*, 139–56, esp. 145).

12. On the English monitoring of the developing alliance between France and the Empire, see *Letters and Papers, Foreign and Domestic, of the Reign of Henry VIII*, ed. John Sherren Brewer, James Gairdner, and Robert Henry Brodie, 21 vols. (1862–1910; reprint, London: HMSO, 1920 [hereafter cited as *LP*]), vol. 13 (1538), pt. 2, 380–81 (no. 915); vol. 14 (1539), pt. 1, 189–90 (no. 490), 216–18 (no. 561), and 375 (no. 782); and vol. 14 (1539), pt. 2, 184 (no. 524), 228–29 (no. 628), and 244–46 (no. 675).

13. The records of Wyatt's involvement with the marriage negotiations are in *LP*, vol. 13 (1538), pt. 2, 186–88, 305–6 (no. 786), 379–80 (no. 914), 383–84 (no. 923), 426–27 (no. 993), 450–51 (no. 1054), and 471–72 (no. 1127); vol. 14 (1539), pt. 1, 37–38 (no. 92), 117 (no. 299), 166 (no. 405), and 189–90 (no. 490), and vol. 15 (1540), 367–69 (no. 781). For Henry's advice to Charles via Wyatt, see *LP*, vol. 13 (1538), pt. 2, 239–42 (no. 622), and for the reply, 411–16 (no. 974)—the quotations appear at 412 and 411. On the usage of "the Spains" to refer to the Spanish nation, see Hugh Seton-Watson, *Nations and States* (Boulder, Colo.: Westview Press, 1977), 53.

14. *LP*, vol. 14 (1539), pt. 1, 236 (no. 603). See also the summary of the nuncio Giovanni Poggio's letter to the pope's vice chancellor Cardinal Alexander Farnese: "Watches the actions, or rather the speeches of this English ambassador and does not weary in soliciting the Inquisitors in his cause, and has good hope of getting rid of him" (218–19).

15. On Wyatt's contacts with Diego Hurtado de Mendoza, see *LP*, vol. 13 (1538), pt. 2, 136–37 (no. 349), 238 (no. 616), 385–86 (no. 925), and 411–16 (no. 974), esp. 413 and 415. Erika Spivakovsky, *Son of the Alhambra: Don Diego Hurtado de Mendoza, 1504–1575* (Austin: University of Texas Press, 1970), is the most recent biographical account; Helen Nader, *The Mendoza Family in the Spanish Renaissance, 1350 to 1550* (New Brunswick: Rutgers University Press, 1979), surveys Mendoza's career as diplomat and humanist in the family context (199–204).

16. John Rattlef calls Wyatt "Don Thomas" in *LP*, vol. 13 (1538), pt. 2, 390–91 (no. 938). On the career of Antonio de Mendoza, who had been appointed viceroy of New Spain in April of 1535, see Arthur Scott Aiton, *Antonio de Mendoza, First Viceroy of New Spain* (Durham: Duke University Press, 1927), and J. H. Elliott, "Spain and America in the Sixteenth and Seventeenth Centuries," *The Cambridge History of Latin America*, ed. Leslie Bethell, 8 vols. to date (Cambridge: Cambridge University Press, 1984–), vol. 1, 293–96. The two Mendoza brothers were in contact during the period of Wyatt's ambassadorship, and Diego Hurtado de Mendoza was manifestly interested in the affairs of New Spain: see *Algunas cartas de Don Diego Hurtado de Mendoza, escritas 1538–1552*, ed. Alberto Vazquez and R. Selden Rose, Yale Romanic Studies 10 (New Haven: Yale University Press, 1935), 2–5, and Angel González Palencia and Eugenio Mele, *Vida y obras de Don Diego Hurtado de*

Mendoza, 2 vols. (Madrid: Instituto de Valencia de Don Juan, 1941), vol. 1, 77. Wyatt is mentioned at vol. 1, 78; Mendoza's friendship with Aretino at vol. 1, 160–77.

17. Lewis Hanke, *The Spanish Struggle for Justice in the Conquest of America* (Philadelphia: University of Pennsylvania Press and London: Oxford University Press, 1949), is an outmoded but helpful source on the encomienda system. Elliott, "Spain and America," describes the struggle in this period over encomiendas, rights, revenues, and geographical claims (287–314).

18. Lesley Byrd Simpson, *The Encomienda in New Spain,* rev. ed. (Berkeley and Los Angeles: University of California Press, 1966), 114–15.

19. The bull is translated into Spanish in *Documentos inéditos del siglo XVI para la historia de México,* ed. P[adre] Mariano Cuevas (Mexico City: Talleres del Museo Nacional de Arqueología, Historia y Etnología, 1914), 84–86, and into English in Hanke, *Spanish Struggle for Justice,* 72–73; it is discussed at length in Hanke's "Pope Paul III and the American Indians," *Harvard Theological Review* 30 (1937), 65–102.

20. The Tuzutlán or Vera Paz experiment is treated in Hanke, *Spanish Struggle for Justice,* 77–81. José M. Gallegos Rocafull, *El pensamiento mexicano en los siglos XVI y XVII* (Mexico City: Centro de Estudios Filosóficos, 1951), describes the controversies over the rights and capacities of the Indians in the sixteenth and seventeenth centuries (15–60).

21. Gallegos Rocafull, *Pensamiento mexicano,* 37–42.

22. On the contexts and results of Vitoria's *relectio,* see Anthony Pagden, "Dispossessing the Barbarian: The Language of Spanish Thomism and the Debate Over the Property Rights of the American Indians," in *The Languages of Political Theory in Early-Modern Europe,* ed. Anthony Pagden (Cambridge: Cambridge University Press, 1987), 79–98.

23. Elliott, "Spain and America," 307.

24. On Wyatt's credit with Charles V, I quote Edmund Bonner's letter of Oct. 15, 1538, in *LP,* vol. 13 (1538), pt. 2, 237 (no. 615).

25. On the hunt conceit in this and other poems, see Rosemond Tuve, *Allegorical Imagery,* ed. Thomas P. Roche, Jr. (Princeton: Princeton University Press, 1966), 305–7; Greenblatt, *Renaissance Self-Fashioning,* 145–49; and Crewe, *Trials of Authorship,* 38–44. Stanley J. Koziskowski, "Wyatt's 'They Flee from Me' and Churchyard's Complaint of Jane Shore" (*Notes and Queries* n.s. 25 [1978], 416–17), reasonably suggests that the woman resembles traditional personifications of Fortune.

26. Anne Lake Prescott, "The Thirsty Deer and the Lord of Life: Some Contexts for *Amoretti* 67–70" (*Spenser Studies* 6 [1985], 33–76), is a particularly useful examination of some sixteenth-century deer and hunt poems as they relate to biblical and liturgical models.

27. Cristóbal Colón, *The Diario of Christopher Columbus's First Voyage to America, 1492–1493,* ed. Oliver Dunn and James E. Kelley, Jr. (Norman: University of Oklahoma Press, 1989), 137 and 158. Columbus's diary was lost sometime in the mid-sixteenth century, and survives in Las Casas's transcription; in the same scholar's *Historia de las Indias,* on which Las Casas worked

for nearly forty years beginning in 1527 and which was published only in the nineteenth century; and in Fernando Columbus's *Historie* of his father's enterprises, which itself survives only in an Italian translation (1571).

28. Richard Harrier, *The Canon of Sir Thomas Wyatt's Poetry* (Cambridge: Harvard University Press, 1975), 131–32.

29. See Stephen J. Greenblatt, "Learning to Curse: Aspects of Linguistic Colonialism in the Sixteenth Century," in *First Images of America: The Impact of the New World on the Old,* ed. Fredi Chiappelli, 2 vols.(Berkeley and Los Angeles: University of California Press, 1976), vol. 2, 568–76, reprinted in Greenblatt, *Learning to Curse: Essays in Early Modern Culture* (New York: Routledge, 1990), 16–39. Here Greenblatt follows the Renaissance convention of the Wild Man, on which poems such as "They fle from me" depend.

30. Richard Hakluyt, comp., *The Principal Navigations, Voyages, Traffiques and Discoveries of the English Nation,* 12 vols. (Glasgow: James MacLehose and Sons, 1903–5), vol. 10, 57.

31. José de Acosta, *Historia natural y moral de las Indias,* ed. Edmundo O'Gorman, 2d ed. (Mexico City: Fondo de Cultura Económica, 1962), 280.

32. Compare McCanles, "Love and Power," 153–54.

33. Thomson tells of the relationship with Boleyn and its light contact with Wyatt's lyrics (*Sir Thomas Wyatt and His Background,* 18–43).

34. José A. Llaguno, *La personalidad jurídica del indio y el III Consilio Provincial Mexicano (1585)* (Mexico City: Editorial Porrúa, 1963), 25. Llaguno summarizes various documents in the Archivo General de Indias in Seville, which are the *pareceres* or opinions of particular informants.

35. Ibid., 25.

36. "Relación sumaria de la información que se trajo de la Nueva España a pedimento de la ciudad de México" (1544), in ibid., 156, 157, 158. The original document is in the Archivo General de Indias.

37. Silvio A. Zavala, *La encomienda indiana,* 2d ed. (Mexico City: Editorial Porrúa, 1973), 55. J. H. Elliott in "The Spanish Conquest and Settlement of America" (*Cambridge History of Latin America,* vol. 1, 192–96) summarily describes the encomienda system between its founding shortly after the Mexican conquest and its adaptations in the New Laws of 1542–43 and subsequent revisions. Simpson, *Encomienda in New Spain,* quotes and paraphrases many documents of this period that engage the aforementioned terms and issues (123–44).

38. "Relación sumaria" (1544), in Llaguno, *Personalidad jurídica del indio,* 155, 156, 158, 25.

39. Compare Anne Ferry, *The "Inward" Language: Sonnets of Wyatt, Sidney, Shakespeare, Donne* (Chicago: University of Chicago Press, 1983), 48: "The speaker in Wyatt's 'They flee from me' remembers ladies 'With naked fote stalking within my chamber,' evoking an atmosphere of dangerous intrigue conducted with difficulty behind the public rooms and courts of great houses."

40. Caldwell summarizes several articles that demonstrate the consensus about what is assumed and what needs demonstration in "They fle from me" ("Recent Studies in Wyatt," 236–37). Compare Greenblatt on a poem often

treated in the same manner, "Who so list to hounte": "There is, in fact, nothing in the poem that is unequivocally about worldly power and appropriation" (*Renaissance Self-Fashioning*, 146).

41. Luís de Camões, *Lirica completa*, ed. Maria de Lurdes Saraiva, 3 vols. (Lisbon: Imprensa Nacional–Casa da Moeda, 1980), vol. 2, 83.

42. Henry Howard, Earl of Surrey, *Poems,* ed. Emrys Jones (Oxford: Clarendon Press, 1964), 3. Perhaps a line from Surrey's epitaph on Wyatt rings out here: "A toung that served in forein realmes his king" (27, l. 17).

43. Harrier, *Canon of Wyatt's Poetry*, 101.

44. *Tottel's Miscellany (1557–1587),* ed. Hyder Edward Rollins, rev. ed., 2 vols. (Cambridge: Harvard University Press, 1966), vol. 1, 32.

45. Cf. Fredric Jameson, "Of Islands and Trenches: Neutralization and the Production of Utopian Discourse," in *The Ideologies of Theory: Essays 1971–1986,* 2 vols., Theory and History of Literature 48–49 (Minneapolis: University of Minnesota Press, 1988), vol. 2, 92. Jameson observes that Thomas More's *Utopia* (1516), a text perhaps two generations older than Wyatt's work, already remarks the passing of the feudal system that "includes, besides the lord and his family, and the peasants and artisans who support them, the feudal retinue which ensures his power." See Raphael Hythlodaeus's speech on the connections between nobles, beggars, and thieves in *Utopia,* ed. Edward Surtz, S.J., and J. H. Hexter, *Yale Edition of the Complete Works,* ed. Richard S. Sylvester et al., 15 vols. (New Haven: Yale University Press, 1963–), vol. 4, 60–64.

46. Thomas Wyatt, *Sir Thomas Wyatt: The Complete Poems,* ed. R. A. Rebholz (New Haven: Yale University Press, 1981), 150–51. Rebholz presents the poem's many variants on 421–22, while Harrier (*Canon of Wyatt's Poetry,* 212–13) gives them interlinearly in his transcription, and calls "What rage is this?" "a remarkable specimen of a poem in the process of being written" (3). Helen V. Baron, "Wyatt's 'What Rage'" (*The Library* 31 [1976], 188–204), describes the revisions and supposes a lost original from which Wyatt might have translated; see Beryl Gray's reply in the next volume and year of the same journal (379–80).

47. As Baron indicates, the poem once opened with the lines "What rage is this? what furour of excesse? / what powre what poyson dothe my mynd opresse?" ("Wyatt's 'What Rage,'" 190). The word "infect" appeared interlinearly as an alternative to the first phrase of l. 2.

48. Alfred W. Crosby, Jr., *The Columbian Exchange: Biological and Cultural Consequences of 1492* (Westport, Conn.: Greenwood Press, 1972), 37–38. Charles Gibson, *The Aztecs under Spanish Rule: A History of the Indians of the Valley of Mexico, 1519–1810* (Stanford: Stanford University Press, 1964), gives a chronological table of epidemics in the Valley of Mexico between 1520 and 1810 (448–51).

49. Gonzalo Fernández de Oviedo, *Historia general y natural de las Indias,* ed. Juan Pérez de Tudela Bueso, 5 vols., Biblioteca de Autores Españoles 117–21 (Madrid: Ediciones Atlas, 1959), vol. 1, 66–67, quoted (in Crosby's translation) in *Columbian Exchange,* 45.

50. Oviedo, *Historia general,* vol. 3, 353.

51. Crosby, *Columbian Exchange*, 39.

52. Paul Slack, *The Impact of Plague in Tudor and Stuart England* (Oxford: Clarendon Press, 1985), esp. 53–78.

53. On the Italian background to Oviedo's career, see Pérez de Tudela's introduction to the BAE edition of the *Historia general*, vol. 1, xxxi, and the historian's own testimony in the abridgement of the *Quinquagenas* entitled *Las memorias de Gonzalo Fernández de Oviedo*, ed. Juan Bautista Avalle-Arce, 2 vols., North Carolina Studies in the Romance Languages and Literatures: Texts, Textual Studies and Translations 1–2 (Chapel Hill: University of North Carolina Department of Romance Languages, 1974), vol. 1, 76, 200, 254, and vol. 2, 544, 639–40. Harold Livermore, *A History of Spain* (London: George Allen and Unwin, 1958), chronicles the ambitions toward Italy held out in this period by Charles VIII of France and Ferdinand II of Aragon (197–203). In books 9 through 11 of his sixteenth-century *Storia d'Italia*, trans. Sidney Alexander (1969; Princeton: Princeton University Press, 1984), Francesco Guicciardini describes the events of 1510 to 1513, including an analysis of the Italian distrust of the Holy League (236–39).

54. *New Iberian World: A Documentary History of the Discovery and Settlement of Latin America to the Early 17th Century*, ed. John H. Parry and Robert G. Keith, 5 vols. (New York: Times Books and Hector and Rose, 1984), vol. 3, 49. Sherburne F. Cook, "The Incidence and Significance of Disease among the Aztecs and Related Tribes" (*Hispanic American Historical Review* 26 [1946], 323), entertains the same possibility.

55. Fray Toribio de Benavente o Motolinía, *Memoriales*, ed. Edmundo O'Gorman, Serie de Historiadores y Cronistas de Indias 2 (Mexico City: Universidad Nacional Autónoma de Mexico, 1971), 21–26. Magnus Mörner, *Race Mixture in the History of Latin America*, defines *calpixque* as an African slave who served as foreman over a village of Indians ([Boston: Little, Brown, 1967], 30).

56. Alonso de Zurita [or Zorita], *Breve relación de los señores de la Nueva España*, in *Nueva colección de documentos para la historia de México*, ed. Joaquín García Icazbalceta, 5 vols. (1886–92; reprint, Mexico City: Editorial Salvador Chavez Hayhoe, [1941]), vol. 3, 164; compare Benjamin Keen's translation, *Life and Labor in Ancient Mexico* (New Brunswick: Rutgers University Press, 1963), 212. In his fine introduction to Zorita's career, Keen summarizes the relation between Motolinía's texts and the *Breve relación*.

57. Thomas Campion, "Observations in the Art of English Poesie," *Works*, ed. Walter R. Davis (New York: W. W. Norton and Company, 1970), 294.

58. "That time that mirth did steer my ship" appears in Rebholz's edition (*Sir Thomas Wyatt: Complete Poems*, 127–28), but is omitted by Harrier (*Canon of Wyatt's Poetry*, 38–41) as spurious; the latter editor confidently and typically asserts that the poem "expresses the resolve of a servant to remain loyal to his lady, whom he has dared to love above his degree" (41), even though the poem says nothing like the second clause.

59. Gutierre de Cetina, *Obras*, ed. Joaquín Hazañas y la Rua, rev. Margarita Peña (Mexico City: Editorial Porrúa, 1977), 13.

60. John Guy, *Tudor England* (Oxford: Oxford University Press, 1988), 409–10. Compare 188, where Guy narrates that "Wyatt, [Thomas] Cromwell's client who witnessed his beheading, wrote his obituary," and quotes the first three lines of "The pillar perished is whereto I leant" without acknowledging Petrarch's original, *Canzoniere* 269, and David Norbrook, *Poetry and Politics in the English Renaissance* (London: Routledge and Kegan Paul, 1984), where the original is mentioned (46). In his edition (*Sir Thomas Wyatt: Complete Poems*, 357–58), Rebholz acutely summarizes the several leaps on which this interpretation relies.

61. For instance, Spearing, *Medieval to Renaissance in English Poetry*, 300–306.

62. H. A. Mason, ed., *Sir Thomas Wyatt: A Literary Portrait* (Bristol: Bristol Classical Press, 1986).

"Holy Wurdes" and "Slypper Wit": John Bale's *King Johan* and the Poetics of Propaganda

DAVID SCOTT KASTAN

"Religion is a sixteenth-century word for nationalism."
—Sir Lewis Namier

"Nations are made by human will."
—Ernest Gellner

Listed among the papers of the reign of Henry VIII and preserved in two manuscript copies is a treatise written by Richard Morison for the king, entitled *A discourse touching the reformation of the lawes of England*. The Calendar of State Papers assigns the document to 1542, though clearly it was written as much as five or six years earlier.[1] The main concern of the Morison tract is a call for the codification of the common law and its translation into Latin, but near the end is an extended digression from its "chief matier," in which Morison rehearses the familiar Protestant charges against the "ungodlynes, hurtes, and evylls" caused by the pope in "every christian realme." Here Morison argues that, "unto the tyme he be destroyed of all prynces," the pope must be resisted by persistently and persuasively declaring the truth of papal tyranny to the English people: "daily by all meanes opened inculked and dryven into the peoples heddes, tought in scholes to children, plaied in plaies before the ignorant people, songe in mynstrelles songes, and bokes in englisshe purposly to be devysed to declare the same at large."

Though obviously aware of the various modes of ideological dissemination and control available to the monarchy, Morison is particularly interested in the capacity of popular drama "to teache and preache." Noting that "into the commen people thynges sooner enter by the eies, then by the eares," Morison sees plays as a medium both "convenyant and most meete" to declare the perfidy of Rome, and accordingly he calls for a revision of the available dramatic forms. "In somer," Morison writes to Henry,

> comenly upon the holy daies in most places of your realm, ther be plLayes of Robyn hoode, mayde Marian, freer Tuck, wherin besides the lewdnes and rebawdrey that ther is open to the people, disobedience also to your officers is tought, whilest these good bloodes go about to take from the shirif of Notyngham one that for offending the lawes shulde have suffered execution. Howmoche better is it that these plaies shulde be forbodden and deleted and others dyvyssed to set forth and declare lyvely before the peoples eies the abhomynation and wickednes of the Bisshop of Rome, monkes, ffreers, nonnes, and suche like, and declare and open to them theobedience that your subiectes by goddes and mans lawes owe unto your magestie.[2]

G. R. Elton, in his *Policy and Police,* certainly the most comprehensive account available of "the enforcement of the Reformation," claims that Morison's call for dramatic propaganda "came to nothing," and Elton seems genuinely relieved to note "that the prehistory of the Elizabethan stage was not littered with pope-hunting plays commissioned by Thomas Cromwell."[3] But, if companies of touring players did not fill their repertories exclusively with antipapal polemic, clearly plays were written to advance the Reformation and were of sufficient concern to provoke a variety of condemnations and prohibitions against polemical drama in the aftermath of the Six Articles Act of 1539, which halted the advance of the Reformation, at least in its Cromwellian form. (Indeed Bishop Gardiner, responding to the unnerving proliferation of anti-Catholic plays in the 1540s, seems to have explicitly reversed Morison's call, forbidding "the players of london" to play anything except plays "of robin hode and litle Johan / and of the Parlament of byrdes and suche other trifles."[4] "Players, printers, preachers," in Foxe's famous phrase, were the reformers' "triple bulwark against the triple crown of the pope."[5] By mid-century, friend and foe alike had come to recognize the constitutive role of theatrical activity in England's reformation. In 1544, Bale commended the players as "godly ministers" of the Reformation, while Abbot Feckenham, in 1559, in a speech in the House of Lords, condemned "the preachers and scaffold players of this new religion."[6] In 1564, while claiming paradoxically that he will "passe ouer here in silence the infamous companie of common minstrelles and enterlude plaiers," Thomas Dorman hysterically sputtered against the role of the players "in publishing the newe ghospell," reluctantly acknowledging them as "one of the engines set vp by god ageinst the triple crowne of the pope to bring him down."[7]

To promote the Henrician reformation, plays unquestionably were written and playwrights patronized. An energetic dramatic campaign, writes David Bevington, "was conducted largely or perhaps entirely under government sponsorship—not under Henry directly, but under his reforming ministers."[8] A troop known as Lord Cromwell's or the Lord Privy Seal's players (perhaps identical with the troop referred to as "the Scycrctars players" in the Leicester borough records) was active between 1537 and 1540; and while it has been suggested that these were the players Cromwell's account book terms "Bale and his ffelowes," this cannot be certainly established. Nonetheless, under whatever name, John Bale and a troop of players did tour and perform plays with government support, and when Bale was twice examined by conservative bishops on charges of heresy, "the pious Cromwell," as Bale calls him, interceded each time and set him free *ob editas comoedias* (i.e., on account of the plays Bale had produced).[9]

King Johan was no doubt one of those plays that earned Bale Cromwell's support, and if not "dyvyssed" explicitly in response to Morison's call for new entertainments to be written to promote the Reformation it was clearly conceived in a similar spirit. In early January of 1538/9, during the Christmas celebrations at Cranmer's house, the play was performed,[10] and at least one spectator that evening clearly got its point: "it ys petie that the Bisshop of Rome should reigne any lenger," declared the eighteen-year-old John Alforde, "for if he should the said Bisshop wold do with our King as he did with King John."[11] Bale's *Johan* is an aggressively antipapal play, designed precisely to show, in the words of Morison's treatise, "the usurped power of the bisshope of Rome, howe he usurped uppon kinges and prynces, howe and wherby he and his adherents wente aboute to distroie this Realme."[12] Indeed in Bale's play, "Usurpyd Powr" is the true name of Pope Innocent III, and King John, the first English king represented on the stage, is not the "wycked" monarch of the chronicles (or of the Robin Hood legend) but, exactly as Morison would have desired, a proto-Protestant martyr, a champion of English integrity, in both senses of the word, and finally, like England itself, a victim of the villainy of Rome.

Bale's play reveals much about the Cromwellian phase of the Reformation that Morison's tract was designed to advance. The emphasis of both is more upon politics than theology. This is not to question the religious commitment of men like Morison, Cromwell, Cranmer, or Bale, but to recognize the degree to which, as Christopher Hill has said, "the Reformation in England was an act of state"[13]—and also, what Hill did not say, an act of state-building.

Notoriously, in 1533, the Act in Restraint of Appeals, drafted by Cromwell himself, had held that "this realm of England is an Empire,"[14] but an imperial sovereignty, whenever it was conceived, was actually secured only with the break from Rome. Only with the creation of the *ecclesia Anglicana,* the Church of England instead of the Church *in* England, does England truly achieve independence from Rome and the papacy; only with the English monarch's assumption of the government of that Church can he truly claim sovereignty in the land. The establishment of an English Church not only denied the supremacy of the pope, fulfilling the imperial desires of Henry that were perhaps apparent even as early as 1509 with his amendments to the coronation promises,[15] but also provided the state (and it is no doubt significant that the use of the word "state" in this sense dates precisely from the 1530s)[16] with resources, both institutional and financial, essential for the effective consolidation of power. Revenue from the dissolution of the monasteries offered at least short-term financial independence to the Crown; and, what was perhaps of even greater consequence than this alienation of church wealth, control of the pulpit and the Church courts (and the system of patronage that accompanied it) provided the crown with necessary apparatuses of social ordering. The powerful ideological and bureaucratic assertions of royal supremacy against the jurisdictional claims of the papacy not only successfully weakened the Church as an institution but were, in fact, what permitted the "Empire," in Cromwell's proud, Erastian term, to organize itself internally as a self-sufficient sovereign state.

It is the same issue of supremacy that is at the heart of Bale's *King Johan,* an issue particularly acute in the winter of 1538/9 when the play was performed, if not actually written. John stands as champion of England against the depredations of the papacy and its clergy. Not merely voicing "England's timeless insular fears of Catholic league and invasion,"[17] the play is a particularly timely articulation of the anxieties of the godly nation in the face of increased Catholic efforts to reimpose papal authority upon it. In December of 1538, the long-suspended bull excommunicating Henry was at last published, and throughout the autumn the government had frantically prepared for Catholic invasion and supporting insurrection of Catholic nobles at home. It could not be accidental, as Greg Walker has noted, "that Bale chose during Christmas 1538/9 to present a play about the occasion on which England was placed under papal interdict and its king excommunicated."[18] Bale's play, as it enacts John's heroic resistance to the aggressions of a worldly Church, if it finally shows the English king resigning "the septer and the crowne" (1729)[19] to the pope's representative, precisely registers both the hopes and the fears of the reformers.

King John enters alone to begin the play and speaks first of how "the scriptur of God" (2) calls for subjects to be obedient to their rulers:

Bothe Peter and Pawle makyth plenteosse utterans
How that all pepell shuld shew there trew alegyauns
To ther lawfull kyng.
(4–6)

John refers to the oft-cited verses of 1 Peter 2:13–14 and Romans 13:1–2, which were regularly invoked in the sixteenth century to justify a doctrine of nonresistance. These familiar claims of absolute obedience are, however, highly charged in the Reformation political controversy. Not understood merely as general demands for the loyalty of a citizenry, the scriptural injunctions were read by many in Tudor England specifically as the authorization of royal supremacy against the temporal claims of the papacy.

"No person," writes Tyndale, "neither any degree, may be exempt from this ordinance of God: neither can the profession of monks and friars, or any thing that the pope or bishops can lay for themselves, except them from the sword of the emperor or kings, if they break the laws. For it is written, 'let every soul submit himself unto the authority of the higher powers.' Here is no man except, but all souls must obey."[20] Tyndale thus holds up the Pauline verse to prove that the clergy themselves, no less than the laity, are subject to secular authority, and that the Church's claims to "the temporal sword" are both unjustifiable and pernicious, clearly "contrary to God's ordinances and Christ's doctrine" (188). The Church, merely a spiritual congregation, has no jurisdictional authority over secular rulers; kings, not "bishops and prelates," are to govern the "worldly" or "temporal kingdom," and are, according to Tyndale, to "rule their realms themselves, with the help of lay-men that are sage, wise, learned, and expert" (206–7). His vision articulates precisely the course the Henrician reformation was to take, and is sufficient reason for Henry to have found *The Obedience of a Christian Man* (1528) "a book for me and all kings to read."[21]

Bale's *King Johan* similarly would advance the claims of supremacy central to the incipient Protestant nation, emphasizing both the king's divine authority, "gevyn from god above" (1342), and the fraudulent claims of the Pope "whych hath no tytle good / Of iurisdyctyon, but of vsurpacyon onlye" (2059–60). John is "a mynyster immedyate vndre God" (2356), ruling by "successyon lyneal" (11), and a just and gracious king, eager "to reforme the lawes and sett men in good order" (20). If John clearly reveals that his notion of "reforme," like that of his Tudor successor, does not extend to any substantive social reorganization (the Anabaptists are as noxious as the Church), he nonetheless convincingly displays his concern for the well-being of his "commynallte" (1573). And yet in spite of John's emphatic right and responsibility, surrounded by hostile forces from abroad and corrupt estates at home, he is finally "compelled" to "resigne . . . both crown and regall poure" (1711–12) in the face of the Catholic force arrayed before him, before receiving it back in fief. Not "cowardness" but "compassyon" (1719–20) determines John's decision to yield; only to prevent the "shedynge of Christen blood" (2957) does he "gyue vpp" his "whole gouernaunce" (1722) to Rome. If his experience provides evidence of "how Antichristes whelpes haue noble princes vsed" (2651), his insistence upon the legitimacy of his authority against the claims of the papacy provides a pattern of godly rule that Henry, "duke Iosue" (1112) to John's "faythfull Moyses" (1107), would fulfill.

But if *King Johan* enthusiastically rehearses the familiar Tudor assertions of monarchical supremacy against the claims of papal jurisdiction, it also unwittingly but necessarily reveals an instability in its own polemical assertions, and perhaps in the imperial claims themselves. *King Johan* enacts Bale's apocalyptic vision of history in John's heroic resistance of the papacy, but it always threatens to collapse its fundamental opposition between godly rule and papal duplicity in the very condition of its enactment. If papal untruth is presented in terms of its manifest "ipocrysy" (432), its deceptive "serymonys and popetly plays" (415), the singular truth of John's proto-Protestantism can be maintained only by impossibly asserting it as something plain and immediate, as something unfeigned; that is, it can be maintained only by repressing the fact of the play itself. John's papal foes are "dysgysed players" (66), "Latyne mummers" (426), performing "spectakles" (767), "pagent[s]" (786), and "sterracles" (997), playing parts that would mask their "falssed" (i.e., falsehood) (263). "The implication," as Greg Walker has argued, "is clearly that any spiritual authority which relies upon costumes, and thus disguise, is in fact worthless, and worse, fraudulent."[22] Characteristically, John does imagine the reformed polity as a community "not of dysgysyd shavelynges / But of faythfull hartes" (429–30). However, Bale's vision of John's authority and of England's integrity is no less a spectacle, available to its sixteenth-century audience only in the representation of "dysgysed players" on a stage. Sedition may "call hymself Relygyon" (544), as John warns, and "chaunge [his] apparell / Vnto a bisshoppe" (296–97), but if this is the sign of Catholic hypocrisy it is also an exact parallel to the merely theatrical doubling practices demanded by the play, where, for example, the stage direction at line 154 calls for England to go out and "drese for" Clergy, and the actor playing Sedicyon apparently is to double not only Stephen Langton but also Verity.[23]

For Bale, of course, the distinction between his plays and the impersonations of his villains is clear and absolute. Bale's play-making is legitimate because its representations conform to the truth; "popetly plays" are immoral because their representations are deceptive.[24] But "the truth" is precisely what is in dispute, and the difficulty of establishing it is apparent not least from the unnerving parallelism between the claims of each. John argues for "princely prehemynens" (352) and England's national integrity; Sedition for "the Popes prehemynence" (220) and an international Church, a "church vnyversall" (83), as England says. The two claims are neatly opposed in a radical binary underwriting a totalizing vision of history itself, but the very neatness may disrupt the opposition it would enforce. Unquestionably, for Bale, one is good and one evil; one "the true Christian church," the other "the proud church of hypocrites,"[25] one of Christ, the other the Antichrist himself. But how, beyond the passionate assertion of difference, is one to be certain which is which? How are we ever, in Thomas More's phrase, "to fynde out whyche chyrche is the very chyrche."[26]

Though this fundamental opposition plays itself out in history, the distinction cannot be securely grounded on historical evidence, since the "Chronycles" themselves are unreliable witnesses, serving the interests of "pristes," as Nobilitie says, determined to "defame / So many prynces and men of notable name" (585–86). Or as Tyndale puts it, in terms no doubt inspiring to Bale: "Consider the story of king John, where I doubt not but they have put the best and fairest for themselves, and the worst of king John: for I suppose they make the chronicles themselves" (338).[27] John himself, in Bale's play, recognizes that "The prystes report me to be a wyckyd tyrant / Be cause I correct ther actes and lyfe vnpleasant" (1402–3). The priests produce the historical record; hence the need for Bale's play to rehabilitate John's tainted name.

John's blackened reputation is but a specific example of the process by which history has been manipulated and deformed. With a true record of the past, Bale and other reformers argued, "Antichrist and hys mynysters are lyke to be better knowne and their tyrannouse vsurpacyons perceyued, how shamefullye they haue abused the dygnyte of kynges,"[28] but that record has long been unavailable, either "tyed vp in cheanes, and hydden vndre dust in the monkes and fryres libarye" (sig. E3r–v) or corrupted by their "execrable lyes and fables" (sig. F3r). History itself must therefore be rehabilitated—thoroughly reinterpreted and rewritten—and freed from the biased, self-serving accounts that clerical chroniclers had regularly substituted for "true hystories" (sig. G4r). "I would wish some learned Englishmen . . . to set forth the English Chronicles in their right shape,"[29] wrote Bale in 1544, and, as he himself is one the few properly "learned Englishmen," he undertakes the task himself, finding the key to "their right shape" not in unreliable historical accounts but in the Bible, particularly in the apocalyptic Revelation of Saint John the Divine. Only its prophecy, Bale writes in *The Image of Both Churches,* can give "full clearance to all the chronicles and most notable histories which hath been write since Christ's ascension, opening the true natures of their ages, times, and seasons."[30]

Scripture must serve, as Bale says, as "a light to the chronicles, and not the chronicles to the text,"[31] but its illumination perhaps dazzles rather than clarifies, its abundant, complex textuality preventing a single, self-evident meaning, as the astonishing history of biblical commentary itself attests. "Twenty doctors expound one text twenty ways," wrote Tyndale (307). The problem, however, is not merely that a single text was dismayingly subject to multiple interpretations, it is also that multiple texts were subject to singular interpretation, texts that could be individually deployed to authorize contradictory positions. John invokes the authority of Romans 13:1–2 to legitimate his authority; Sedition quotes Matthew 16:19 as the proof-text for his: "Quodcumque ligaveris" (97): "And I will give unto thee, the keys of the kingdom of heaven: and whatsoever thou bindest upon earth shall be bound in heaven: and whatsoever thou loosest on earth shall be loosed in heaven."[32]

Like the Pauline verse which was seized upon to authorize the reformers' political position, the apostolic verse was often invoked in support of the Church's claim of authority over secular rulers. Thus, in the margins of the 1535 translation of Marsilius of Padua's *Defence of Peace* (1324), Matthew 16:19 is cited as "the first authoritie of scripture which semeth to make the popes powre." In his efforts to counter the claims of papal jurisdiction, efforts that two centuries later struck a particularly responsive chord among English and continental reformers, Marsilius recognizes the necessity to dispute the interpretation of the biblical passage, since, as he writes, "of those wordes, certayne bysshopes of Rome haue chalenged & taken to themselues, the auctoryte of hyghest iurysdyccion aforesayd / for by the keyes graunted to saynt Peter by christ they wyl to be vnderstood the fulnes of powre of al wordly gouernance."[33]

Certainly the verse from Matthew concerns the exercise of authority but it is, in fact, provocatively silent about the *nature* of that authority. The text's application to "worldly gouernance" depends completely upon operations of an interpretive "wyl" that can be both contested and reversed. "Whatt call ye those kyes?" asks Nobility; and Clergy replies: "Owr holy fathers powr and hys hygh avtoryte" (621–22). But they could well be otherwise called. The scope of the pope's power and authority is not transparently indicated by the scriptural citation. While

Catholic commentators often interpreted the keys given to Peter as the sign of the primacy of the Church over temporal rulers, reformers held that they indicate only its spiritual authority. Marsilius, for example, devotes an entire chapter to "the auctoryte and powre of the keyes" (sig. k6r), arguing that they do not signify "the fulness of powre" (*plenitudo potestis*) claimed by the pope but rather refer exclusively to the sacerdotal power (*potestas ordinis*) to rebuke and pardon sin. Luther writes a sermon on "the true use of the keyes"[34] in which "the very true keye" is revealed as God's "holy woorde" while the false keys of the pope and the Catholic clergy are exposed as mere "tradicions and not Cryst onelye" (sig. A2v). Tyndale similarly argues that "The keys wherof they so greatly boast themselves, are no carnal things, but spiritual" (205), insisting that "the authority that Christ gave them was to preach" (211).

The reformers energetically reject the reading of Matthew 16:19 that claims temporal jurisdiction for the papacy, but they do so only by acknowledging that "the sacred scripture of God" demands interpretation, implicitly denying that it is by itself plain and articulate. The keys of St. Peter may well not refer to a wordly kingdom of Christ, but even the reformers admit the keys signify something other than literal keys. The 1602 Geneva gloss, for example, explicitly identifies them as "a metaphore." Yet if the reformers, like Tyndale, prove their determination "not to expound the scriptures carnally and worldly" (207), in their desire to understand the keys as spiritual rather than temporal authority, they perhaps win only a pyrrhic victory for the reformed faith by their tacit concession that the Scriptures must be expounded at all. The word of God is evidently available not plainly and immediately but, exactly as for their Catholic opponents, only in the mediations of their interpretive practices. To the degree that the reformers' reinterpretation of Matthew 16:19 has successfully undercut a prop of the argument for the pope's temporal rule, it has done so at the cost of the major weapon of the reformers' cause: their appeal to the unmediated authority of Scripture as the supreme word of God.

The reformers held, of course, that Scripture, rather than the accumulated traditions of the Church, contained all necessary truth and that this truth was "open and manifest,"[35] in Tyndale's phrase, in the Bible. Nothing was essential unless, as Bale wrote in January of 1537, "yt is playnlye expressyd in the sacred scripture of God."[36] And yet, in spite of the insistence on "the scriptures openyng" (1393), it was clear that God's word was often less open and plain, less "puer and cleane" (79), than the claims made in its name would admit. Tyndale may well attack "allegories" as the source of "this blindness wherein we now are"

(307), holding that scriptural meaning "is ever the literal sense," but he must also allow that it is a literal sense regularly signified by "proverbs, similitudes, riddles, or allegories" (304), and therefore in need of interpretation. Though Tyndale believed that these allegories ultimately can be read and reduced to some "open conclusion of the scripture" (343), since "the scripture giveth records to himself, and ever expoundeth itself by another open text" (320), the idea of a self-sufficient and self-interpreting Scripture depends upon a logically circular account of how the text regulates and corrects a reading: we discover the true and literal meaning of Scripture as we are lead from the figurative passages to the open text that underlies it; but we are lead from "doubtful" texts in need of expounding to the putatively "open" text that explains them only by our prior sense of the true and literal meaning of Scripture. Not only is the relation of open and doubtful texts necessarily uncertain, constituted by an interpreter rather than the text itself, but also the very "openness" that is claimed for some texts is a product of a critical practice and not a textual effect. In no proper hermeneutic sense can it be said of Scripture that it "ever expoundeth itself," although its prodigious textual density seemingly does ever demand expounding. "Prove yt by scriptur," says John, "and than wyll I it alowe" (1435), but undoubtedly more things can be proven "by scriptur" than are dreamt of either in his or in the reformers' philosophy.

The hermeneutic difficulty reveals itself in Bale's play ironically with the very scriptural citation John chooses to prove the authority of Scripture. When John berates Nobility for his disloyalty, Clergy intervenes, scornfully protesting that John has "nothyung . . . to allege to vs but scripture." "What shuld I allege elles, thy wycked pharyse?" replies John, anticipating the *sola scriptura* theme of the Reformation; "Dothe not the lord say, *nunc reges intelligite:* / The kynges of the erth that worldly cawses iuge, / Seke to the scriptur, late that be yowr refuge" (1463–69). But the biblical text cited to prove the authority of Scripture oddly undercuts the assertion. First of all, both A and B versions of the play offer an incorrect reading of the passage from Psalm 2. What all modern editions have corrected, following the Vulgate, to "intelligite," in both texts actually reads "intellige." The emendation thus erases what the conscious or unconscious error reveals: that scriptural texts are never immediately accessible, present as what Tyndale called "the pure word of God," but are always and necessarily transmitted and received through various mediations. Like any text, the biblical text is read—indeed could be said to exist—only through the interference of interpretive and material activities.

Second, and perhaps more consequentially, the text that John cites, "be wise now therefore, ye kings" (as the Geneva translators rendered *nunc reges intelligite*), is not, in any case, obviously about the authority of or over Scripture. Admittedly Christopher St. Germain had cited the same verse to refute the clerical monopoly on scriptural interpretation: "For it appereth. Psalm ii. that it is said thus to kynges and princes, 'O ye kynges, understand ye: be ye learned that iudge the world."[37] But, although St. Germain, like Bale's John, sees the psalm authorizing the monarch's authority over the interpretation of Scripture, the psalm goes on to speak of the ruler's need to know God's anger rather than His holy word: "Be learned ye Iudges of the earth. / Serve the Lord in feare, reioyce in trembling. Kisse the sonne, lest he be angrie, and ye perish in the waie, when his wrath shall suddenly burne" (Psalm 2:10–12). The text John cites to justify Scripture as his "refuge" in fact serves only if its context and literal meaning are ignored. "Yt was neuer well," complains John, since the Scriptures were left "for menns ymagynacyons" (334–35), intending to differentiate the interpretation of the Bible by Catholic authorities from the unadulterated word of God that the faithful could readily apprehend. But John's own interpretations demonstrate how fully the word of God is inevitably reconstructed in the "ymaginacyons" of its hearers.

Indeed the problem of stabilizing the word of God is clearly revealed when John and Clergy argue about the proliferation of monastic orders. Clergy attempts to justify their existence and "prove yt by Dauid substancially," quoting Psalm 44:10: "a quene, sayeth Davyd, on thy right hond, lord, I se, / Apparellyd with golde and compassyd with dyversite" (134–37). Clergy interprets the biblical passage to refer to and authorize the multiplicity of orders: "this quene ys the chyrch, which thorow all Christen regions / Ys beawtifull, deckyd with many holy relygyons" (434–40). John, however, disputes Clergy's reading: "Davyd meanyth vertuys by the same diversyte, / As in the sayd psalme yt is evydent to se, / And not mvnkysh sectes" (463–65). But John's interpretation is no more "evydent" than Clergy's, no more plainly present in the text.

Both readings are allegorizations, each attempting to establish and fix a referent for the text's opaque "dyversyte." Clergy stakes his reading solely on the interpretive authority of the pope: "Of owr holy father in this I take my grownd, / Which hathe awthoryte the scriptures to expound" (467–68); but Civil Order, joining in to support John, has already challenged Clergy's authorized interpretation, providing another and apparently firmer "grownd" on which to base a reading of the text: "Me thynkyth yowr fyrst text stondeth nothyng with yor reson, / For in Davydes tyme wer no such sects of relygyon" (461–62). History is offered as the stable and sustaining basis of interpretation, invalidating the tendentious papal reading of the biblical text. But, by the play's own logic, history, at least in the inevitably textualized form in which it is available, has been revealed to be itself unreliable and interested, demanding Scripture, as Bale argued, to "open" its "true nature." The circularity of Bale's procedure is unmistakable and inescapable: history demands Scripture to be known truly, and Scripture demands history.

To observe this circularity is neither to discredit Bale's project nor the parallel project of the godly nation, but merely to observe that the assertion of royal supremacy on which the Protestant nation depends rests on something other than the unconditional supports it claims for itself. Indeed, it may be that inevitably, as Ernest Gellner provocatively argues, "Nationalism is not what it seems and not what it seems to itself."[38] The Protestant nation is not—and cannot be—something historically grounded or divinely authorized but is, like every nation, a necessarily ambivalent and contested form of, what Homi Bhaba has called, "social and textual affiliation"[39]—a form of cultural signification claiming an imaginary necessity as the very condition of its being.

In spite of Cromwell's effort in the Act in Restraint of Appeals to ground his political vision in history, declaring that royal supremacy is "manifestly declared and expressed" in "divers sundry old authentic histories and chronicles,"[40] quite obviously the chronicles, as Tyndale and Bale both anxiously see, do no such thing; indeed precisely what motivates Bale's *King Johan* is the desire to correct their inadequacy. And yet neither can royal supremacy confidently be based on biblical authority, for, although passages can be marshaled to validate the claim, their meaning is never "evydent" but rather dependent upon the interpretive procedures not different in kind from those used to argue the opposite, on allegorizations of a biblical text that can be—and often was—allegorized differently. History needs Scripture and Scripture history if either is to serve to authorize the English nation, but their reciprocal need reveals them both to *require* grounding rather than to provide it, reveals their authorizations, that is, to be contingent and rhetorical rather than logical and absolute.

However unwittingly, then, Bale's play admits what it most wants to deny. If it attempts to witness to the powerful authorizations that underwrite the nation, it testifies instead that the godly nation is, in fact, inevitably *written* rather than underwritten, purposefully constructed as a form of political rationality rather than comfortably inhabited as a pre-given geopolitical reality. The processes by which England, as a sovereign state, comes in the first half of the sixteenth century to be the primary affiliation granting a sense of identity to its people seems to confirm Gellner's hypothesis that "nationalism is not the awakening of nations to self-consciousness: it invents nations where they do not exist."[41]

But even within its polemical assertion, if the nation must be written, clearly it must be written, as Peter Stallybrass has acutely observed, so as to deny that it "could be written otherwise."[42] And the only way to insure the necessary singularity of its articulation is to do what Bale has done in *King Johan;* that is, to repress the necessarily partial and tendentious act of writing that is the play's political vision and transform it into an act of apparently uncontested and uncontestable reading, to locate the nation in the past (in history) and in the future (in prophecy) that it may, in the present, come into being.

Notes

A version of this paper was presented in Chicago at the MLA in December of 1990. I would like to thank Peter Herman for providing me the opportunity to deliver the paper then and to present it here in revised form, and also to express my gratitude to David Bevington, Mary Cregan, John King, Claire McEachern, Allison Outland, Jim Shapiro, Peter Stallybrass, and Edward W. Tayler for comments and criticism that have greatly improved the paper in its successive versions.

1. G. R. Elton argues that Morison must have been "working on the book round about 1535 or 1536." See his "Reform by Statute: Thomas Starkey's *Dialogue* and Thomas Cromwell's Policy," *Proceedings of the British Academy* 54 (1968), 178.

2. All quotations from this document are from Sydney Anglo's transcription of a section of Morison's tract (London, British Library, Cotton Faustina C.ii, fols. 15v–18v), published in "An Early Tudor Programme for Plays and Other Demonstrations against the Pope," *Journal of the Warburg and Courtauld Institutes* 20 (1957), 176–79.

3. G. R. Elton, *Policy and Police: The Enforcement of the Reformation in the Age of Thomas Cromwell* (Cambridge: Cambridge University Press, 1972), 185–86.

4. William Turner, in *The Rescuynge of the Romishe Fox* (Winchester [for Bonn], 1545), a reply to Stephen Gardiner's *Examination of the Hunter,* cites this inhibition, quoting it "as it was told me" (sig. G2r).

5. John Foxe, *Acts and Monuments of John Foxe,* ed. S. R. Cattley, rev. Josiah Pratt (London: Religious Tract Society, 1877), vol. 6, 57.

6. [Henry Stalbrydge, pseud.], *The Epistel Exhortatorye of an Inglyshe Chrystian unto his derely beloued country of Ingland* (Basel?, 1544), sig. C5r; *Proceedings in the Parliaments of Elizabeth I, 1558–1581* (Leicester: Leicester University Press, 1981–), vol. 1, 31.

7. Thomas Dorman, *A Provfe of Certeyne Articles in Religion . . .* (Antwerp, 1564), sig. li3v. Quoted in Thora Blaslev Blatt, *The Plays of John Bale* (Copenhagen: G. E. C. Gad, 1969), 131.

8. David Bevington, *Tudor Drama and Politics: A Critical Approach to Topical Meaning* (Cambridge: Harvard University Press, 1968), 96–97.

9. *Catalogus* I, 702; quoted in Blatt, *Plays of John Bale,* 13.

10. Though see Sydney Anglo's skepticism that the play at Cranmer's household and Bale's *King Johan* are the same in *Spectacle, Pageantry and Early Tudor Policy* (Oxford: Oxford University Press, 1969), 269, n.

11. *The Miscellaneous Writings and Letters of Thomas Cranmer,* ed. J. E. Cox (Cambridge: Cambridge University Press, 1946), 387.

12. "Early Tudor Programme," ed. Anglo, 178.

13. Christopher Hill, "Social and Economic Consequences of the Henrician Revolution," in his *Puritanism and Revolution* (1958; reprint, Harmondsworth: Penguin, 1986), 41.

14. "Act in Restraint of Appeals" (24 Henry VIII, c. 12), in *Tudor Constitutional Documents A.D. 1485–1603,* ed. J. R. Tanner (Cambridge: Cambridge University Press, 1951), 40. But see Walter Ullmann, "This Realm of England Is an Empire," *Journal of Ecclesiastical History* 30 (1979), 175–204; and John Guy, "Thomas Cromwell and the Intellectual Origins of the Henrician Revolution," in *Reassessing the Henrician Age: Humanism, Politics and Reform 1500–1550,* ed. Alistair Fox and John Guy (Oxford: Basil Blackwell, 1986), 151–78.

15. See Ullmann, "This Realm of England," 183.

16. According to the *OED,* "state," meaning the "body politic as organized for supreme civil rule and government," is first used by Thomas Starkey in 1538 in his *Dialogue between Cardinal Pole and Thomas Lupset.*

17. Bevington, *Tudor Drama and Politics,* 103.

18. Greg Walker's fine essay, in his *Plays of Persuasion: Drama and Politics at the Court of Henry VIII* (Cambridge: Cambridge University Press, 1991), includes an extended discussion of the correspondences between the play and the events of 1538/9 (194–200, quotation 196).

19. John Bale, *King Johan,* ed. Barry B. Adams (San Marino: Huntington Library, 1969). All quotations from the play are from this edition and are cited parenthetically by line number. I have throughout silently expanded contractions but have otherwise followed the original spelling. Adams's edition is, of course, based on the unique copy of the manuscript that is in the Huntington Library, a manuscript written, as Adams says, "in two distinct hands at different times." What "we have," according to Adams, is "not just a composite manuscript but two separate versions of the play," an incomplete "A-text," a scribal copy of the play written about 1538, and an expanded "B-text," written in Bale's own hand sometime after 1558, probably in 1560. See Adams's account of the text (1–24) and also Greg Walker's thoughtful consideration of the text and plausible reconstruction of the missing A-text material in his *Plays of Persuasion* (173–78).

20. William Tyndale, *The Obedience of a Christian Man,* in *Doctrinal Treatises and Introductions to Different Portions of The Holy Scriptures,* ed. Henry Walter (Cambridge: Parker Society, 1848), 178.

21. Quoted in J. J. Scarisbrick, *Henry VIII* (Berkeley and Los Angeles:

University of California Press, 1968), 247, from Strype's *Ecclesiastical Memorials* I, 1, 172. The story of Henry's notorious response to Anne Boleyn's presentation to him of Tyndale's *Obedience* seemingly has no contemporary source but apparently originates in a letter of 1579 from John Louthe to Foxe, claiming to report what was told him by one of Anne's ladies-in-waiting. A complete narrative of the exchange can be found in *Narratives of the Days of the Reformation,* ed. John Gough Nichols (London: Camden Society, 1859), 52–57.

22. Walker, *Plays of Persuasion,* 191.

23. See the doubling charts in appendix 4 of Peter Happé's *Complete Works of John Bale* (Cambridge: D. S. Brewer, 1985), vol. 1, 152–53.

24. Ritchie D. Kendall, in *The Drama of Dissent: The Radical Poetics of Nonconformity, 1380–1590* (Chapel Hill: University of North Carolina Press, 1986), shrewdly explores "the opposition between godly stagecraft and Catholic playing" in Bale's work (101–31).

25. John Bale, *Image of Both Churches,* in *Select Works of John Bale,* ed. Henry Christmas (Cambridge: Parker Society, 1849), 251. For extended and intelligent accounts of Bale's place within early Tudor apocalyptic thought, see Katharine R. Firth, *The Apocalyptic Tradition in Reformation Britain 1530–1645* (Oxford: Oxford University Press, 1979), esp. 32–68; and Richard Bauckham, *Tudor Apocalypse* (Appleford: Sutton Courtenay, 1978), esp. 54–90.

26. Thomas More, *The Confutation of Tyndale's Answer,* in *The Complete Works of St. Thomas More,* vol. 8, pt. 1, ed. Louis A. Schuster, Richard C. Marius, James P. Lusardi, and Richard J. Schoeck (New Haven: Yale University Press, 1973), 480.

27. Other sources for Bale's treatment of John include Simon Fish's *A Supplycayon for the Beggers* (1524) and Robert Barnes's *A Supplicacion unto the most gracious prynce H, the viii* (1534). See Carole Levin's *Propaganda in the English Renaissance: Heroic and Villainous Images of King John* (Lewiston, N.Y.: Edwin Mellen, 1988), esp. 55–104, for an account of the creation of John's "heroic image" and its use in the religious controversies of Tudor England.

28. John Leland, *The Laboryouse Journey and serche of John Leylande for Englandes Antiquities . . . with declaracyons enlarged by J. Bale* (London, 1549), sig. F2r.

29. John Bale, *Chronicle of the Examination and Death of Lord Cobham,* in *Select Works of John Bale,* ed. Christmas, 8.

30. Bale, *Image of Both Churches,* 253.

31. Ibid., 253.

32. Quoted from *Tyndale's New Testament,* ed. David Daniell (New Haven: Yale University Press, 1989), a modern-spelling edition of the 1534 translation.

33. Marsilius of Padua, *The Defence of Peace: lately translated out of laten in to englysshe,* trans. William Marshall (London, 1535), sig. h5v. Marshall's translation of Marsilius of Padua's *Defensor Pacis,* "badly done and severely edited in the interests of monarchy," at least in the judgment of its modern editor, C. W. Previté-Orton (*Proceedings of the British Academy* 21 [1935], 163), was certainly undertaken with the approval and financial backing of Cromwell if not actually at his behest. The English edition, however, was hardly an instant suc-

cess. Marshall wrote Cromwell asking for the money he had been promised, explaining that the book "has not sold" (*Letters and Papers, Foreign and Domestic, of the Reign of Henry VIII,* ed. John Sherren Brewer, James Gairdner, and Robert Henry Brodie, 21 vols. [1862–1910; reprint, London: HMSO, 1920], vol. 11 [no. 1355]; hereafter *LP*). That the edition did at least succeed in causing distress in some circles is clear from a letter Jasper Fyllol wrote Cromwell reporting that twenty-four copies of the edition Marshall had sent to a monastery were returned three days later as "commanded" by their president, and John Rochester "took one and kept it four or five days and then burnt it, which," Fyllol reminds Cromwell, "is good matter to say to them at the time when your pleasure shall be to visit them" (*LP,* vol. 9 [no. 523]). Although Elton claims Marshall's translation was "the first printed edition" (*Policy and Police,* 186) of Marsilius's text, a Latin edition of *Defensor Pacis* had been issued thirteen years earlier at Basel.

34. Martin Luther, *Sermon uppon the Twentieth Chapter of Johan of absolution and the true use of the keyes,* trans. Anthony Scoloker (Ipswich, 1548); quoted in John N. King's indispensable *English Reformation Literature: The Tudor Origins of the Protestant Tradition* (Princeton: Princeton University Press, 1982), 192.

35. "William Tyndale, yet once more to the Christian Reader," *Tyndale's New Testament,* 15.

36. Quoted in *The Complete Plays of John Bale,* ed. Happé, vol. 1, 4.

37. Christopher St. Germain, *An Answer to a Letter* (London, 1535), sig. G3r. See John A. Guy's *Christopher St. Germain on Chancery and Statute* (London: Seldon Society, 1985), esp. 41–45. Guy discusses St. Germain's belief that it was "kynges and princes . . . with theire counsell spirytuall and temporall," rather than a clergy whose disinterestedness could not readily be assumed, who should "make exposycyon of such scripture as is doubtful."

38. Ernest Gellner, *Nations and Nationalism* (Ithaca: Cornell University Press, 1983), 56.

39. Homi K. Bhaba, "DissemiNation: Time, Narrative, and the Margins of the Modern Nation," in *Nations and Narration,* ed. Homi K. Bhaba (London: Routledge, 1990), 292.

40. "Act in Restraint of Appeals," *Tudor Constitutional Documents,* ed. Tanner, 40.

41. Ernest Gellner, *Thought and Change* (London: Weidenfield and Nicholson, 1964), 169.

42. Peter Stallybrass, "Time, Space and Unity: The Symbolic Discourse of *The Faerie Queene,*" in *Patriotism: The Making and Unmaking of British Identity,* ed. Samuel Raphael (London: Routledge, 1989), vol. 3, 200.

When Did the Renaissance Begin? The Henrician Court and the Shakespearean Stage

BILL READINGS

In societies where modern conditions of production pre-
vail, all of life presents itself as an immense accumulation
of spectacles. Everything that was directly lived had
moved away into a representation.

—Guy Debord, *The Society of Spectacle*

Prologue

First Beginning: A Historical Perspective

An opening assumption: the Renaissance has something to do with
spectacle and representation. This assumption governs not merely our
own accounts of the Renaissance but also Shakespeare's *Henry VIII*. In
this essay I'm not going to talk about Tudor spectacle per se but about
what it means to view the Tudor Renaissance in terms of spectacle—
about the spectacle of Renaissance spectacle.[1] My contention is that if
the Renaissance gives a new value to spectacle, that value is the value of
the new, of modernity itself. The specificity of Renaissance spectacle has
less to do with a new pomp, a new material accumulation, than with
loss. Specifically with the understanding of the present as a moment of
loss, as poised against a lost past. This primary separation from the past
is what enables historical perspective. The past must have died, if its
appearance in the present can take on the quality of a rebirth or renaissance rather than a permanent authority. And the sense that the past has
been lost also grounds the Renaissance as a period of new confidence
in human powers, a new humanism. For the hope of futurity is precisely for the redemption of the present, a recovery of the lost origin hidden by the distantiation of the past.

The modernity of the Renaissance, its inscription of the present as the site of loss, is evidenced in the new visibility of the past, which depends upon the notion that the past is over, that it is past, rather than present as authority or unquestionable tradition. The critical independence of Renaissance modernity thus rests upon a sense of the present as lacking which likewise marks the theatricality of the stage and the court as the twin poles of public life. Furthermore, as my epigraph from Debord on twentieth-century consumer culture indicates, the intersection of loss and spectacle that is the very ground of historical perspective seems to characterize our own modernity in a most unhistorical and anachronistic fashion. To be blunt, a sense of the growing unreality of a world newly born into spectacle is a constant complaint from Thomas More to the Situationists. Historical writers are always finding that the modern world has become a mere representation but this owes less to Henry VIII or late capitalism than to the structure of modernist historical "perspective." The problem is perhaps new to the Renaissance but the paradigm is inescapable for us as long as we try to see historically something that we still are, for perspective itself ("perspectivity") is precisely that on which it is impossible to take a perspective. As Descartes's *Optics* show, perspective thinks of itself as blindness, by the analogy of a blind man feeling his way with sticks. To put this another way, the objective claim of modernist history is always that of writing from a position somehow separated from history, not itself historical. Events can only be seen clearly once they are presumed to be definitively over, once it is claimed that the dust thrown up by history's pageant has settled.

Second Beginning: Dating the Renaissance

It is because the visibility of the past derives from the characterization of the viewer's present in terms of loss that anachronism arises, since this loss seems always to have just happened, to be the ground of the viewer's modernity. Thus for contemporary critics as for Shakespeare, the birth of the Renaissance as a certain sense of spectacle or theater, a new kind of visibility, causes a confusion as to historical time. Something about the nature of the Renaissance makes it very hard to say when the Renaissance begins, as the very visibility of this new culture of spectacle gives rise to anachronism.[2]

Orthodox accounts of Renaissance literature tend to pass over the court of Henry VIII as a period of preparation: as Wyatt and Surrey struggle to work out how to write a Petrarchan sonnet in English, they serve only to prepare the way for the messianic flowering of the Elizabethan literary Renaissance.[3] One's most immediate response to this would be to perform a detailed examination of those relegated to obscurity by the misfortune of having predated Elizabeth. Such a study would tend to show them worthy to be numbered among the ranks of Renaissance women and men. What I am trying to do is something slightly different—to ask why this relegation might have occurred, more specifically, what about the Renaissance makes it difficult to think of its beginning? For the political and religious stakes in the relative erasure of pre-Elizabethan culture are obvious. However, we find Shakespeare interested in recovering the court of Henry VIII for the benefit of James.[4] What I shall argue is that there is a particular problem with the historicity of the Renaissance which has led us (who are presumably now less wedded to the need to defend the values of the Elizabethan court) to tend to want to say that the English Renaissance both does and does not begin in the court of Henry VIII, that it is somehow clear that it's about to start at any minute. For me, this problem is bound up with a sense of visibility and spectacle, and I shall trace it through a consideration of these terms in a series of accounts of the origin of the Renaissance.

In dating the rise of a culture of spectacle, not merely Shakespeare but also a number of contemporary historical critics and theorists produce wildly differing historical explanations. This is not so much a product of any willfulness on their part as of the particular problems for historical understanding that spectacle raises. The difficulties of the historical and theoretical explanation of spectacle are tied on the one hand to the modernity of renaissances and on the other, to the fact that theory itself is bound up with notions of spectacle and gaze. Two questions present themselves here. The first is the great conundrum of "when did the Renaissance begin?": the question that Marxists tend to pose as that of "transition" from a feudalist to a capitalist mode of production. Normally, whenever anyone asks "when did the Renaissance begin?" one knows to expect the answer "sooner than you think."[5] My examination of this issue will consider the grip that the question has upon us and our inability to answer it. The second question concerns theory and whether there can be a theory of spectacle, if theory is itself etymologically linked to spectacle (Lat. *theoria*, a procession) and spectatorship (Gk. *theoros*, a spectator). Since theory is bound up with spectacle, theory always tends to find spectacle wherever it looks, to identify a society newly given up to spectacle and hence newly available for purely theoretical consideration.

Against this, I shall argue that the lesson of Shakespeare's *Henry VIII* in its difficulties of staging or failure as drama is a hard one for the modern critic, the critic concerned with the classic modernist question of the datability of the English Renaissance. Rather than the homeless

modern time-traveler, master of all she or he surveys of our first beginning, the historian would have to become one whose time is made un-
comfortable (time is no longer his or her "own") by the persistence of
the past as remainder or ruin, its resistance to being "dated." For such
a (postmodern?) historian, the theater would catch fire, as we shall see.

Third Beginning: That Shakespearean Stage

Thus, I shall make the ludicrous argument, with all the seriousness that
I can muster, that the sheer contingency of the Globe's having burnt
down at the first (?) performance of *Henry VIII* is somehow implicit to
the structure of the play as spectacle. And this, let me be clear, is not an
argument about the fire risk of certain scenery or props; it is an argument about the extent to which historical perspective is prey to the raw
contingency of the event that it seeks to exclude. I want to focus on
Shakespeare's *Henry VIII* because the light of spectacle in the Henrician era provokes in Shakespeare not merely a relinquishing of the concern for chronological sequence shown in his previous history plays but
nothing less than a repudiation of the very dramaturgical task in terms
of which we are inclined to judge those plays: the synthesizing of historical events into causal patterns, the move from post hoc to propter
hoc.[6] Recent critics have been inclined to dismiss traditional readings
of Shakespeare's treatment of history as mere moralistic obfuscation of
ideological agendas, to insist that what is at stake is not the revelation
of moral universals but Tudor particulars.[7] What strikes one in the case
of *Henry VIII* is the fact that the way in which the play stages the Henrician court renders the revelation of any such causal agenda, moral or
political, intensely problematic. It does so because what seems to matter about the spectacles presented is no more and no less than their
condition as spectacle. We might even call this the relinquishment of
history for a purely theorized politics; a politics become entirely visible
as theater.

To put this another way, we seem in Shakespeare's account of the
Henrician court to be in the world identified by my epigraph from
Debord, a society of spectacle, where everything exists only as representation, representation of nothing other than itself. Except that Debord
must be wrong, since "modern conditions of production" did not pre-
vail in the Henrician or even the Jacobean period. What I want to propose is not a creative anachronism that may solve the problem of
Shakespeare's *Henry VIII*. To claim to set spectacle in context by bringing historically displaced texts, either "marginal" contemporary writings or posterior theorizing, to bear on it would be to ignore the problematic historicity of spectacle and Renaissance. Nor do I lay claim to

absolute historical fidelity, being as inclined as anyone else to rest upon my theoretical posterior.

Fourth Beginning: Representing the Renaissance

In fact, I'm presently less concerned with getting Shakespeare right than with setting him alongside some commentators of our own day who find a similar emphasis upon representation crucial to the comprehension of the Renaissance. Representation has come to be a key term in the study of Renaissance culture—we might even go so far as to say that a certain manipulation of the term has been responsible for the substitution of Renaissance culture for Renaissance literature in our critical activities. Of course, to suggest that the wider horizons of cultural history are entirely new in Renaissance studies would be to ignore the tradition established by the Warburg Institute on the one hand and the Marxist analysis of ideological superstructures on the other. Moreover, a generalized notion of culture is something that is embedded within the Renaissance itself. In her lucid study of Burckhardt, Michael-Ann Holly has pointed to the way in which the broad yet balanced perspective that he evokes as the desideratum of historical writing is itself the reflection of the very values that Burckhardt finds Renaissance painting to have established.[8]

My own contention will be that Shakespeare's *Henry VIII* is not so much a representation of Renaissance history as an attempt to instantiate renaissance through the understanding of history as representation.

Shakespeare and the Henrician Society of Spectacle: The Theater of Politics and the Politics of Theater

As we shall see, to point out that Shakespeare's *Henry VIII* finds in the Henrician court a concern with spectacle and display that distinguishes it markedly from Shakespeare's other history plays can hardly claim the title of a "rethinking."[9] The play, after all, opens with a description of the Field of the Cloth of Gold, the first modern example of combat by conspicuous consumption.[10] The drama proceeds to thematize political power as expressed by the "big look" of Buckingham (I.i.118), understanding matters of state in terms of Anne Bullen's having "caught the king" (II.iii.77) by display of beauty and honor when brought to the king's eye in act I scene iv. The well-being of state is no less than the right regulation of the royal gaze: Wolsey seizes power as Henry's eye sleeps in viewing him (II.ii.42), the royal gaze usurped by virtue of its blinding. The play relinquishes historical sequence and aetiological unity in order to present a series of vignettes whose diegetic isolation lends them the quality of purely visual tableaux.[11] This is a more naked juxtaposition of events than even that of the chronicle history plays: order is now visual rather than temporal, the passage of time marks merely the interval between aetiologically sterile tableaux. Scenes are almost entirely encapsulated, passing over temporal gaps without comment, thematic unity apparently sacrificed to the logic of the slide show. Cranmer's final prophecy does not appear as an optimistic conclusion, because preceding events seem almost entirely irrelevant to it. These are exhibited pictures of a court rather than the matter of historical comprehension: the logic of each incident is entirely internal to it.

If a narrative sequence that offers simple succession rather than thematic continuity tends to accent the visual quality of static display in scenes, this effect is heightened by the inclusion of scenes that are little more than pure display: masques, processions, formal occasions. Elaborate stage directions detail the processional entry of Wolsey at I.i. and of Henry at I.ii., the order of the masque in I.iv., the divorce court at II.iv., the coronation of Anne at IV.i., the council of state at V.iii., and the christening of Elizabeth at V.v. In each case, rank and power are explicitly effects of sequence before the eye, of positioning within an order of procession. In this sense, the play's purely sequential plotting mirrors the procession scenes: political power is to be understood less as a matter of actions in causal patterns giving rise to effects than as a question of momentary precedence within an order that is given to the eye. These processions do not in fact move in narrative time. Rather, they are an accumulating succession of spectacles of power—we might say that each one moves only in order to give the viewer a sense of in which direction to read the order of power unfolded there.

My own interest here can only be situated in the light of recent criticism's increased awareness of the political nature of the Renaissance stage. In a sense, Shakespeare's *Henry VIII* is not merely an example of the political nature of Renaissance or "early modern" theater. As a meditation on the acute visibility of political power in the Renaissance, it may be said to precede a critical claim to find any hidden political agenda in the drama. In this sense, the play is metahistorical, less concerned with historical events than with the conditions imposed upon the viewer by the nexus of history, politics, and theater that characterizes the modernity of the English Renaissance. That is why the return to static tableaux is qualitatively different from the medieval drama of, say, *Everyman*. That is why these are not feudal pageants, since what is at stake is not so much a new kind of show as a new kind of visibility, one that we may characterize as the historical consciousness of modernity.[12] Thus, to speak easily of the politics of theater (as Tennenhouse does) is perhaps to miss the extent to which the visibility of the political is at issue in this drama. On the other hand, to understand the Renaissance theatricalization of politics as making historically visible a shift from the real to the illusory (as Greenblatt does) is to fail to recognize that the historical coordinates of critical subjectivity are under examination in the historical object being viewed.

Seeing History: The Moment of Renaissance and the Gaze of Theory

To understand the way in which an attention to Renaissance spectacle involves a threat of heuristic hubris for the gaze of the theorist or the historian, we should consider how the Renaissance as such is bound up with questions of visibility, of light. And this is not just because Italy was sunnier than medieval Europe. If the Renaissance "begins" it does so in a way that is bound up with the question of what it means to look at history. From Vasari on, the thought of the Renaissance is bound up with the condition of possibility of art history as a kind of seeing. And it is in reading Vasari that Panofsky finds the possibility of art history, when "The First Page of Giorgio Vasari's 'Libro'" turns out also to be the first page in the historical study of art.[13] According to Panofsky the Renaissance begins as a consciousness of the Gothic as not simply a (bad) "taste but also a style," by virtue of the gesture of enframing with which Vasari presents Cimabue's sketches in a Gothic frame and with a Gothic inscription: "Here [in Italy] the Renaissance movement itself had with one fell swoop established that distance between Gothic and contemporary art . . . this opposition to the Middle Ages compelled and enabled the Renaissance really to 'confront' Gothic art, and thereby, even through glasses tinted by hostility, to see it for the first time— to see it as an alien and contemptible, yet for this reason truly characteristic, phenomenon which could not be taken too seriously."[14]

The Renaissance is not simply a new movement in art history, it is the possibility of understanding art as a history of movements. The Renaissance invention of "perspective" is not merely technical, for Panofsky, for with the Renaissance comes the very possibility of any historical "perspective" on the arts at all: "Thus Vasari's inconspicuous 'Gothic' frame bears witness, at a relatively early date [between 1550 and 1568], to the rise of a new attitude toward the heritage of the Middle Ages: it illustrates the possibility of interpreting mediaeval works of art, regardless of medium and maniera, as specimens of a 'period style.'"[15]

It is by virtue of this gesture of distancing and enframing that the historical perspective becomes possible. This is why, despite the fact that just about any of Burkhardt's historical assertions can be challenged, his account of the Renaissance persists. It does so (and here again I draw on Holly's argument) not so much by virtue of its persuasiveness as because it subjugates historical writing about the Renaissance to the conditions of visibility that the Renaissance itself introduces—perspectival clarity, compositional variety and balance. What does it mean to have a single perspective on the Renaissance when it is to the Renaissance that we owe the possibility of one-point perspectival construction?[16] In trying to answer the question of when the Renaissance begins, we have to reckon with the fact that we are dealing not merely with the historical moment of a certain "look," a new sense of the meaning(lessness) of courtly spectacle, but also with the moment of a certain historical way of looking. If for Vasari, in Panofsky's description, the Renaissance ushers in the possibility of history, how does this fit with the apparent suspension of the connectedness of historical action in courtly spectacle? Precisely because history has become the object of a gaze, something to be looked at—as Shakespeare's insistent thematization of the audience present at "historical events" such as the coronation of Anne Bullen suggests. History is thus inseparable from a certain theoretical grasp of historicity as pageant, procession. And it is in this way that the static pageant of the Henrician court in *Henry VIII* belongs to the Renaissance rather than to the fixed pyramid of feudal power—because its politics are theatrical: this spectacle of power theorizes its spectator.[17] It is very important to understand this, since otherwise my argument would be unable to distinguish the significance of spectacle in the Henrician court from the importance attached to pomp and circumstance in the feudal court. What changes is the temporality of vision: historical vision installs the sense of the present as the theatrical site of loss. We can draw a parallel between Vasari's enframing of Cimabue and Shakespeare's inclusion of the spectator: each prices consciousness at the cost of an internal differentiation. Like the frame, the spectacle of the spectator is implicated in a parergonal space, outside the inside yet inside the pure exteriority of world or theater. No simple untangling is possible here. However, we can say that the thought of the Renaissance as a historical moment is bound up with the Renaissance as the moment of the thought of historical moments, a thought that is owed to a certain theatricalization or enframing of the possibility of representation, a splitting of representation against itself.

In light of this, I shall characterize the Renaissance, and specifically the Henrician court, as spectacular in a double sense. On the one hand, a new visibility triumphs over the past, over the Dark Ages. The possibility of historical perspective and historical difference arises when the past becomes spectacle for Shakespeare, when art becomes art history for Vasari. At the same time, however, the present political world itself becomes newly visible, displaced toward the condition of spectacle, of theater, in a way that renders a present grasp of the past as spectacle problematic. I shall call the displacement into visibility of both viewed and viewer theatrical, though in a sense different from that in which we are accustomed to claim theater as "the most representative of the age's forms."[18] In the sense in which I wish to try to think it, theatricality names a certain internal differentiation that makes representation unable either to reflect a world felt as real or to inhabit fully its own condition as pure simulacrum.[19] We owe the problem of anachronism in writing about the Renaissance to a critical habit of taking theater as transparently reflective of either a real world or its own condition (the condition of primacy over the real). In a sense, then, I am linking the Renaissance to a "thickening" of the theatrical condition into figurality, a becoming-opaque of theatrical space, the rise of a theater that marks the necessary and yet finally untranslatable intersection of a political theater and a theatrical politics.

The New Historicism: Representation and Anachronism

If we wish to understand this fusion of the theatrical and the political, the appearance of Stephen Greenblatt's *Renaissance Self-Fashioning* in 1980 marks a shift in the way in which the term *representation* may be held to function in Renaissance culture. Nor is Greenblatt a lone voice, since he shares the field with a number of others whose work, often loosely classed as "New Historicist," similarly focuses on the issue of representation as constitutive of, rather than merely instrumental for, Renaissance culture.[20] The Renaissance offers a notion of culture that we now understand as composed by and in representation rather than as mirroring or reflecting presences in its artefacts.

Although most subsequent work has concentrated on representation in Elizabethan and Jacobean culture, Greenblatt found in his reading of Sir Thomas More the strongest and most persuasive figure of an identity wholly inscribed within a realm of representation: "In More, appearances have a more problematical relationship to reality. His is a world in which everyone is profoundly committed to upholding conventions in which no one believes; somehow belief has ceased to be necessary. The conventions serve no evident human purpose, not even deceit, yet king and bishop cannot live without them. Strip off the layer of theatrical delusion and you reach nothing at all."[21]

The metaphor that ties a world of simulacra and delusion to theatricality is not incidental; Greenblatt speaks in convincing detail of the "theatricalization of public life in the society dominated by Henry VIII and Cardinal Wolsey," a society where authority and wealth are confirmed only as display, where power is not so much exercised as shown.[22] Leonard Tennenhouse finds Shakespeare's *Henry VIII* doing the same thing, although if "the production of art . . . comes squarely under a political imperative to display wealth and title," he is concerned to establish that imperative as specifically Jacobean, in contrast to the chronicle history plays of the Elizabethan Shakespeare.[23] Tennenhouse is clearly correct in pointing to the fact that Henry does not actually do very much: surrounded by bureaucrats, the king has merely to show or withhold favour in order for history to be made: "It is worth noting that Henry VIII, unlike the political heroes of an earlier stage, does not have to overpower those who possess the symbols of authority in order to make his line legitimate. Quite the contrary, in possessing the blood, his body is a living icon in relation to which all other signs and symbols acquire meaning and value."[24]

Wolsey is a figure of naked and all-encompassing power who the Lord Chamberlain fears "will have all" (II.ii.11):

> *Norfolk:* All men's honors
> Lie like one lump before him, to be fashioned
> Into what pitch he please.
> (II.ii.47–9)

The contentless nature of Wolsey's power, its indifference to all previously encoded forms of power, underlies its absolute capacity for expansion. Power thus plays the political equivalent of the role of money in the rise of capitalism: void ground of a purely virtual system of representation. Power alienates force or ability as money alienates labor. As with Machiavelli's *virtù*, power has become a meaningless principle of sheer translatability: everything is up for grabs. Power is thus the unit of representability in *Henry VIII*, a common denominator of representation which owes its invasive or inflationary force to the fact that it is, in itself, *meaningless*. Wolsey will hold power insofar as he incarnates the prince as blind spot, void center of the system of power, for as long as the monarch's eyes will have "slept upon" him (II.ii.42). He incarnates the king as blind spot of the system of political power, and once the king sees him (becomes himself his own central blind spot), Wolsey vanishes. Nor is this specific to Shakespeare: More's Utopia where display is frowned upon meets Castiglione's court of Urbino where knowing how to fake *sprezzatura* is everything, in that the limpid politics of the former and the theatrical opacity of the latter are each underpinned by a central vanishing point or blind spot.[25] The "dark city" of Amaurot or the empty figure of the duchess (who regulates games without taking part)[26] lie at the center of each political space, marking the point from which the rejection of "display" or "affectation" becomes visible. *Sprezzatura* is the display that makes itself invisible, Utopia the totally visible society that suppresses all ostentation. Each can thus only legitimate its own visibility as project at a secondary level, as critical reflection upon an essentially empty and hence purely formal principle: Utopia is so totally political that nothing can happen; *sprezzatura* is a *non so che* about which nothing empirical can be stated. Thus Utopia has as few laws as courtiership has rules: each is not so much a worldly practice as the search for its own principle, each has as its project the more fully proper definition of itself. Thus the courtiers in Castiglione's Urbino begin with the metagame, the game of choosing which game to play, proceeding to the game of metacourtliness, in which one seeks to be courtly in defining the nature of courtliness. These texts do not simply present theories of society: they position the understanding of the social as a preeminently theoretical task, the task of a spectator who must imagine what it is to occupy the blind spot or vanishing point of society, that of the Prince, whose authority in each case owes its absolute quality to its pure visibility and its practical emptiness.[27] Like Henry, neither the ruler of Utopia nor the duchess actually *does* anything, indeed their power is registered in the very fact that their inactivity is what renders society visible to the critical theorist.

For Tennenhouse, this shift to a world of pure spectacle is an effect of the succession of James I and VI, which demanded a new account of political legitimacy in response to different forms of opposition. For Greenblatt, it is constitutive of a new, modern, sense of subjectivity arising out of the ironic realization of the general relativity of cultural forms and our place among them. Is Greenblatt merely reading More under the anachronistic influence of Jacobean cultural forms? Or will Tennenhouse have to claim that More's problems arise from his subterranean prediction of a succession crisis analogous to that of James, if he wishes to preserve the historical specificity of his argument? After all, if Cranmer ends *Henry VIII* by predicting the reign of Elizabeth and succession of James, why shouldn't More? The problem we have struck here is one that should give us pause, since what is at stake is much more than a historical quibble as to whether the agreed theatricality of the Henrician court is the product of contemporary or Jacobean perception, whether More's fondness for theatrical metaphor is significant in his own time or only in the light of later stress upon the possibilities of theater, only after the work that Shakespeare will have done.

Greenblatt and Tennenhouse make utterly opposed claims for the historical genesis of the notion of the Henrician court as theatrical or spectacular, which is to say, they make utterly opposed claims as to the point at which the Renaissance says it begins in England. However, neither of them is wrong. Rather, in saying that politics are theatrical in the Henrician era, Greenblatt assumes that we know what theater is, while Tennenhouse's claim for the theatricality of politics as a Jacobean effect rests on a similar assumption as to the self-evident nature of the political. Hence Greenblatt's radical claim is that politics are theatrical, while Tennenhouse asserts a parallel shock value for his claim that theater is political. And a historical gap yawns between the two, between the death of More in 1535 and the writing of *Henry VIII* in 1612–13, three years before Shakespeare's death. To ask whether Greenblatt's and Shakespeare's shared perception of the Henrician court is accurate or merely the effect of Jacobean influence (as Tennenhouse might claim), would be like trying to assess the validity of Debord's account of spectacle by considering the extent to which modern conditions of production prevailed in Henry's court. Instead of inquiring whether or not Cardinal Wolsey was England's first public relations executive, I prefer to focus on the peculiar anachronism that accompanies the spectacle: anachronism that is not a matter of historical inaccuracy but of a certain slippage of time between the theatrical and the political.

Shakespeare's *Henry VIII* owes its strangeness to the way in which the relation of theater and politics is obscured by the light of the spectacular. The spectacular qualities of *Henry VIII* are acknowledged by Schoenbaum—in the light of Greenblatt's linking of Renaissance spectacle to a world become mere representation or "theatrical deceit," this casts an ironic shadow on the play's presumed subtitle, *All is True*.[28] Well-documented difficulties in the public staging of the play that is held to assert the theatricality of all forms of public life add a further historical irony. At what was possibly the first performance of *Henry VIII* in 1613, the very attention to pomp and pageantry that marks this play caused the Globe Theater to burn to the ground, possibly when the ceremonial cannon announcing the entrance of the masked Henry VIII at act I scene iv caught fire.[29]

The fading of that "insubstantial pageant" in flames stands, like the gap of over a hundred years between More and Shakespeare, as a warning to us not to assume too readily that an attention to the term *representation* will allow a pure isomorphism between the theatrical and the political. Rather than saying that politics and theater are the same thing, an attention to the reciprocal implication of theater and politics in the Renaissance might lead us to conclude that each differs from itself in the light of the other. Thus, "representation" would not merely un-ground the real in the spiral of simulacra that Baudrillard has named "precession."[30] Rather, we may understand the anxiety of representa-tion in Renaissance culture as linked to an inevitable failure fully to the-atricalize politics or to politicize theater, a failure that is not incidental but constitutive of the respective possibilities of politics and theater as poles of public life.[31]

Furthermore, this failure and the representational anxiety that ac-companies and accomplishes it are themselves the constituents of the sudden possibility of public life that marks the English Renaissance. To put this another way, in reading Shakespeare's appropriation of Henry VIII's court we can come to understand not only the peculiarity of this not-quite-history play in its politicization of the very condition of the-ater but also the problems inherent in what I tend to see as the particu-lar Henrician attempt to invent a court that will ground the central-ization of state power in a theatricalization of politics.[32] Our more general gain may be an understanding of the preeminence of represen-tation and worries about it in the Renaissance as something more trou-bled than merely an abandonment of referential anchoring in the face of a world of appearances.

The failure of *Henry VIII* as a Shakespearean history play arises from its insistent thematization of the condition of historical representation. *Henry VIII* is as obsessed with its own difficulty in being a play as Hen-ry was with the problem of fathering heirs. The prologue counterposes a claim for "truth" (9) and tragedy to the mere "show" (18) of a "mer-ry bawdy play" (14), to either "fool" or "fight" (19). What is interest-ing here is that the shield is ruled out along with the jester's cap and bells. A claim for accurate representation (realism) is grounded in an attention to the politics of a court rather than the historical vicissitudes of war. Authenticity rests upon a refusal to pander to the audience, a certain rejection of conventional theater that is, however, accomplished by the inclusion of the audience within the drama, as the internal con-dition of appearance for characters:

> Think ye see
> The very persons of our noble story
> As they were living. Think you see them great,
> And followed with the general throng and sweat
> Of thousand friends. Then, in a moment, see
> How soon this mightiness meets misery;
> (Prologue, 25–30)

The play claims seriousness in that it refuses to acknowledge the gaze of the audience, yet the seriousness it presents is that of a world in which to be is to be looked at, "followed with the general throng." The play becomes authentic as theater insofar as it rejects its own conventional theatricality to be, rather than show, the theatricality of the political world it represents. This is an engagement with theatricality that goes beyond the conventions of the stage play world, in which drama does not encounter its own identity as pure theater but its difference from itself in the representation of a world already haunted by the specter of theatricality, already modern. Its success as a play requires a giving up of theater to become politics. Hence the play fails as Shakespearean drama in the ways to which I have alluded. The critical claim for multiple authorship is perhaps motivated by the sterile succession of tableaux and the lack of organic resolution (Elizabeth appears effectively as infant deus ex machina) which lend the play a fragmented appearance. This is underlined by the failure to establish dramatic causality in the rise and fall of characters such as Buckingham and Wolsey (or the rise and preservation of Cranmer), and by the indifference of the drama to the passage of time between episodes, which appears as a failure to generate an organic temporality internal to the play.

What we get instead is a drama of looks. Witness for instance the elaborate stage directions at I.i.114, which establish the rivalry between Buckingham and Wolsey: "Enter Cardinal WOLSEY, the purse borne before him, certain of the GUARD and two SECRETARIES with papers. The cardinal [Wolsey] in his passage fixeth his eye on BUCKINGHAM, and BUCKINGHAM on him, both full of disdain." Events do not so much progress as process, parade—characters alternately fall under and out of the king's eye, an eye that in itself seems to stare blindly. This is a drama in which political power is a matter of vision, where power is the unit of calculation of *representability*. As such, no conventional reading of the play as moral *fabula* is possible, which is why a critic such as Lily B. Campbell simply omits it from consideration. There is nothing to be said about power in the play, since power has no content: it is nothing but the void ground of representability itself.

Conversely, within the play, political success rests upon the capacity of a Cranmer to relinquish political argumentation (the illusion of content) when upon trial so as to remind his prosecutors that they are merely actors in the eye of the monarch:

> Look there, my lords.
> By virtue of that ring, I take my cause
> Out of the gripes of cruel men, and give it
> To a most noble judge, the King my master.
> (V.iii.97–101)

It proves very difficult to restrain our own modernity here. We want to greet this gleefully as proof either that politics is merely theater or that theater is entirely political. Our very sense of the mutual transparency of the two terms reenacts the spectacularity that we want to criticize as illusion. We want, that is, to erase the difference between theater and politics and along with it the difference between Henrician modernity and our own alienation from a world in which commodification seems to have replaced productive agency with passive consumerism. The ground of historical accuracy within modernism, the possibility of dating an event, rests upon the replacement of the event qua happening by the event qua visible element within a historical schema of datability. And as such, all that the historical critic can do is blindly repeat the lack that characterizes her or his own present, so that writing history becomes the finding of loss more or less everywhere. The sense of history as having newly become visible is nothing less than the finding of history as the text of our own alienation, as a sense that the past is over, mere spectacle. History's error will have been the attempt to put things in their place, to take a perspective, to reduce the error of anachronism, to eliminate the risk of a past that will not stay dead or remain clearly visible. Yet such an attempt must always repeat its own anachronism, the assumption that history can be written from a site of alienation, from a pure present which is no time at all.

Henry VIII may be said to offer two options, if we recognize that the one I would wish to uphold is hardly an option at all, more of a chance, more of a risk attendant on the modernist staging of history as perspective. On the one hand history may be made visible as representation, at the price of instituting an ineradicable anxiety about our own alienation from a past become mere spectacle. On the other hand, history may, as it were, catch fire, but at the price of obscuring history, making it appear opaque and putting our own position as historians at very real risk. A marginal event from the stage history of this play dramatically illustrates the way in which, pushing the issue of historical representation to the limit, it enacts the structural possibility of dramatic failure that is lodged at its center, in a logic which no amount of care as to the handling of flammable stage properties can control.

The most obvious spectacle of this drama, and the one that is hardest to see without endangering the modernist's universe, or at least his or her Globe, is that of the historical critic blinded by a play which can only reinscribe his or her own alienation in offering itself so neatly for critical attention. In the very readability of Shakespeare's appropriation of the Henrician court we find the problems of thinking the English Renaissance inscribed as pure spectacle—offering a historical obviousness that leads to inevitable anachronism and a theoretical transparency that erases difference and blinds us with our own reflection. Such is the challenge, and the risk, of writing after Renaissance texts, after multiple beginnings that each claim authenticity as original.[33] The Renaissance is always beginning (and has never *begun* in any simple sense) because we are not yet out of it, nor perhaps will ever be.

Notes

1. On Renaissance spectacle as a historical phenomenon, see Werner L. Gundersheimer, *Ferrara: The Style of a Renaissance Despotism* (Princeton: Princeton University Press, 1973); Frances A. Yates, *Astraea: The Imperial Theme in the Sixteenth Century* (London: Routledge and Kegan Paul, 1975); and Norbert Elias, *Power and Civility,* trans. Edmund Jephcott (New York: Pantheon, 1982). The historical parameters of such a survey would have to stretch far wider than is in my power, dealing with such matters as the introduction of Burgundian manners at the court of Henry VII. I can only reiterate that my concern is with the critical awareness of the Renaissance of spectacle, which I wish to see as a legacy of the Renaissance itself rather than as a judgment passed from any secured historical vantage point.

2. Thomas Greene's *A Light in Troy: Imitation and Discovery in Renaissance Poetry* (New Haven: Yale University Press, 1982) addresses this issue: his fine chapters on "Historical Solitude" and "Imitation and Anachronism" are particularly worth studying. An excellent summary of the problem of anachronism in Renaissance historiography is provided by Phyllis Rackin in *Stages of History: Shakespeare's English Chronicles* (Ithaca: Cornell University Press, 1990), 5–12.

3. For example, Julia Briggs's synthesis of critical orthodoxy runs as follows: "At the court of Henry VIII, Sir Thomas Wyatt and the Earl of Surrey had set themselves to compose Petrarchan sonnets, but it was above all through the examples of Sidney and Spenser that Renaissance poetic practices and habits of mind were naturalized" (*This Stage-Play World* [Oxford: Oxford University Press, 1983], 2).

4. Cranmer's closing prediction of the effects of Elizabeth's birth introduces an interesting proleptic fold into the historical revaluation of Henry VIII. Clearly, this play can only be written after Elizabeth's death, which seems to allow historical origins to become visible. Of course, that death also lifts a direct risk of censorship.

5. An exception to this statement is to be found in William Kerrigan and Gordon Braden, *The Idea of the Renaissance* (Baltimore: The Johns Hopkins University Press, 1990), who argue that the Renaissance began just when you always thought it did. My cavil here would be that they fail to give Burckhardt his due by paying too little attention to the effort involved in *inventing* the Renaissance, for Burckhardt as for Michelet and Pater.

6. An example of the orthodox reading of the chronicle histories to which I am alluding would be Lily B. Campbell's *Shakespeare's Histories* (London:

Methuen, 1964), which is concerned to show how Shakespeare makes the scattered and chance events of historical chronicle into patterns that we may consider universally significant.

Wilson-Knight's reading of the play in terms of the pattern of the late romances that he noted in *The Crown of Life* (London: Methuen, 1966) seems to me to ignore the play's quality as performance almost entirely. Wilson-Knight's "Note on *Henry VIII*" finally rests its argument on the optimistic note struck in the final prophecy that Cranmer makes. His exemplary attention to Shakespeare's language ends up by ignoring the implications of the very displacement of dramatic structure that Wilson-Knight notes ("A Note on *Henry VIII*" in *Shakespeare and Religion* [London: Routledge and Kegan Paul, 1967]). I would tend to agree with Phyllis Rackin, who also notes that Cranmer's prophecy must be understood as a "move beyond drama" (*Stages of History*, 105), while preserving a sense that this resolution is itself already a moment of nostalgia for a lost presence that is beyond representation. What strikes one about *Henry VIII* here is precisely the way in which dramatic plot (insofar as we can speak of one in the play) is refused the possibility of resolution in its own terms.

7. Jonathan Dollimore and Alan Sinfield provide an exemplary polemic on this topic in their "History and Ideology: The Instance of Henry V" in *Alternative Shakespeares*, ed. John Drakakis (London: Methuen, 1985).

8. Michael-Ann Holly, "Burckhardt and the Ideology of the Past," *Journal of the History of the Human Sciences* 1 (Summer 1988).

9. All references are to William Shakespeare's *The Famous History of the Life of King Henry the Eighth*, ed. S. Schoenbaum (New York: New American Library, 1967). I refer throughout to the author as "Shakespeare," since the question of attribution is not specific to my argument.

10. In the words of Michelet, "un duel de dépense." (*Renaissance et réforme: histoire de France au XVIe siècle* [Paris: Editions Robert Laffont, 1982], 273).

11. In act I the Field of the Cloth of Gold is reported, Wolsey engineers the fall of Buckingham, Henry initiates a divorce against Katherine of Aragon, the French influence in court manners is mocked, and Henry meets Anne Bullen at a masque. In act II Buckingham is executed, Wolsey exerts his influence, Anne receives favor, the divorce court meets. In act III Katherine argues with Wolsey fruitlessly, Wolsey falls from favor. In act IV Anne is crowned and Katherine tactfully dies. In the fifth act Cranmer speaks with the king while the birth of Elizabeth is reported, is kept waiting before his trial, has the charges against him dismissed, and then presides at the christening of Elizabeth, prophesying a glorious future for her and for her successor, James.

12. I would thus want to distinguish between the tableaux of *Henry VIII* and the nostalgia for an imagined medieval world that Rackin finds underpinning the appeal of spectacle in *Richard II* (*Stages of History*, 47–48).

13. Erwin Panofsky, "The First Page of Giorgio Vasari's 'Libro,'" in his *Meaning in the Visual Arts* (Chicago: University of Chicago Press, 1982). For a more detailed discussion of the centrality of the Renaissance to Panofsky's

account of the possibility of art history, see Georges Didi-Huberman, *Devant l'image: questions posées aux fins d'une histoire de l'art* (Paris: Minuit, 1990).

14. Panofsky, *Meaning in the Visual Arts,* 184 and 186–87.

15. Ibid., 223–24.

16. The most detailed and thoughtful attempt to think perspective whilst remaining aware of the heuristic force of the perspectival apparatus itself is Hubert Damisch's *L'Origine de la perspective* (Paris: Flammarion, 1987). As Damisch points out: "The eminently paradoxical status of perspective, considered as a cultural formation, makes the task of the historian particularly difficult and leads to all sorts of anachronisms. Thus it is claimed that a new notion of space is introduced with Alberti—the very mathematical ideal for which Descartes, two centuries later, produced the concept of the extended, understood as homogeneous, continuous and infinite. This forgets that the geometry of the Greeks, to which the author of *Della pittura* refers, was a finite geometry, which did not take space as its object but rather shapes and bodies as they are described or delineated by their limits, that it is a matter of the outline which circumscribes them or the surfaces that enclose them, to take up the definition of Alberti himself" (*L'Origine de la perspective,* 11 [my translation]).

17. On the thematization of the audience throughout Shakespeare's histories, see Phyllis Rackin, *Stages of History,* esp. 123–25. Her helpful reminder that the theatrical public is itself socially heterogeneous and plural neatly resolves the impasse of the argument over containment and subversion in Shakeapearean political criticism. I am less convinced by her attempt to erect "audience manipulation" into a principle of reading. The metaphor of orchestration to which she appeals returns us to the paradigm of reader-response criticism, with the difference that multiple and divided responses are interposed as a critical fiction that will allow the continuation of author-centered criticism by other means. The text exists only as response, but that response turns out to be itself the object of an authorial strategy. My own interest in the destruction of the Globe by fire implies an interest in performance that exceeds this model of reception aesthetics. For more on reader-response, see my "On the New Forcers of Conscience: Milton's Critics," *Oxford Literary Review* 7 (1985), 131–47.

18. The quotation is from Julia Briggs's *This Stage-Play World,* 161.

19. My thinking on theatricality is much indebted to Michael Fried's *Absorption and Theatricality: Painting and Beholder in the Age of Diderot* (Chicago: University of Chicago Press, 1980). However, I want to insist upon the inescapability of the theatrical condition rather than counterpose it to the high seriousness of absorption as Fried does.

20. For example, Jonathan Goldberg's *James I and the Politics of Literature* (Stanford: Stanford University Press, 1989) first appeared in 1983. A sense of the range and fecundity of work on Renaissance representation performed in the eighties may be gleaned from three roughly contemporaneous collections: *Rewriting the Renaissance: The Discourses of Sexual Difference in Early Modern Europe,* ed. Margaret W. Ferguson, Maureen Quilligan, and Nancy J. Vickers (Chicago: Chicago University Press, 1986); *Shakespeare Reproduced,* ed. Jean

E. Howard and Marion F. O'Connor (New York: Methuen, 1987); and *Representing the English Renaissance,* ed. Stephen Greenblatt (Berkeley and Los Angeles: University of California Press, 1988). The last contains essays published between 1983 and 1986.

21. Stephen J. Greenblatt, *Renaissance Self-Fashioning: From More to Shakespeare* (Chicago: University of Chicago Press, 1980), 14.

22. Ibid., 28.

23. Leonard Tennenhouse, *Power on Display* (London: Methuen, 1986), 99.

24. Ibid., 97.

25. Thomas More, *Utopia,* ed. and trans. Paul Turner (Harmondsworth: Penguin, 1980); Baldassare Castiglione, *The Book of the Courtier,* trans. Thomas Hoby, ed. J. H. Whitfield (London: J. M. Dent and Sons, 1975). Of course, each author enframes the passage to the critical level: More with the dialogue in his garden that gives way to monologue and is then questioned by the character "More," Castiglione with the opening lament for the fact that the court of Urbino no longer exists. Each, that is, abstracts himself as viewer from the purely visible society, the author becoming the counterpart of the prince/duchess as absent or empty center.

26. The duchess does not participate but remains present as a purely formal condition of regulation. Thus when Emilia Pia asks her to choose who will speak of the perfect courtier she delegates the task to Emilia herself while retaining her authority: insisting that Emilia must not disobey her by not making a choice. Purely virtual power is power without activity (the prerogative of a duchess throughout the ages?).

27. *The Book of the Courtier* begins with the empty figure of the duchess, whose main virtue is her existence in purely virtual space; it ends by proposing the figure of an absolute prince who is the unmediated product of the direct advice of the very courtiers whom his rule must protect.

28. As Schoenbaum puts it in his introduction, "*Henry VIII* on the stage was the super-spectacle of its own day" (xxx).

29. The description comes from a letter of July 2, 1613, written by Sir Henry Wotton: "The King's players had a new play called *All Is True,* representing some principal pieces of the reign of Henry VIII, which was set forth with many extraordinary circumstances of pomp and majesty, even to the matting of the stage; the Knights of the Order with their Georges and garters, the Guards with their embroidered coats, and the like: sufficient in truth within a while to make greatness very familiar, if not ridiculous. Now, King Henry making a masque at the Cardinal Wolsey's house, and certain chambers being shot off at his entry, some of the paper, or other stuff, wherewith one of them was stopped, did light on the thatch, where being thought at first but an idle smoke, and their eyes more attentive to the show, it kindled inwardly and ran round like a train, consuming within less than an hour the whole hous to the very grounds" (cited by E. K. Chambers, *The Elizabethan Stage,* 4 vols. [Oxford: Clarendon Press, 1923], vol. 2, 419–20).

The tendency of spectacle to blind one to events is here indicated by Wotton at the moment that *Henry VIII* brings to an end one incarnation of the theater, stretching the representational capacity of the old Globe beyond its limits in its insistence on the show of realistic detail.

30. See Jean Baudrillard, *Simulations,* trans. Paul Foss, Paul Patton, and Philip Beitchman (New York: Semiotext(e), 1983).

31. To be fair, Greenblatt does stipulate that More is not simply claiming that politics is absurd—yet he doesn't make more of this than an observation upon the nuances of More's character as a cipher for the problem of all liberal humanist subjectivity. I'm not sure that this adds up to much more than the observation of William S. Preston, esquire, a San Diemas teenager in the film *Bill and Ted's Excellent Adventure,* that Socrates' (pronounced So-crates) assertion that "the greatest wisdom is to know that we know nothing" describes himself and his companion perfectly. The power of Greenblatt's own writing perhaps gets in the way of his argument here: the negative capability with which he evokes More's self-presentation leads him to accept its terms perhaps too readily.

32. In speaking of Henry VII's and VIII's "invention" of the court I allude to Norbert Elias's insistence upon the royal court as central to the process of the development of the monopoly state (*Power and Civility,* 258–59). Although the transformation of warriors into courtiers is a lengthy historical process, the emphasis on pomp and spectacle introduced by the Tudors is a crucial step, most obviously in the case of the Field of the Cloth of Gold. This makes what Tennenhouse calls "Shakespeare's inability to write an Elizabethan chronicle history play for a Jacobean audience" (*Power on Display,* 99) equally an inability to write a medieval chronicle history of Renaissance political events, as much an effect of the Henrician court as of the Jacobean.

33. Thus Vasari in his *Lives of the Artists* credits successive artists with having "broken" with prior practices to bring the art of painting in Italy back to life: such is the task of being "modern and original" that belongs to Masaccio as much as to Giotto or Cimabue (Giorgio Vasari, *Lives of the Artists,* ed. and trans. George A. Bull, 2 vols. [Harmondsworth: Penguin, 1986], vol. 1, 125). A study of the repeated rebirths that Vasari charts would require another essay altogether.

CONTRIBUTORS

W. Scott Blanchard has written articles on Ben Jonson and Italian humanism that have been published in *Studies in Philology* and the *Journal of Medieval and Renaissance Studies*. He is an assistant professor at College Misericordia. His book *Scholar's Bedlam: Menippean Satire in the Renaissance* is forthcoming from Bucknell University Press.

Barbara L. Estrin teaches at Stonehill College. She has published *The Raven and the Lark: Lost Children in the Literature of the English Renaissance* (Lewisburg: Bucknell University Press, 1985), and she is currently completing a manuscript tentatively entitled *The Muse in the Maze: Uncovering Laura in Wyatt, Donne and Marvell*. She has also published numerous articles in such journals as *ELH, Texas Studies in Language and Literature,* and *Philological Quarterly.*

Roland Greene is Professor of Comparative Literature and English and Director of the Program in Comparative Literature at the University of Oregon. His articles on Spenser and Sidney have appeared in *Spenser Studies* and *SEL*. He has published *Post-Petrarchism: Origins and Innovations of the Western Lyric Sequence* (Princeton: Princeton University Press, 1991), and has a book forthcoming entitled *Unrequited Conquests: Love and Empire in the Colonial Americas.*

Alexandra Halasz teaches at Dartmouth College. She is working on the history of the pamphlet writers in the sixteenth and seventeenth centuries.

Peter C. Herman is an assistant professor at Georgia State University. He has published articles in *The Sidney Newsletter, SEL,* and *Chaucer Review*. His article on Shakespeare's *Henry V* and the crisis of the 1590s will appear in *Tudor Political Culture,* ed. Dale Hoak (Cambridge: Cambridge University Press, forthcoming). He is currently working on a book on Renaissance antipoetics.

Skiles Howard, a doctoral student at Columbia University, is completing a dissertation entitled "The Politics of Courtly Dancing," with the assistance of a Charlotte Newcombe Fellowship. She has published two articles in *Theatre Survey* on casting practice in the King's Company. Before embarking on her academic career, she enjoyed a career as a Broadway "gypsy" and as a solo dancer at the Metropolitan Opera.

David S. Kastan is Professor of English and Comparative Literature at Columbia University. He is the author of *Shakespeare and the Shapes of Time* (Hanover, N.H.: University Press of New England, 1982) and the forthcoming *Proud Majesty Made a Subject: Representation and Authority in the Drama of Early Modern England* (Routledge). He has also, with Peter Stallybrass, edited *Staging the Renaissance: Reinterpretations of Elizabethan and Jacobean Drama* (New York: Routledge, 1991). Presently he is editing *I Henry IV* for the Arden Series.

John N. King, Professor of English at Ohio State University, has written *English Reformation Literature: The Tudor Origins of the Protestant Tradition* (Princeton: Princeton University Press, 1982; paperback ed., 1986), *Tudor Royal Iconography: Literature and Art in an Age of Religious Crisis* (Princeton: Princeton University Press, 1989), and *Spenser's Poetry and the Reformation Tradition* (Princeton: Princeton University Press, 1990). He has also co-edited *The Vocaccyon of Johan Bale* with Peter Happé for the Early English Text Society (1990) and serves as editor of *Literature and History*.

Janel Mueller is Professor of English at the University of Chicago and the editor of *Modern Philology*. Publications on Donne's poetry and prose span her career to date; she has also published on medieval and early modern women authors (Margery Kempe and Queen Katherine Parr), Milton's poetry and prose, and on the development of early modern English as a literary medium in *The Native Tongue and the Word: Developments in English Prose Style, 1380–1580* (Chicago: University of Chicago Press, 1984).

Bill Readings is Professeur Agrégé of Comparative Literature at the University of Montréal. He is the author of *Introducing Lyotard: Art and Politics* (New York: Routledge, 1991) and of diverse essays on Renaissance literature and literary theory. He is currently working on a study of Milton.

Paul G. Remley is an assistant professor in the Department of English at the University of Washington. He has published articles in such journals as *English Studies, Anglo-Saxon England,* and *Peritia*. He works on medieval and Renaissance manuscripts, Anglo-Latin of all periods, and is completing a book on the poetry of Oxford, Bodleian Library, MS. Junius 11.

W. A. Sessions is Professor of English at Georgia State University. His books and monographs include *Henry Howard, Earl of Surrey* (Boston: G. K. Hall, 1986),

Francis Bacon's Legacy of Texts: "The Art of Discovery Grows with Discovery" (New York: AMS, 1990), and "Spenser's Georgics," in a special issue of *English Literary Renaissance*. He has published essays in such collections as *"Bright Shootes of Everlastingness": The Seventeenth-Century Religious Lyric* (Columbia: University of Missouri Press, 1987) and *"Too Riche to Clothe the Sun": Essays on George Herbert* (Pittsburgh: University of Pittsburgh Press, 1980). He is currently working on a biography of Surrey, a chapter of which appeared in *History Today* (June 1991). In addition, he is a prize-winning playwright.

INDEX